# MEN
# AND
# MORALS

THE SCHOOL OF ATHENS

# MEN
# AND
# MORALS

## *THE STORY OF ETHICS*

WOODBRIDGE RILEY

FREDERICK UNGAR PUBLISHING CO.
*NEW YORK*

*First published 1929*

*Republished 1960*

Printed in the United States of America

Library of Congress Catalog Card No. 60-9101

# CONTENTS

## THE PAGEANT OF MORALS

## *Part One*

## THE DAWN OF MORALS

## *Part Two*

## THE GREEK SCHOOLS

v

# CONTENTS

# LIST OF ILLUSTRATIONS

# THE PAGEANT OF MORALS

"IT IS universally acknowledged, that there is a great uniformity among the actions of men, in all nations and ages, and that human nature remains still the same, in its principles and operations. The same events follow from the same causes. Ambition, avarice, self-love, vanity, friendship, generosity, public spirit; these passions, mixed in various degrees, and distributed through society, have been, from the beginning of the world, and still are, the source of all the actions and enterprises which have ever been observed among mankind. Would you know the sentiments, inclinations, and course of life of the Greeks and Romans? Study well the temper and actions of the French and English: you cannot be much mistaken in transferring to the former most of the observations which you have made with regard to the latter. Mankind are so much the same, in all times and places, that history informs us of nothing new or strange in that particular. Its chief use is only to discover the constant and universal principles of human nature, by shewing men in all varieties of circumstances and situations, and furnishing us with materials, from which we may form our observations, and become acquainted with the regular springs of human action and behaviour. These records of wars, intrigues, factions, and revolutions, are so many collections of experiments, by which the politician or moral philosopher fixes the principles of his science; in the same manner as the physician or natural philosopher becomes acquainted with the nature of plants, minerals, and other external objects, by the experiments which he forms concerning them. Nor are the earth, water, and other elements, examined by Aristotle and Hippocrates, more like to those which at present lie under our observation, than the men, described by Polybius and Tacitus, are to those who now govern the world."—DAVID HUME, *Essays, Moral, Political, and Literary.*

## I. THE ANCIENT WORLD

WHY should I read a book of morals; why trouble myself with problems of conduct which have agitated others? Ask a kindred question and an answer is suggested. Why should I read a book of plays? Why go to the theatre to see how some author untangles difficult situations? Combine these questions and the answer is given. The individual mind is a little theatre in which the present repeats the past, in which the individual recapitulates the experience of the race. Take the infancy of man; then fear, and wonder, and confusion fill the mind; and childish notions as to ghosts and spirits and mysterious powers disturb the imagination. This was the age of primitive man and of the pioneers; the age of "silly nonsense," as the Greeks called it. Next came the age of free inquiry and speculation, the age of adolescence when bold philosophers and doubting Sophists questioned the validity of the tribal mores or customs and when Socrates was punished for impiety. Plato, too, possessed this same spirit of "flaming youth" when he kicked against the conventions and propounded his radical solution of the problem of sex among other problems of an ideal republic. This spirit of venturesome experiment was inevitably followed by an age of maturity, with Aristotle advocating moderation through the golden mean, and giving such sage advice as to food and drink, as to pleasure and prosperity, that his lines are worth learning to this very day.

Meanwhile the scene shifts from West to East, from Greece to India, where a people had aged more rapidly and where Buddhism advised resignation to the evils of life and Gautama preached a form of pessimism which has seemed to many but a lean philosophy of senility. This gray outlook on life was later reflected in the system of the Nineteenth Century thinker Schopenhauer, who read the Sacred Books of the East, while its tone may still be caught in the writings of the so-called Western Orientals, Tolstoy, Turgenieff, and Dostoyevski. Yet it would be an error to paint all the moralities of Asia in drab colours. Confucianism is cheerful, and the teachings of the Five Loyalties so entered into the bone and sinew of the great Middle Kingdom that China has had the longest recorded history of any people, and its civilization, based on the solidarity of the family, has survived when Greece perished, Rome rose and fell, and mediæval and modern nations were wiped off the map.

The scene shifts again and we return to the West. In Greece hard times had come, for first from Macedon, and then from Rome, the land of Socrates and Plato felt the iron heel of the oppressor. New philosophers arose to meet the situation, Diogenes who withdrew into his tub and Epicurus into his garden; the one a growling cynic, the other a smiling seeker of moderate pleasures. But greater than these two schools were the Stoics, who wandered about in their philosophers' cloaks and like strolling players gathered about them in forum and market place all who cared to listen. From the time when Greece fell, through the century of mystery and massacre, when Spartacus and his gladiators hung crucified on the road from Rome to Capua, through the nightmare reign of Nero they taught the gospel of courage in an age of cruelty and oppression. It was a gospel because it reached high and low, from the lame slave Epictetus to the harassed statesman Seneca. It was a gospel because it made many determined never to give in; in this it influenced characters as far apart as St. Paul, who from his Stoic teacher learned to fight the good fight, and young Roman aristocrats who, seeing the tortured Christians in the arena, said to themselves: "We will become like these, the noblest Stoics of them all."

## II. THE CHRISTIAN EPIC

YET not all Christians were Stoics. When to the terrible persecutions were added the catastrophes of barbarian invasion a veritable failure of nerve afflicted some. Of such was St. Augustine, whose great drama of the Christian life, the *City of God*, was really a defeatist drama. The old city, the wicked city of the West, had fallen before the rude onslaught of Alaric the Goth, but Christians should not despair, for the new city, the City of God, is in sight. Relentless Rome is being punished for its persecution of the saints, but the New Jerusalem is to recompense not only the martyrs but all who believe in the coming kingdom. Those who have suffered are soon to be rewarded; theirs is the assurance of a happy future, for God has divided mankind into two cities according to two moralities. There is a fundamental conflict between good and evil, between Deity and Devil, but those who have abandoned the pagan gods, and followed the one only true God, are safe. The crimes, the impieties, and the falsehoods of paganism are now being visibly punished, but by the same mark those who have suffered are to be recompensed. Scripture has said it. From the very days of Adam and Eve the Almighty has divided men into two classes—the Cains and Abels, the sinners and saints, the elect and non-elect. The majority of mankind belongs to this wicked world, as shown by the teeming millions in the imperial city, but there is a remnant which shall be saved, the little band of Christians, who, being purified by Divine Grace from the taint of original sin, shall inherit the kingdom of heaven.

For this strange document a new interpretation is needed. It is an historical monstrosity, but psychologically it can be understood. What the critics have missed is this: that Augustine's theology had an abnormal basis; that his *City of God* is a counterpart of his *Confessions;* and that this outburst against the great Babylon arose from the fact that while he himself had escaped from the "city of sin" by abandoning his concubine and being received into the church, he still hankered after his mistresses—"those vanities of vanities."

The confessions of Augustine the saint are matched only by the confessions of Rousseau the sinner, and in both cases an erratic youth led to a splenetic age. The churchman reviled Rome and condemned unbaptized infants to crawl on the floors of hell; the Swiss sentimentalist condemned French society, sought a return to nature, or man's primitive age of innocence, and abandoned his children on the steps of the foundling hospital. Yet both Augustine and Rousseau had enormous influence; both held out the hope of change, the one by means of fiction to frighten, the other by means of fiction to please: "Flee from the wrath to come," said the theologian. "Flee from civilization into the past," said the revolutionary.

Both these figures are pathological and both pathetic; in each may be seen failure of nerve and the working out of an inferiority complex. Augustine in the last resort is a weak character, but his logical successor in the history of the Church is not. It was Thomas Aquinas who took over the rôle of defender of the faith, and by liberalizing the old doctrine made it stronger. The church persecuted became the church triumphant, and in the centre of the stage, as in some miracle play, stands the confident figure of the "Angelic Doctor." This greatest of the scholastics had the personal assurance of one of high birth. Born in the castle of his father, Count Aquino, in the territories of Naples, of noble lineage and related to kings, he nevertheless determined to start at the bottom and make his own way in the world of wisdom and scholarship. Despite the opposition of his strong-minded mother he joined the Dominican order and started on a plodding journey, symbolic of his long exploration in that new world of knowledge opened up in the Thirteenth Century. Thus as a preaching monk, carrying nothing but satchel and breviary, he was sent on his first pilgrimage of learning from Rome to Cologne. He and his companion, Friar John, journeyed some fifteen hundred miles through Lombardy in November, across the Alpine passes in December, and so on to Paris and finally down the Rhine. It was in the same painstaking and thorough way that Aquinas spent his life in the paths of learning, refusing all high office, and devoting his years to scholarship. To this cosmopolitan thinker the pagan world was no Vanity Fair, since the cardinal virtues of the Greeks were not incompatible with the Christian virtues of faith, hope, and charity. Still this subtle spiritual adviser of the Middle Ages could not rid the mediæval system of its illiberal elements. The notion that the privileges of salvation were only for the elect still persisted, and the Stoic doctrine that man was by nature good was counterbalanced by the doctrine of original sin, a notion which hung like a weight upon men's necks until the age of the Renaissance, or rebirth of knowledge. But then the revolt came with a vengeance and a bold adventurer in morals like the Italian Machiavelli wiped out the church's arbitrary division of mankind into good and evil by pointing out that in this world the most unscrupulous are the most successful. To such might is right, and the Prince who uses the cloak of religion to mask his schemes is perfectly justified. Mediæval morals, with its fine distinctions between venial and mortal sins, now gave way to the morals of opportunism, and the diplomat of the Fifteenth Century advocates the familiar and persistent notion that a country is not saved by morality, but by subtlety in statecraft.

## III.  FROM THE MIDDLE AGES TO THE RENAISSANCE

AT THE Renaissance there took place an entire change of plot as well as of cast. The Middle Ages had offered a series of mystery and miracle plays based, for example, on the mystery of man's fall and the miracle of infused grace. But now men become more interested in humanity than in heaven; life is no longer a weary pilgrimage, a vale of tears, but an exciting adventure, a place of joy. Fresh vistas are opened up; the new explorations unroll space, the new knowledge unrolls time; science and history combine to stimulate men's minds. As Francis Bacon, Lord Verulam, declares: "Lands, seas, and stars have been immensely revealed in our times."

That which is an old story to us was a new story to the men of the Renaissance. There was the long and glorious roll of explorers and circumnavigators—Columbus, Magellan, Vasco da Gama, Ferdinando de Soto, and Ponce de Leon, searching for the fountain of youth. There was also the long line of gentlemen-adventurers like Drake, Frobisher, and Sir Walter Raleigh. To these lists must be added the other list of explorers and adventurers in the heavens— Copernicus, Tycho Brahe, and Galileo. Finally, besides exploring space, the new age explored time, and with the fall of Constantinople the scholars, driven out by the Turks, brought to Italy the manuscripts of classical antiquity. One of the scholars thus affected was Machiavelli, the Italian diplomatist, who was enabled to draw inspiration for the unification of Italy out of the history of Livy, just as the Fascists now, with their axes and fasces, employ the very symbols of ancient Rome. So, like the Roman rulers, Machiavelli advocated a form of morals without scruples, where might is right and nothing succeeds like success.

Thus it came about that the entire tone and aspect of the pageant of morals were changed. Moving adventures on land and sea, exciting discoveries in the skies, and the very dangers arising from the mingling of diplomacy and duplicity, of force and craft, drew men's minds away from the Middle Ages. They were no longer interested in looking at life as if it were a melancholy procession of the Misericordia, black-robed figures chanting mournfully as they marched slowly through the streets. To the most, life became less saintly and, because of that, more exciting. Instead of reading Augustine on the City of God and Aquinas on the theological virtues of chastity, poverty, and obedience, they read Machiavelli's, *Prince* and Boccaccio's *Decameron*. This at least for the majority. For the minority, the lesser band of "heroic souls," a thinker like Giordano Bruno offered plots not of backstairs diplomacy or of amorous intrigue, but drama in the grand manner, drama based on the new cosmic discoveries when men were to fight their way over mountains of difficulty in this life and have for reward in the future life "Eternity for duration, immensity for place, and omniformity for realization."

This, of course, is a personal philosophy. Bruno distinctly says that it is meant for "rare souls"; but, taken in connection with the current contempt for the theological virtues and with the whole rich and lurid literature of Renaissance novels, plays, and poems, it represents a tremendous change in the outlook of the majority. It is the same change that is occurring in the so-called renaissance in America. Take but one feature of this change, the stage; put, for example, a mediæval revival like *The Miracle* alongside a current sex play and consider the contrast. In the one there is the solemn organ note, symbols of suffering and death, and an atmosphere of magic; in the other there is frivolity, the pursuit of pleasure, and for all that an atmosphere of reality, for miracles do not happen nowadays, but other things do.

This is but a single aspect; it represents in an outward and

visible way something more profound. Some have called the present
state of affairs the new paganism versus the old Puritanism. The
phrase will do if, for example, it betokens an unconscious reaction
against one's New England ancestry. Here there are certain ideas
bred in the bone against which the modern brain revolts, while the
old symbols appear not awful, but merely absurd. It is not necessary to go back to obsolete literature like Cotton Mather's *Wonders
of the Invisible World*, or Michael Wigglesworth's *The Day of Doom*.
These productions, along with the *New England Primer*, are nowadays considered curiosities of literature, yet at one time they left
their marks on the ancestral nerve tracts. So did more outward
symbols which cheered the nurseries of New England homes—
pictures of weeping willows drooping over tombs, and pictures of
the Tree of Sin with red apples, marked alphabetically from adultery to wantonness, to represent the temptations to which human
flesh is prone.

In this connection it does not require much imagination to reconstruct a Sabbath in New England; the child dragged from the
nursery to listen with its elders to a sermon lasting two turnings of
the hourglass; a walk after a cold dinner in that ancient substitute
for a park, a graveyard, and home for supper and after that the
reciting of the *New England Primer* with its alphabet of woes: "In
Adam's Fall, We sinnèd All"; "Youth forward slips, Death soonest
nips."

"Dear old, mediæval America!" as George Bernard Shaw once
exclaimed. It is still with us in the back of the minds of even the
emancipated. And what is the reaction? If anybody does not know
let him go back and study the reaction of the Italian Renaissance
to mediæval morals; when Machiavelli flouted the lantern-jawed
Dante and Boccaccio recounted his tales on the sunny slopes of
Fiesole.

## IV. FROM THE RENAISSANCE TO THE ENLIGHTENMENT

THIS reaction is also to be found in the strange works of Rabelais,
whose breed of giants, it has been said, was representative of the
man of the Middle Ages, freeing himself from the shackles of the
period and at last finding an outlet for fundamental instincts which
had long been repressed, and revelling in the enjoyment of human
life, in the thirst for knowledge, in the struggle for a freer political
and religious society.

To utilize this interpretation of a brilliant French critic, we can see how the first of this breed of giants was Niccolò Machiavelli, whose first name led some to consider him the original of "Old Nick," and whose last name has given us a word of sinister significance—Machiavellian. This was because this advocate of mingled subtlety and violence considered that the end justifies the means, in his case the end being the unification of Italy and the means diplomacy, duplicity, and finally force. In spite of his reputation Machiavelli was a patriot. The ropes and the pulleys of the rack could not extort from him a confession that he had conspired against his native city, while neglect and poverty could not keep him from his dreams of an Italy restored to the glories of Rome. Here is an account of these studies which led to the writing of his greatest work, *The Prince:* "The evening being come, I return home and go to my study; at the entrance I pull off my peasant clothes, covered with dust and dirt, and put on my noble court dress, and thus becomingly reclothed I pass into the ancient courts of the men of old, where, being lovingly received by them, I am fed with that food which is mine alone; where I do not hesitate to speak with them, and to ask for the reason of their actions, and they in their benignity answer me; and for four hours I feel no weariness, I forget every trouble, poverty does not dismay, death does not terrify me; I am possessed entirely by those great men."

Another Rabelaisian giant of the Renaissance was Giordano Bruno, the passionate pilgrim through life, who sought by means of the new knowledge to enlarge men's minds. As Machiavelli the diplomat sought a greater Italy, so Bruno the monk sought to put before men the vision of a greater universe. To the Middle Ages this earth on which we dwell was the chief part of a single world visible to the naked eye. But when Galileo, seizing his telescope, exclaimed: "Vanish ye dark vaults of heaven," Bruno went even further, filled the universe with a plurality of worlds, and offered to man a glorious view, for he declared it unworthy of the divine goodness and power to create a finite world when able to produce besides it endless particular worlds similar to this of the earth.

This was heresy, but the church, when it burned Bruno at the stake, only lit a torch which lighted all Europe. Nevertheless, that act frightened some. There was René Descartes of France, who did not dare publish his laborious work treating of the world as a machine, and also Thomas Hobbes, who, in fear of the established church of England, confessed that the study of spirits, angelic and divine, was beyond human power. Hobbes consequently confined himself to amusing the Merry Monarch, Charles II, and to moralizing over the social compact whereby mankind originally prevented a war of all against all. Although a political fiction, this view had an immense influence later. It meant that men could covenant and agree together to overthrow an oppressive government, as did those American and French revolutionaries who drew inspiration from Hobbes.

At this point we have passed from the Renaissance to the Enlightenment. The stage is no longer lit with the lurid flames that consumed Bruno; we no longer hear the muffled cries of the victims of Cesare Borgia, the "hero" of Machiavelli's *Prince*. Instead the curtain lifts and the light of reason shines forth from the person of Voltaire, while his voice rings over Europe in those terrible invectives: "The Case of the Calas," and "The Cry of Innocent Blood." Voltaire, with his hatchet face, his wig awry, and his walking stick supporting a feeble body, is not an heroic figure to look upon, but his place in history is that of a hero. Almost singlehanded he fought "the Infamy," that sinister combination of church and state which sent him to the Bastille for an alleged insult to the crown, or tied a poor peasant, like a human X, to die on the St. Andrew's cross. In attacking the infamy of bigotry and cruelty, Voltaire was no St. George spearing from horseback a clumsy dragon; he was rather a duellist of the intellect whose thrusts and parries of irony and wit left his opponents nonplussed. "If this is the best possible world," said his character Candide, shaken amid the ruins of the Lisbon earthquake, "what must the worst be like!"

Voltaire was let out of the Bastille on condition that he go to England. From there he wrote his famous letters of mingled wit and wisdom which, among other things, said that, while England had thirty kinds of religion, it had only one kind of soup, and while it had a king and court, it nevertheless allowed liberty of thought. The trip to England was the turning point of Voltaire's life, and for the rest of his days he determined to carry on the fight against the Infamy as the double-headed monster of political oppression and intellectual tyranny. Switzerland at last became his refuge and from there he directed that literary bombardment which frightened both the crown and the church and made its echoes heard across the Atlantic.

Alongside of Voltaire we may put his rival, Rousseau, the young sentimentalist who was everything that the older rationalist was not. To Voltaire the civilization of his day was complicated, but not utterly corrupt. To Rousseau that civilization was so bad that it should be swept away. Our morals, he argues, are corrupted in proportion as our arts and sciences progress. Before art had fashioned our manners and taught our passions to speak a borrowed language, our morals were rude but natural.

Here starts the familiar and fatuous attempt to restore "the good old times" by going back to Arcadian simplicity. It is by a return to nature, or the natural man, that total equality shall be reached. As an antidote to the artificiality and boredom of the day there were offered as ideals of conduct characters like the "noble red man" and the "pious Peruvian," characters as fictitious as that popular hero of the simple life, Robinson Crusoe. It was the day of sentimental morality, when, as Rousseau expressed it, only within himself could man find peace, only under the stars could he discover the Supreme Being that made the world.

## V. THE REDISCOVERY OF THE INNER LIFE

IN SPITE of its flimsy historical basis Rousseau's message contained two principles which a deeper thinker was to make fundamental. In almost identical language the German, Immanuel Kant, declared that there were two things which filled his mind with an ever new and rising admiration and reverence: "The starry heavens above, the moral law within." This moral law can be summed up in the famous formula: "Act so that the maxim of thy will can always hold good as a principle of universal legislation." But this profound principle of the moralist beyond the Rhine was not gained without difficulty, since Kant had first to overcome the shattering doubts of a thinker beyond the Channel. It was David Hume, the Scottish skeptic, who sought to resolve all morality into mere human experience. Custom, he held, was the guide of life and the rule of living was simply this: "When in Rome, do as the Romans do."

To the German, with an early background of humble pietism, a religious persuasion based on the inner light of conscience, the conventional standards of polite society would not do. To him the individual is not to follow mere custom, not to drift with the tide, but to struggle for a principle higher and better than all previous principles. From the Epicurean doctrine of private happiness, through the mediæval doctrine of the will of God and the modern doctrine of convention or easy acquiescence in the customs of the day, the moral systems have been either artificial or shallow. But

in reaching out after a universal law man should pay no attention
to the lower desires, nor to outside authority, whether divine or
human, but should strive only for the good will as the supreme test.
Underneath all lies the fundamental principle of self-sufficiency, of
individual reliance on a self-created "categorical imperative,"
a law which is called an imperative because the good will is a command to itself, and categorical because it says: You *must* act thus
and so.

In a way, and in spite of Kant's notion that he had superseded all
previous systems, much of this was a revival of the ancient Stoic
doctrine which in hard times put iron into the hearts of men. At any
rate, this new school of discipline inspired the rising generation, as
was shown in Fichte's addresses to the German people to throw off
the yoke of Napoleon and in the valiant but vain attempts of the
revolutionists of 1848 to gain the rights of a written constitution for
the Fatherland. But along with the subsequent political reaction a
certain moral reaction set in and, despite the high ideals of self-will
and self-government put forward by Fichte and Schelling, there were
other romanticists for whom the principle of liberty became an excuse for license, and the rule that you must do thus and so degenerated into: You may do anything you please.

This "new freedom" has been given the high-sounding title of
"personal idealism," and while it did inspire to good conduct many
of the strong-minded, at the same time it furnished sorry excuses
for those whose spirit was willing but whose flesh was weak. There
were youths who bore the strange device "Excelsior"; there were
also young men and maidens who went in for "elective affinities" or
other equally romantic excuses for illicit relations. Hence to the
young romanticists of the "storm and stress" period Kant, with his
pietistic ancestry and his categorical imperative, was a kind of moral
"Old Ironsides." So what took place in England, when the Pro-
tectorate of Cromwell was succeeded by the Restoration of King
Charles, was reproduced in Germany when the principle of self-
sufficiency was turned into a principle of self-indulgence.

And still another reaction set in when the easy-going optimism of
the romanticist was succeeded by the stern doctrine of the pessimist.
What one member of the Jena circle had called "the merry whirligig" Arthur Schopenhauer now replaced by the figure of "the wheel
of life," the notion of the sad cycle of existence taken from the
Sacred Books of the East. Both the romanticists and the pessimists
thought of the world as Will and Idea, but an entirely different
meaning was given to the two words by the two parties concerned.

The will so far had been interpreted as ranging from the good will to the free will, and the idea expanded into high hopes of perfection and human happiness. But to Schopenhauer the will means the world will, relentless, implacable, caring nothing for man; and the idea mere illusion, vanity of vanities, the Web of Maya. With these phrases, taken from the wisdom literature of ancient India, Schopenhauer transvaluates the values of the romanticists. Man is not the master, but the product; not a creative first cause, but the latest manifestation of vast cosmic processes. So while the romanticist begins with energy and ends with the joy of living, the pessimist begins with energy and ends with ennui. We may start with self-assertion; we are bound to end with self-abnegation. Man emerges on the scene full of appetites and desires, but in the last act he is bound to give way to remorse and the stings of conscience. Selfishness is the disease which he must eradicate. Like the preacher of old and the Christian saints of the Middle Ages, he must realize that all is vanity, and like Gautama Buddha he must cease to will anything, must guard against attaching his will to anything, must seek to cultivate in himself the greatest indifference to anything.

Through his contact with what to his generation was an almost forgotten system of the East, Schopenhauer may be said to have brought the mental climate of India into Europe. But this artificial adoption of a depressing atmosphere is less of an explanation than Schopenhauer's own experience and personality. The wrongs and cruelties of Western civilization—wanton wars and the industrial oppression of men, women, and children—so affected him that pessimism became a protective covering for his feelings; he suffered himself, he could not help suffering for others. Thus pessimism, which so many of the Western world denounced as sheer intellectual perversity, when rightly understood contains a quality of mercy lacking in the shallow optimism of idealism. In fine, while Schopenhauer's system had a tinge of the pathological, it may be counted profound in its searching insight into the darker recesses of life.

Schopenhauer, the arch-pessimist, has been dismissed by many as a mere degenerate. So has his ardent follower, Friedrich Nietzsche, who seized upon the former's principle of the world will, turned it into a principle of the will to power, and boasted of being the first immoralist. Nietzsche is the young and brilliant thinker whose last days were clouded by insanity and whose doctrines were perverted into the principles of sheer ruthlessness by the later advocate of Prussian militarism. To vindicate Nietzsche is one thing; to explain him another. Like his master Schopenhauer, his system is another

defense mechanism, another valiant method to erect a mental
screen against the sorrows of life. The universe is evil, he declared,
cruel like a dissonance of notes, and the soul of man, dissonant like
the universe, suffering from itself, would detach itself from life,
if it did not invent some illusion, some myth which deceives but
appeases him and procures it a refuge of beauty.

Is this philosophy of illusion legitimate? In the case of a nation,
no; in the case of an individual, yes, provided it furnishes a means
of escape from suffering. Writing to his sister, Nietzsche uses three
phrases, the last of which shows that it was not a philosophy of
despair, but a philosophy of courage, which animated him: "For the
strongest and highest the will to life," he explains, "does not find
expression in the miserable struggle for existence, but in a will to
War, a will to Power, a will to Overcome." Two of these fatal phrases
were seized upon by the militarists, but the last was utilized by
Nietzsche himself, a life-long invalid, as a will to overcome pain, to
hide his suffering, to show a brave face to the world. One dislikes to
use the harsh and ungenerous expression "the inferiority complex,"
yet while Nietzsche was doubtless oppressed by such a complex,
still he rose above it and like Giordano Bruno, with his appeal to the
heroic soul, overcame mountains of difficulty. Hence arises the
paradox of his personality: his system advocated immoralism, but,
as his sister declared, he had "the soul of a Christian knight"; it
advocated an ethics of self-assertion and pride, but from all accounts
Nietzsche by nature was modest and tractable; it finally held out
as the highest model of humanity the superman who, like Machiavelli's Prince, works on the doctrines that might is right, that there
is no law for the overlord, and that politics has nothing to do with
ethics.

## VI.  THE RETURN TO UTILITY

FROM this fevered philosophy, this metaphysical mirage, it is a
relief to return to a system built up by a succession of cool and
practical minds. In contrast to master morality and privileged supermen, the English utilitarians, whose motto was "the greatest
happiness of the greatest number," had meanwhile been constructing a morals based on democracy and aiming toward the equal
rights of all. Early in the Eighteenth Century Lord Shaftesbury
had argued that, since man was originally a social being, he derived
his greatest happiness from that which makes for the existence of

society and the common weal. After Shaftesbury, Francis Hutcheson developed a moral arithmetic in terms of the net benevolence of the agent, that is, the excess of benevolence over self-interest. To this he added a kind of calculus in which virtue is in proportion to the number of persons to whom the happiness shall extend.

All this has been criticized as too mercantile, and as a lowering of high ideals on the part of a nation of shopkeepers. But as old Jeremy Bentham sarcastically remarked, "The *summum bonum*—the sovereign good—what is it? It is this thing, and that thing, and the other thing—it is anything but pleasure—it is the Irishman's apple-pie made of nothing but quinces." What Bentham was attacking here was not morals as such but the elbow-chair moralist who talks glibly of the sense of duty and benevolence and so misses the real motives at work in the advancements of mankind. To Bentham it was an open question whether the unadorned desire to better one's condition is not on the whole a more effective tool of social reform than appeals to idealism and philanthropy however noble.

This crusty critic, writing about the time of the American Revolution, left two suggestive principles—that of enlightened self-interest and that of the greatest happiness of the greatest number—but failed to work out their mutual connections. This task remained for the mid-Victorian, John Stuart Mill, who followed his father, James Mill, in exploiting the possibilities of the "expediency" philosophy. In his standard of morals the older man, according to his autobiography, was Epicurean, taking as the exclusive test of right and wrong the tendency of actions to produce pleasure and pain. But in his personal qualities the cynic predominated, for he would sometimes say that if life were made what it might be by good government and education, it would be worth having. Like father, like son. The younger Mill had no delusions regarding man as by nature good; he declared that there may be germs of virtue in human nature, but the weeds of vice dispute the ground with these beneficent germs. Sympathy, though in a sense natural, requires a good deal of cultivation, while veracity, one of the highest virtues, is plainly artificial, for all savages are liars. It is here that the cultivation of virtue by education comes in, for the greatest recorded victory which education ever achieved over a whole host of natural inclinations in a people was that of Sparta. Furthermore, that victory was reënforced by public opinion in its two aspects: its attractive power was the love of glory, praise, and admiration; its deterring power the fear of shame and ill-repute.

## VII.  PERSONAL LIBERTY

AT THIS point Mill reaches his chief message to his age by clarifying the perplexing problem of modern civilization concerning the struggle between liberty and authority. In the old days liberty meant protection against the tyranny of the political rulers, and the aim of patriots was to set limits to "the king of the vultures bent upon preying on the flock." In modern times the tyrant is public opinion, the tyranny of the majority that enslaves the soul itself. In the old days, again, patriots obtained certain immunities, called political liberties or rights; in the new the struggle concerns the inner domain of conscience and man's liberty of conscience, liberty of thought, and absolute freedom of opinion on all subjects, practical or speculative, scientific, moral, or theological. But at this juncture public opinion comes in with its deterring power, and, as the public is made up of a few wise men and many fools, individual progress is slow.

This, then, is the paradox, the problem. Public opinion, which with its positive power fostered the common defense against tyrants, now with its negative power of disapprobation threatens itself to become the tyrant. In the English-speaking countries not only is public opinion growing, but it is controlled by the spirit of Puritanism and by some of those modern reformers who, while placing themselves in strongest opposition to the religions of the past, have been no way behind either churches or sects in their assertion of the right of spiritual domination. There is an instance of this in the curious infirmity in English minds which makes them take a preposterous pleasure in the assertion of a bad principle; for example, in the assumption that the oath of a person who does not believe in a future state is worthless, a kind of intolerance which, though it kills no one, neverthless induces men to disguise their opinions.

Among Americans a similar state of things obtains in legislation prohibiting the use of liquor, as if legal enactment made drinking a wrong in itself. This, declares Mill, writing when only one half the United States was under such restrictive legislation, is a monstrous principle, since it violates the more fundamental principle that every man is free to do that which he wills, provided he does not infringe upon the equal freedom of any other man.

Such is the principle of *laissez faire*, of letting each man live as seems good to himself, but not compelling each to live as seems good to the rest. This principle, enunciated by Mill in his famous essay "On Liberty," was followed by Herbert Spencer in a statement that acts of Parliament do not originate morals, but in many cases simply preserve discarded notions. Thus legislation concerning the Sabbath and restrictions on amusements simply illustrate the survival of the unfit, for much political tradition, living in the past, is mere dying prejudice in the present. The whole is an instance of the conflict between two codes, the primitive and the progressive. Thus early man was one whose happiness was obtained largely at the sacrifice of the happiness of others. But while conquest and enslaving might at first have been justified, yet primitive man must give way to the ultimate man who can obtain his own happiness without deducting from the happiness of others. Human character has changed slowly because it has been subject to two conflicting sets of conditions. On the one hand the discipline of the social state has been developing it into the sympathetic form, while, on the other hand, the necessity for self-defense, partly of man against brute, partly of man against man, and partly of societies against each other, has been maintaining the old unsympathetic form. Consequently, in the immense course of social evolution there have arisen two codes of ethics, the ethics of amity and the ethics of enmity, and only when warfare has largely ceased can the former code, which is to develop into the code of the perfect man, have a normal and reasonably rapid development. Unfortunately, this ideal is still far off, for, as Spencer says, the civilized races are at present in an intermediate position, since the pre-moral stage still persists into the moral stage.

## VIII.  THE MORALS OF PRACTICALITY

Such, in brief, is evolutional ethics, whose problems are carried on by one of the latest schools, named the pragmatic after the title of one of William James's books. This book, advocating the morals of practicality, the author dedicates to John Stuart Mill "as one whom fancy likes to picture as our leader were he alive to-day." This dedication is significant since James virtually accepts the utilitarian principle that actions are right in proportion as they tend to promote happiness; wrong as they tend to produce the reverse of happiness. Now apply this principle to modern civilization and it is evident that out of all factors war is that which, by and large, produces the greatest unhappiness to humanity. But here, as James says, the war against war is going to be no holiday excursion, or camping party. We inherit the warlike type, our ancestors have bred the pugnacity into our bone and marrow, and thousands of years of peace will not breed it out of us. The war party is assuredly right in affirming that the martial virtues, although originally gained by the race in war, are absolute and permanent human goods. Patriotic pride and ambition in their military form are, after all, only specifications of a more generous competitive passion. They are its first form, but that is no reason for supposing them to be its last form. Men now are proud of belonging to a conquering nation, and without a murmur lay down their persons and their wealth, if by so doing they may fend off subjection. But who can be sure that *other aspects of one's country* may not, with time and education and suggestion enough, come to be regarded with similarly effective feelings of pride and shame? Why should men not some day feel that it is worth a blood tax to belong to a collectivity superior in *any* ideal respect? Why should they not blush with indignant shame if the community that owns them is vile in any way whatsoever? Individuals, daily more numerous, now feel this civic passion. It is only a question of blowing on the spark till the whole population gets incandescent, and on the ruins of the old morals of military honour a stable system of morals of civic honour builds itself up.

Such is the pragmatic suggestion for a "Moral Equivalent of War," propounded but four years before the great world conflict and in the mind of William James the most burning question before mankind. Here, he confesses, it is plain that on this subject civilized man has developed a sort of double personality, two natures struggling within him, two codes of morals still existing side by side. In concluding, then, this survey of the pageant of morals it is necessary to turn back and to point out that this conflict of ideals between the pursuits of war and the pursuits of peace emerges on the very first pages of history. To these pages we may hereupon turn and attempt to trace the faint beginnings of the ideas of right and wrong, first with primitive men struggling with one another and with the forces of nature, next with the fighters of the Homeric Age, and so on to the emergence of true morals with Socrates, of an ideal republic with Plato, of political justice with Aristotle; in a word, those early conceptions, developed by the thinkers of classical antiquity, which persist to this very day.

# PART ONE

## THE DAWN OF MORALS

# I. THE SCHOOL OF ATHENS

"WE ARE placed in this world, as in a great theatre, where the true springs and causes of every event are entirely concealed from us; nor have we either sufficient wisdom to foresee, or power to prevent those ills, with which we are continually threatened. We hang in perpetual suspense between life and death, health and sickness, plenty and want; which are distributed amongst the human species by secret and unknown causes, whose operation is oft unexpected, and always unaccountable. These unknown causes, then, become the constant object of our hope and fear; and while the passions are kept in perpetual alarm by an anxious expectation of the events, the imagination is equally employed in forming ideas of those powers, on which we have so entire a dependence. Could men anatomize nature, according to the most probable, at least the most intelligible philosophy, they would find that these causes are nothing but the particular fabric and structure of the minute parts of their own bodies and of external objects; and that, by a regular and constant machinery, all the events are produced, about which they are so much concerned."—DAVID HUME, *Essays*.

In the "Pageant of Morals" we have been spectators of a procession of moving figures passing before us in historic succession down the ages. We may now go back and examine the earlier of these figures at rest, standing before us as Raphael represents them in his great masterpiece, The School of Athens. In this picture, where Athens really represents the whole of Greece, Aristotle and Plato are the central figures, the first appealing to nature, the source of his own prodigious studies, the second pointing to heaven, the fount and cause of all knowledge. To the right stands Socrates—with his snub nose and flattened features—talking to a group of friends of whom Xenophon, in the uniform of a general, is most conspicuous. Before the central group lies a great cynic, Diogenes, bare-armed and barelegged, resting his elbow on the steps and reading his tablets. To his left, in the right-hand corner of the picture, stands Ptolemy, holding a celestial globe studded with stars, symbolizing thereby that false ancient notion of the earth as within that globe and thereby the centre of the universe, a notion which became later not only a hindrance to the advancement of science, but even to the advancement of morals. Finally, in the left-hand corner there sits a great mathematician, Pythagoras, writing in a book a table of harmonies, those harmonies which govern not only the courses of the stars above, but the moral conduct of man below.

Such are the figures of the philosophers which have been identified in this masterpiece of the Renaissance. If to them we add the conjectured figures of Epicurus and of Boetius, a later Roman whose *Consolation of Philosophy* was written in the earlier Stoic style, we have an almost complete cast of the chief characters of what we may call the great morality play of Greece.

This play had three acts; the last was played by the Stoics and Epicureans who in troublous times sought, the one by stern renunciation, and the other by moderate pleasure, to withstand the vicissitudes of fortune. Those who played these rôles were of the introspective type, the very opposite of that objective type represented in the first act by the legendary heroes who did more fighting than thinking. Midway between the last sophisticated and the first unsophisticated group there stands in the centre of the stage, as in the centre of the actual picture, the great trio, Socrates, Plato, and Aristotle. As for them, it seems as if some wise power, some cosmic impresario, had cast the parts. Between them they represent the most divergent types conceivable, Socrates standing for the man in the street, Plato for the man of culture, and Aristotle for the scientist and tester of theories. But they need to be examined more closely. Socrates was one who could hold his own, not only with all sorts and conditions of men, but with all sorts and conditions of women. A friend of Alcibiades and other young bloods of Athens, he could drink the rest of the company under the table. Yet in spite of his own strong head he advocated temperance and considered a drunkard a fool. Toward women his attitude was more or less the conventional Greek attitude of superiority, but with a touch of humour. When friends chided him for enduring the tantrums of his wife Xanthippe, he used to say that one ought to live with a restive woman, just as horsemen manage violent-tempered horses; "and as they," said he, "when they have once mastered them, are easily able to manage all other; so I, after managing Xanthippe, can easily live with anyone else whatever." His attitude toward the demimonde, the hetairæ or "companions" of Athens, was also quizzical, witness his conversation with the fair Theodote whom he advised not to "hunt friends, the noblest game in the world," by such crude methods as she employed, but to be more subtle in her ways.

So much for Socrates, who stood for the morality of the plain man, a rough diamond, yet nature's gentleman. Plato was the aristocrat, proud of his lineage, yet admiring most the character of Socrates and seeking to extol his master's bodily endurance and strength of will as an antidote to the physical softness and moral flabbiness of the gilded youth of the day. It was for this reason that his ideal commonwealth, the Republic, advocates the strenuous life and would employ the selective draft and the training camp to sift out the best rulers or guardians for the state.

We come to the last of this remarkable cast of characters, Aristotle, the scientist and tester of theories who turned Socrates's practice of moderation into the principle of the golden mean—nothing in excess, but everything in proportion. Plato's system he also modified, and he tamed the wild theories of selective breeding and severe censorship with this sensible rule of moral education: "From youth upward to be accustomed to be good." These three men had three different rôles, rôles which between them covered about all the important problems of conduct, Socrates standing for the problem of the individual, Plato for that of the family, and Aristotle for that of the state. But lest a formula like this appear too trite and obvious, it should be added that these three men were innovators who put new business into their parts. Socrates is not an individualist in the sense of being a crank, but because he made his views not only characteristic of himself, but also workable for others. Plato, too, was original, almost too original in his free handling of the family, where he would substitute "public hymeneals" for private matrimony. But the aim in all this was not to shock public opinion but to better the miserable conditions of the married woman at Athens. So finally Aristotle; bare statements of his principles of being accustomed to be good and of his golden mean are but empty frames unless filled out with the countless details he furnishes as to how to bring up children, how to make and keep friends, how to be generous in time and money towards the state, and how to fill up those last years of life when leisure to so many seems mere boredom.

Socrates, Plato, Aristotle—the mere recital of these names suggests a veritable cycle of plays for the civilized man because these three are veteran actors in their respective parts. With their combination of urbanity and worldly wisdom, of free inquiry and sound speculation, they rightly stand as the central figures in the picture. And logically, also, they stand midway between the too sophisticated and the too unsophisticated. After them came Epicurus whose garden was a refuge for the hypersensitive, and the Stoic, whose cloak was a covering for proud endurance. Before them came the fighters of the Homeric Age with their rough virtues, and back of these the pioneers, primitive men struggling with one another and with the forces of nature, dim and shadowy figures in whom may be traced the beginnings of the ideas of right and wrong. These are the figures far in the backstage; they do not speak in the polished lines of the finished actor, they rather act in pantomime; while inarticulate, they are yet interpretable; they have left us not a literature but ceremonies, symbolic actions coming down the ages. It may be gestures and groupings of the Greek chorus, wild gestures of despair at the pursuit of the Furies and strange huddled groupings which represent the fear of fate, all being but reflections of the ancestral terrors of primitive man before forces which he could neither control nor comprehend.

## II. THE PIONEERS

"THE immense force and domination of Fear in the first self-conscious stages of the human mind is a thing which can hardly be exaggerated, and which is even difficult for some of us moderns to realize. But naturally as soon as Man began to think about himself —a frail phantom and waif in the midst of tremendous forces of whose nature and mode of operation he was entirely ignorant—he was beset with terrors; dangers loomed upon him on all sides. Even to-day it is noticed by doctors that one of the chief obstacles to the cure of illness among some black or native races is sheer superstitious terror; and Thanatomania is the recognized word for a state of mind ("obsession of death") which will often cause a savage to perish from a mere scratch hardly to be called a wound. The natural defence against this state of mind was the creation of an enormous number of taboos—such as we find among all races and on every conceivable subject—and these taboos constituted practically a great body of warnings which regulated the lives and thoughts of the community, and ultimately, after they had been weeded out and to some degree simplified, hardened down into very stringent Customs and Laws. Fear does not seem a very worthy motive, but in the beginning it curbed the violence of the purely animal passions, and introduced order and restraint among them. Simultaneously it became itself, through the gradual increase of knowledge and observation, transmuted and etherealized into something more like wonder and awe, and (when the gods rose above the horizon) into reverence. Anyhow we seem to perceive that from the early beginnings (in the Stone Age) of self-consciousness in Man there has been a gradual development—from crass superstition, senseless and accidental, to rudimentary observation, and so to belief in Magic; thence to Animism and personification of nature-powers in more or less human form, as earth-divinities or sky gods or embodiments of the tribe; and to placation of these powers by rites like Sacrifice and the Eucharist, which in their turn became the foundation of Morality. Graphic representations made for the encouragement of fertility became the nurse of pictorial Art; observations of plants or of the weather or the stars, carried on by tribal medicine-men for purposes of witchcraft or prophecy, supplied some of the material of Science; and humanity emerged by faltering and hesitating steps on the borderland of those finer perceptions and reasonings which are supposed to be characteristic of Civilization."—EDWARD CARPENTER, *Pagan and Christian Creeds*.

In the search for the origins of morals we must peer back to those nameless shifting figures in the dimness before the dawn of civilization; for the beginnings of Western morals we must re-experience those bonds of savagery and of irrational conviction which were at last broken by the force of the Greek genius. The historian Herodotus claimed that the Greeks of his day, the Fifth Century before Christ, were free from "the silly nonsense of the barbarians." But at the time that statement was made the Greeks had largely outgrown magic and mythology, hence we must go back of even Herodotus and investigate what he called "silly nonsense."

The earliest surviving Greek literature, such as the Iliad and the Odyssey of Homer and Hesiod's *Works and Days* and his *Theogony*, or *Generation of the Gods*, preserved savage customs and primitive usages which survived like fossil remains of prehistoric creatures, remains of a remote past which now call for skilful scientific interpretations. These interpretations have shown how age-old mores, or customs, were refined in later ages into moral codes, just as the rude flints of the cave men became civilization's instruments of precision. At the least, these primitive usages and customs expressed the first dim gropings of humanity toward religion and ethics. They may be taken as crude mental games with the powers of nature, which seemed generally hostile but yet amenable to diplomatic handling by magic. At the first it was apparently a case of hide and go seek in the dark, with haunting spirits of the wood, with creatures of the underworld, with the departed souls of the dead as one's terrifying companions. So in fear of being caught unawares man invented schemes of ghost avoidance, of animal propitiation, and of purifications by fire.

Even Homer, with his healthy-minded outlook on life, preserves in his epics traces of this dark backward and abysm of time. Where can you find better examples of ghost avoidance by the wearing of black and the disfigurement of the person by wounds or dust? Or of animal propitiation? Recall the ægis, or breastplate, or Athena, which consisted of serpents and points to snake worship. Recall again the burning of the body of the hero Patroclus and the sacrifice of twelve wretched Trojan captives at that time, and you have a splendid instance of an ancient funeral ceremony.

In reading the earliest available Greek literature we find ourselves in a mythological maze. Like Theseus we need a guiding thread out of this labyrinth, and a thread is perhaps best furnished in a single conception, that of animism. By this is meant man's projecting into the great world about him the image of his own mind. When that mind is very primitive, says one authority, the images so projected are those of fragmentary intelligences, the spirits and gnomes of the age of magic. When the mind rises to distinct consciousness of itself the reflections of it are anthropomorphic gods, when finally it reaches the universal, or cosmic state, it perceives the presence of a universal Being behind all phenomena.

This is a convenient generalization by whose aid we can go slowly backward into the more remote times, for in the present age most men pin their moral faith on some universal Being, either a personal God, or "a power that makes for righteousness" or more vaguely "some far-off divine event towards which the whole creation moves." Such is a comparatively late and developed stage of thought, but long before that there existed the age of anthropomorphism, when men made gods in their own image, an age when the sculptors fashioned their deities in figures "divinely tall, divinely fair" —Zeus, Poseidon, Apollo, and the rest of the glittering procession of the Greek pantheon. But this was not all. Back of these gods were others less well known. Thus Herodotus learned at Dodona, the seat of the oracle, that the Pelasgians worshipped nameless "gods" who had set all things in order, and all dispensations were in their hands. The historian then adds his explanation of how these impersonal powers became personalized, individualized, veritable objects of literary art: "It was only yesterday, so to speak, that they learnt of what parentage was each God, or whether they were all from everlasting, and what they were like in figure. For, in my opinion, Homer and Hesiod lived not more than four hundred years before my time; and it was they who composed a theogony for the Hellenes, gave the gods their titles, apportioned to them their functions and arts, and made clear their figures."

In this reference to the Pelasgians Herodotus has an inkling of the antiquity of religious and moral history, but he did not go far enough. Behind this primitive people of Greece lay countless millennia of social development of which neither he nor any of the ancients knew much, but which modern scholarship attempted, and with fair success, to reconstruct. Here comparative religion has been aided by anthropology and the twilight of the gods has been partly explored. A recent philosopher, Friedrich Nietzsche, has spoken of this remote age as one "beyond good and evil." By this is meant an age when good and evil had not so much the meaning of "moral and immoral" as of "allowed and forbidden." As the traditional gods were sublimated men, so behind religion lay social customs as the structure of human society. Now this meaning of morals as mores, mere social customs, is still evident even in trivial acts. Thus it is right to salute an acquaintance; it is wrong to eat fish with a knife. However, primitive religion, if so it be called, constituted no shallow book of etiquette. It concerned matters of life and death to the tribe; matters such as the right and wrong time to plant crops, the right and wrong way to treat wandering or departed spirits. In other words, morals dealt chiefly with magic. For example, that mass of beliefs called "totemism" concerned itself with matters fundamental to the existence and continuity of the tribe. The ordinary and superficial knowledge of totems and totem ceremonies has led us into the attitude of the sophisticated Greeks toward "the silly nonsense of the barbarians." Thus we have been surprised at the reluctance of the Oregon tribes to sell their totem poles, of the Sioux to give up their snake dances, or of Hiawatha to offend the spirit of the corn. In this we are dense-minded because unsympathetic, while scholarship understands because sympathetic. Primitive man, as exemplified by many existing savage races, possessed a genuine social consciousness based on the unity of the totemic group. As the matter has been explained: The members of a totem clan normally believe themselves to be descended from a totem ancestor, who is often half human and half plant or animal— a mythical representation which significantly symbolizes the identity of the clan and its totem species. By virtue of this descent they are of one blood; and we may conceive the blood as a continuous medium running through the whole group, as it were the material substratum of its solidarity. Through it every part of the group is in vital sympathy with every other, so that in the blood feud the group is collectively responsible, or the blood may be thought of as the life of the totem—the one life derived from the common ancestor and immanent throughout the clan.

Such is the age of magic, and in that age we have reached the very roots out of which religion and morals are to grow. To dissect this primitive mass is like making a cross section of a bulb, in which may be seen, as yet undeveloped, the bud from which the flower will later bloom. In the magic age, then, we have in embryonic form shadowings of what is subsequently to come into being. Here there is a worship not of definite gods but of spirits, the process of personification being only partial and the placation of the powers being made by bloody sacrifices, not by a humble and contrite heart. A process of evolution is presaged, but the unfolding has not yet taken place. Man still does not know the difference between the figures which visit him in his dreams and ephemeral phantoms and ghosts. Before he achieves full-grown gods—the human form made divine —he has half-gods—strange combinations of man and beast such as the horse-headed black Demeter, the minotaur of Crete, the owl-eyed Athena, or Hercules hidden in the hide of a lion. Finally, the placation of these powers, ghostly, animal, or half human, is made by grossly material means. As evidence of the motive of fear at the bottom of religion we have the pouring out of the blood of human victims on the ground in order that the ghostly visitors of the underworld may suck it up; or the sacrifice of children to the totem animal of the tribe; or the "tribute of youth" to the monster of Crete, half man, half beast; or the purification by the sacrificial blood of the bull in the worship of Mithras, that ancient cult, the true soldier's religion which the Christian Church found so hard to dislodge in the Roman Empire.

Thus in the most primitive age of magic religion and morals had not yet been differentiated, nor had the functions of the leaders of the tribe. Like a semi-barbarous monarch who is executive, legislative, judicial in one, the tribal head is magician, king, and god in one. It is here that modern scholarship has shown that the personality of king and god alike has developed out of the medicine-chieftain whose business was to be food producer and rain maker. Here the king is not the strong man, the able man, the man who "can," as

A great moralist's death—Socrates drinking the hemlock

has been falsely said, but since the savage is ruled by hope and fear more than by force, the king must have magic behind him.

Here, then, is the strange figure that has been reconstructed out of the fragments of the past: The king as magician and medicine man must be what the Greeks call blameless, that is, physically without spot or blemish because upon his strength and vitality there are dependent not only the life of his people, but all those natural things by which the tribal life is nourished. Fertility, flocks and herds, rain and sunshine are wrapped up in the king's life; if that life wanes pestilence and famine will surely follow. So by savage logic the king must never be allowed to grow enfeebled and by a primitive paradox he must, if necessity arise, be put to death in order to save his life. But there are degrees in the execution of this strange sacrifice of the saviour-king. Sometimes death is declared by common consent of the tribes; at other times the king's son is the proxy; at still others a sacred beast—the tribal totem; occasionally a chance stranger is the substitute, and finally—as a mere remnant of the real killing of the king—a puppet is used as the royal representative.

The scholars have gathered cues from all quarters to make up this composite picture; but more familiar literature furnishes hints of the same thing. The pious Plutarch would have liked to think of his gods as dwellers on Olympus—serene, beneficent, immortal— hence he was greatly puzzled to discover in his travels rites of tearing to pieces, of deaths and dismemberments, of resurrections and re-generations, not only in Egypt and Asia Minor but in Greece itself in connection with his own god Dionysos. But this is not all; besides the notion of the medicine man and a king-god there is the primitive ritual of the fertility play, or year-drama, typifying the cycle of the life of man with the life of the year. Thus in the rude drama of the dying god Dionysos the fight and the death are swiftly followed by the resurrection. In its variant and world-wide forms this fight of summer and winter is disguised as the fight of the old year and the new, of darkness and light, of the old king and the new, of the father and the son, of the hero and the monster. In other words, these rites have been interpreted as the utterances of man's ardent desire and the commemoration with magical intent of nature's annual doings, since on these doings all man's life and prosperity depend.

The rudiments of morals are to be found in these magic practices, good and evil being symbolized in the succession of the seasons, of glorious summer and the winter of discontent. Here the vintage stands for the blood of the dying god Dionysos, and the sprouting of the vine in the spring for his resurrection; or in another form the seasons are portrayed in the departure of Persephone to the dark realms of the underworld and her coming again clad in flowers at the return of spring.

This drama of the year should not be considered as mere poetry, mere Tanglewood Tales, but as a profound portrayal of man's career, checkered with good and evil. In this symbolism of summer and winter, of life and death, is intertwined a dim notion of the play of destiny. As the seasons come and go there must be some law in the orderly processes of nature, since destiny, or "Moira," in its primitive use means "allotted portion." The physical order, it has been said, is guarded by the same powers that punish moral transgression. Those ministers of justice, the Moirai, are those who "if the sun should overstep his bounds would find him out."

Such is the conception of a philosopher some centuries later than the poet Homer. But even in the Iliad the same conception is found. The gods themselves are subject to Moira, destiny, personified as the Lady of Lots. Thus Zeus one day awakes to find the Trojans hard-pressed in battle by the Greeks, assisted by Poseidon. Thereupon he sends Iris with a threatening message, commanding Poseidon to cease from war and battle, and to withdraw among the tribes of the gods or into the bright sea. Poseidon is very angry and protests: "Alack," he says, "strong though he be, these words are past all bearing, if he will constrain me by violence against my will, though I am his equal in rank. For we are three brothers, born of Kronos and Rhea, Zeus and I, and Hades is the third, the lord of the dead. And in three lots were all things divided, and each took his appointed domain. When we shook the lots, to me fell the hoary sea, that I should dwell therein forever; and Hades drew the misty darkness, and Zeus the broad heaven among the æther and the clouds; the earth and high Olympus are yet common to all. Therefore never will I live according to the mind of Zeus; no, masterful though he be, let him stay quiet in his own third part."

Back of the traditional gods lay a remoter age when destiny ruled. She may be personified, yet she is not personal but is rather a blind, automatic force, a power as indifferent as the dice which are thrown in the casting of lots. Destiny stands for the allotted portions, but in this the Lady of Lots is impersonal and without purpose. The high gods may have their favourites, Zeus helping the Trojans, Poseidon the Greeks, but destiny plays no favourites. She is higher than the high gods and so represents that law of the necessary and the just of which the Greeks made so much. There are metes and bounds beyond which men must not pass, for if they do, vengeance awaits them. Overweening pride goes before a fall; overmuch prosperity is followed by adversity; there is in all things a kind of poetic justice which came to solace many. As one of the poets said: "The son of Kronos has not appointed to mortal men a lot free from pain, but sorrow and joy come round to all, as the Bear moves in his circling paths. Nothing abides in one stay for men; not starry night, nor calamities; nor yet wealth; in a moment it is gone, and another has his turn of gladness or of loss."

It is not until the Stoics that this notion of the neutrality of nature was fully worked out and that they could preach that consolation of philosophy, even-handed justice. Yet Homer himself did something to help the development of this idea. As the maid Nausicaä says to the shipwrecked Odysseus, the hapless suppliant: "It is Olympian Zeus himself that giveth weal to men, to the good as to the evil, to each one as he will, and this thy lot doubtless is of him, and so thou must in any wise endure it."

Mighty Zeus, then, came to be regarded as the dispenser of fate, representative of that destiny to which he himself had once submitted. As he distributes their lots to me, so, as supreme ruler, he does to the gods. Thus the poet Hesiod speaks of the time when Zeus "was reigning in Heaven, himself holding the lightning and glowing thunder-bolt, when he had overcome by might his father Kronos; and he distributed fairly to the immortals their portions and declared their privileges."

All this brings forward the problem of moral necessity with which the philosophers were to wrestle. The primitive notion of necessity, as will be seen, was a reflection of the social obligation of the tribe, the totem representing what could be done, the taboo what could not. These social obligations, in characteristic Greek fashion, were personified as Moirai and Erinyes, who "hold the tiller of necessity." Even cloud-compelling Zeus cannot escape the decrees of fate. The potent ruler of Olympus is the representative of destiny, yet only in part. The powers delegated to him are not supreme; back of him lie the decrees of fate. He himself laments that it is fated that the best-beloved of men, his son Sarpedon, must die at the hands of Patroclus. And as Zeus stands under the higher destiny, so do men stand beneath the Olympians as representatives of fate. The opening lines of the Iliad show this, for the poet begins with this invocation: "Sing, goddess, the wrath of Achilles, son of Peleus, the ruinous wrath that brought on the Achaians woes innumerable, and hurled down into Hades many strong souls of heroes, and gave their bodies to be a prey to dogs and all winged fowls; and so the counsel of Zeus wrought out its accomplishment from the day when first strife parted Atreides, king of men, and noble Achilles."

## III. THE HEROIC AGE

"THE invaders who perhaps in the second millennium B. C., brought the Greek speech with them into Greece, Ionia, and the islands, were far from savages, though they may have been no more than barbarians; and they found, and were highly impressed by, a culture already at least a thousand years old, much of which they assimilated. Building on this good foundation, they achieved by the date of their earliest surviving document, the Homeric poems, a civilization politically rather like that of mediæval Europe, but so far as we can judge, less brutal, less priest-ridden, less infected by cloudy mysticism, and much more capable of original thought and action; in a word, younger in outlook despite its greater age. From this again developed, not without struggles and set-backs, but with no eclipses of civilization such as those of the Seventh Century A. D. in Western Europe and the early Twentieth in Russia, the marvellous classical culture, to which belongs nearly everything of value in the modern world, including the beginnings of that great forward movement of the sciences which after long interruption was resumed about the Seventeenth Century and still continued."—H. V. ROSE, *Primitive Culture in Greece*.

Men, supermen, and gods, Myrmidons, chieftains, and Olympians formed the three groups in the unfolding story of the Homeric epics. The Iliad and the ten years' siege of Troy, and the Odyssey, or the wanderings of the wily Odysseus, may be fiction, but they present a body of beliefs, a code of conduct which long affected the Western world. The heroic age is filled with battle, murder, and sudden death, but intermingled with acts of bravery, chivalry, and hospitality which do much to offset the dark side of the picture. The heroes of the Trojan War have been called supermen, as if they lived in an unmoral realm beyond good and evil. This is as futile as calling them "perfect, gentle knights." They followed no Christian code of an advanced age of chivalry, yet they had their own ten commandments of which this list has been given: Bravery, wisdom, self-control, justice, vengeance belonging to the wronged, family affection, patriotism, generosity, magnanimity, and truth. Bravery goes without question. The opening book of the Iliad treats of the strife of kings. With bravery goes wisdom; Nestor, speaking of the quarrel between Achilles and Agamemnon, says: "In all this tale of strife between you twain, ye are the chiefest of Danaans in counsel and chiefest in battle." As for self-control even Socrates in a later and better age often quoted the words of Odysseus: "Be patient, now my soul; thou hast endured still worse than this."

Regarding the fourth cardinal virtue, justice, the name may not be used in Homer, but the sentiment exists. Even the goddess Athena was accused of rank injustice in assuming the form of Hector's brother, in order to deceive him and by the false promise of her help to persuade him to withstand Achilles. It may seem strange to call vengeance a virtue, yet a certain feeling of moral satisfaction arises when Hermes, messenger of the gods, predicts Orestes' killing of his father's murderer. Alongside of this "splendid sin" may be put the homelier virtue of family affection, as when the chief motive of the Trojans' long-continued fight was the defense of their wives and children, or when Odysseus declares that man's deepest sorrow is in burying his son. Respecting patriotism, there is this ever-memorable line: "One omen is best for all—to fight for one's fatherland."

As for generosity, this is best seen in Homeric hospitality. The very motive of the Trojan War lay in its broken laws when Paris fled with Helen, the wife of his host, Menelaus. That this was no petty scandal is shown by the deep indignation of Menelaus when he makes his prayer to Father Zeus: "King Zeus, grant me revenge on him that was first to do me wrong, even on goodly Alexander, and subdue thou him at my hands; so that many an one of men that shall be hereafter may shudder to wrong his host that hath shown him kindness."

Magnanimity is a unique Homeric virtue. Many of the heroes are called great-souled, and it is Achilles the leader who utters the famous statement: "Hateful to me even as the gates of Hades is he that hideth one thing in his heart and uttereth another." And this leaves the last of the "commandments," more honoured in the breach than in the observance. Truthfulness was not a highly developed virtue of the Greeks. If the epithet for Achilles is "magnanimous," that for Odysseus is "wily," and the whole plot of the second epic depends upon its hero's ability to lie, deceive, and weave fabrics of falsity as involved as the web of his wife Penelope. Odysseus depended upon deceit from the time when he set forth on his wanderings, after he had sacked the sacred citadel of Troy, to the time when he returned to his palace in Ithaca in disguise, and slew the suitors.

This discrepancy between magnanimity and deceit is the kind of contradiction that makes the Homeric heroes real. Their cardinal virtues may have been bravery, wisdom, self-control, and justice, but there are plenty of cases where the opposite qualities are shown. Hector flees thrice about the walls of Troy; Achilles boasts in a foolish fashion; Paris gives way to tears; and as for justice, the gods themselves do not decide the fate of Hector according to his deserts, but leave it to the chance decision of the lots. In the death of Hector a rank injustice is apparently excused by the actions of a vacillating god, but what excuse can be given for the dragging of Hector's body about the walls of Troy and the subsequent mutilation of the corpse? Here the Greeks wonder at the beauty of Hector's form, but at the same time stab him with their spears and exclaim: "Of a truth it is far easier to handle Hector now, than when he burnt the ships with blazing fire."

The excuse for all this may be sought in the demoralization due to a long war. After ten years of fighting atrocities may be expected and there is a consistent note of savagery in the countless descriptions of bloody combat. This moral license is not to be passed off as poetic license, for there is an element of fact in the Homeric fiction. The Trojan War represents a transition stage between the earlier barbarism of the invading Northmen and the later settled civilization represented by Plato, who would exclude Homeric tales from his ideal Republic, because they presented a sorry picture of warring men and erring gods. But this very picture has historical value. It is a frank portrayal of the mingled good and evil in its characters. Thus Achilles feels two natures struggling within him. When the aged and helpless King Priam begs for the return of the body of his son, the chieftain addresses him: "No longer chafe me, oh sire; of myself am I minded to give Hector back to thee, for there came to me a messenger from Zeus, even my mother who bare me, daughter of the Ancient One of the Sea. And I know, O Priam, in my mind nor am unaware that some god it is that hath guided thee to the swift ships of the Achaians. For no mortal man, even though in prime of youth, would dare to come among the host, for neither could he escape the watch, nor easily thrust back the bolt of our doors. Therefore now stir my heart no more amid my troubles, lest I leave not even thee in peace, old sire, within my hut, albeit thou art my suppliant, and lest I transgress the commandment of Zeus."

This very frankness of description which shows Achilles in violent anger extends from the heroes to the gods. The Olympians in later times were raised into the very heavens, serene and immutable; but in the Homeric world they are but magnified men, superhuman in power, but as human in their anger, their deceit, and their love affairs as were the fierce Achilles, the wily Odysseus, and the weak and amorous Paris. Since men made gods in their own image there resulted a mixed mythology, the Olympians being sometimes looked upon as supernatural powers, at others as fettered by human conditions. Even the use of magic was turned to personal account. Athena, by the aid of the helmet of Hades, "the cap of darkness," makes herself invisible to Ares and drives her spear into the belly of the god.

The supernatural powers of the divinities also served as excuses for mortals. Fair Helen of Troy is not to blame for succumbing to Paris, but was weak of will because the victim of Aphrodite, the irresistible goddess of love. Helen has been considered by some as a mere lay figure and, like Milton's definition of poetry, a mere incarnation of the simple, the sensuous, and the passionate. The English poet refers to Helen's face as that which "launched a thousand ships and burned the topless towers of Ilium," as if she were a mere mechanical cause of the Trojan War. Homer, however, presents in her case certain redeeming features—her shame at her lover's cowardice, and her words of repentance to his father Priam: "Revered art thou to me and dread, dear father of my lord: would that sore death had been my pleasure when I followed thy son hither, and left my home and my kinsfolk and my daughter in her girlhood and the lovely company of mine age-fellows. But that was not so, wherefore I pine with weeping." It is this touch of conscience that leads old Priam to offer a tactful excuse when he calls to Helen on the first day of battle: "Come hither, dear child, that thou mayest see thy former husband, thy kinsmen, and thy friends. Thou art not to blame in my sight: the gods are to blame, who brought upon men the tearful war of the Achaians."

If men, then, are affected by the will of the powers of Olympus, so the gods themselves are limited by still higher powers. There is a kind of vague faith which leads Athena to utter the sorrowful saying: "Death, which is common to all, the very gods cannot avert even from the man they love, when the ruinous doom shall bring him low of death that lays men at their length." If, beyond Olympus and the gods, there is another and higher realm, this shows that the Olympians themselves were but sublimated men: in other words, that thought had undergone a process of what has been called an Olympianization of the overlords of a former age. Behind the scenes of history and before the curtain lifts on the siege of Troy there were movements of whole peoples whose mentality and morality are partly reflected in the pages of Homer. His gods have been described as a dissolute and quarrelsome aristocracy. Thus Zeus is a sort of easy-going but all-powerful Agamemnon, ruling over a number of turbulent, self-willed lesser gods, who are perpetually trying to evade and thwart his commands. At intervals he wakes up and terrifies them into submission by threats, but it is evident that he can count on no higher principle. Hero, Poseidon, Ares, Aphrodite, Pallas, all are thoroughly insubordinate, and loyal to one thing only, that is, their party. Faction, as among the Greeks of Thucydides, had clearly usurped the place of principle, and we are actually presented with the strange picture of a city of gods more immoral, more faithless, and more depraved than the world of men.

The Homeric gods are worse than the Homeric heroes because they are in part reflections of an earlier and more barbarous age. The beautiful joyousness of the Greek polytheism is only a poetic modern fiction. The poet Hesiod, successor of old Homer, knew better when he spoke of the prototypes of these gods, the men of the last migration, as "the race of iron, whose righteousness is in their fists." In other words, the Homeric deities represent an age before good and evil, an age when might was right. Hence, if any excuse were wanted for evil actions or evil deeds the Homeric warriors could find it in the elemental passions of the earlier overlords. Thus, in a conflict with the gods in the plain of Troy, Athena hits Ares in the neck with a large stone and overthrows him; Aphrodite then leads him from the battle "groaning continually, for scarce gathered he his spirit back to him." These unlovely characters, as Plato later calls them, are nevertheless better off than men. While men are mortal, the gods are ever young; while men toil and sweat, the gods are at ease; while men consume bread and wine, the gods feast on nectar and ambrosia; while men dwell on the dark earth, the gods inhabit Olympus where the air is pure and there are no storms. In short, the gods are sublimated and superior chieftains who live on the heights, while their vassals live below.

From these details it is clear that the Olympian pantheon is but a glorified picture of the Homeric aristocracy, those chieftains who watched from the hills and exacted tribute from the people of the plains. As Plato puts it, Zeus in his "castle of heaven" reflects those

men of might who have castles as nests for their eggs, robbers covetous of money which they hoard in dark places.

As the heroes were to the henchmen, so were the gods to the
heroes. They demanded sacrifices as the price of protection and those
who paid the highest tolls were especially favoured. So Zeus says of
Hector: "Dearest to me also, since he never failed in acceptable
gifts. For never did my altar lack a proper feast, neither libations
nor savour." Odysseus, too, is praised because he surpasses in sacrifices which he offers to the immortals. There was nothing moral in
this;the arrangement was purelymercantile;sacrifices were contracts
for favours received or about to be received, insurance against
danger on land or sea. Sin, in the sense of neglect of the gods, demanded reparation, not repentance; it was not a question of remorse but of restitution, as in the case of Odysseus' followers who
slew the cattle of Hyperion and proposed repayment by building
a rich shrine to the god.

Religion, then, was largely a matter of services rendered. The
Olympian overlords would carry out the bargain, if the promise
were kept, but would punish swiftly any neglect. Indeed the Iliad
opens with the plague sent upon the Greek army by Apollo, when
for nine days the shafts of the god ranged through the hosts. In consequence of this Achilles summoned the folk to the assembly in
order to inquire of some soothsayer and priest "who shall say wherefore Phœbus Apollo is so wroth, whether he blame us by reason of
vow or hecatomb; if perchance he would accept the savour of lambs
or unblemished goats, and so would take away the pestilence from
us."

All this means that the Homeric religion was less one of abject
fear, and more one of business. Comfortable relations could be assured between men and gods, provided the latter were propitiated.
The great exception lay in the case of mortals who were overprosper-
ous. In this the gods were intensely jealous and that characteristic
Greek notion of moderation, of nothing in excess, came out in a
kind of balancing of accounts. Thus Achilles soliloquizes:"If I abide
here and besiege the Trojans' city, then my returning home is taken
from me, but my fame shall be imperishable; but if I go home to my
dear native land, my high fame is taken from me, but my life shall
endure long while, neither shall the issue of death soon reach
me."

In this testing of alternations there is a trace of the developed
doctrine of fate in the form of a universal law of balance to which

even the gods are subject. Zeus himself is bound by fate, when, in doubt concerning the outcome of the combat between the two chief contestants, the poet recounts how he "hung his golden balances and set therein two lots of dreary death, one of Achilles, one of the horse-taming Hector, and held them by the midst and poised. Then Hector's fatal day hung down and fell to the house of Hades." From such a passage it seems Homer brings forward the problems of fatalism and free will but makes no attempt to solve them. Responsibility is sometimes laid on the gods, and sometimes pushed back to mysterious forces behind the gods themselves. As Agamemnon says: "It is not I who am the cause, but Zeus, and destiny and Erinys who walketh in the darkness, who put into my soul fierce madness on the day when in the assembly I, even I, bereft Achilles of his meed. What could I do? It is the deity who accomplisheth all; Ate, eldest daughter of Zeus, who blindeth all, a power of bane."

The problem of moral responsibility in Homer is not solved but shelved. The like occurs in the problem of the hereafter. There was a kind of objective optimism obtained by not dwelling upon thoughts of "the dark portals of death." There was none of that later pessimism when death was looked upon as a release from the evils of life. Instead there was a longing for life. As the shade of Achilles says to Odysseus when he meets him in the plain of Asphodel: "I should rather be upon the fields as the servant of another, of one who had no land and little property, than be the king of all the dead."

The existence desired by the Homeric characters was one of sunshine and the open air, of the willingness to struggle for existence at all odds. Odysseus, indeed, once meditated upon making an end to himself when, on nearing his native land, a storm carried him away, but his soliloquy did not lead to suicide. "And the violent blast seized my men and bare them toward the high seas weeping, away from their own country; but as for me, I awoke and communed with my great heart, whether I should cast myself from the ship and perish in the deep, or endure in silence and abide yet among the living. Howbeit I hardened my heart to endure, and muffling my head I lay still in the ship."

To conclude: In the Homeric epics there is little of the spirit of Hamlet; the characters are not "sicklied o'er with the pale cast of thought"; they are objective, men of action, not of introspection. In short, the tone of the heroic age is one of healthy-mindedness where adventure, struggle, and death itself may be fine. Three sayings serve to show this: "A man finds joy in evils when they are past"; "A man has no greater glory so long as he lives than the athletic prizes he wins with his hands and his feet"; "It is glorious to die fighting for one's land."

## IV. FROM MYTHOLOGY TO PHILOSOPHY

"GREEK religious experience, being but part of universal religious experience, craved also gods who gave help and guidance, and groped after the God who knew the meaning of the word 'alas.' The more fortunate and the more spiritual might, indeed, sustain themselves on the level of the Olympian worship and adore, for the sake of their sheer beauty and happiness, its splendid visions of that complete and perfected existence after which all men yearn. But to the less fortunate, and the less assured, to the simple and the ignorant, to the great mass of mankind on whom the injustice and imperfection of life bore more heavily and evoked a more naïve response, the presence of evil in the world was a more important and compelling fact than the vision of the Good. To them the prime function of religion was not to portray however nobly the Ideal, but to afford man relief and escape from his present sorrows and infirmities. Man might reverence from afar the sorrowless life of the august Olympians, but his immediate need was for salvation from his own imperfection. So it is that we find side by side with the Olympian cult, with its stress upon the perfection of the divine life, another religious movement, with its stress upon the imperfections of human life and responsive to the cry for redemption from evil." —B. A. G. FULLER, *History of Greek Philosophy.*

Homer, or the school of Homeric poets, had struggled in vain with the profound problem of moral necessity. The Homeric cycle represented a compromise. To Zeus were delegated but partial powers, for even the ruler of high Olympus was subject to higher forces— the Moirai and Erinyes that "hold the tiller of necessity." This conception of an overruling destiny was thus older than the heroic age. It was a primitive notion, nowadays interpreted as a reflection of the social obligation of the tribe, the totem representing what could be done, the taboo what could not. Such remote and primitive ways of thinking—so remote and so primitive that the Greeks of classical times had but dim notions of them—persisted to Homer's day and even beyond into the era of the rational philosophers. But in the meanwhile social conditions were changing and the problem of destiny became more complicated. The idea of universal law and order is partly derived from the old tribal feeling; it is also partly a reaction against political absolutism. The earliest Greek thinkers lived in Asia Minor, not far from the places where the Homeric heroes struggled, but their struggles were not so much among themselves as against the growing despotism of the great empires of the Near East. These philosophers lived in self-governing cities like Miletus and Ephesus. Becoming political-minded, they began to look upon the universe as if it were an enlarged city-state—an empire which governed itself not in the fashion of arbitrary monarchy, but of a constitutional state. In this commonwealth the gods might be the aristocracy and men the common people, but both were subject to legal limitations. This state of affairs serves to explain certain developments in the problem of destiny. There are here three stages: First, the social structure determines the destinies of the individual—he can go thus far and no farther; next, it determines the destinies even of the gods; lastly, it is projected to include the order of nature and we have natural law identified with moral law. Just as to Zeus was given the sky, to Poseidon the sea, and to Hades the realms below, yet over all destiny, so nature itself is divided into the realms of air, water, and earth, and over all fire, which in its constancy, subtlety, and life-giving powers is counted the noblest of the elements. Thus one of the early philosophers of nature, Empedocles, of Sicily, said of these elements: "Each is lord of a different function, each has its wonted range, and in turn they gain the mastery, as the cycle of time comes round." This is genuine naturalism, but a tinge of the supernatural remains when the same interpreter gives to the elements the names of divinities: "Hear first the four roots of all things: brightly shining Zeus, life-bringing Hera, Aidoneus, and Nestis, who bedews with her tears the wellspring of mortals."

This was a concession to current usage. To this rationalist the gods were mere names, to other rationalists they were not only nonentities but nonsense. To us they may be interesting as the mountain gods of the old invading Northmen, reflections of those heroic buccaneers who fought and quarrelled, feasted and played. But to a thinker like Xenophanes, of Asia Minor, they were anything but objects of worship. According to him, "Homer and Hesiod have ascribed to the gods all deeds that are a shame and a disgrace among men: thieving, adultery, fraud. . . . Mortals fancy gods are born, and wear clothes, and have voice and form like themselves. . . . Yet if oxen and lions had hands, and could paint with their hands, and fashion images, as men do, they would make the pictures and images of their gods in their own likeness; horses would make them like horses, oxen like oxen."

To the rationalist the Olympians, as products of a sorry fancy, had simply faded away. This left the field free for natural science and for that extraordinary group of thinkers who turned from imaginary gods to the real elements. This group gradually refined these elements down into the smallest conceivable bodies, the atoms, and explained the workings of the world as due not to design but to chance. This was the great advancement of science made by Eastern Greeks in Ionia and Western Greeks in Italy, and that before the age of Socrates and Plato. This advancement might do for one type of mind, yet not for another. It was impossible for many and perhaps the most to find solace in a universe which had come into being through the war of the elements and the clash of atoms. Hence arose a demand for something more satisfying. Blind chance and harsh necessity were to them too mechanical, too impersonal. In its place sentiment demanded something moral, something personal. The old gods had gone, other gods were needed, and these, strangely enough, were found by going past the Olympians and back to those more intimate powers whose worship lingered among the people. There were the old gods of high heaven, there were also older gods of earth, and now the Olympian cult is supplanted in the minds of many by the Orphic. This cult took its name from the legendary hero Orpheus, who with the aid of Hermes sought to lead his wife Eurydice from the realms of the dead. Orphicism was a form of salvationism and as such offered a hope of personal immortality. It had its defects due to an admixture of Eastern occultism such as rites of purification and baths of blood. But it lent itself to a partial rationalization at the hands of Pythagoras, the mathematical philosopher of southern Italy, from whom it passed on to Plato. At the least Plato puts in the mouth of Socrates, on the day of his death, a discussion of "that ancient doctrine, that souls pass out of this world to another, and there exist, and then come back hither from the dead and are born again."

This notion, refined and ennobled in Socrates's last talk before his death, has been considered a reformation of the old Dionysiac religion, the cult of the dying god who comes to life again, symbol of the seasonal round of vegetation, with its death in winter and rebirth in the spring. This is the primitive notion of reincarnation, exemplified in the harvest festival and the spring festival, represented by a mathematical symbol, the cycle of existence, the wheel of life, which is again divided into two half-circles of light and of darkness, of summer and winter, through which the life of the individual, like the life of nature, continuously revolves. To learn of this life, then, is the way of salvation. But "the way" was almost purposely obscured by the occult. The followers of Pythagoras banded themselves into a secret society, whose mysteries were unfolded only to the initiate. They referred to "the master" as "He," and for authority simply explained "He said it." This *ipse dixit* is a cause of irritation to the rationalist who avoids dogmas and secrets and prefers diagrams and science. Yet the latter were not wholly lacking. There was the wheel of life and the analogy of the circling seasons. If plants and animals appear and disappear in annual cycles, why should not the soul go through a similar process?

There have here been preserved fragmentary sayings which may appear both fantastic and comic, yet were uttered by the rationalists themselves Thus Empedocles declares: "I was once a bird, a fish, a maiden, and a bush," and Xenophanes is reported to have expostulated in behalf of a beaten dog because he recognized in its howls the voice of a departed friend.

There was in all this that imaginative quality of the Greek which sees some reason in all things. However, it was the problem of reminiscence as connected with the doctrine of rebirth that especially puzzled them. The things we perceive with the senses, we are told, remind us of things we knew when the soul was out of the body and could perceive reality directly. We recognize because we have cognized in a previous state of existence. At any rate, Pythagoras, and after him Plato, thus reasoned in regard to the mathematical axioms: "We have never seen equal sticks or stones, but we know what equality is, and it is just by comparing the things of sense with the realities of which they remind us that we judge them to be imperfect." Or take triangles. Pythagoras enunciated the proposition, still named after him, that the square of the hypotenuse of a right-angled triangle is equal to the sum of the squares of the other two sides. Why can we assert that as absolutely true, though no measurement of actual triangles would come out absolutely accurate? This, it is answered, is because we have seen the perfect triangle in a previous state of existence, an archetype, or supreme model, of which all triangles in this lower world are ectypes, or copies.

This, at least, is the explanation of the Pythagorean Plato, and to him it was but a step from mathematics to morals. The reason why we recognize goodness in this man or that, political justice in this state or that, is because in a former, preëxistent stage the

soul has envisaged "white transparent thoughts" of perfect goodness, truth, beauty—that trinity of celestial excellences which
once the soul beheld before it descended to this mundane sphere.

Such is the high realm of speculation where Plato's fancy winged
its roving flight. But meanwhile, in this poetic search for the highest
good another more prosaic mind had been at work. This was the
practical Socrates who dealt with things about him and, in the
language of Cicero, brought philosophy from heaven to earth.

# PART TWO
## THE GREEK SCHOOLS

# I. SOCRATES AND THE SOPHISTS (469–399 B. C.)

"BETWEEN the years 440 and 400 B. C. a visitor to Athens would
have seen, during the forenoon in the market-place, at other times in
one of the gymnasia or of the covered walks which were found in all
Greek cities, a strongly built but ugly man talking to a small group
of people. These Greeks would be discussing the meaning of religion
and irreligion, discussing what are beauty and ugliness, what are
justice and courage, what are the qualities that make men good
rulers, and how to define 'city' or 'government.' . . . Generals,
cavalry officers, courtesans, painters, country gentlemen, aspiring
or disappointed politicians came to discuss their affairs with Socrates, and went away enlightened on subjects as various as house-
building, painting, picnicking, operations of war, indigestion, and
physical exercise."—R. W. LIVINGSTONE, *The Greek Genius and Its
Meaning to Us.*

Socrates, the first of the great moralists of Greece, is a paradox.
His features were plain and so was his birth, yet men were attracted
to him in spite of his looks, while aristocrats like Plato and Alcibiades
were proud to be counted his disciples. Behind this walking "Mask
of Silenus," with its prominent eyes and upturned nose, there was a
mind that baffled Athens. The man whose face was his fortune,
because it was conspicuously ugly among a crowd of handsome men,
had such a sense of humour that it took its very name from him. It
was Socratic irony that led him to say that the art of midwifery,
which his mother had practised in regard to the body, he himself
practised in regard to the soul, by bringing to birth and consciousness truths held before unconsciously. It was Socratic irony that
made him accept the message from the Delphic oracle that he was
the wisest of men with the words: "Yes, because I know my own
ignorance." It was Socratic irony that led him at his trial to call himself the gadfly of the state, thereby implying that the state was an
old horse that needed prodding.

Socrates's strange face and his biting tongue were not all; within,
deeply within, behind the ironic mask, lay a power of moral appeal.
In later days Plutarch, recalling the confessions of the self-indulgent

but repentant Alcibiades, declared that "outwardly Socrates to those who met him appeared rude and uncouth and overbearing, but within was full of earnestness and of matters that moved his hearers to tears and wrung their hearts." But Socrates did not gain this reputation of moral earnestness until after his tragic death. The majority preferred the professional teacher to the casual talker. The snobs employed the Sophists, with their purple robes and gorgeous vocabularies, to educate their sons, and looked down on this son of the people who wore one garment summer and winter and used the language employed by butchers, bakers, and candlestick-makers.

We know that Socrates was a rare case of a self-made man who did not worship his own creator, yet respectable Athenians thought he was only posing when he declared that he was but a searcher after truth who had to go to all sorts and conditions of men in order to find out what was right. Their ideal teacher was the solemn Sophist who dressed to kill; they did not relish this plain man who put on no airs, who, as Xenophon describes him, used to go early in the morning to the public walks and gymnasia; and when the market was full he was to be seen there, and the remainder of the day he was always where he would meet most people.

The snobs did not see that a man can come up from the streets and yet be a great leader. They wanted the equivalent of a college education, whereas Socrates had only the equivalent of a common school education except for what he could pick up from the cheaper Sophists. As he again ironically remarked, he could not afford the fifty-minæ course but had to be content with the single-mina course of instruction. Thus Socrates was a graduate of the school of hard knocks who learned to talk by talking and to preach what he had himself practised. His two main tenets were self-control and self-knowledge, and here the stories about him are quite consistent. When he made friends with people of means he could enjoy their luxuries. He outdrank Aristophanes at Agathon's banquet, but generally he preferred not to drink too much lest he might think too little. He believed in temperance, not in prohibition, and when made symposiarch, or leader of the feast, he called for "little cups." Good food he enjoyed, but he could endure the poor cooking of his wife. The same with clothes. During the campaign at Potidæa, when others were clad in sheepskins and furs, he walked barefoot on the snow. But unlike many moral reformers Socrates did not insist that what he did was the only thing to do. If the Greeks had smoked tobacco he would not have belonged to the Anti-Nicotine League.

No, his doctrine of self-control seemed to be this: "I can do with, and I can do without, as I please, and I trust that you can do the same." Or, as he put the matter, when present at the fair: "How many things there are which I do not need."

To Socrates material things might be matters of indifference, but self-knowledge was not a matter of indifference. He took as his motto the Delphic utterance, "Know thyself," for to know one-self is to know the world, since the motives that move other men are the same as those that move oneself. But this subject is not so simple as it looks, for out of the sayings of Socrates quite opposite schools arose. Because he could do without luxuries the Cynics railed against luxury and Diogenes retired to his tub. Because he was a good judge of wine and enjoyed the sight of dancing girls, not Epicurus but his degenerate followers concocted their philosophy of sensual pleasures.

Socrates has been compared to Luther, who had two sides to his nature—the ascetic monk who practised penances and the jovial host who enjoyed good beer, good music, and good table talk. In other words, people can find what they want in complex characters. Lincoln may be known by some as a retailer of tavern stories, by others as "a man of God"; Walt Whitman may be known as a "magnificent idler" or, on the other hand, the American poet who has best succeeded in showing that nature is indeed "that fair appa-rition that shines about us."

Socrates was not only two-sided by many-sided. A speculative philosopher, he was also a good soldier and a good judge. Of the four cardinal virtues we have already learned of his wisdom and tem-perance, the latter in the sense of doing nothing in excess. As to bravery and justice, he exhibited the former when he rescued Alci-biades, while he showed a combination of bravery and justice on three separate occasions: first, when he alone protested against condemning without a hearing certain generals who were charged with neglecting to save the wounded; again, when in the reign of terror under the Thirty Tyrants he was told to assist in the arrest of an innocent citizen; and finally, when at his own trial he refused the suggestions of his friends to escape the death penalty by bribing his jailers. Socrates was many-sided, but he held to this single principle: to obey the oracle, the voice of conscience. His last words bore this out: "Strange indeed would be my conduct, O men of Athens, if I, who, when I was ordered by the generals whom you chose to com-mand me at Potidæa and Amphipolis and Delium, remained where they placed me, like any other man facing death—if now, when, as I conceive and imagine, God orders me to fulfil the philosopher's mission of searching into myself and other men, I were to desert my post through fear of death or any other fear; . . . and I might justly be arraigned in court for denying the existence of the gods if I disobeyed the oracle because I was afraid of death, fancying that I was wise when I was not wise."

Such was the character of Socrates, who learned a little music in his youth and all his life played on the emotions of men. He made enemies by his irony, for it is not pleasant to be criticized before the public for one's self-conceit; he made friends by his sympathy, for even Alcibiades declared that he was the only man that made him ashamed; he made devoted disciples by his ability, for Xenophon wrote in his *Memorabilia* that his teacher was "of men the best and happiest," while Plato declared that Socrates was the "best, the most sensible, and the most just man of his age."

These praises of Socrates's two most famous followers were called out because of all available teachers he was to their minds the foremost. In character he was the golden mean between two extreme types of thinkers. At one end of the scale were the skeptics where, as Democritus said, "truth lies at the bottom of the well," and where, as Socrates himself remarked, it would take a Delian diver to get at the meaning of the current speculations about the cosmos. At the other end were the dogmatists, the teachers who promised much but accomplished little. These were largely the foreign philosophers of Asia Minor and southern Italy who, in the Golden Age of Pericles, were drawn to Athens as the literary mart of the Greek world.

While Socrates was partly skeptical of the philosopher of nature he was wholly skeptical of the Sophist. The word, which originally meant "the wise man," speedily lost its value, when the professional wise man claimed to teach virtue in a few sittings. Now the Sophists have been called half journalist and half professor because they sought publicity and received pay; they might also be called promoters of get-wise-quick schemes, not in the way of a correspondence course, but of a conversation course. They guaranteed that by asking questions and obtaining answers people might be taught social manners, ability to win law cases, and the fundamentals of political justice—all in short order.

Where is Socrates to be placed in this scheme? Aristophanes in his comedy entitled *The Clouds* satirizes him as partaking of the weaknesses of both sides. He is "up in the air" like the speculators upon nature; he also runs a "philosophy shop" like a mercenary Sophist and offers to sell any virtue for a price. This is unfair. A truer statement was made by Cicero when he declared that Socrates was he who first brought philosophy from heaven to earth. By this was meant that he was the first to bring ethics out of the realm of the doubtful and into the realm of the practical, his attitude being that those who reasoned about law and order in the world above had not yet brought that law and order into the world below, the world of man and of the state. He himself did not believe, as did Anaxagoras, that what made life worth living was contemplating the heavens and the universal order. He preferred the task of finding a common element in the conduct of human affairs. Plato makes Socrates say that the things in the heavens were the chief studies in his youth, but that he did not find them worth while, since the physical philosophers had proved with equal effectiveness that nature is one and many, finite and infinite, with and without change.

It took generations of hard thinking to reconcile these discrepancies, to obtain a working model of the universe, and to point out man's place in that universe. Aristotle worked toward that problem and the Stoics almost solved it, but that was in a later age. Meanwhile the path before Socrates was to find some common element in the business of life, to search for some law of conduct which might guide all men; in short, the Socratic quest was the quest of justice in the affairs of family and friendship, of partnerships and business, and of peace and war, as Plato puts it in that ideal commonwealth, the Republic.

To Socrates the proper study of mankind was man. Now while the Sophists had made a start in the moral sciences, it was a false start. The trouble is they made the thing too easy and persuaded people to think that learning to be virtuous is like learning any ordinary accomplishment. What Socrates, the true philosopher who taught for the love of teaching, had here to contend with was the charlatan who as a perfect jack-of-all-trades had taken up with the latest fad—the art of being good. Here Socrates cites the case of two brothers, Dionysodorus and Euthydemus, who are the chief performers. They are natives of Chios who in former days appeared at Athens as teachers of rhetoric and of the art of fighting in armour. To this they have now added a new fighting accomplishment, the art of eristic, or fighting with words, which they are likewise willing to teach, "for a consideration." But they can also teach virtue in a very short time and in the very best manner. In this ironical account Socrates is made to say: "Here I offer my old person to Dionysodorus; he may put me into the pot, like Medea the Colchian, kill me, pickle me, eat me, if he will only make me good." To this

Ctesippus adds, "And I, Socrates, am ready to commit myself to the strangers; they may skin me alive, if they please, and I am pretty well skinned by them already, if only my skin is made at last, not like that of Marsyas, into a leathern bottle, but into a piece of virtue."

While Socrates satirizes the charlatans among the Sophists, he is willing to acknowledge that there is some good among those of better reputation. Protagoras is the chief of these, and while he was charged with earning more by his tongue than did the sculptor Phidias by his chisel, yet his teaching is by no means sophistry. So to understand Socrates's attitude toward the better type of Sophists we may turn to the debate which took place at the house of Callias. Education and admonition, declares Protagoras, commence in the first years of childhood, and last to the very end of life. Mother and nurse and father and tutor are quarrelling about the improvement of the child as soon as ever he is able to understand them: he cannot say or do anything without their setting forth to him that this is just and that is unjust; this is honourable, that is dishonourable; this is holy, that is unholy; do this and abstain from that. And if he obeys, well and good; if not, he is straightened by threats and blows, like a piece of warped wood. At a later stage they send him to teachers, and enjoin them to see to his manners even more than to his reading and music; and the teachers do as they are desired. And when the boy has learned his letters and is beginning to understand what is written, as before he understood only what was spoken, they put into his hands the works of the great poets, which he reads at school; in these are contained many admonitions, and many tales, and praises, and encomia of ancient famous men, which he is required to learn by heart, in order that he may imitate or emulate them and desire to be like them. Then, again, the teachers of the lyre take similar care that their young disciple is temperate and gets into no mischief; and when they have taught him the use of the lyre, they introduce him to the poems of other excellent poets, who are the lyric poets; and these they set to music and make their harmonies and rhythms quite familiar to the children, in order that they may learn to be more gentle and harmonious, and rhythmical, and so more fitted for speech and action; for the life of man in every part has need of harmony and rhythm. Then they send them to the master of gymnastic, in order that their bodies may better minister to the virtuous mind, and that the weakness of their bodies may not force them to play the coward in war or on any other occasion. This

is what is done by those who have the means, and those who have
the means are the rich; their children begin education soonest and
leave off latest. When they have done with masters, the state again
compels them to learn the laws, and live after the pattern which
they furnish and not after their own fancies; and just as in learning
to write the writing master first draws the lines with a style for the
use of the young beginner, and gives him the tablet and makes him
follow the lines, so the city draws the laws, which were the invention
of good lawgivers who were of old time; these are given to the young
man, in order to guide him in his conduct whether as ruler or ruled;
and he who transgresses them is to be corrected, or, in other words,
called to account, which is a term used not only in your country, but
also in many others. Now when there is all this care about virtue,
private and public, why, Socrates, do you still wonder and doubt
whether virtue can be taught?

## THE SOCRATIC QUEST

We have just had an example of the Socratic method of getting
at the truth. Here two alternatives appear. There are those who
would guarantee success in fighting with words as they do in fighting with armour; there are those who, like Protagoras, make the
attaining of virtue a long and laborious process. The latter was the
ideal of higher education cherished at Athens which called the
Sophists into being. How could this ideal be attained? Plato warns
against the false Sophists who deceive by the illusion of words just as
the painter deceives by the illusion or perspective, yet he leaves room
for the true Sophist like Socrates, who may be skeptical as to physics but is certain as to ethics. This certainty may be attained provided that these two steps are taken: first, a consciousness of one's
ignorance, and second, the attainment of clear general notions regarding the cardinal virtues.

The Sophists were not wrong in holding that goodness could be
taught, for Protagoras had just presented a scheme of education
which is almost Socratic. However, they were wrong in making no
distinction between philosophic and popular goodness, between
goodness that is constant and invariable depending on intellect, and
goodness that varies because depending on mere custom. Therefore
what Socrates sought was a habit of mind that would enable its
possessor to pursue goodness steadily, in short, moral efficiency.
Practices are one thing, principles another, and these principles

Socrates summed up in four great virtues or habits of mind—wisdom, courage, temperance, and justice, the greatest of these being justice in the sense of harmony between the other three.

Man's efficiency is then threefold: in his reason he should show wisdom, in his spirited element, bravery, in his appetitive nature, temperance. Put in everyday language, his head, heart, and natural appetites should work together to attain harmonious ends. Such is man the noblest of the animals, tripartite in capacities, virtues, and organs, and all to be exercised judiciously, with "nothing in excess"; not too intellectual, nor too spirited, nor too appetitive, but all working in accord like the three classes in the state—the rulers, the warriors, and the workers.

Socrates started this famous threefold scheme in his search for the good man and Plato carried it on in his search for the ideal commonwealth, for, as the author of the *Republic* says, the state is but "man writ large." But since this is only the first sketch the details must be gone into. To Socrates moral relations are threefold—duty to oneself, duty to one's friends, and duty to one's state. The moral quest, then, starts at a specific point and develops in ever-widening circles. First to be true to oneself is to show self-control in one's wants and desires. Moderation is the corner stone of all the virtues, yet such independence as to worldly wants does not mean cynical independence of other men. The cynic Diogenes is no true Socratic when he retires grumbling into his tub. There is a nobler side of life and that is friendship. On this topic and the kindred factors of sympathy and love there has been much misrepresentation. The friendship between Socrates and his younger followers has been confounded with the worst of Greek vices; sympathy has been identified with the maudlin sentimentality of the symposium or drinking bout, and love between man and man turned not into something truly disinterested and Platonic—"the marriage of kindred mind"—but something quite Plutonic, partaking of the lower regions.

These are interpretations of later evil-minded days. Socratic friendship was healthy-minded; Alcibiades said of Socrates that he was the only man that ever made him feel ashamed; and Socrates as the symposiarch, or master of the banquet, specified that the wine should be mixed with plenty of water. Yet he was no sentimental prohibitionist who talked glibly of the feast of reason and the flow of soul; but like any sensible ancient he was not averse to the cup that cheers, although he did intimate that the strength of an argument varies inversely with the strength of a drink.

Friends, therefore, to Socrates are not mere boon companions any more than love is based on the sensual conception of Eros. Friendship to him is a moral relation and it can exist only between virtuous men, since friendship between bad men is really as rare as honour among thieves, and no man can expect to preserve the friendship of another if he is contemptible to another. It is this compelling power of mutual respect that keeps a man on the straight road; conscience is here like a charioteer who does not want to let the public see that he cannot control his steeds. This is the negative side, the side of the moral check. There is also the positive, the side of the moral spur. The Socratic circle was not a mutual admiration society. Socrates and his friends did not fool themselves that way. There is not a single dialogue where the master does not give some sly digs to his pupils and where the pupils do not return the compliment. Often when Socrates professes ignorance he is ironical; when the fierce Thrasymachus comes at him like a roaring lion he may pretend to be frightened, but before the dialogue is over this advocate of the principle that might is right is flustered and out of breath. Often, too, the younger men turned the tables on the older. As Socrates strutted through the streets he was compared to a meditative pelican, while his very looks were utilized in asking the sophistical question: "If Socrates were handsome, would he still be Socrates?"

The Socratic circle was not a mutual admiration society nor was the symposium mere horseplay. There was a bohemian spirit; there was also good breeding. The contestants did not gather together for the sake of showing themselves off, or of showing others up; the Sophists might argue for pay and the "Eristics" for victory, but Socrates argued for certainty in so far as that might be attainable in the three moral relations. In regard to the individual this meant self-knowledge and self-control; in regard to friendship mutual respect and confidence; in regard to the state service to the commonwealth and obedience to the laws. In this last relation, as in the first two, Socrates practised what he preached. In the Peloponnesian War he did his duty as a citizen-soldier and in one of the battles saved the life of Alcibiades. In both the affairs of the generals at Arginusæ and of Leon of Salamis he voted against the majority when they tried to override the law and condemn the accused without fair trial.

But his great service to the state was criticizing it. The two affairs just mentioned were political crimes, one on the part of the old democracy, the other on the part of the Thirty Tyrants, and in both cases lack of intelligence was shown. Now since the attempted crime was a stupidity Socrates reasons that knowledge would be the cure of injustice. But how can such knowledge be attained? Democracy represents the rule of the majority, but democracy, being a "many-headed monster," can hardly act intelligently. Again an oligarchy, like the Thirty, is too often based on birth or wealth, and neither of these accidents of fortune guarantees a high intelligence quotient. It was his unhappy political experiences that led Socrates to his great maxims that goodness is based on wisdom, and that the wise man is bound to be the good man. Apply this to the administration of Athens and see what Socrates is bound to advocate. In place of the equality of all he demands government by professional adepts; in place of an aristocracy of birth or wealth he demands an aristocracy of brains—in short, what modern democracies threatened by swollen fortunes are demanding. These measures, advocated more than two thousand years ago, still hold good. In a strong presidential cabinet one can generally count on a majority consisting of college-bred men; in an efficient diplomatic service one chooses men not for their looks, but for their knowledge of languages; and in a municipal government one prefers a city manager to an idol of the people.

In regard to the state the wise man is in the long run the good man; this is fairly obvious. In regard to the individual the same maxim is somewhat dubious. Alcibiades was trained by Socrates but was a traitor to his country; several of the Thirty Tyrants had the best education that wealth could afford, but feathered their own nests. To say that knowledge and virtue are identical is to awaken doubt in the mind. How can the wise man be the good man, when at the bottom of the social scale the cleverest criminals are the most dangerous, and when at the top of the state stands a Machiavelli advising the "perfect Prince" to educate himself in craft, deceit, and guile?

We ask Socrates this question. Let us imagine that he is among us, having just come over on tourist third class. "By the dog of Egypt," he might reply, "you doubt that a wise man is the good man? Then consider the case of the bad man who sees how foolish he has been. There is one of your burglars who has recently written a work entitled *It Doesn't Pay*. What did he mean by that? His conclusion was that crime in the long run brought him less reward than steady industry, and that as an honest janitor he would have had more in the bank than as an agile porch climber." "Well," we would answer, "this might apply to the small fry, but how about male-factors of great wealth; are they not very astute? According to popular morality, it is a sin to steal a pin, but is not so wicked to prostitute a people, if only dust can be thrown into their eyes by charity, by subsidizing great foundations of research, by erecting religious edifices, from altars to unknown gods to Y. M. C. A. buildings."

To these questions Athenian Socrates might have no answer. The problem of swollen fortunes corrupting a whole people hardly existed in a city of some thirty thousand inhabitants. However, Socrates's pupil, the imaginative Plato, did have an answer and in his latter descriptions of the baser forms of government tells us what might be done with the mighty malefactors, however clever and unscrupulous. Socrates the moralist, advocating intelligence as the chief criterion, has been accused of lack of intelligence, but it must be remembered that the greater problems of a complex civilization had not yet loomed over his horizon. Still another criticism of his system had been made, and that is that to make virtue a matter of calculation would result in a kind of moral mathematics. If we knew what would be the results of our acts, then virtue would be prudence, and we would have the drab utilitarianism of a Franklin—honesty is the best policy, because it pays the best in the long run. Now Socrates had little of this in his make-up. When it comes to great issues, as when the jury at his trial tells him that it would pay him to keep his mouth shut, he makes this reply: "If you were to say to me, We shall let you go free but on this condition, that you give up this quest of yours and philosophize no more. If you are caught at it again you shall die. If, I say, you were to let me off on these terms, I should reply: Fellow Athenians, I love you, I am devoted to you; but I shall obey God rather than you, and while breath and strength hold out I shall never cease from pursuing wisdom."

The Socratic pursuit of wisdom was, in its final form, ethical. Knowledge is virtue because truth and right are the same for all and it is only ignorance, mistake, confusion, which make them seem different to different men. Here are some examples of the wisdom of virtue: He is wise who distinguishes between the excess and the defect of a quality such as minding one's business and not intruding into the affairs of others above or below him; he is brave who distinguishes between what is really dangerous and what is not, and knows how to guard against risks as the sailor in a storm at sea; he is temperate who can distinguish between the real and apparent good in food and drink and gymnastics; finally, he is just who properly harmonizes those parts of his nature corresponding to the above virtues. To take them in reverse order from lower to higher: He will exercise control against the concupiscent principle which in every man forms the largest portion of his nature; in like manner, we call an individual brave in virtue of the spirited element of his nature, when this part of him holds fast, through pain and pleasure; and we call him wise in virtue of that small part which reigns within him and issues these instructions.

## SOCRATES: HIS TRIAL AND DEATH

Socrates's definition of justice as the last and highest virtue resolves itself into political justice and as such is expounded at length by Plato in the *Republic*. It fits into the characteristic Greek insistence on limitation or avoidance of extremes, like the golden mean of Pythagoras and the ancient motto: "Nothing in excess." Theoretically this is admirable, but does it work practically? Turn to the *Republic* and see what pages of question and answer are required to gain the first notion of this ideal. Besides Socrates as interlocutor there are in this dramatic dialogue three characters who take as many points of view. There is the aged Cephalus, who stands for the simple morality of former times and has an intuition for right and wrong, but no theory. Besides this gentleman of the old school is his son Polymarchus, who takes the definition of justice from Simonides as a Sophistic art. His motto seems to be: "Keep just within the law." There is next Thrasymachus, whose very name suggests boldness, who looks upon old-fashioned maxims as absurd, favours new views of morality, holds that the claims of tradition may be broken by reason, and concludes that man should be guided by nature, because nature says: "Enjoy yourself." There is finally Socrates himself, who inclines toward the view that both reason and nature may be nearer to the old traditional view than to "the new freedom."

All these views sound familiar. They are so because they are founded on human nature. Take Cephalus: personally he may be a fine old man, but logically his principles sound rather hollow. He offers several definitions which are each in turn demolished by Socrates simply by pointing out what lies behind them. Cephalus says first that justice is the subjection of the senses, but as an old man who has outgrown his passions he makes a virtue out of a necessity. Next he states that happiness is the result of justice and that contentment is its criterion, but as he has fair health and moderate wealth he ought to be contented. Finally he states that justice consists in telling the truth and paying one's debts, but as he has no need to lie and a genteel sufficiency of this world's goods, these are not such difficult virtues. In all these qualities he reminds one of Major Pendennis, that kind of paragon with beautiful manners who so exasperated his nephew, young Pendennis.

The old man's rather simple morality having been disposed of, his son Polymarchus, the fighter, takes up the cudgels in favour of this definition: Justice is to do good to friends and ill to enemies, in war, peace, and partnerships. This sounds better, for it is the everyday morality of practical men and follows the old Greek view, handed down from Homer, that the true manly character is shown in the power and will to favour friends and injure enemies. But see the consequences of this, retorts Socrates: Many a man who is ignorant of the world has had friends and to these he ought to do harm; also he has good enemies whom he ought to benefit, and thus we arrive at the exact converse of the proposition of Simonides.

This is too subtle for the restive Thrasymachus, representative of a rough-and-ready morality. He bursts into the discussion with the exclamation: "Away with such watery stuff. Let us have some system that will bring results and that right quickly. Listen, then: I proclaim that might is right, justice the interest of the stronger." This sounds simple, but what, asks Socrates, is the meaning of this? "You can't mean to say that because Polydamus, the Pancratiast, who is stronger than we are, finds the eating of beef for his interest, that this is equally for our interest who are weaker than he is?"

All this is a sample of the Socratic method of disposing of his adversaries. He sweeps away the trivial definitions already given in order to clear the ground for something better. As finally understood, justice resolves itself into political justice, when the end of government is not the multiplication of wealth, not the selfish doing as one likes, not the domination of a faction, but the virtue and true happiness of the individual and the order and harmony of the whole. Such, at least, is the city portrayed by Plato, highly idealized, yet based on the practical results already gained by Socrates. Plato had been listening to his master for some eight years and here takes advantage of that relentless logic which Socrates employed to the very last. This method of combined reasoning and irony is best seen in Socrates's Defense of Himself as reported by Plato in the *Apology*. This title, taken in its modern sense, is misleading. The ancient apology was a defense, and the defense, in turn, an attack on one's enemies. So at his trial Socrates, now seventy years of age, faces his accusers and uses the same words that he was accustomed to use in the market place, at the table of the money changers, or wherever he might be. The charges against him are threefold: He is accused of atheism in prying into things in the heavens and not believing in

the gods; he is accused of corrupting the youth of Athens in making
the worse appear the better; and finally he is accused of being unpatriotic in pointing out the defects of the democracy. To these
several charges he replies that he has nothing to do with physical
speculations such as that the sun is a stone and the moon earth, but
that he does believe in divine agency. There is, he declares, "a certain supernatural and divine sign that comes to me and which I have
had ever since I was a child, a sort of voice that speaks to me and
dissuades me from doing what I was on the point of doing." This,
he continues, is a divinity far superior to those believed in by the
people, such as those "sons of gods"—natural sons, as it were, by
nymphs or some other mortal mothers as rumour makes them.

As for the charge of corrupting the youth, Socrates disposes of
this by describing how that charge arose: "Young men of the richer
classes, who have not much to do, come about me of their own accord: they like to hear the pretenders examined, and they often imitate me, and examine others themselves; there are plenty of persons,
as they soon discover, who think that they know something, but
really know little or nothing; and then those who are examined by
them, instead of being angry with themselves are angry with me.
This confounded Socrates, they say; this villainous misleader of
youth. And then if somebody asks them, Why, what evil does he
practise or teach? they do not know, and cannot tell; but in order
that they may not appear to be at a loss, they repeat the ready-made
charges which are used against all philosophers about teaching
things up in the clouds and under the earth, and having no gods, and
making the worse appear the better cause; for they do not like to
confess that their pretense of knowledge has been detected—which
is the truth; and as they are numerous and ambitious and energetic,
and are all in battle array and have persuasive tongues, they have
filled your ears with their loud and inveterate calumnies."

As for being unpatriotic, that charge is absurd. Continues Socrates: "Fellow Athenians, when the generals whom you had chosen
to place over me assigned me my post at Potidæa, at Amphipolis,
and at Delium, I remained where they had put me, facing death like
any other man. Strange indeed then would be my conduct if, through
fear of death or of anything else, I were now to desert the post where
God has placed me, as I am firmly persuaded that he has, commanding me to spend my life in the search after truth and in examining myself and others."

As for the connected charge of criticizing the state, that charge

PLATO

Meditating on immortality before Socrates, the butterfly, skull, and poppy

Socrates acknowledges as true and turns with crushing irony upon his accusers:

"So, fellow Athenians, I am not making the present defense just to save my own life, as might be supposed. Not at all. I am doing so to save you from sinning against God and rejecting his gift to you by condemning mé. For if you kill me you will not easily find another man who like me will, at God's bidding, literally stick to the state like a gadfly to a horse—if you'll pardon a rather ludicrous comparison. For the state is like a huge horse of noble breed, but rather sluggish from his very size, and needing the gadfly to wake him up. And I think God has given me to the state to play the part of just such a gadfly and I keep lighting upon you any and everywhere, and spend the live-long day waking you up, and persuading you and rebuking you. My friends, you will not easily find another man like that, and if you take my advice you will spare my life. However, it is quite possible that you are irritated, like drowsy men when they are awakened, and that you will listen to Anytus and crush this gadfly, lightly putting me to death. Then you could sleep on in peace for the rest of your day—unless God in his care for you were to send you another tormentor. That it is God himself who has given me to the state you can see from this: no mere human motive would account for my having neglected all my own affairs, allowing my private interests to go to ruin during all these years, while at the same time always looking after your welfare, going to you all, one by one, like a father or an elder brother, and urging you to pay heed to virtue. If I had taken a fee for my exhortations, and made any money out of them, my conduct could be accounted for. But now you yourselves see that my accusers, though they have accused me of everything else with such effrontery, hadn't the face to try to show that I ever either asked or received any fee. I offer you, I fancy, in my actual poverty an incontrovertible witness to the truth of my words."

To be the gadfly of the state—such, declares Socrates with superb assurance, is his mission, a mission which has been assigned to him by God, who has made his will known through oracles, dreams, and in every other way by which the divine providence has ever imposed any duty upon man. Such was the final argument in Socrates's *Apology*. The defense became an accusation and, added to all that was said before, so wrought upon his judges that they found him guilty and sentenced him to death. At this moment Socrates turned upon his condemners, first with a prophecy as to their future in this life, and then with a confession as to his own high hopes for life after death:

"I want to prophesy the future to you who have condemned me. For I am about to die, and that is the time when men are most gifted with prophetic power. I say to you, you who have condemned me to death, that the moment I am gone punishment will overtake you, yes, by heaven, a punishment far more severe than the penalty of death which you have inflicted on me. You have now done this thing in the belief that you are going to be free from the necessity of giving an account of your lives. I assure you that the result will be quite to the contrary. There will be many more to call you to account, men whom I have thus far been holding in check though you didn't perceive it. And they are younger, and will be so much the harder upon you, and you will be so much the more angry with them. For you are much mistaken if you think that by putting men to death you can keep people from reproaching you for your evil lives. That way of escape is certainly not possible, nor is it honourable. The way that is at once easiest and most honourable is, not to be silencing the reproaches of others, but to be making yourselves as perfect as you can. With this prophecy, then, I take my leave of you who have condemned me.

"But with you who have voted to acquit me I would gladly converse about this thing that has happened, while the officers are busy, and before I go where I must go to die. Pray stay that long with me. my friends, for there is no reason why we should not talk together about our beliefs while we may. I want to explain to you who are my friends the meaning of what has just befallen me. For a very strange thing has happened to me, my judges—for I am surely right in addressing you as judges; my familiar prophetic voice, the divine sign, has up to the present time always been in the habit of opposing me even in most trifling matters, when I was on the point of acting wrongly. But now you yourselves see what has just happened to me, a thing which one might think, which is generally considered the greatest possible evil. But the divine sign did not oppose me as I was leaving my house this morning, nor as I was mounting the platform here in court, nor did it oppose me once in my speech in what I was about to say. Yet often on other occasions it has stopped me right in the middle of a speech. But now, in this affair, it has not opposed a single word or deed of mine. What do I take to be the meaning of this? I will tell you. This thing that has happened to me must be a blessing, and we who think that death is an evil are surely mistaken in our belief. I have received striking evidence of this, for it is impossible that the divine sign should not have opposed me, unless indeed I am going to fare well.

"Again, look at the matter in this light, too, and we discover high hope for believing that death is a blessing. There are just two alternatives with regard to death: either the dead man has lost all power of perception, and wholly ceased to be; or else, as tradition has it, the soul at death changes its habitation, moving from its home here to its home yonder. And as there is no perception at all, and death is like a sound sleep unbroken even by a dream, then it is a wonderful gain. For I think if one were called upon to select the night in which he slept so soundly that he did not even dream, and to compare all the other days and nights of his life with that night, and to declare after careful consideration how many days and nights of his life he had passed better or more agreeably than that night, I think that no one, whether private citizen or even the great king himself, would find them very easy to count in comparison with all the rest. If then that is what death is like, I for one say it is a gain, for in that case all eternity is but a single night. If, on the other hand, death is a journey to another world, and if the traditional belief is true that all the dead are there, what blessing could be greater than this, O my judges? If on arriving in the underworld one is free from these pretended judges here and finds the true judges who are said to sit in judgment there, Minos and Rhadamanthus and Æacus and Triptolemus, and all the other demigods who in life were themselves just—wouldn't that be a journey worth taking? Again, to associate with Orpheus and Hesiod—what would you not give for that privilege? For my part I am ready to die over and over again if these beliefs are true; for I should find wondrous pleasure in the life over there, meeting with Palamedes and Ajax, the son of Telamon, or any of the other men of old who met their death through an unjust judgment. It would be no small pleasure, I take it, to compare my own experiences with theirs. And, best of all, I could spend my time examining and questioning the men over there, as I do the men here on earth, finding out which of them are wise, and which of them thinks himself wise when he is not. What would one give, O my judges, to examine him who led the great expedition against Troy, or Odysseus, or Sisyphus, or countless other men and women who might be named? What inconceivable happiness to be with them, to converse with them, and examine them! One thing at least is certain: they do not put a man to death over there for asking questions. For the men of that world, besides being happier than we are in all other respects, are once and for all immortal, if the tales that are told are true. You, too, my judges, are to face death full of hope. You ought to meditate on this truth; no evil can possibly befall a good man, in this life or after death. His interests are not neglected by the gods. And it is no mere chance that has brought him to this pass. No, I see clearly, that it is better for me to die now and be released from trouble. That is why the oracle did not once turn me back; that is why I am not at all angry with these men who have condemned me, or with my accusers. To be sure, it was not with this in mind that they condemned me, or brought the accusation against me, but because they thought to do me harm. For that, indeed, I may fairly blame them.

"However, I have this request to make of them. When my sons grow up take your revenge on them, gentlemen; plague them just as I have plagued you, if you find them setting their hearts on riches, or on anything else more than on virtue. If they think they are something when in reality they are nothing, reproach them, as I have reproached you, for not caring for the things they ought to care for and for thinking they are worth something when they are worth nothing at all. If you do this I shall have received justice at your hands, I and my sons too.

"But the time has come for us to depart—I to die, you to live. Which of us is going to the better lot God alone clearly knows."

## II. PLATO (427-346 B. C.)

"The biography of Plato is interior. We are to account for the supreme elevation of this man in the intellectual history of our race —how it happens that in proportion to the culture of men they become his scholars; that, as our Jewish Bible has implanted itself in the table talk and household life of every man and woman in the European and American nations, so the writings of Plato have preoccupied every school of learning, every lover of thought, every church, every poet,—making it impossible to think, on certain levels, except through him."—Emerson, *Representative Men*.

There is significance in the very name of Plato, given him because he was broad of shoulder and broad of brow; for his system stands not only for intellect but for athletics, in a word, for a sound mind in a sound body. All through the greatest of his works, the *Republic*, this double motive is evident, since in this ideal commonwealth the future rulers of the state are selected at birth itself for soundness of limb, and through a long life of mental training are finally fitted to become philosopher-kings.

The name of Plato has significance, so has the place in which he lived. The Athens of his day was the mother of arts and eloquence; it was also the richest of Greek cities, and to Plato, as to the poet, that land is "to hastening ills a prey, where riches multiply and men decay." So Plato, fearing that ease and luxury might smother the best in men, advocates plain living and high thinking and deprecates high living and plain thinking. Philosophy is put forward as a way of salvation, for the love of knowledge is a means of progress from the sensual to the intellectual, and morality is the fulfilment of philosophy, since reason, like a charioteer, does not give rein to the passions, but guides the spirited element in man.

Plato demanded for his ideal ruler what he had undergone himself, a long course of physical and mental gymnastics. As a youth he wrestled at the Isthmian games, and legend has it that he was twice victor, once at the Nemean and once at the Olympian games. At any rate, he had some eight years of intellectual wrestling with Socrates, years which amounted to more than the work in modern preparatory and college courses. In addition he had what might be called a postgraduate course of travel, for, after the death of his master, he journeyed possibly to Egypt, probably to southern Italy, and quite certainly to Sicily. From the first it is said that he gained such a reverence for antiquity as to explain the saying attributed to an Egyptian priest: "You Greeks are boys." From southern Italy, the home of the Pythagorean brotherhood, it is conjectured that he obtained that knowledge of music and mathematics which plays so large a part in his doctrines of harmony and proportion. Finally, from Sicily he derived from painful personal experiences that loathing of tyranny as the lowest form of government, for when he used plain speech to the luxurious and unscrupulous Dionysius I of Syracuse the latter had him sold into slavery, from which he was fortunately ransomed by a friend. Whether or not these stories are true Plato was absent from Athens much of the time during the dozen years after the death of Socrates and until he founded the Academy. This has been declared the most important event not only in his life, but also in the history of European science. While the Republic was imitated in theory by many other political utopias, the Academy was imitated in reality by the Lyceum of Aristotle, the garden of Epicurus, and the museum of Alexandria, institutions which in turn generated similar learned societies through the Renaissance up to the most modern times.

Like the ancient monument at the gates of the Academy, which was used as a starting point in the torch races, Plato's school handed on the torch of learning to his own and later ages. It did this because it was thorough. Before this time those who wished a general education had gone to the Sophists, who were usually foreigners demanding high fees for imparting their knowledge. Plato had the same contempt for these men that a college professor had, let us say, for visiting mahatmas and yogis from the Far East, since he denounces them as smatterers and pretenders to philosophy. But the course he himself offers is thorough. It ranges from mathematics to morals, and from morals to politics. The art of conduct, whether individual or social, is especially important; it must be as truly scientific as other arts. If the carpenter has to be scientific in material things, so must the moralist and statesman be scientific in virtue, as the art of happiness, and in politics, as the royal art. The Sophists have offered only pretended knowledge in these branches, their rhetoric being merely the art of persuasive speech and their politics the tricks of the trade. But the real statesman, who follows the royal art, must be a genuine philosopher-king.

Plato's ideal was perhaps too high. In Europe there has never been a perfect prince who at the same time was deeply versed in science, and while America has had the scholar in politics it has only recently put a scientist in the White House. Yet while Plato's ideal was never carried out as a whole, it was in part. The Academy turned out a mathematician like Eudoxus, an orator like Demosthenes, a thinker like Aristotle, tutor to a king and critic of constitutions. Furthermore, the influence of the Academy can be traced down through the ages. It was a training school for rulers and legislators; it also became the nucleus of the University of Athens, to which for one thousand years pupils came not only from Hellendom, but from the greater Roman Empire; it furnished a model for the mediæval university, and its influence can be traced from Europe to England and from England to America through scholars like John Locke, who devised a constitution for the Carolinas, and statesmen like Thomas Jefferson, who wrote the Virginia Bill of Rights.

## THE CITY OF THE PERFECT

The Socratic quest ends with the goal of the city of the blessed, not that Homeric underworld of flitting shadows—a nightmare of half reality—but a future abode where real persons gather in a congenial company. The Platonic quest is of like nature, but its goal is here on earth. Patterned on a celestial city, its locality is terrestrial. The quest of Plato is also broader than that of Socrates. The latter explored the individual conscience, but did not try to elaborate a political realm, seeking rather to build character than to frame a constitution. Plato went further. Upon the foundations built by Socrates in the way of forming men of wisdom, bravery, and temperance he would construct a composite picture of the perfect state, compact of all the virtues and ruled by the greatest virtue— justice. Our whole state, he declares, is an imitation of the best and noblest life. The state as "man writ large" was then a combination and magnification of what his master had taught. In short, it stood for political justice, an adjustment of the parts to the whole, of the many to the one. In other words, Socrates emphasized what man owed to himself as a sentinel placed by God at his post, Plato what the social classes owed each other, civic harmony resembling in a way the heavenly harmony where all things work together for good.

The Republic was designed to be the city of the perfect, where man's end was not to make himself happy but the state strong. Here the iron element of self-control which made Socrates the soldier stand fast at Potidæa, is the first test in citizenship. Those who can control their appetites are promoted to the military class and in turn those who can rule themselves are to rule over others. But this policy was not sheer militarism. Plato considered the defect of the soldier to lie in a certain stupidity; "theirs not to reason why, theirs but to do and die" was not his motto. No, above the soldier with the virtue of bravery was the ruler who possessed not only control of his appetites and the spirited element of his being, but in his required military service exhibited marked intellectual efficiency. The soldiers are the watchdogs, but the rulers are their masters, and governance is to be finally lodged in the best minds. From the top down there are to be three classes. First there are the guardians or cultured class who were to guide and rule the state because they had the capacity to conceive abstract thoughts and rule their brethren by intellectual power. Psychologically they represent the mind of the social organism. Next there are the warrior-guardians, who should support the first class and maintain order in the state because they have executive force. These represent the passions and the will power of man. Finally there are the artisans and farmers, who support the upper classes because they are controlled and protected by those whose duties are contemplative and executive. They are the productive classes because, like hunger, thirst, and desire, they "lead to something being done."

Such is the bare outline of the ideal commonwealth, the rough sketch on the canvas which is later to be as crowded with figures as was that panorama of Greek life, the Olympic games. Plato himself compares his commonwealth to that great contest with its three divisions. Here the rulers correspond to the observers, who are sharp critics of what goes on; next the warriors resemble the contestants, who in the original Greek are called those who "agonize" in the manly sports; and lastly, in the lowest estate, the appetitive classes are compared to the hucksters and hangers-on who have never borne the heat and burden of the day.

In this stratification of society Plato exhibits a certain note of contempt for the bulk of the population, the masses. He had never forgiven that democratic assembly which had condemned his dear master to death. Yet this disparagement was in a way justified. Those at the top of the scale had already performed the duty of a soldier, just as the Athenian citizen had engaged in sport and kept himself fit on the running track of the gymnasium and in the wrestling bout of the dusty palæstra. The rabble, therefore, represents those who have not engaged in either physical or mental gymnastics, that horde of spectators who take their exercise in watching others exercise. But in the coming commonwealth this matter will be corrected. Every child will go through the school of athletics; sweat will be the doorstep not merely of manly virtue, but girls as well as boys will have their bodies trained as we know they did at Sparta from the statue of the running maiden, for it was the Spartan plan that Plato had here in mind.

## AN EXPERIMENT IN EUGENICS

In this first view of the *Republic* there is nothing particularly startling. It emphasizes the obvious virtues of wisdom, bravery, and temperance; it offers a familiar classification of the state into the ruling, fighting, and working classes and advocates an apparently moderate programme of education for boys and girls alike. But Plato was no milk-and-water reformer, for this last suggestion as to coeducation, after the Spartan model, was the entering wedge of the most radical reforms imaginable, reforms that advocated the abolishing not only of private property, but of the family itself, reforms with so wide a range as to be comparable to the communism of the Russian Soviet government and even their views of free marriage.

People who talk of Plato as an ideal philosopher in the sense of chasing the rainbows of the good, the true, and the beautiful do not know what they are talking about. They should read the fifth book of the *Republic*, where the author not only forbids the rulers to hold private property, but openly advocates a sheer form of eugenics. By the latter is meant "public hymeneals" at the prime of life, when "brave fathers ought to have as many sons as possible," and "mating seasons" when wives will be drawn by lot, but with the proviso that the rulers will invent some ingenious kind of lots which the less worthy may draw on each occasion of meeting and all to the end that the breed of the guardians may be kept pure.

As there is no smoke without some fire, so there is no radical philosophy without something to reform. Things were in a bad way in the Fifth Century. In the self-indulgent spirits of an Alcibiades Plato saw softness threatening the Athenian youth, and in the defeats of the Peloponnesian War weakness and cowardice. So he turned to Sparta, where the laws of Lycurgus had bred generations of perhaps the strongest and bravest men ever existing on the face of the earth, where men lived, ate, and owned property in common, where women were brought up on an equality with men, and where bravery was taken for granted and adultery almost unknown.

The practical results of the laws of Lycurgus had become proverbial in what were known as Laconic sayings; as when Leonidas said to his little band at Thermopylæ threatened with annihilation by the Persian hosts: "Breakfast here, supper in Hades"; or where the Spartan mother, dismissing her son to battle, exclaimed: "Return either with your shield or on it." Not only the proverbs but the anecdotes exhibit bravery and endurance as twin results of the iron system of Lacedemon. There is the story of the Spartan boy who endured the gnawings of the stolen fox beneath his cloak without uttering a word. There is also the passage in a play of Aristophanes where an Athenian lady welcomes a Lacedemonian wife with the words: "O dearest Spartan, O Lampito, welcome! How beautiful you look, sweetest one; how fresh your complexion, how vigorous your body. You could throttle an ox." "Yes," says she, "I think I could, by Castor and Pollux, for I practise gymnastics and leap high."

Though expressed in everyday anecdote and even in comedy these Spartan qualities of courage and endurance were not deemed trivial. Plato took them seriously; they seemed to him means for strengthening the state. The salient feature of his reform was communistic coeducation, and this, impossible as it seemed in practice, had a logical basis. The philosopher knew that Athens had tried several forms of government, from that of the Thirty Tyrants to that of the "many-headed monster," the democracy which had killed the "divine" Socrates. And there was this additional fact: numerous forms of government had been experimented with, but through all these experiments one half of the population had been politically inactive. The women had been left out. Everything, then, pointed to the possibility of a new and bold experiment, a scheme which ranged from the abolishing of private property to a form of trial marriage, from a participation of both sexes in politics to a common education which could raise up an efficient breed of rulers, not only of governors but of "governesses"—to use the word in its original sense.

Feminism was no fad with Plato. Aristophanes in the play just cited may have invented half ironically the plot of putting an end to the war between Athenians and Lacedemonians by combined feminine action from all parts of Greece. Propounded in jest, the suggestion might be taken seriously. Here was Sparta where the women played their part. As nothing succeeds like success, victorious Sparta should furnish the model for a new republic. But Plato goes Lycurgus one better. Women shall not only be strong mothers of sturdy offspring, but also soldiers, capable of bearing arms and "manning" the walls. The girls are to be taught early to race in the light armour of the Greek soldier and later to follow the examples of the fighting women of Scythia and Sarmatia. The Amazons might be but mythical and Athena in shield and helmet never come down from her pedestal, but here are to be women ready to form battalions of death.

Yet Plato does not overemphasize this point. He anticipated modern military preparedness of a nation in arms and the mobilizing of the so-called weaker sex in case of dire necessity, but back of his doctrine of the equal right to fight lay his broader principle of equal right to engage in all the activities of men. This general principle had a particular cause. It was derived in the way of mental reaction against the state of affairs Plato found at Athens. On the one side there was the conventional wife whose duty was to "remain inside and to be obedient to her husband," as described by Xenophon. On the other side was the unconventional hetaira or "companion" such as Aspasia, the mistress of Pericles. Plato's message, then, to the Athenian woman was to come out of the kitchen and imitate even the "stranger-women," who sought to be the intellectual companions of well-known political leaders. Like the intelligentsia of the present day who deride the Victorian ideal of woman as the plaything of man, the timid mouse, the shrinking violet, Plato resented as a pattern of perfection the customary ideals of what an Athenian spouse should be. Here one need but turn to that other biographer of Socrates, Xenophon, to see what that ideal meant. Take this passage from the *Œconomicus*, or a *Discussion on Estate Management*. Socrates is supposed to be the interlocutor and asks this question of the householder: "Did you yourself train your wife to be of the right sort, or did she know her household duties when you received her from her parents?" "Why, what knowledge could she have had, Socrates, when I took her for my wife? She was not yet fifteen years old when she came to me, and up to that time she had lived in leading strings, seeing, hearing, and saying as little as possible. If when she came she knew no more than how, when given wool, to turn out a cloak, and had seen only how the spinning is given out to the maids, is not that as much as could be expected? For in control of her appetite, Socrates, she had been excellently trained; and this sort of training is, in my opinion, the most important to man and woman alike."

This is not all. Even if the wife of a wealthy man was more a mistress over her servants and slaves than a household drudge, her life was pretty dreary. Up to marriage at fourteen or fifteen she knew little of the outside world. What she had enjoyed in the way of entertainment was scarcely more exciting than a Sunday-school picnic, to judge from this passage from the play *Lysistrata:* "When I was seven years of age I carried the mystic box in procession; then when I was ten I ground the cakes for our patron goddess, and then clad in a saffron-coloured robe, I was the bear at the Brauronian festival; and I carried the sacred basket when I became a beautiful girl."

So far the Athenian ideal for woman appears strangely like that alliterative line for the German *Hausfrau: "Kinder, Küche, Kirche"* —children, kitchen, church. But there was one exception, the escape offered by the ritual of Bacchus, when for a few days a Greek woman became a free creature allowed to roam at large upon the mountains. But these Bacchanalia, like the Saturnalia at Rome, were frowned upon by the respectable. In general, the Greek woman's life has been described as the stifling seclusion of the harem home. This description is borne out by the facts. There was an historical reason for it. When Athens extended her political borders across the Ægean she took over from Ionia, neighbour to the Eastern empires, the notion of women as inferior creatures. This notion was Oriental and so was that badge of servitude worn by the Athenian woman, the *kredemnon* or veil, which protected her face from the gaze of strange men. And still more Oriental was the conviction that women, like slaves, were the property of their husbands, a conviction summed up in the indignant protest of the strong-minded Medea, who exclaims: "Oh, of all things that draw breath and have understanding, we women are the most miserable; we are merely a thing that exists."

It was against this state of affairs that Plato revolted. There was no stimulus to the state in the passive ideal of "silence and discretion" and "to remain quiet within doors." Thus it was that the notion of women as property to be hidden at home led to Plato's description of the ordinary woman's lot as "a life of darkness and fear." In place of this negative notion Plato would put the positive ideal of the equality of the sexes and a common education for all. Here he gained an inkling of what women might become as the intellectual equals of men from the hetairæ, whose morals might be low, but whose intelligence and sagacity were high. Hence in his new society he boldly declares that there is no difference between the natures of the man and the woman, but only various degrees of weakness and strength. Therefore, he continues, we shall have to select duly qualified women also to share in the life and official labours of the duly qualified men, since we find that they are competent to the work and of kindred nature with the man.

In these proposals Plato is well aware that he will meet opposition from all sides. There was the conventional Athenian wife who was shocked by any talk of sex equality, and there was the ordinary Athenian husband, lord and master over his wife, who, like Chief Powhatan in the affair of Pocahontas, held that woman's place is in the wigwam. Thus Plato had to meet a double opposition from the ladies who were confined in their houses and from their lords who were absent most of the day and had no idea of discussing the serious business of politics with their wives. So he speaks through the mouth of Socrates as but a doubting inquirer and acknowledges what a hornet's nest of words he is arousing. Nevertheless, he must take the risk, for fair play demands that the sexes be treated alike: "The men have played out their part, and now comes the women's turn; of whom I shall proceed to speak, and the more so as I am invited by you. For men born and educated like our citizens, the only way, in my opinion, of arriving at a right conclusion about the possession and use of women and children is to follow the principle which has been already laid down about the men: that principle was that they were to be the guardians and watchdogs of the herd.

Now dogs are not divided into he's and she's, nor do we take the masculine gender out to hunt and leave the females at home to look after their puppies. They have the same employments, the only difference between them is that the one is stronger and the other weaker. But if women are to have the same employments as men, they must have the same education—they must be taught music and gymnastics, and the art of war. . . . And can there be anything better for the interests of the state than that the men and women of a state should be as good as possible? There can be nothing better. And our course of music and gymnastics will accomplish this? Certainly. Then we have made an enactment not only possible but in the highest degree advantageous to the state? True. Then let the wives of our guardians strip, having virtue for their robe, and share in the toils of war and the defense of their country; only in the distribution of labour the lighter labours are to be assigned to the women, as being the weaker vessels, but in other respects, their duties are to be the same."

Plato is so conscious that this view will be criticized that he compares the opposition to a storm at sea. Still, he contends, the first wave has not swallowed us up alive for enacting that the guardians of either sex shall have all their pursuits in common, since to the utility and possibility of this the argument is its own witness. But a much greater wave is coming and you will not think much of this when you see the next. This is the law that the wives of these guardians are to be common, and their children also common, and no parent is to know his own child, nor any child his parent.

This "wave" certainly takes one's breath away, but let us make a distinction. The utility of this proposition is one thing, the possibility quite another; yet, argues Plato, one may be allowed to feast his mind as do daydreamers when they are walking alone. "Suppose that in the capacity of legislator you have selected those men who are to be rulers. You will now select the women who are most akin to them and give them to them and they will live in common houses and meet at common meals. None of them will have anything specially his or her own; and they will be together and associate at gymnastic exercises, and be brought up together. And so they will be drawn by a necessity of their natures to have intercourse with each other: necessity is not too strong a word, I think."

In this proposal, put in a hypothetical way, Plato has put forward two distinct propositions, one being the prohibition of separate property, the other prohibition of the separate family—propositions which men generally count as mere aberrations of history, impossible of fulfilment and ever destined to failure. Examples spring up from all quarters. Thus the Christians of the First Century, with the best of intentions, tried to pool their property, and found an Ananias and Sapphira in their midst, and John Noyes of the Nineteenth Century, founder of the Oneida community, camouflaged as "spiritual wifehood," was suppressed by an outraged public opinion.

Dissension within and opposition without have been too much for communistic experiments, with one great exception, an exception which Plato had in the back of his mind when he made his bold proposal. His idea was that the individual exists for the whole, and in Sparta that idea had already been largely carried out. The Spartan state, even in peace, was a camp: morals, exercises, recreations, even sleeping places were in common for the male population, just as for the army in the field. This may be called militarism, but militarism may also be considered a form of communism where the spirit of "one for all" is the driving force. Those that decry militarism have perhaps not had experience in the school of the soldier where one is willing to undergo discipline for the sake of the whole and where the mere contact with numbers, working in unison, is an inspiration. This was the spirit of Sparta which Plato admired, just as one nowadays can admire the West Point spirit. The unlocking of human energy by drill, by discipline, and by the stimulus of companionship is a potent factor which the anti-militarists ignore, but which Plato did not ignore. Judging from the results of the Peloponnesian War, he found the Spartan community spirit efficient and was willing to go far in carrying out its principles.

In the southern military oligarchy boys at the tender age of seven were taken from the home and organized into divisions or "packs." These "packs" were fed together, slept on reeds, and wore only a single garment winter and summer. It was an intensified Boy Scout movement, for thus only could children be taught a soldier's ideal of obedience, courage, and self-devotion. Plato took over this scheme and applied it not only to both sexes but to all ages. Children at birth were taken in charge by the guardians and the most promising selected for further training, while the guardians themselves were supported at the public expense, living together in barracks, keeping themselves fit by public gymnastics, and devoting all their energies to the betterment of the state.

In this programme Plato had two principles in mind; one was that the child mind, like a piece of fair white cloth, took a permanent dye very early, the other that the individual must sacrifice himself to the state, not the state to the individual. In all this the *Republic* may be seen as a protest against certain political and social conditions at Athens. The Athenian ideal was the assertion of the individual; if man be the measure of all things, he bulks larger than the state; he may even defy public opinion as in the case of Alcibiades and his companions who in a drunken frolic mutilated the sacred statues of Hermes. Against this extreme Ionian ideal of the self-sufficiency of the individual Plato would put the Dorian or Spartan ideal, which, like the very Doric order of architecture, stood for a simpler and severer type.

Plato's admiration for the Spartan system can be understood; both his companion Xenophon and his pupil Aristotle shared in the general admiration of Greece for such a going concern as that of Lacedemon. But neither of these other political speculators could go the whole road as did Plato in advocating the exposure of weakly or deformed infants as practised by the Spartans. The Athenians were familiar with this practise as in the plot of Œdipus who, in spite of his lameness, became king; but they must have revolted at Plato's suggestion that unfit infants shall be "hurried away to places unknown," which meant hurried away to destruction. In a later work of his Plato partially relents as to this cruel doctrine and directs that the children considered as unworthy shall be secretly distributed among the remaining community. In his original proposition, which followed the laws of Lycurgus that no child was allowed to be brought up until it had been inspected and approved by the public nurses, Plato was carrying out the negative side of a relentless system of eugenics. But he went even beyond this in the proposal that in place of permanent marriages there should be only occasional matings. Disguised under the name of public hymeneals, sanctioned by religious solemnities, this was but a stark system of the breeding of that higher animal—man. As put in the dialogue between Socrates and Glaucon, this is Plato's "dream of what might be": "In the first place our rulers will enforce the laws and make new ones where they are wanted, and their allies or ministers will obey. You, as legislator, have already selected the men; and now you shall select the women. After the selection has been made they will live in common houses and have their meals in common and will be brought together by a necessity more certain than that of mathematics. But they cannot be allowed to live in licentiousness; that is an unholy and unlawful thing, which the rulers are determined to prevent. For the avoidance of this, holy marriage festivals will be instituted, and their holiness will be in proportion to their usefulness. And here, Glaucon, I should like to ask (as I know that you are a breeder of birds and animals) do you not take the greatest care in the mating? Certainly. And there is no reason to suppose that less care is required in the marriage of human beings. But then, our rulers must be physicians, and use many medicines in their treatment of the body corporate; some falsehoods, too, which are allowed by us in the practice of medicine. The good must be paired with the good as often as possible, and the bad with the bad as seldom as possible, and the offspring of the one must be reared, and of the other destroyed; this will be the only way of preserving the flock in prime condition. But how can this be accomplished? The hymeneal festivals will be celebrated at times fixed with an eye to population, and then the brides and bridegrooms will meet, but not too often: and by an ingenious system of lots the rulers will contrive that the brave only deserve the fair, and that those of inferior breed are paired with inferiors; the latter will ascribe to chance what is really the invention of the rulers."

Such is the most extraordinary scheme of eugenics ever propounded in history. In its religious aspect it resembles in a way the "revelation on spiritual wifeism," received by Joseph Smith, Jr., the founder of Mormonism, and also the doctrine of "spiritual marriage" proposed by John Noyes, the lecherous leader of the Oneida community. But this precious pair had no such excuse as did Plato. They based their belief on the scriptural injunction to "be fruitful and multiply," and justified themselves on the ground that to increase the population was a patriotic service. But Greece was not America; on the contrary the problem of congested populations was a serious one in a land of limited area whose communities thickly pressed upon one another. Owing to large families, to numerous poor freemen, and to thousands of slaves, a city like Athens fairly spilled over its walls. There were no wide-open spaces on the narrow peninsula of Greece proper. Not only was arable land limited and the water supply defiled but the available land along the shores of the Mediterranean had been pretty well settled by colonists from the Greek cities which suffered both from the pressure of their own populations and the pressure of the growing empires of the Near East.

It was this situation which led even the astute Aristotle to reason that if all the children it was possible for adult couples to produce were born and brought up a fearful aggravation of poverty, with all its accompanying troubles and suffering, would be inevitable. The laws of diminishing return and of the margin of cultivation were as yet the far-off formulas of the days of Malthus, but the same principles were at work then in crowded Greece as later in the congested slums of England. It was an understanding of these principles that led Plato to advocate, as the chief check on population, preventive restraint. He went the limit. Instead of leaving birth control to the individual, he handed it over to the state and, in order to prevent overpopulation, with its attendant evils of misery and vice, he would allow the guardians to take complete charge of the situation, even to the employment of deceit where, "by an ingenious system of lots, the rulers will contrive that the brave only deserve the fair." Because of its famous, or infamous, fifth book the *Republic* of Plato has been declared to set forth anything but an ideal commonwealth. It shocked the Mrs. Grundys of Greece, was anathema to the church fathers, is skipped by college classes nowadays, and in general has had a hard time of it. By most this "daydream" of a speculative philosopher has been considered a nightmare of jumbled notions. But recalling Dr. Johnson's definition of a prude as "a person with a nasty mind," it is possible to look even on this part of the *Republic* with objective eye and pick out some of the propositions that have come true. This fifth book was not written with the almost insane irony of Dean Swift in his *Modest Proposal* for eating children in order to keep down the population of Ireland. It was written, as has already been shown, in order to substitute Spartan hardness in place of Athenian softness, devotion to the state in place of indulgence of self, compulsory public education of both sexes in place of haphazard private instruction for boys only, equality of the sexes in political life, and, most attractive of all, outdoor work and life-long athletics for every man, woman, and child in the commonwealth. Discard what is morally offensive or cruel, or what is economically impossible because economically unsound, cancel all desperate remedies, and you still have left these five points common to all progressive commonwealths, as yet by no means actualities, but prophesied as potentialities by Plato more than two thousand years ago.

## THE REPUBLIC: ITS RIVALS

Such is the social system of the *Republic*, a flexible framework beginning with experimental eugenics and ending with practical problems of promotion and demotion and all determined by the tests of the cardinal virtues—reason or wisdom, courage or manliness, temperance or good form, and through all justice, a harmony of the whole. This is the positive side in "the game of cities which

men play." But there is another side, the negative, in which men
do not play the game, but selfishly seek their own interests. Plato
has often been misrepresented as a blank idealist whose perfect
state is like a marble temple shining on a hill. The *Republic* has
inspired a host of utopias, cities of nowhere, from Augustine's
*City of God* to Edward Bellamy's *Looking Backward*. All these might
better be called dream cities than might Plato's masterpiece, for the
*Republic* contains a note of stark realism based on the author's sorry
political experience. Plato may advocate a real aristocracy in the
sense of a rule of the best, but he also knows that there are inferior
forms of government. This leads him to draw up a scheme of "the
order of badness in states" and to point out a descending scale of
bad, worse, and worst. After the best form of society comes the
second-best, the "timocratic" state, where personal ambition rules;
next comes the oligarchy, which turns out to be a plutocracy, a rule
of wealth; then, after a rule of the few, comes the democracy, the
rule of the many, the reign of Demos, "the many-headed beast";
finally we reach tyranny, the rule of a single despot.

Of these four great types of inferior forms of government Plato
himself had personal experience. In the Peloponnesian War those
military men of spirit, the timocratic Spartans, had sold their
services for Persian gold; in the time of the Thirty Tyrants of
Athens these oligarchs had feathered their own nest; and again in
Athens that "great beast," the democracy, had slain the "divine"
Socrates; finally, if we are to believe the *Letters* attributed to him,
Plato had suffered painful experiences at the hands of Dionysius I,
the last tyrant of Syracuse, a ruler far removed from the perfect
prince.

To these four baser forms of government correspond four types
of men which Plato describes with such verisimilitude and vividness
that they seem to live again. Here one is tempted to suggest examples. For the spirited, timocratic man, a Roosevelt; for the oligar-
chical, a Trotsky and a Lenin; for a triumphant democratical man,
a Carnegie; for a despotic, tyrannical man, a Mussolini. But this is
dangerous ground, historical parallels are never exact, and comparisons are odious. Still there are general forms of government and
corresponding types of rulers wherein history more or less repeats
itself. Plato's ideal, like that of all political philosophers, was to
portray a rule of the most efficient; literally an aristocracy, or rule
of the best. This may take the form of government by a few rulers,
an oligarchy, or by one masterful man, a monarchy. In the former
case an artificial selection of "golden minds" determines the survival

of the fittest. This selection is both intellectual and physical, a combination nowadays represented by a permanent civil service with a series of successive examinations for promotion, and by gymnastic tests through which fat armchair generals are weeded out.

But in the second case, that of the monarchy, what guarantee is there of a continuation of a good government? There is practically none. Even if the reigning sovereign is all that a sovereign should be, the crown prince is seldom a perfect prince. Plato knew too much of the monarchies of his day to put his trust in princes, for able fathers do not mean able sons, and heredity is more or less of a gamble when left to individual caprice.

At this point begins the decline in governments since the guardians of the ideal republic will break the established laws of public hymeneals, will beget children out of due season, and an inferior generation will arise. Along with the neglect of these provisions will come a neglect of education and the severe mental tests demanded for the highest ruling class will be abated. So the culture of the mind will be neglected for the culture of the body and we will have young barbarians at play, as Matthew Arnold described the undergraduates of his day. Plato, it must be remembered, was an educational reformer ever fighting against the downward tendency to substitute brawn for brains. Like Socrates, he was a believer in sweat as the doorstep to manly virtue, and the Academy itself was next door to a gymnasium. Yet Plato, who started the first university, would have a surprising time visiting one of our universities where the stadium costs more than the laboratories, where the Sophists might envy the salary of the football coach, and where education, to judge from the newspapers, begins at the feet and stops at the eyebrows.

Plato lived in the land of athletics, of stadia, of Olympic games, of marathon races, but he warned his countrymen lest physical force should have preference over wisdom. If public opinion, he goes on, does not demand that the rulers of the state shall belong to the highest, the intellectual class, then they will fall to the next lower. Our state, then, he continues, will be ruled by soldiers, and organized rather for war than for peace. Then the timocrat will arise. He is a lover of honour, for such is the meaning of "Timocrat," but he is also a lover of power; claiming to be a ruler, not because he is a speaker, or on any ground of that sort, but because he is a soldier and, as a soldier, has performed feats of arms. Now such a character may be in many ways admirable: he is not only a lover of honour, but also of gymnastic exercises and of the chase. But will he not be more interested in sport than in statesmanship? So it seems. When the timocrats get together they are good fellows, but do they give us good government? It does not appear so. There may be outward loyalty to the laws but this will not be of paramount importance. To put the thing in modern terms, to keep up the pace of belonging to country clubs, of going off to the woods to hunt or fish, and of keeping in with the sporting crowd costs money. But money may be made easiest by keeping just within the law. So, Plato resumes, the guardians may profess respect for the old traditions, but all the time they are seeking to gratify their growing avarice quietly and by stealth.

Such is the second-best society, timocracy, where the personal ambitions of the "man of spirit" take the place of unostentatious service to the state. Such a character may often be found in the aspiring son of an excellent father who has met with misfortune. Here Plato draws this picture: Suppose the representative of timocracy to have a son: at first he begins by emulating his father and walking in his footsteps, but presently he sees him strike all in a moment on a sunken reef, which is the state, and he and all that he has are lost; he may have been a general or some other high officer who is brought to trial under a prejudice raised by informers, and either put to death, or exiled, or deprived of the privileges of a citizen, and all his property taken from him. . . . And the son has seen and known all this—he is a ruined man, and his fear has taught him to knock ambition and passion head foremost from his bosom's throne: humbled by poverty he takes to money making and by mean and small savings and doings gets a fortune together. Is not this man likely to seat the concupiscent and covetous elements on that vacant throne? They will play the great king within him, and he will array them with tiara and collar and scimetar.

Although put in antiquated language, with similes drawn from the rule of the Great King, the Persian monarch with his fabulous wealth, the lesson still holds good. An oligarchy of wealth—a plutocracy, to be precise—is a decline from a rule where public service is a public trust, and where efficiency and not property is the prime qualification of the ruler. But here Plato is no socialist in the sense of being one who is envious of the wealthy. As his pupil Aristotle showed in describing "magnificence" as a virtue, men of large fortune can do much in benefiting and beautifying a city from the motive of civic pride. But the rich, who amass fortunes under the protection of the state and do nothing in return, they are to be counted drones in the national hive. Anyone can supply instances of this type of man, and one of Plato's interpreters has compared such a man to the founder of an American millionaire family, who despises education, counts honesty the best policy— because it pays—but never loses a chance to make a dishonest profit provided he is not found out. This interpreter might have added the type of the politician who is in politics for what he may make out of it, some city boss who cuts down school appropriations because the three R's were good enough for him, who can see no wrong in "honest graft," and, if he is engaged in some business on the side, talks a great deal about "service," which people may take to mean public service, but which he knows means private profit. Such men existed in Greece, and Plato did not spare them. There were the Thirty Tyrants, who were not in politics merely for their health; there were also the "metics," or resident foreigners, who sometimes gained citizenship from the city fathers by putting up a temple or erecting a monument in gratitude for the chance to make money.

But worse than oligarchy, the small group which allowed such things, was the democracy, "the many-headed monster." To belivers in democracy Plato's strictures on the rule of the majority may appear extreme, but it must be remembered that it was "triumphant democracy" that put Socrates to death. The party in power did this ostensibly on the ground of Socrates's impiety, but really on account of his criticisms of their way of carrying on the government. Of course, modern democracies do not count unorthodoxy, or the critical spirit, political crime, nor visit it with the extreme penalty. Nevertheless, experience shows that any political candidate who differs from the majority in religion, or who points out the faults of an administration, has but a slim chance for high office.

Leaving aside the bitterness of Plato's attack on the government by the people as a far remove from the government by the best, certain of his observations still hold good. Liberty and equality were not to his taste, the first because it allows every true democrat to do pretty much as he likes, and the second because it contradicts the principle of the selection of the fittest to govern. From the liberty of doing as one likes, says Plato, arises the "forgiving spirit" of democracy, and the "don't care" about trifles, and the acquiescence in the shady transactions of the "people's friend"—the popular political leader known among us as the "easy boss." Plato's language sounds as if it were taken from the manifesto of some good-government club which, disgusted with a corrupt city or national

government, is starting a campaign to "turn the rascals out." But
these hard words are not as significant as the more fundamental
criticisms which Plato raises against the rule of the many. The
principle of equality, taken in a wider sense than equality before
the law, is a false principle. Liberty allows a man to serve, or not
serve, the state as he pleases; but equality allows anyone, and that
without special qualifications, to take part in determining the
government's policies. In other words, the first principle of democracy is that there shall be no selection of the "fittest to govern"
because all men are equal, all "uncrowned kings." Taken literally,
these glittering generalities are sophistries, and any modern democracy does all it can to obviate them. One means is education, yet
even here popular education, in the sense of instructing all the
children of all the people, is a misnomer. Only a small fraction
receives a college education, the equivalent of what Plato demanded
for his rulers, and when the smaller fry try for political jobs competitive examinations sift out the unfit. In other words, the
easy-going principle of equality and the iron law of the survival of
the fittest to both natural and artificial selection—this is the eternal
conflict which Plato brings before us.

Pure democracy as the cult of incompetence is an inferior form of
government; but even lower than that in the scale is tyranny, the
unfettered arbitrary rule of a single despot. Of tyrannies there
are all grades from partial to total. Plato knew or had experience
of these from the rule of Pisistratus at Athens to the career of the
elder Dionysius in Sicily. But these historical parallels are nothing
without the historic principles beneath them. A tyrant is a tyrant
under any other name, whether he is called a city boss in Chicago,
a president in Venezuela, a dictator in Spain, a regent in Hungary,
or a leader in Italy. What Plato offers is a composite portrait of the
"people's friend" who by successive steps gradually descends into
the abyss of despotism. There are all grades of tyrants, but generally
the force of circumstances is too much for them. There is the dema-
gogue who starts with promises of good government but ends with
relying on picked bands of ruffians who frighten law-abiding citizens
into submission. This is seen in a city which begins with the reform
mayor and ends with "racketeers." Again there is a country which
has a written constitution based on universal suffrage but where
bullets are found more effective than ballots. Certain "republics"
south of the Rio Grande furnish illustrations of such a state of
affairs. And if we go to another hemisphere history furnishes plenty
of parallels. Julius Cæsar started as the champion of the plebs but

was murdered before he could make himself their master. Machiavelli's *Prince*, treating of the Borgias and their bravos, shows how ecclesiastical rulers, professing themselves guardians of the people, were forced to surround themselves with foreign mercenaries and to banish, imprison, or kill all rivals. So, too, Victor Hugo's *The History of a Crime* shows how a tinsel tyrant like Napoleon III, elected president by a plebiscite, had final recourse to a bloody coup d'état and at last, in order to distract the attention of the people, undertook a disastrous war.

From the ancient tyrant who aped the regalia of the Persian king to the modern dictator rattling his sabre, Plato's composite portrait applies in varying degree. Lastly, he says, we will go and view the city of tyranny and he, the protector of whom we spake, is not fallen in his might, but, himself the overthrower of many, is to be seen standing up in the chariot of state with the reins in his hand, no longer protector, but tyrant absolute.

No doubt, he said.

And now let us tell of the happiness of the man, and also of the state, in which this sort of creature is generated.

Yes, he said, let us tell of that.

At first, in the early days of his power, he smiles upon everyone and salutes everyone—he to be called a tyrant, who is making promises in public and also in private; liberating debtors, and distributing land to the people and to his followers, and wanting to be kind and good to everyone.

That is the regular thing.

But when he has got rid of foreign enemies, and is reconciled with some of them and has destroyed others, and there is nothing to fear from them, then he is always stirring up some war or other, in order that the people may require a leader.

Yes, that may be expected of him.

Has he not also another object, which is that they may be impoverished by payment of taxes, and thus compelled to devote themselves to their daily wants and therefore less likely to plot against him?

Clearly.

Yes, and if he suspects any of them of having notions of freedom, and of being disloyal to him, he has a good pretext for destroying them by giving them up to the enemy; and for all these reasons the tyrant is always compelled to be getting up a war.[1]

------

[1] *The Republic*, Jowett trans., pp. 404–405.

### III. ARISTOTLE (385–322 B. C.)

"THERE are a few philosophers whose influence on thought and language has been so extensive that no one who reads can be ignorant of their names, and that every man who speaks the language of educated Europeans is constantly using their vocabulary. Among this few Aristotle holds not the lowest place. We have all heard of him, as we have all heard of Homer. He has left his impress so firmly on theology that many of the formulæ of the churches are unintelligible without acquaintance with his conception of the universe If we are interested in the growth of modern science we shall readily discover for ourselves that some knowledge of Aristotelianism is necessary for the understanding of Bacon and Galileo and the other great anti-Aristotelians who created the 'modern scientific' view of nature. If we turn to the imaginative literature of the modern languages, Dante is a sealed book, and many a passage of Chaucer and Shakespeare and Milton is half unmeaning to us unless we are at home in the outlines of Aristotle's philosophy. And if we turn to ordinary language, we find that many of the familiar turns of modern speech cannot be fully understood without a knowledge of the doctrines they were first forged to express. An Englishman who speaks of the 'golden mean' or of 'liberal education,' or contrasts the 'matter' of a work of literature with its 'form,' or the 'essential' features of a situation or a scheme of policy with its 'accidents,' or 'theory' with 'practice,' is using words which derive their significance from the part they play in the vocabulary of Aristotle."—A. E. TAYLOR, *Aristotle*.

Aristotle the thinker and Alexander the conqueror have been called "the great twin brethren" without whom the whole course of human development must have been different. While the dominion of the soldier soon passed away, that of the philosopher lasted on, and to-day science, law, philosophy, theology, and ethics bear the marks of that philosophic governor for whom Plato longed. As Socrates moulded Plato, so did Plato mould Aristotle, and in turn the last of this speculative triumvirate handed on Greek culture to those new worlds which Alexander the Great conquered.

It was at Stagirus, a Greek colony in Thrace, that Aristotle was born in the year 385 B. C. Coming to Athens at the age of seventeen, he studied for a score of years with Plato, and the master had so high an opinion of the pupil that he called him the intellect of the school.

In turn, the pupil said of Plato that he was the character who first showed by word and deed how a man may be at once good and happy.

While the admiration between master and pupil was mutual their spirit was different. They both take as a common subject political justice, but while one looks at the forms of social life as a picture, the other looks upon them as a map. Plato gives intimate personal portraits of characters ranging from the timocrat to the tyrant; Aristotle broadly surveys the field of humanity and points out the logical limitations of different motives and aims, such as goodness and happiness, wealth and wisdom. In general Plato appeals to the imagination, Aristotle to reason, and in the long run reason wins. As the great advocate of the golden mean Aristotle was paradoxically called "moderate to excess," yet it is this very moderation which has made men go back to him for reference, as they would to an encyclopædia which presents all sides of a question.

Aristotle had a cool and calculating mind and preferred as his ideal the life of quiet contemplation, yet his own life was not without colour and movement. Born in Thrace, where his father was court physician to King Amyntas II, he early became acquainted with those plots and counterplots which agitated the royal house of Macedonia. This knowledge of what we would now call Balkan disturbances intensified in Aristotle's mind that distinction between Greek and "barbarian" which has been compared to the colour line drawn by an American brought up in a Southern state. Further contact with the barbarians arose when on the death of Plato Aristotle went to reside with his friend and fellow-student Hermias, who had become ruler of two cities in Asia Minor, and who was cruelly put to death by the Persian king. Two years later, in his forty-second year, Aristotle was invited by King Philip of Macedon to undertake the education of his son Alexander, then at the age of fourteen. Aristotle taught the young crown prince for three years, but although he did not keep him from copying his aggressive father, King Philip, the relations between master and pupil remained cordial. When Alexander ascended the throne and undertook those conquests which extended as far as India he remembered his old teacher and not only sent him zoölogical specimens, but helped him financially in his studies. These studies covered an enormous range, and Aristotle must have been a walking encyclopædia of knowledge, to judge from the more than two score titles of his books, books which had a strange history, since after lying buried for nearly two hundred years they were brought to Athens and there became part of the loot which Sulla carried off to Rome.

The year after Alexander's mounting the throne Aristotle returned
to Athens and there founded his famous Lyceum, whose varied
curriculum was but the master's brain turned inside out. Here
Aristotle taught a scant dozen years, for on the death of Alexander
his position in Athens became precarious. The city was at this time
no longer free, but was ruled by a Macedonian vicegerent with
whom Aristotle was on terms of friendship. Really because of this,
though ostensibly on a charge of impiety, Aristotle was indicted.
To escape death he fled the city, declaring, as the story goes, that
"Athens must not sin a second time against philosophy." He sought
refuge in the neighbouring island of Eubœa, but did not long enjoy
that contemplative life to which he looked forward, for he died in
the following year at the age of sixty-two.

## GOODNESS AND HAPPINESS

Aristotle said of Plato that he was the character who first showed
by word and deed how a man may be at once good and happy.
These two adjectives are the keywords to Aristotle's system of
morality. It begins with the search for the highest good: Every
art and every kind of inquiry, he declares, and likewise every act and
purpose seem to aim at some good; so it has been well said that the
good is that at which everything aims. And surely from a practical
point of view it much concerns us to know this good; for then, like
archers shooting at a definite mark, we shall be more likely to attain what we want.... Now that which is pursued as an end in itself
is more final than that which is pursued as means to something else,
and that which is never chosen as means than that which is chosen
both as an end in itself and as means, and that is strictly final which
is always chosen as an end in itself and never as means. Happiness
seems more than anything else to answer to this description: for we
always choose it for itself, and never for the sake of something else;
while honour and pleasure and reason, and all virtue or excellence, we
choose partly indeed for themselves (for, apart from any result,
we should choose each of them), but partly also for the sake of happiness, supposing that they will help to make us happy. But no
one chooses happiness for the sake of these things, or as a means to
anything else at all.

All this has an air of dogmatic finality in picking on a single principle—happiness—as man's chief aim. But analysis vindicates the
exclusion of other aims: honour, especially political honour, often
turns out to be a hollow mockery; pleasure, especially as it affects the

senses, is fleeting; while reason is not an end in itself, but a means toward that happiness which all men desire. And lest this single argument of finality seem one-sided, let us take another point of view. We seem to be led to the same conclusion, continues Aristotle, when we start from the notion of self-sufficiency. The final good is thought to be self-sufficing (or all-sufficing). In applying this term we do not regard a man as an individual leading a solitary life, but we also take account of parents, children, wife, and, in short, friends and fellow-citizens generally, since man is naturally a social being. Some limit must indeed be set to this; for if you go on to parents and descendants and friends of friends you will never come to a stop. But this we will consider further on: for the present we will take self-sufficing to mean what by itself makes life desirable and in want of nothing. And happiness is believed to answer to this description.

There is a kind of natural common sense in this reasoning which explains the high authority of Aristotle in matters of conduct. In later ages the cart was put before the horse when it was held that this was true "because Aristotle said it." Here it seems that Aristotle said it because it was true; in other words, there is a persistent sanity in these moral remarks that makes them almost commonplace. In Plato there is a dramatic quality, an enormous enthusiasm which carries the reader along; but Plato was by that led into such absurdities as a doctrine of communism in wives and children. There is no such extravagance as that in his pupil, for with Aristotle the family is considered the fundamental unit of the state and the state a happy family. And as the higher animals spend much time in bringing up their young, so man as a "political animal" must have had a long preliminary training to fit himself for citizenship.

Aristotle's motto for moral education is: "From youth upward to be accustomed to be good." It is not that children are born good, stamped at birth with virtue as a coin is stamped with the superscription of the great king. No, virtue seems more acquired than innate, for it is practice that makes perfect. So Aristotle's chief moral treatise, the *Nicomachean Ethics*, proceeds in language that is to become proverbial: youth is not a sufficient span in which to attain virtue but there must also be a full term of years for this exercise; for one swallow or one fine day does not make a spring, nor does one day or any small space of time make a blessed or happy man. . . . And as at the Olympic games it is not the fairest and strongest who receive the crown, but those who contend (for among these are the victors), so in life, too, the winners are those who not only have all the excellences, but manifest these in deed.

To attain happiness by means of virtue is a hard and a life-long task, yet happiness is not merely subjective, not solely dependent upon the effort of the individual. Happiness, continues the common-sense philosopher, plainly requires external goods, too, as we said; for it is impossible, or at least not easy, to act nobly without some furniture of fortune. There are many things that can only be done through instruments, so to speak, such as friends and wealth and political influence: and there are some things whose absence takes the bloom off our happiness, as good birth, the blessing of children, personal beauty; for a man is not very likely to be happy if he is very ugly in person, or of low birth, or alone in the world, or childless, and perhaps still less if he has worthless children or friends, or has lost good ones that he had. As we said, then, happiness seems to stand in need of this kind of prosperity.

However, the man richly endowed with worldly goods is not of necessity happy; this would be giving the case away to the seekers after pleasure as the highest good. As with material things so with moral. Passive acceptance is one thing, active use another. The virtues, without which no man can be happy, are not implanted in us by nature; nature merely gives the capacity for acquiring them and this is developed by training: we acquire the virtues by doing the acts, as is the case with the arts, too. We learn an art by doing that which we wish to do when we have learned it; we become builders by building, and harpers by harping. And so by doing just acts we become just, and by doing acts of temperance and courage we become temperate and courageous. . . .

This is analogous to palpable things like strength. Strength is produced by taking plenty of nourishment and doing plenty of hard work, and the strong man, in turn, has the greatest capacity for these. And the case is the same with the virtues: by abstaining from pleasure we become temperate, and when we have become temperate we are best able to abstain. And so with courage: by habituating ourselves to despise danger, and to face it, we become courageous, and when we have become courageous we are best able to face danger.

Such is the highly workable view of the plastic moral nature. It runs counter to the extreme optimists who claim that man is by nature good and to the extreme pessimists who claim that he is by nature bad. To Aristotle nature is neutral: our natural emotions and impulses are in themselves neither good nor bad; they merely furnish the moral material out of which man is made. This view is neither optimistic nor pessimistic, yet in view of Aristotle's later goal—the growth of the great social community where men are associated for the sake of some advantage—it leans toward meliorism or the hope of social betterment. Virtue, Aristotle says, lies in observing the mean, but as this is also called the golden mean such an aim might properly be counted optimistic. Nevertheless, Aristotle never portrayed an ideal republic, as did Plato, where men could be made good willy-nilly. Virtue and vice, he insists, are voluntary, and lest the reader should lose sight of the rôle of free will, he states the case in all its alternatives: virtue depends upon ourselves; and vice likewise. For where it lies with us to do, it lies with us not to do. Where we can say no, we can say yes. If, then, the doing a deed, which is noble, lies with us, the not doing it, which is disgraceful, lies with us; and if the not doing, which is noble, lies with us, the doing, which is disgraceful, also lies with us. But if the doing and likewise the not doing of noble or base deeds lie with us, and if this is, as we found, identical with being good or bad, then it follows that it lies with us to be worthy or worthless men.

Because we are in the position of freedom of choice it follows that there are three classes of men: the wicked who deliberately follow a wrong rule of life; the morally weak who know what is right but let their tempers and appetites run away with them; the morally strong who like good athletes follow the rules of training. But here the objection may be raised that some are born bad and are not morally responsible for their acts. This, retorts the logician, is confusing inanimate objects with rational beings. For instance, a stone naturally tends to fall downward, and you could not train it to rise upward, though you tried to do so by throwing it up ten thousand times; nor could you train fire to move downward, nor accustom anything which naturally behaves in one way to behave in any other way.

There is, indeed, a certain perversity in inanimate objects, but such perversity is only seeming in man. You cannot train fire to go opposite to its natural place, but you can train a hot temper to confine itself to righteous indignation toward wrongdoing, and not to give way to a sheer defiance of lawful authority.

In all things man, "the rational animal," should follow the golden mean, for virtue is a fixed habit of mind, resulting from effort and principle, which, with reference to our own particular nature, is equidistant from excess or defect. However, to keep to the middle of the road is not easy. The attainment of virtue is an art, and art is long; it takes much time to learn to be a prudent man. Indeed the knowledge of morality is as difficult to attain as the knowledge of medicine. It is not the mere using or not using the knife, administering or not administering certain drugs, which constitute medical treatment or curing, but doing these things in a certain particular way.

And a further warning must be given. When men think it is no great instance of wisdom, the knowing what is just and what is unjust, because it is not hard to comprehend those things of which the laws speak, they forget that these are not just actions, except accidentally. To be just they must be done and distributed in a certain manner and this is a more difficult task than knowing what things are wholesome, for in this branch of knowledge it is an easy matter to know honey, and wine, and hellebore, and cautery, and the use of the knife, but the knowing how one should administer these with a view to health, and to whom and at what time, amounts in fact to being a physician.

## THE GOLDEN MEAN

The way to moral wisdom is a long way, but lest men be discouraged this rule may be given to help one in keeping to the middle of the road: Moral virtue is acquired by a repetition of the corresponding acts. These acts must be such as reason prescribes. They cannot be defined exactly, but must be neither too much nor too little. Virtue is not an emotion, nor a bare faculty, but a trained faculty or habit of choosing the golden mean. This is the royal road, yet it is not easy, for one may go wrong in many different ways (because, as the Pythagoreans expressed it, evil is of the class of the infinite, good of the finite), but right only in one; and so the former is easy, the latter difficult; easy to miss the mark, but hard to hit it: and for these reasons, therefore, both the excess and defect belong to vice, and the mean state to virtue. But to be more precise: virtue is a middle state between two faulty ones, in the way of excess on one side, and defect on the other. However, it must not be supposed that every action or every feeling is capable of subsisting in this mean state, because some there are which are so named as immediately to convey the notion of badness, as malevolence, shamelessness, envy; or, to instance in actions, adultery, theft, murder; for all these and such like are blamed, because they are in themselves bad, and not the having too much or too little of them.

Now to apply this definition to particular instances. We have lost Aristotle's table of the virtues and vices, which he probably sketched out and exhibited to his audiences, but we have notes of what might be called the ten commandments of this metaphysical Moses, from which this table may be reconstructed. Thus there is a sphere of anticipated evils where the defect is timidity, the excess foolhardiness, and the virtue courage. Into this scheme certain proverbs will fit, as: "He who fights and runs away will live to fight another day." "Fools rush in where angels fear to tread." The next sphere is that of bodily pleasures where the defect is insensibility, the excess intemperance, and the virtue temperance—a classification often lost sight of by advocates of sumptuary legislation, extremists who substitute absolute prohibition for a wise self-restraint. As for the sphere of probity the defect is stinginess, the excess prodigality, the mean liberality.

So the table continues into further spheres of wea.th, greatness, honour, provocation, companionship, conversation, and recreation. Out of this elaborate list a few of the characteristic vices and virtues may be selected. Take the case of suicide. This is not as with Socrates a wilful desertion of the post assigned to us by God, but a form of injustice toward the community which needs every man's services: Dying to escape from poverty, or the pangs of love, or anything that is simply painful, is the act, not of a brave man, but of a coward, because it is mere softness to fly from what is toilsome, and the suicide braves the terrors of death, not because it is noble to do so, but to get out of the reach of evil.

These strictures are connected with the characteristic view of Aristotle regarding the virtue of great-mindedness, whose defect is little-mindedness and excess pompousness. The ideal is really that of the self-respecting gentleman who values himself highly and at the same time justly, because, as great-minded, honour is his criterion. This virtue seems to be a kind of ornament of all the other virtues, in that it makes them better and cannot be without them, and for this reason it is a hard matter to be really and truly great-minded; for great-mindedness cannot be without thorough goodness and nobleness of character.

There is, however, a vulgar opinion which must be combated, for the gifts of fortune are commonly thought to contribute to high-mindedness. These are the marks of the great-minded: He is not a man to incur little risks, nor does he court danger, because there are but few things he has a value for; but he will incur great dangers, and when he does venture, he is prodigal of his life, as knowing that there are terms on which it is not worth his while to live. He is the kind of man to do kindnesses, but he is ashamed to receive them; the former putting a man in the position of superiority, the latter in that of inferiority. Further, it is characteristic of the great-minded man to ask favours not at all, or very reluctantly, but to do a service very readily; and to bear himself loftily toward the great or fortunate, but toward people of middle station affably. It is a property of his also to be open, both in his dislikes and his likings, because concealment is a consequence of fear. Likewise to be careful for reality rather than appearance, and talk and act openly. Neither is his admiration easily excited, because nothing is great in his eyes; nor does he bear malice, since remembering anything, and especially wrongs, is not part of great-mindedness, but rather overlooking them; nor does he talk of other men, in fact, he will not speak either of himself or of any other; he neither cares to be praised himself, nor to have others blamed; nor, again, does he praise freely, and for this reason he is not apt to speak ill even of his enemies, except he means to give offense. Again, he is the kind of man to acquire what is beautiful and unproductive, rather than what is productive and profitable; this being rather the part of a man who is sufficient to himself.

Great-mindedness is perhaps the most significant of the Aristotelian virtues, because it leads on to the final end of the ethics, the highest aim of life being not the carrying on of business, or politics, or war, but the noble employment of leisure at the time of life when we are our own masters, "the last of life for which the first was made."

Lest this result of magnanimity appear selfish, the author praises the corresponding virtue of magnificence where services to the public have their widest scope. This ideal is to be connected with what was said of the magnanimous man who is wont to acquire what is beautiful and unproductive rather than what is productive and profitable. It is characteristic of the magnificent man, says Aristotle, to build his house suitable to his wealth, for this also is in a way a public ornament, and again to spend rather upon such things as are of long duration, these being most honourable. He will consider also how a thing may be done most beautifully and fittingly, rather than for how much it may be done, and at the least expense. Such cases of expenditure which we call honourable are dedicatory offerings to the gods, and the furnishing of their temples, and sacrifices, and in like manner everything that has reference to the Deity, and all such public matters as are objects of honourable ambition, as when men think in any case that it is their duty to furnish a chorus for the stage splendidly, or fit out and maintain a trireme, or give a general public feast.

ARISTOTLE
"Master of them that know"

The Aristotelian magnificence has seemed to many an artificial and unnecessary virtue, in fact anything but a virtue, as contrary to moral humility. Yet even the humble Christian of the early centuries looked forward to a city of magnificence in the future life, a fair city with streets of gold and with gates of precious stones, all being a compensation for what he had missed in this life. Magnificence, again, has been criticized as not ethical because not disinterested. In the strong language of modern politics, there have been malefactors of great wealth who have sought to atone for their ill-gotten gains by belated civic liberality and the endowment of great public foundations. It is true that in Athens there were such acts of magnificence as when certain resident merchants from abroad sought to gain citizenship by their lavish gifts to the city. But the motive which Aristotle puts forward is neither one of atonement nor of self-interest, but one of æsthetic enjoyment. The Greek craving for beauty was to be satisfied. As in the Middle Ages the cathedral was the poor man's picture gallery, so in Athens the people were accustomed to being surrounded by things of beauty—marble temples, decorated colonnades, the pomp of processions, and public spectacles.

The magnificent man was a public benefactor in appealing to the pride of the eye. To a high degree this was a virtue, for civic pride in the appearance of one's city is but an enlargement of the individual's pride in his personal appearance. Historically this notion was important. It influenced Mæcenas, patron of art; it influenced Italy of the Renaissance. Lorenzo the Magnificent was clearly inspired by this ideal in what he did for Florence, just as were later rulers—the Grand Monarch of France with his palace at Versailles, and the two Napoleons with their bridges and boulevards, and so on down to the city fathers of Paris who with lavish illumination keep up the reputation of the city of light.

The criticism of this notion of magnificence is that it is economically unsound and leads to unproductive industries. To a certain degree Aristotle conceded the point in conjoining the beautiful and the unproductive. But recently some have argued that there is a close interrelation between the fine arts and the industrial arts. The movement for the city beautiful has no doubt a sordid side, yet even hard-headed boards of directors are in favour of beautifying banks, and real estate speculators of adorning skyscrapers.

Magnanimity and magnificence are two characteristic doctrines which have been censured as too aristocratic. As a man of property and companion to a crown prince, Aristotle has been pictured as a dreadful example of his own definition of snobbishness as the "excess of wealth." His views on friendship belie this, for to him its essence is disinterestedness. He grants that there are several types of friendship, based in turn on the good, the pleasant, and the useful. But he contends that of these three the first only is perfect, for true friendship is unselfish, since those whose motive to friendship is utility love their friends for what is good to themselves, and they whose motive is pleasure do so for what is pleasurable to themselves. That, then, is perfect friendship which subsists between those who are good and whose similarity consists in their goodness, for these men wish one another's good in similar ways, in so far as they are good (and good they are in themselves). And those are specially friends who wish good to their friends for their sakes, because they feel thus toward them on their own account, and not as a mere matter of result; so the friendship between these men continues to subsist so long as they are good, and goodness, we know, has in it a principle of permanence.

This is the ideal, but there are variants which though not disinterested are still called friendships: Men who are rich or possessed of authority and influence are thought to have special need of friends, for where is the use of such prosperity if there be taken away the doing of kindnesses of which friends are the most usual and most commendable objects? . . . In poverty, moreover, and all other adversities, men think friends to be their only refuge. Finally, friendship seems to be the bond of social communities, and legislators seem to be more anxious to secure it than justice, even. I mean, unanimity is somewhat like to friendship, and this they certainly aim at, and specially drive out faction as being inimical.

The rich, the poor, and the politicians all have use for friendship, but as riches, poverty, and occupation are but the accidents of life, the essence of friendship must be sought elsewhere. The perfect relation, then, subsists between those who are good and whose similarity consists in their goodness. Of course, bad men may be friends to one another from motives of pleasure or profit, but disinterestedly for the sake of one another; plainly the good alone can be friends, for only between good men does mutual confidence exist. As for the politicians, those demagogues who talk about being "friends of the people" are merely talking: to be a friend to many people, in the way of the perfect friendship, is not possible—just as you cannot love many at once. It is, so to speak, a state of excess, which naturally has but one object; and besides, it is not an easy thing for one man to be very much pleased with many people at the same time, nor perhaps to find many really good. In spite of all this there is a certain valuable relation between political friendship and justice. Men address as friends, for instance, those who are their friends by sea, or in war, or in other forms of communion.

In these observations Aristotle is rising toward his conception of the great social communion, the state as a whole which is more precisely defined in the *Politics* as a community of good life, embracing both families and tribes, intended to promote full and independent existence. This sounds well, but in the application to the Greek family and the foreign tribe we find the golden mean gone wrong. In the case of the family the relation of husband, wife, and children is one of autocracy and not of equality. The three parties are described as the head of the house, the dutiful wife, and obedient offspring. This is of course the conventional classic scheme of grades of subordination. If Aristotle had been consistent he might have been the prophet of equality of the sexes with perfect friendship between man and wife, and even the prophet of that final step, when children, as far as possible, are to be treated as equals, or at least as small rational beings whose opinions are worth listening to.

However, the golden mean of equality was not so applied in the family and much less in the relation of the Greek state to foreign tribes. Defining man as a social animal, Aristotle compares the great social communion to other creatures with their coöperation for a common end, yet even as the social bees and wasps have their stings ready for intruders, so does the philosopher. In regard to those outside Hellendom, so-called barbarians, he makes this astonishing statement: Barbarism and slavery are by nature identical. Finally he quotes with approval the poet's line: "Let the alien serve the Hellene, they are bounden, we are free."

To uphold this preposterous piece of snobbishness, Aristotle presents this elaborate piece of reasoning: The peoples of the cold North and of Europe are courageous, and therefore remain in undisturbed possession of their freedom; but they lack intelligence and skill in the arts; for this reason they have no good political institutions and are incapable of ruling their neighbours. The Orientals, on the other hand, are distinguished by their intelligence and their skill in the arts; but they lack courage; hence they are perpetually dominated and enslaved. But just as Greece occupies a middle position, so the Greek people shares the advantages of both. This people is at once courageous and intelligent. Hence it preserves its freedom, possesses the best political institutions, and would be able, could it attain constitutional unity, to rule over all.

This reminds one of certain statements made before the World War and still reëchoed in the myth of Nordic supremacy. In his excessive national conceit Aristotle's usual sanity has given place to sophistry and we miss in him that Socratic irony which Plato employed when he propounded this quizzical question: "Just as the Greeks contrast all others with themselves, might not some other race of intelligent creatures, say the cranes, become inflated with pride, and balance themselves against all other living beings, lumping into one mass all that are not cranes, men included, and dubbing them all alike 'beasts'?" Yet there was a certain historic irony in Aristotle's position. The Stagirite himself came from the cold North and was tutor to a conqueror who founded such a cosmopolitan city of Hellenes and barbarians as Alexandria. However, Aristotle's position as to barbarians being potential slaves, and slaves "animated tools," did a certain amount of good in the way of arousing revolt. The Stoics seized on his statements and as citizens of the world and in many cases slaves themselves bitterly resented all doctrines of chattel ownership. Some of the Stoics as prisoners of war were in the position of barbarians. How then, as Aristotle reasoned, were they "destined by nature" to slavery? As the matter has been well put: by founding slavery on natural rights Aristotle provoked thought and protest, and led the Stoics to reject with indignation his theories and to proclaim the moral equality of master and slave, of Greek and barbarian. Moreover, his declaration that slaves are merely animated instruments, are men incapable of virtue, worked as powerfully in destroying ancient slavery as the Dred Scott Decision of the Supreme Court of the United States, maintaining that Negro slaves have no rights which the white man is bound to respect, worked for the destruction of Negro slavery in the Southern states.[1]

Aristotle's bark was worse than his bite, for he finally argues for the educating of slaves and offers as a reward for good behaviour emancipation itself. As a wealthy man he characterized slaves as "absolutely one's own," but in his last testament he made such provisions as these: "I also will that Aubrachis shall have her liberty and that there shall be given to her five hundred drachmas. . . . I also will that Tychon shall have his liberty when his daughter is married, and Philon, and Olympius, and his son. Moreover, of those boys who wait upon me, I will that none shall be sold, but my executors may use them, and when they are grown up then they shall emancipate them if they deserve it."

---

[1] P. V. N. Myers, *History as Past Ethics*, p. 203.

Aristotle's moral system has these two blots—an excessive national conceit and its correlate, the enslavement of barbarians. In these respects he did not rise above his contemporaries, but in another respect he did. His final ideal for the virtuous man is to lead the life of contemplation, in order to attain that vision of the highest good, "the goal after which all beings strive," where wonderful pleasures, wonderful in their purity and their permanence, are afforded by philosophy or science. By contemplation is meant the pursuit of the knowledge of things beautiful and divine, the works of nature and the nature of God himself. To show what this double aim was, we have two passages, one preserved by Cicero, and the other the words of the great master himself:

Imagine a race of men, says the Roman, who had always lived under ground in beautiful houses adorned with pictures and statues and every luxury of wealth. Suppose that some dim rumour of a divine being had reached them in their subterranean world. Then suppose that the earth were to open and they ascended up from their dark abodes and saw before them all the wonders of this world. Could they doubt, when they beheld the earth and the sea and the sky with its gathering clouds and its mighty winds, and the glory and majesty of the sun as he floods the heaven with the light of day, and then the starry heaven of night, and the varying brightness of the waxing and the waning moon, and the regular movements of all the heavenly bodies and their risings and settings governed by an everlasting and unchanging law—could they doubt that the gods really existed, and that these mighty works were theirs?

But the height of contemplative speculation is reached in Aristotle's description of the divine reason: God's life is like that of which we catch a transient glimpse when our life is at its best. Thus, indeed, his life always is (a thing which is impossible for us), for his very self-activity is bliss. And that is why we find greatest pleasure in being awake, in feeling and in thinking, and in the hopes and memories that come through these activities. But thinking, pure thinking, has for its object that which is in itself the best, and such thinking when most perfect has for its object the supreme good. The intellect thinks itself in grasping the intelligible, for it becomes intelligible in laying hold upon and thinking its object. Therefore, the intellect and the intelligible are the same thing; for to be able to receive the intelligible and the real is what we mean by intellect, and the intellect actually lives in doing this. And it is this actual life of the intellect, rather than the intelligible as object, that seems to be the divine element in the intellect, and pure speculative vision is what is best and most enjoyable. If then God is always as well off as we are now and then, how wonderful it is! And if he is always better off, it is still more wonderful. But such is the fact. And life belongs to him; for the activity of the mind is life, and he is that activity. Pure self-activity of reason is God's most blessed and everlasting life. We say that God is living, eternal, perfect; and continuous and everlasting life is God's, for God is eternal life.

# PART THREE

## ASIATIC SYSTEMS

# I. BUDDHISM

## THE WAY OF THE BUDDHA

ARISTOTLE has brought us far on the road of virtue and happiness
—virtue depending on the training of the soul and happiness on the
imitation of the divine nature. It is now necessary to turn back and
examine a more ancient way of wisdom. This was the system of
Gautama, the Buddha, or Enlightened One, the greatest of the moralists of India, who held that there is no soul, in the proper sense
of the word, and no God, in the sense of a supreme personal being.

Without these two postulates it would seem to the Occidental
mind as impossible to construct an ethics as it would be to describe
an ellipse without two foci. But the attempt was made, and with a
no-soul psychology and an atheistic metaphysics there was erected
a system that was so successful that it favourably affected the lives
and characters of perhaps more millions in the East than any
morality could lay claim to in the West.

The backgrounds of Buddhism are, of course, remote. Its doctrines
of Karma, which virtually denied human personality, and of Nirvana,
which dispensed with any absolute being, were gained both by borrowing and by rejecting certain tenets of the older Brahmanism.
The priests of this older cult, like the thinkers in the Homeric age,
had struggled with the problems of destiny and had concluded that
it was not a blind power against which human wisdom and endeavour are weak, but only results of one's former actions in previous
states of existence which counted. Now attach this to the notion
of transmigration, a notion which many a Greek cherished, and turn
it into a set of causes which can be understood, and the formula
becomes rational. Whatsoever a man has sown, that shall he reap,
since in every case there shall be "a fruit similar to the action."
For example, a murderer will be short-lived; a thief will be poor;
an adulterer will have an unfaithful wife. In short, Karma explains
everything.

Such, briefly, was the doctrine as developed in the Sixth Century
before Christ by Gautama, the Aryan aristocrat, who preferred the
way of speculation and meditation to the privileges of the highest

ruling caste. But while the notion of Karma was borrowed from the Brahmans, that of Nirvana, though verbally borrowed, was actually offered as a substitute for the earlier belief in Brahm, that spirit or power deeply interfused through the universe, a being into whose bosom the faithful were ultimately to be received. Over against this notion of absorption, with the attached idea of a power not ourselves that saves us, Gautama put the notion of Nirvana, a supreme condition of blessedness engendered by the efforts of the single saint. The way to Nirvana is the way of self-salvation; the gods have nothing to do with it; the individual alone swims the current of adversity. Nor can he expect a miracle to intervene; a pious wish will not bring the opposite bank of the river over to him when he stands trembling on the brink. As Gautama himself inquires: "The self is the protector of the self; what other protector could the self have?"

These are statements taken directly from the Sacred Books of the East. Despite their figurative nature they exhibit the stern logic of events. The chain of Karma is a rational chain of cause and effect, a natural law in the spiritual world that allows for no mystery or miracle. As contrasted with Western thought, blame cannot be put upon the shoulders of destiny as the Homeric age was wont to do, nor upon the original sin of our first parents as was the fashion in the later Christian Era. No, the individual is the fashioner of his own fate: he sows and he reaps; he sins and he suffers, and countless ages of right action and right thinking are needed to wipe out the debt and thus to reach that ecstatic state of freedom from illusion, when the debt is paid, the mortgage lifted, the account cleared. Perhaps this way of thinking seems too mercantile, but it was suited to the temper of the Oriental, past master as a trader and a merchant. So, in its first aspect, Buddhism appears to be built up on a veritable system of double-entry bookkeeping. Yet, while the account is checked up at every turn, many an extension of time is allowed; there are countless lives in which expiation may be made, but in the end full settlement must be rendered.

This to the Western mind is scarcely a philosophy that warms the heart. It is as cold-blooded as banking. It does not appeal to those who would have recourse to some outside benefactor who is expected to erase the record by an act of forgiveness. According to Buddhism, while one is urged to wipe out the debts of others, he cannot count on others to wipe out his, and above all there is no supreme power who can interfere with Karma. So there lies before him an inevitable day of reckoning—the day of death when the balance is struck be-

tween moral debits and credits, and the next stage of existence is to
be in accordance with this balance.

"All that we are is the result of what we have thought and done"
—this saying sums up the matter in its first aspect. The formula
is logical and even scientific; it suggests a kind of conservation and
correlation of energy in the moral sphere, when no more can be got
out of this life than has been put into it by former lives. Yet this
problem remains: How can debit and credit be talked of without
postulating a person who is either a debtor or a creditor? How can
sin and guilt, virtue and merit, be attributed to a being who is not
a self, a soul, an entity? The Buddhist says, "No doer is there, naught
save the deed that is found." What is meant by this? Technically, the
matter is explained by asserting that there is no real self but only
a series of conjoined phenomena, or, as the Buddhists put it figuratively, man is like a chariot made up of the body, wheels, and pole,
but the individual is no more a thing in itself than the chariot is a
chariot in itself.

So far as popular belief goes, the Buddhist is negative, he defines
man as selflessness and does not admit the existence of an ego, a
permanent individual. Here the founder Gautama, in protest against
popular thought, was opposing the Brahmanic view of the soul as
an airy something, a survival of the. old animistic belief in the
ghostly self which leaves the body not only in dreams but in death
and after the dissolution of the body passes into another body—
that of some beast if this life has been evil, that of some noble, or
hero, or saint if this life has been good. According to this view the
soul, as Atman, or breath, is imperishable; the body may moulder in
the grave, but the soul goes marching on. To this popular, this primitive, belief the master objected, and in its place substituted a view
which left the primitive view so far behind as to approach the most
subtle modern speculations on the meaning of the self. Put in the
language of the Twentieth Century, the self is not a substance,
however attenuated, but a stream of consciousness; all that actually
exists is a series of states of consciousness, one of which may be a
consciousness of those states, but no one of which may be fastened
on as the true self, permanent, perdurable, everlasting. If we think
that we possess a self to which we should be true we are deceiving
ourselves; the self as soul is but the ghost of primitive man's ghost,
the faint echo of a prehistoric squeak unworthy even to be considered an object worth thinking about.

Such, in modern terms, is the gist of the Hindu speculations of
over twenty centuries ago. The matter as subtly developed by the

later Buddhists has been thus summed up: There is not a self, a permanent substantial unity, but there is a person to be described as "a living continuous fluid complex" which does not remain quite the same for two consecutive moments, but which continues for an endless number of existences, bridging an endless number of deaths, without becoming completely different from itself.[1] In short, man is but a nucleus of predispositions and the individual is as "soulless" logically as a corporation is legally.

Under this theory of no-soul how can a system of morality be possible? If there is no self what becomes of personal responsibility? If the world is "void of self or of aught of that nature," as the Buddhist says, the vast hierarchy of Hindu gods may be got rid of as mere fancied beings, and man too would seem to disappear in this process of erasure. Now in all this has not the Buddhist, in freeing himself of a burdensome mythology, destroyed psychology itself and with it the very connective tissue of morality? So at first sight it might appear unless we connect this no-soul psychology with the Buddhistic philosophy of causation as suggested in the doctrine of Karma. The latter was seen to be a kind of correlation and conservation of ethical energy, when evil deeds would never be wiped out by miraculous means, nor good deeds discounted as to their consequences. Both the good and the evil that we do live after us and our future lives represent the resultants in the parallelogram of forces engendered in this and in previous states of existence. In the cosmos nothing is lost; energy may be dissipated, but is never destroyed. Karma, then, represents ethical energy and Karma as a process of causation is a self-recording process registered on the unfolding roll of time. Now how may the self, not as a permanent unity, but as "a continuous fluid complex," be fitted into this scheme? The soul is not a semimaterial body, an impalpable something as the earlier animists thought; it is rather a condition of stress and strain, a transitory bundle of conflicting sensations, cognitions, and volitions, in a word, states of mind without a mind as such. There are perceptions, says the Buddhist, but we do not know the perceiver. In answer to the statement of King Milinda, who declared that he came in a chariot, the Buddhist sage retorted: "There is no chariot, for neither the pole, nor the axle, nor the wheels, nor the frame, nor the yoke, nor any part of the chariot is the chariot." Or put in other language, just as the word "chariot" is but a mode of expression for the constituent members, in exactly the same way

---

[1] D. V. Poussin, *The Way to Nirvana*, p. 35.

the words "living being" and "ego" are only modes of expression for a complex of bodily and non-bodily constituents.[1]

This is the problem of the whole and the parts, over which the Buddhist held abstruse and age-long discussions, coming to the conclusion that the self is but a name for a chance totality, a mere notion of an aggregate. Meanwhile, and here is the rub, with a no-soul psychology the Buddhists developed a fine morality and for generations kept on developing characters whom to know is to admire. How is this to be explained from the Western standpoint, such as that of Aristotle, who reasoned that without a soul, an informing principle, there could be no free will and consequently no responsibility? And how again can we reconcile this no-soul theory with a passage like the following, where the sinner meets the sage and hears this question and answer: "Have you, O man, when you reach old age, thought within yourself: I am subject to death; well, then, I will do good in thought, word, and deed. . . . These your evil deeds your mother has not done, nor your father, nor your brother, nor your sister, nor your friends and advisers, nor your connections and blood relatives, nor ascetics, nor Brahmans, nor gods. It is you alone who have done these evil deeds; you alone will enjoy their fruit."[2]

The solution of this subtle difficulty seems to lie in the doctrine of Karma, which in brief is cosmic causation, a vast network in which humanity and all creatures are enmeshed. Hence as men it is not the gods but we ourselves who forge the links of this chain of cause and effect. We can no more escape the consequences of our acts than coefficients can lie outside of a mathematical series. As the numbers add themselves together in a sum, so our acts pile up a store of merit or demerit. From this process of causation, this process of summation, no one can escape; it lies in the nature of things; it is part of the cosmic stream of events, the rushing metamorphosis from which no one can dissociate himself and yet of which each one forms a part. But it is the task of the wise man to learn how small that part is as compared to the mighty Whole, for his reality does not consist so much in his personal identity in this little span of life, as in the sense of union with all that was, is, and shall be. In short, this life is but one in an endless series of past existences, a series which is to project itself in like manner into an endless series of future existences, unless, by some prodigy of insight, by some

[1]Poussin, p. 42.
[2]*Ibid.*, p. 47.

miracle of meditation, one can step aside from the chain of causation and escape this devouring machinery of the inevitable. This escape, this way of salvation, is Nirvana. This does not mean absorption into the bosom of the absolute, for there is no absolute; it does not mean the coalescence of the soul of the individual with the soul of the world, for properly there are no souls, human or divine.

To the Western mind, revolving about the twin doctrines of God and soul, this notion of Nirvana seems atheistic and unnatural, and the adjurations of Gautama to attain it an invitation to intellectual suicide. Still, it was hardly that, but rather an attempt to escape from a prison house of popular belief in which the Indian mind of Gautama's day was fettered. The notion of transmigration existed, of course, in Greece in the form of the myth of the cycle of the seasons which, as in the story of Demeter and Persephone, was enlarged and rationalized in the form of a cycle of existences, not only for the vegetable kingdom, but for animals and men. This myth lent itself to art and to the playful fancies of Plato, as in his vision of Er, but outside of the limited circle of Pythagoras, contemporary with Gautama, it had comparatively few adherents. But in India the belief in transmigration was held by millions and in its crowded population took the form, not of the poetic fancies of the Greeks, but the form of the swastika, the symbol of the unending, hopeless wheel of life. In regard to this belief a well-known authority has said: The terrible thing was not a rebirth in hell so much as the far more staggering and terrifying conception that there was no escape from the round of transmigration at all. A being in a state of misery, or in a state of happiness, might be perfectly sure that that state would sooner or later come to an end; but it would come to an end only by the commencement of another state, of another birth. And that birth would be inevitably attended by all the results inherent in the limitations of individuality, and the struggle necessary to keep the individuality alive would bring with it fresh cares and troubles, old age and death, grief, lamentations, wailings, and despair. This is the evil to be avoided.[1]

## MEDITATION

Buddha said, "Avoid desire and hatred, attain patience, be calm, meditate," and forthwith this became the Buddhist's rule of life, whether he understood it or not. The happiness sought by the Buddhist was also a happiness in heaven till he learned a loftier goal, and

[1] Rhys-Davids, *Buddhism*, p. 154.

then the Nirvana which he attained was like the unconscious bliss
of the Brahman's union with the All-soul. To the virtuous, but not
philosophic, man were offered in both cases a reward in heaven and
high birth again on earth; while to the philosopher was offered also,
by Buddhist and by Brahman alike, escape from birth followed by
bliss ineffable in the loss of individuality (extinction of self). Ethically, every good act aims at the highest goal for the philosopher, as
every good act, as he is capable of understanding and performing it,
aims at the passing joy of heaven and "good rebirth" for the man of
limited mind and hope. The act brings happiness (passing joy hereafter or bliss eternal) because it is good. However, the basic value of
goodness is capable of being measured by the result of the act in
terms of emancipation. Buddha saw as pressing realities the miseries
of rebirth and the need to escape from them, and argued that escape
was possible only through elimination of desire (thirst), which was
inherited by each individual from a precedent birth and appeared
in any one birth as a predisposition. Gratification of desire therefore
only bound one the more, and the way of escape was to eliminate
desire of everything except of the highest goal, which was to be
reached eventually by absolute indifference; but the way to it was
found in a preliminary elimination of everything tending to post-
pone the desired state. Now to acquire even the approach to indifference one must subdue certain inherent traits such as longings
and aversions and hatreds, which were therefore evil in a varying
degree. For example, serenity implies an equable mind fostered by a
calm and friendly environment. Hence one must cultivate amity and
a wide love for all beings; but when thereby one has attained the state
of serenity one must renounce love and advance further to indifference. Kindly feeling and love for all are stages toward perfection.[1]

## KARMA

"The Indian philosophers called character, as thus defined,
'karma.' It is this karma which passed from life to life and linked
them in the chain of transmigrations; and they held that it is modified in each life, not merely by confluence of parentage, but by its
own acts. They were, in fact, strong believers in the theory, so much
disputed just at present, of the hereditary transmission of acquired
characters. That the manifestation of the tendencies of a character
may be greatly facilitated, or impeded, by conditions, of which self-
discipline, or the absence of it, are among the most important, is

[1]E. W. Hopkins, *Ethics of India*, pp. 140–141.

indubitable; but that the character itself it modified in this way is by no means so certain; it is not so sure that the transmitted character of an evil liver is worse, or that of a righteous man better, than that which he received. Indian philosophy, however, did not admit of any doubt on this subject; the belief in the influence of conditions, notably of self-discipline on the karma, was not merely a necessary postulate of its theory of retribution, but it presented the only way of escape from the endless round of transmigrations.

"Accepting the prevalent Brahminical doctrine that the whole cosmos, celestial, terrestrial, and infernal, with its population of gods and other celestial beings, of sentient animals, of Mara and his devils, is incessantly shifting through recurring cycles of production and destruction, in each of which every human being has his transmigratory representative, Gautama proceeded to eliminate substance altogether, and to reduce the cosmos to a mere flow of sensations, emotions, volitions, and thoughts, devoid of any substratum. As, on the surface of a stream of water, we see ripples and whirlpools, which last for a while and then vanish with the causes that gave rise to them, so what seem individual existences are mere temporary associations of phenomena circling round a centre, 'like a dog tied to a post.' In the whole universe there is nothing permanent, no eternal substance either of mind or of matter. Personality is a metaphysical fancy; and in very truth, not only we, but all things, in the worlds without end of the cosmic phantasmagoria, are such stuff as dreams are made of.

"What then becomes of karma? Karma remains untouched. As the peculiar form of energy we call magnetism may be transmitted from a loadstone to a piece of steel, from the steel to a piece of nickel, as it may be strengthened or weakened by the conditions to which it is subjected while resident in each piece, so it seems to have been conceived that karma might be transmitted from one phenomenal association to another by a sort of induction. However this may be, Gautama doubtless had a better guarantee for the abolition of transmigration, when no wrack of substance, either of Atman or of Brahma, was left behind; when, in short, a man had but to dream that he willed not to dream, to put an end to all dreaming.

"This end of life's dream is Nirvana. What Nirvana is the learned do not agree. But, since the best original authorities tell us there is neither desire nor activity, nor any possibility of phenomenal reappearance for the sage who has entered Nirvana, it may be safely said of this acme of Buddhistic philosophy—'the rest is silence.'"— THOMAS H. HUXLEY, *Evolution and Ethics*, pp. 62–63, 66–68.

The Great Buddha having attained Nirvana

## THE PATH TO NIRVANA

With this widespread Indian belief, in Karma before him the founder of Buddhism, after his long meditations under the bo-tree, strives to erect a defense mechanism, a screen of speculation which will shut out these haunting fears. The secret of Buddhism is here said to be the escape from the wheel of life by way of Nirvana. The meaning of this term, made hazily familiar by the modern theosophists, and generally translated as a state of nothingness, is most difficult to grasp. Its primitive meaning is twofold, on the one side "becoming cool," on the other "blowing out." In the former case it means the cooling of a man who is heated with desire; in the latter the extinction of individual existence, like the snuffing out of a candle. From these interpretations are derived two main ideas: on the one hand Nirvana means the sanctity attained by one who is no longer inflamed by the fire of the passions; on the other it means extinction of a saint after death. But here a further distinction must be made and that is between the ordinary man and the sanctified man. One who has not overcome his desire for existence will have to continue on the weary round, the treadmill of transmigration, whose phases will be determined by the merit and demerit of Karma. On the contrary, the saint who, like Gautama himself, has overcome all desire for any future life has "destroyed rebirth." But there are steps in the path to Nirvana. The future goal is not to be reached at once. Here the very portal to the great deliverance is said to be the breaking of the first "fetter," the delusion of self. But at what a cost is this achieved. The Buddhist "conqueror" would seem to be a Samson Agonistes who escaped the prison treadmill by destroying not only the building but himself along with it. Yet such is the Buddhist message: Destroy the delusion of self and there shall be no rebirth; we cannot be selfless and survive.

There now follows the second fetter concerning doubt. By overcoming doubt as to the delusion of self one has reached a salvation from the sorrows of life in a changed state of mind which sums itself up in the conviction of the folly of a craving after a future life. This is a strange doctrine, as difficult to understand as to practise. It was scarcely made clear to the Western mind until the neurotic Schopenhauer, after his contact with certain Sacred Books of the East, proclaimed that the way of deliverance consisted in suppressing the will to live, that salvation lay not in self-assertion but in self-abnegation; that ultimate satisfaction might be reached by giving up the struggle, and that one's motto should be: "Seek the eternal quiet."

To the West this message made comparatively little appeal. A few took literally what Schopenhauer had to say on suicide; a few more became quietists and in peaceful meditation sought relief from the complexities of life; but in general the philosophy of self-surrender did not suit the European temper; even the "tender-minded" English poet Clough exclaims: "Say not the struggle naught availeth," while the German Nietzsche's poetic fancies on "the eternal return," which implies a mere drifting in the whirlpool of existence, are far outweighed by his insistence on the duty of "the noble soul" to practise self-assertion and not self-surrender.

Such protest and such reactions show that the West was but little sympathetic to the mental patterns of the East, especially to the fundamental pattern, symbolized by the swastika, of the wheel of life, the cycle of existence—that image substitution, that great idol that dominated the Indian mind. Plato the Greek used it in one of his myths, but he also derided it as meaning an inevitable return of previous states of existence. Gibbon the Englishman employed it in his *Rise and Fall of the Roman Empire*, while Vico the Italian, formulating his law of flux and reflux in the affairs of men, was forced to modify the cyclic view of history with epicycles of exceptions, and finally, and more recently, Spengler, in his *Downfall of Western Civilization*, has had the spokes knocked out of his pessimistic wheel by the phenomenal rise of America.

But to the Indian thinkers of twenty-five centuries ago the great symbol was taken literally and the pattern of the wheel became fatally stamped upon their minds. Brahmans as well as Buddhists thought in circles, and for the latter the way of escape from this dreary round was not to fly off on a tangent of independent action, but to strive to stop the giddy whirl of life as far as one's existence was concerned. The logical step was to go aside and deny the logic of events. So, as a French critic has wittily said, they did so, for "they were not Hindus for nothing." One Oriental trait—and all men are more or less Oriental—is bland denial of what we do not care to believe. When, for example, William James speaks of the will to believe, he suggests as its correlate the will to disbelieve, and it is to the credit of the imaginative Oriental that he wills to disbelieve in that which the Occidental almost universally takes as the most fundamental of facts—the self itself. Among British thinkers, at least, the confidence in self-consciousness was so ingrained that when David Hume declared that the mind is but a name for a bundle of sensations his contemporaries paid little attention to his views. There had, of course, been much discussion of the mind, the soul, the self, but the skeptical Scotchman took the very core out of this apple of discord and was considered a fool for his pains. When he declared that in seeking for the self he always "tumbled on some particular perception," and could find no indwelling soul, or spirit, or ego, he issued a challenge which it took the great Kant over twenty years of thinking to counter, if indeed he ever did counter it. But here twenty-four hundred years ago the Buddhists had attacked this problem and reached the paradoxical conclusion that the worst doubt was not to doubt the existence of the self. This, then, was the second fetter of Gautama—to doubt the truth of the impermanence of the self. To the Enlightened One the self is but an eddy in the stream of existence. It is not a permanent substantial unity but, as already described, a "fluid complex." Now if the doctrine of Karma may be explained in terms of the correlation and conservation of energy, which never gains and never loses aught of its totality, so may the doctrine of the impermanence of the self be illustrated by the vortex theory as an attempt to explain the forms which energy takes. This fluid complex is not only the whirlpool in the water, but the whirlwind in the air, now rendered visible through dust, now through leaves caught up in the circling currents. Under this aspect the complex of the self is not to be considered a thing in itself, but merely an empty form, an impalpable wheel of existence which whirls onward in its course not only inanimate bits of matter, but all animate existences, up to men and the gods themselves. What can be done to arrest its inexorable sway? For the wise man the answer is to check the functioning of this cycle of existence. Hence the advice of the Master: Cease striving and you stop the wheel of life itself, so far as you are concerned. In the quiet hour, freed from all disturbing emotions, the saint may attain that sense of tranquillity which is described as a state of victory over the world and over birth and death, a state of inward peace that never can be shaken, of a joy that can never be ruffled. This is the condition of Nirvana as further described in one of the poems put into the mouth of a convert to Buddhism:

> That state of peace I saw, wherein the roots
> Of ever fresh rebirth are all destroyed, and greed
> And hatred and delusion all have ceased,
> That state from lust for future life set free,
> That changeth not, can ne'er be led to change.
> My mind saw that! What care I for those rites?

Poetic ecstasy is perhaps an unsatisfactory answer to the puzzles of Buddhism. Just as denying the debts incurred by Karma would be a mere subterfuge, a kind of moral moratorium, so to deny the doctrine of the whirlpool of rebirths would not rid a Hindu of his haunting fears unless some positive cure were offered. Such a cure was suggested by Gautama, for like all religious founders, he was a physician of souls. Nirvana, then, does not mean mere nihilism, but a positive state of happiness reached through the negation of the burdens of life. Literally Nirvana signifies a "going out," as of the flame of a lamp; figuratively, in its moral sense, it stands for the going out of the threefold fire of lust, ill will, and delusion. In another of its primitive meanings Nirvana also stands for "cooling, becoming cool." Ethically interpreted, this could describe the intense relief of one who has escaped the fervent heat of the emotions. By these secondary interpretations the Buddhist has escaped the full rigours of the doctrine of Nirvana as annihilation. Like other practical reformers, Gautama has made a compromise with common sense, just as the Stoics did later when they modified their dictum of indifference to the goods of life and allowed the enjoyment of harmless goods. In other words, Buddhism, like many another reforming movement, turned from strict to loose construction, from the "dangerous truths" of absolute selflessness and annihilation to a more workable rule of living. This meant that, while the professional saint may strive for an end of suffering by putting an end to all feeling, the layman may enjoy the goods of life in moderation, and may look forward to a series of future lives in which he will work off his indebtedness to Karma. And here, just as the harsh doctrine of Nirvana was modified by a drift from the extreme to the moderate view, so was the notion of Karma. Instead of meaning an overburdening sense of the crushing chain of causality, it was turned into a sense of solidarity with all creatures. Our lives may appear to be like the chance loads hurried along on a conveying belt, but at the same time they are akin to other existences in the vast organic mechanism. Because of this common carrier there arises in us not only a sense of union with humanity, but with all animate creatures.

At this point there arises one of the most attractive features of Buddhism, a belief which starts with the idea of the brotherhood of man and ends with the idea of our brotherhood with brutes. At times this reaches fantastic extremes, as when the Buddhist monk was supplied with a crude filter to strain his drinking water lest he destroy any forms of life invisible to him. But in general this teaching of a gentle affection for all that lives meant not only the forming of an informal society for the prevention of cruelty to animals, but what was of vaster importance, an ingrained abhorrence for the taking of life in war. It is true that the Emperor Asoka, when he became a Buddhist, issued his famous proclamation against the slaying of men after he had slaughtered thousands of his enemies; nevertheless, his message goes on to say not only that "His Majesty feels remorse on account of this conquest," but also that hereafter no animal may be slaughtered in his capital for sacrifice. "Formerly in His Majesty's kitchen thousands of living creatures were slain every day to make curries. At present only two peacocks and one deer are killed daily and the deer not invariably. But in future even these three creatures shall not be slaughtered."[1]

To realize the humanness of applied Buddhism we may here compare this edict engraven on rock with the state of mind of the Romans who at this time were starting the first of their Punic wars, a series of bloody conflicts which ended with that perfect motto of militarism: "Carthage must be destroyed." It is true that alongside of such relentless sentiments should be put the historian Pliny's tales of animal intelligence and Æsop's inimitable fables, but the sources of both of these were Indian and both went back to those ancient "bestiaries" where kinship and sympathy between man and beast bear unmistakable traces of Buddhist influence.

As compared with the Western moralist, the Buddhist was a professional pacifist, but if comparisons are considered odious the odium falls on the Christian nations. No Buddhist hell compares in horror with the hell of the World War, and while there were militant monks among the Buddhists there were no such advocates of militarism as that true son of the church, Machiavelli, who utilized the cloak of religion to cover up the crimes of his Prince, nor for such defenders of ruthlessness as Treitschke and Bernhardi, who conjoined the policy of frightfulness with the motto: "God with us."

But to argue the pros and cons of ethnic systems of morality is futile; it leads to that very fetter of ill will which the Buddhist sought to escape. In fine, it was the process of purging the mind of envy, malice, and all uncharitableness which was Gautama's positive contribution to human thought. Here is a summary of his practical morality, and somewhat in the manner of Aristotle with his golden mean, the Buddhist offers the middle way between two extremes, between the pleasures of sense, and especially of sensuality, and the habitual practise of self-mortification, "a practise painful, unworthy

---

[1]E. W. Hopkins, *Ethics of India*, p. 154.

and equally of no abiding profit." This middle way is found in the "Noble Eightfold Path," That is to say:

"Right Views (free from superstition or delusion)—
"Right Aspirations (high, and worthy of the intelligent, worthy man)—
"Right Speech (kindly, open, truthful)—
"Right Conduct (peaceful, honest, pure)—
"Right Livelihood (bringing hurt or danger to no living thing)—
"Right Effort (in self-training and in self-control)—
"Right Mindfulness (the active, watchful mind)—
"Right Rapture (in deep meditation on the realities of life)."

## II. CONFUCIANISM

### THE FILIAL RELATIONS

"ONCE upon a time Confucius was sitting in his study, having his disciple Tseng Ts'an to attend upon him. He asked Tseng Ts'an: 'Do you know by what virtue and power the good emperors of old made the world peaceful, the people to live in harmony with one another, and the inferior contented under the control of their superiors?' To this Tseng Ts'an, rising from his seat, replied: 'I do not know this, for I am not clever.' Then said Confucius: 'The duty of children to their parents is the fountain whence all other virtues spring, and also the starting point from which we ought to begin our education. Now take your seat, and I will explain this. Our body and hair and skin are all derived from our parents, and therefore we have no right to injure any of them in the least. This is the first duty of a child.

"'To live an upright life and to spread the great doctrines of humanity must win good reputation after death, and reflect great honour upon our parents. This is the last duty of a son.

"'Hence the first duty of a son is to pay a careful attention to every want of his parents. The next is to serve his government loyally; and the last to establish a good name for himself.'"—*The Book of Filial Duty*.

Confucianism has been called the cement of a social structure that has outlasted all others in the social world, since it furnished an ideal of character that for more than three thousand years exercised an incalculable influence upon the moral life of probably a fourth of the human race. Unlike Buddhism, it was not the system of a recluse but of a man of affairs; it was not directed toward perfection in saintship, but in the ordinary duties of life; and had as its goal not the monastery, but the family. Family life was its norm of activity, and from the peasant in his hut to the prince on his throne the prime virtue was filial piety. That which bound son and father also bound husband and wife, elder and younger brother, friend and friend, and sovereign and minister.

These are the famous five relations, or duties of universal obligation. Now every relation has a double aspect, hence the five relations give rise to ten fundamental virtues. These are kindness in a father, filial piety in a son; gentleness in an elder brother, obedience in a younger; righteousness in a husband, submission in a wife; kindness in elders, deference in juniors; benevolence in a ruler, loyalty in a minister.

These passages may appear to be mere counsels of perfection, about as ineffective as a set of trite wall mottoes; but if a way is shown how these virtues may be obtained they become dynamic and not merely static. This way is given in a passage of practical advice: "He who knows how to exemplify what a son should be can afterward exemplify what a father should be. He who knows how to exemplify what a minister should be can afterward exemplify what a ruler should be. He who knows how to serve others can afterward employ them." In all this it should be noted that filial piety is put first and foremost among the virtues in accordance with the significance of one of the oldest characters in the Chinese system of writing where the symbol of filial piety was originally the ideograph, or picture, of a youth holding upon his shoulders an old man. But lest the advice upon filial piety should seem too vague and general Confucius splits it up into its constituent parts. A filial son, he says, has five duties to perform to his parents: He must venerate them in daily life. He must try to make them happy in every possible way, especially when the meal is served. He must take extra care of them when they are sick. He ought to show great sorrow for them when they are dead. He must offer sacrifices to his deceased parents with the utmost solemnity. If he fulfils these duties, then he can be considered as having done what ought to be done by a son.

This advice from *The Book of Filial Duty* has been criticized by many as being based on mere blind devotion, reënforced by an abject superstition—the so-called worship of ancestors. Neither of these charges appears to be true. It is specifically said that when unrighteous conduct is concerned a son must by no means refrain from remonstrating with his father. As for ancestor worship, the best authorities consider this cult more a form of communion with the departed than a superstitious attempt to propitiate the spirits of the dead. Confucius himself was not inclined to bolster up his system by the aid of supernaturalism, for he put the ancestral sacrifices last in the list, as a harmless, prevailing custom. Yet even the latter custom had its uses; it projected the family honour into the past just as living parents should project it into the future by admonishing their children ever to live an honourable life and never to stain the family name. This is, of course, a form of old-fashioned loyalty, a kind of abstract advice difficult to convey to the younger members of the family. But the matter was made easier by the teaching of Confucius that, while the son should admire and imitate the father, the father should make himself a human being whom the son might admire and imitate. The subtle thing about all this is that the principle of imitation works both ways, and furnishes a principle of self-improvement which applies to fathers as well as to sons. If the son is to copy the father, the father must be a decent example to the son and so the family standards are kept up by younger eyes and ears ever on the watch. To see ourselves mirrored in our children, our acts of rudeness mechanically repeated and ugly habits of speech fatally reëchoed by young mouths, is a disconcerting discovery against which Confucius made provision. This was done in his famous principle of reciprocity. When a disciple asked him if there is one word which should be taken as fundamental, the Master replied: "Is not 'reciprocity' such a word? What you do not want done to yourself, do not do unto others."

This has been called the Negative Golden Rule of Chinese morality; it should rather be considered a psychological principle to bind the family together. If we wish our children to admire and imitate us, declared *The Book of Filial Duty*, we should establish our character by the practise of the filial course and thereby glorify our parents.

Thus in successive links the unbroken chain of family life and family honour is preserved. This is far from the abject worship of ancestors, for by the principle of reciprocity the principle of self-respect is also insured. Here, while Confucius left no written word, yet according to well-founded tradition, one disciple heard the Master say that "of all that the Heaven produces and Earth nourishes there is none so great as man. His parents give birth to his person all complete and to return it to them complete may be called filial duty." The same ancient book amplifies this in the further statement that "the superior man's respect extends to all. It is at its greatest when he respects himself. He is but an outgrowth from his parents; dare he do otherwise than preserve his self-respect? If he cannot respect himself, he injures them." As still another incentive to preserving the honour of the family there is the additional principle that human nature is good. Every Chinese schoolboy is taught the doctrine that "man commences life with a virtuous nature." Whether or not this Eastern dogma is true, it is ethically more valuable than the theological dogma of the West that man is conceived in sin and ever prone to evil. When the Chinese schoolboy is further taught that "man is born for uprightness," this is as much as to say that he himself is expected to be good, that it is assumed by society that he will do his best. As a pedagogical principle this seems far superior to the old Puritanic attitude that children were "little vipers," "limbs of Satan" from whom nothing but mischief and maliciousness was to be expected, unless, by some miracle of grace, they were converted from the evil of their ways. In the West this latter way of thinking can be traced from the days of St. Augustine's *City of God* to the days of the *New England Primer*, where the first letter of the alphabet taught that "In Adam's Fall, We sinnèd All."

Meanwhile, in the East the children of Confucian parents were taught not only that man begins life with a virtuous nature, but that "an accordance with this nature is called the path of duty." However, this does not mean an easy complacency, a placid conceit that whatever one does is right. As Confucius put it: "If on self-examination I find I am not upright, shall I not be in fear even of a poor man in his loose garments of haircloth? If on self-examination I find that I am upright, I will go forward against thousands and tens of thousands."

Self-examination further means self-reliance; a man is saved neither by miracles nor by other men, hence, says Confucius, "Let every man consider virtue as what devolves upon himself; he may not yield the performance even to his teacher." Yet the mere desire for self-development means nothing in itself. As was said by Confucius' disciple Tsze-Chang: "When a man holds fast virtue, but without seeking to enlarge it, and credits right principles, but without firm sincerity, what account can be made of his existence or non-existence?" There is need, then, for a motive power to bring self-development about, and this power is furnished by the will. Countless Confucian sayings bring this out: "If the will be set on virtue there will be no practice of wickedness. . . . When the will rests upon set purpose, based upon purified desire, nothing can withstand it. . . . The commander of the forces of a large state may be carried off, but the will of even a common man cannot be taken from him."

There is a spirit of Stoicism in all this and especially in a notable passage where Confucius praises another for preferring virtue over all else: "With a single bamboo dish of rice, a single gourd dish of drink, and living in a mean, narrow lane, while others could not have endured the distress, he did not allow his joy to be affected by it." By this praise Confucius did not mean to uphold the doctrine of the ascetic recluse who lives apart from the world. To him the social good included harmless pleasures: "To find enjoyment in the discriminating study of ceremonies and music; to find enjoyment in speaking of the goodness of others; to find enjoyment in having many worthy friends—these are advantageous. To find enjoyment in extravagant pleasures; to find enjoyment in idleness and sauntering; to find enjoyment in the pleasures of feasting—these are injurious." Still further these two contrasted attitudes are to be found in two contrasted characters: "They who are without virtue cannot abide long either in a condition of poverty and hardship or in a condition of enjoyment, but the way of the superior man is threefold—virtuous, he is free from anxiety; wise, he is free from perplexity; bold, he is free from fear."

## THE SUPERIOR MAN

We are now introduced to the heart of the Confucian ethics, the moral ideal as embodied in the character of the "superior man," or the "princely man." But lest these phrases imply either the prig or the snob, they are also to be translated the "higher type of man," the "nobler sort of man," or, even more simply, the "good man." Briefly, the Confucian ideal of character is a blend of the gentleman and the scholar, of the man of manners and the man of brains. This ideal should be started early in life. At home, says Confucius, a young man should show the qualities of a son; abroad, those of a younger brother. He should be circumspect but truthful. He should have charity in his heart for all men, but associate only with the virtuous. After thus regulating his conduct, his surplus energy should be devoted to literary culture.

This may appear an impossible ideal; but it is based on that spirit of optimism and expectancy at the bottom of the Confucian philosophy. All men are born good, declares Confucius, hence a youth is to be regarded with respect, for how do we know that his future will not be equal to our present? But while all men are born good, in the sense of possessing moral potentialities, this does not mean that they all know what morality is. Much as Shakespeare spoke of riches does Confucius speak of morals: "Some men are born with the knowledge of these moral qualities; some acquire it as the result of education; some acquire it as the result of hard experience. But when the knowledge is acquired it comes to one and the same thing. Some exercise these moral qualities naturally and easily; some because they find it advantageous to do so; some with effort and difficulty. But when the achievement is made it comes to one and the same thing." The moral qualities here spoken of are three—benevolence, wisdom, and courage. "The princely man had three great virtues," Confucius once said, "which I cannot claim for myself. He is truly benevolent, and is free from care; he is truly wise, and is free from delusions; he is truly brave, and is free from fear."—"Nay," replied Tzu Kung, "these virtues are our Master's own."

In spite of his disciple's polite disclaimer Confucius knew that no man possessed the three cardinal virtues in equal proportion. Hence he pointed out that in the two halves of China there were, broadly, two types of men. Thus when another disciple asked what constituted force of character, Confucius replied, "Do you mean force of character of the people of the Southern countries or force of character of the people of the Northern countries; or do you mean force of character in an absolute sense? To be patient and gentle, ready to teach, returning not evil for evil: that is the force of character of the people of the Southern countries. It is the ideal of the moral man. . . . To lie under arms and meet death without regret: that is the force of character of the people of the Northern countries. It is the ideal of the brave man."

Now combine these two types, Southern and Northern, and we approach the moral ideal. As Confucius continues: Force of character in an absolute sense is another thing. Wherefore the man with the true force of moral character is one who is easy and accommodating and yet without weakness or indiscrimination. How unflinchingly firm he is in his strength! He is independent without any bias. How unflinchingly firm he is in his strength! When there is moral social order in the country, if he enters public life he does not change from what he was when in retirement. When there is no moral social order in the country he holds on his way without changing even unto death. How unflinchingly firm he is in his strength!

Such is the absolute moral ideal; naturally only a few attain it;

for men can be divided into three classes: First there are those who seek perfection that they may leave a name to posterity; again there are good men who try to live in conformity with the moral law, but who when they have gone halfway, throw it up; lastly, there are truly moral men who unconsciously live in entire harmony with the universal moral order and who live unknown to the world and unnoticed of men without any concern. It is only men of holy, divine natures who are capable of this.

These are excellent generalizations, but they are less interesting than Confucius' thumb-nail character sketches. Here the first type that he attacks is the man who tries to take virtue by storm. This is brought out in a dialogue with a disciple: Tzu Chang asked: What must a man do in order to be considered distinguished?—The Master said: What do you mean by the term "distinguished"? —Tzu Chang replied: I mean one whose fame fills both his own private circle and the state at large.—The Master said: That is notoriety, not distinction. The man of true distinction is simple, honest, and a lover of justice and duty. He weighs men's words, and observes the expression of their faces. He is anxious to put himself below others. Such a one is truly distinguished in his private and his public life. As to the man who is merely much talked about, he puts on an appearance of charity and benevolence, but his actions belie it. He is self-satisfied and has no misgivings. Neather in private nor in public life does he achieve more than notoriety.

According to this dialogue, the first step in the way of virtue is modesty, and Confucius brings this out in two parables: In the practise of archery, he explains, we have something resembling the principle in a moral man's life. When the archer misses the centre of the target he turns round and seeks for the cause of his failure within himself. . . . Again, the true gentleman is never contentious. If a spirit of rivalry is anywhere unavoidable, it is at a shooting match. Yet even here he courteously salutes his opponents before taking up his position, and again when, having lost, he retires to drink the forfeit cup. So that even when competing he remains a true gentleman.

While modesty and freedom from contention are good, they are only a kind of negative good, as another question and answer show. When a disciple asked: "To refrain from self-glorification, to subdue feelings of resentment, to control selfish desire—may this be held to constitute perfect virtue?"—the Master replied: "These things may certainly be considered hard to achieve, but I am not so sure that they constitute perfect virtue." What Confucius had in mind

AN EARLY UTILITARIAN
"The moral codes of Confucius have guided one quarter
of the human race for more than three thousand years"

was that the above virtues might be excellent in themselves, but they brought no positive results. Hence, he adds a list of moral qualities which have practical consequences, because moral virtue simply consists in being able, anywhere and everywhere, to exercise five particular qualities. Asked what these were, he said: Self-respect, magnanimity, sincerity, earnestness, and benevolence. Show self-respect, and others will respect you; be magnanimous, and you will win all hearts; be sincere, and men will trust you; be earnest, and you will achieve great things; be benevolent, and you will be fit to impose your will on others.

Confucius was evidently no believer in the hollow doctrine that virtue is its own reward. He was a utilitarian and sought what the pragmatists of a later day called "moral cash values." To him it paid to exercise the virtues anywhere and everywhere, as when he declared: "In private life, show self-respect; in the management of affairs, be attentive and thorough; in your dealings with others, be honest and conscientious. Never abandon these principles, even among savages."

Here is a suggestion for a proper colonial policy, and at this point Confucius shows how the attainment of personal morality in the individual can be utilized in affairs of state. Rulers are not so much born as made, and capacity to rule is reached only gradually. Thus, he explains, when a man understands the nature and use of these moral qualities he will then understand how to put in order his personal conduct and character. When a man understands how to put in order his personal conduct and character he will understand how to govern men. When a man understands how to govern men he will then understand how to govern nations and empires.

This is going too fast. Such advice is fit for the true prince; in the meanwhile the ordinary man wants to know how to attain a decent moral character, and Confucius helps him out in a series of pithy contrasts such as these: The higher type of man is calm and serene; the inferior man is constantly agitated and worried. The nobler sort of man emphasizes the good qualities in others, and does not accentuate the bad; the inferior sort does the reverse. The nobler sort of man is dignified but not proud; the inferior man is proud but not dignified. The nobler sort of man is accommodating but not obsequious; the inferior sort is obsequious but not accommodating. Here Confucius is certainly a practical utilitarian, for, as he elsewhere remarks, the moral law is not something away from the actuality of life. So he offers a series of further antitheses which teach one what to avoid. Thus, when the solid outweighs the orna-

mental we have boorishness; when the ornamental outweighs the
solid we have superficial smartness. Only from a proper blending of
the two will the higher type of man emerge. . . . The man of high
station who has courage without righteousness is a menace to the
state; the common man who has courage without righteousness is
nothing more than a brigand.

Much of this has been compared to Aristotle's golden mean and
to the Greek maxim, "Nothing in excess." With Confucius this was
called the "just medium" and was summed up in the aphorism:
"To go beyond is as wrong as to fall short." The matter is also expressed in the answer to the disciple who asked: "If you, sir, had the
conduct of three legions, whom would you associate with yourself in
the command?"—"I would not," replied the Master, "choose a
man who would attack a tiger unarmed, cross a river without a
boat, or sacrifice his life without a moment's regret. Rather should
it be one who would not embark on an enterprise without anxiety,
and who was accustomed to lay his plans well before putting them
into execution."

Such was the principle of prudence, hard to attain, for while art
is long, life is short. Confucius consistently followed this principle,
for, as his disciples asserted of him, he had no foregone conclusions,
no arbitrary predeterminations, no obstinacy, and no egoism. So
while he held the cheerful view that man is born to righteousness in
the way of possibility of moral development, he said of himself: "I
am not one who was born in the possession of knowledge; I am one
who is fond of antiquity and earnest in seeking it there."

And yet in spite of his knowledge of the filial relations, Confucius
finally made this confession: "There are three things that I have not
been able to do. To serve my sovereign as I would expect a minister
under me to serve me: that I have not been able to do. To act toward my elder brother as I would expect my younger brother to
act toward me: that I have not been able to do. To be the first to
behave toward friends as I would expect them to behave toward me:
that I have not been able to do."

In a way, that which began with a note of cheer ends with a note
of gloom. But lest Confucius be considered a pessimist, because of
his extreme modesty, we should consider a prophetic vision attributed to him. He had been talking of the "Great Principle." When
this prevails, he went on, the whole world becomes a republic; they
elect men of talents, virtue, and ability; they talk about sincere
agreement, and cultivate universal peace. Thus men do not regard
as their parents only their own parents, nor treat as their children

only their own children. A competent provision is secured for the aged till their death, employment for the middle-aged, and the means of growing up for the young. The widowers, widows, orphans, childless men, and those who are disabled by disease are all sufficiently maintained. Each man has his rights, and each woman her individuality, safeguarded. They produce wealth, disliking that it should be thrown away upon the ground, but not wishing to keep it for their own gratification. Disliking idleness, they labour, but not alone with a view to their own advantage. In this way selfish schemings are repressed and find no way to arise. Robbers, filchers, and rebellious traitors do not exist. Hence the outer doors remain open, and are not shut.

# PART FOUR

## STOICS AND EPICUREANS

# I. STOICISM

"GREEK philosophy, like Greek art, is the offspring of Greek political independence. In the whirl of public life everyone is thrown on himself and his own resources. Thereby, and by the emulation begotten of unlimited competition for all the good things of life, the Greek had learned to make full use of his intellect. Consciousness of his dignity—which a Greek associated far more closely than we do with the privilege of citizenship—and independence of the necessity of struggling for daily food, had taught him independence of mind, and enabled him to devote himself to the pursuit of knowledge without any ulterior aim. With the decline of political independence the mental powers of the nation were broken past remedy. No longer borne up by a powerful *esprit de corps*, weaned from the habit of working for the common weal, the majority gave themselves up to the petty interests of private life and personal affairs. Even the better disposed were too much occupied in contending against the low tone and corruption of their times to be able to devote themselves in moments of relaxation to independent speculation. What could be expected in such an age as that which preceded the rise of the Stoic and Epicurean systems, but that philosophy would become practical itself, if indeed it were studied at all?

"An age like that did not require theoretical knowledge, but it did require moral bracing and strengthening. If these were not to be had from popular religion in its then state, was it matter for wonder that philosophy should be looked to to supply the deficiency, seeing that in all cultivated circles philosophy had already taken the place of religion? If we ask in what form, and in what form only, philosophy could supply the deficiency under the then circumstances, the answer is not far to seek. There was little room for creative effort, plenty for sustained endurance; little for activity without, plenty for activity within; little room for public life, plenty of room for private life. So utterly hopeless had the public state of Greece become that even the few who made it their business to provide a remedy could only gain for themselves the honour of martyrdom. As matters stood, the only course open for the best-intentioned was to withdraw entirely within themselves, to entrench themselves within the safe barriers of their inner life against outward misfortunes, and to make happiness dependent entirely on their own inward state.

"Stoic apathy, Epicurean self-contentment, and Sceptic imperturbability were the doctrines which suited the political helplessness of the age, and they were therefore the doctrines which met with the most general acceptance. There was yet another which suited it— viz., the sinking of national distinctions in the feeling of a common humanity, the severance of morals from politics which characterises the philosophy of the Alexandrian and Roman periods. The barriers which kept nations apart had been swept away, together with their national independence: East and West, Greeks and barbarians, were united in large empires, brought into communication and forced into comparison with one another in matters the most important. Philosophy declared that all men are of one blood and are equally privileged citizens of one empire, that morality rests on the relation of man to man, and is independent of nationality and position in the state; but in so doing it only explicitly stated a truth which was partly realized and partly implied in actual life."—ZELLER: *Stoics, Epicureans, and Sceptics.*

## THE SCHOOL OF DISCIPLINE

To Aristotle the highest happiness is found in the vision of truth, in the pursuit of wisdom as such. In this he connects himself both with his predecessors and his successors. The old Pythagorean brotherhood had a similar aim, so had the Platonic Academy, and now Aristotle's own school, the Peripatetic, under Theophrastus, sought to carry the quest forward. But the scene changes. With the overlordship of Macedonia and Rome, Greece lost its liberty. The Athenians were no longer free men who could vary their political activities with philosophic speculations. Hence the philosophic schools changed their character and became a mental refuge, just as did the colleges in the South after the Civil War when the soldier often became the scholar. The analogy is curiously close when we read that after the conquest of Alexander thoughtful and original men sought in scientific ethics an occupation for the loss of public life, and consolation for the misconstruction put upon their retirement by noisy patriots.[1]

Such a mental refuge was the Stoa, that public porch or colonnade of Athens which gave the school its name. Here another change

---

J. P. Mahaffy, *Greek Life and Thought,* p. 4.

took place. Serious men might turn to philosophy, but philosophy itself was turned to ethics rather than metaphysics, to practical happiness rather than to speculation as an end in itself. In many cases the results were remarkable. The Stoics were valued both privately and publicly. They were sometimes called in professionally to minister to those in sorrow; at other times to negotiate with foreign powers as when a trio of representative philosophers were sent to Rome to obtain better terms from the conqueror.

In general the Stoic was a creature of practical morality and came to be a familiar figure throughout the Roman Empire, known outwardly by his cloak and staff, inwardly by his insistency on the majesty of duty, the splendour of devotion, the dignity of self-denial. To understand what this ancient travelling thinker meant to the public, we may compare him to Emerson, who was welcome by the men and women of the far frontier who had a hard row to hoe and were braced by the Sage of Concord, preaching his doctrines of courage and self-reliance. The Stoics were the best known of the later Greek moralists; in fact, their influence was so strong as to justify the ancient paradox that captive Greece led Rome itself into captivity. In the terrible times of the civil wars and the nightmare reign of Nero the Stoics were especially effective. They consoled those who needed the consolation of philosophy, teaching that the accidents and misfortunes of life are nothing to him who has a serene belief in providence.

This is Stoicism in its simplicity. Its rise and development, however, were complicated. The school had its rivals. There were the Cynics, who took their name from their doglike manners, as when Diogenes growled from his tub that the only favour he wanted from the great Alexander was that the latter should keep out of his light. There were the Epicureans, who sought a state of undisturbedness, and were so opposed to the strenuous life that they held that happiness consisted in the avoidance of all excitements and disturbances. The garden of Epicurus, with its freedom from perturbations, was for many a place of perpetual vacation, far from the madding crowd, a place where it was bad form to discuss public questions, and where disagreeably earnest people were not wanted. This, at least, was the school as it was portrayed by its critics. But Epicurus himself was no sterile dilettante and his doctrine was not one of mere self-indulgence. Still, many an Epicurean looked forward to the "garden" as a means of escape from the cares and troubles of this world, just as a weary man of affairs dreams of ending his days on the Riviera.

But to return to the Stoic. Those who prefer the Epicurean land of the lotus-eater have portrayed him as a dismal Johnny, a mere kill-joy belonging to that species of social reformer and uplifter for whose suppression the easy-going citizen often longs. Such a portrayal is an exaggeration. The Stoic had much sense and moderation and was above all practical. Zeno, the founder, arrived in Athens as a stranger from Cyprus and, according to the story, first came into contact with Crates the Cynic. From the latter and his followers he learned the principle of self-sufficiency, but did not follow them in their churlish disregard for the social amenities. As the saying is, he accepted Diogenes without the tub. The Cynic was wont to withdraw into his shell, to avoid public affairs, and to disdain the current beliefs in patriotism and religion. But the Stoic, though meditative, did not identify the inner life with isolation; he advised his disciples to mix in affairs, to attain the larger patriotism of the citizen of the world, and to see that in all religions there was a common element, the providential care of the gods for men.

Cynicism was one thing, civilization another. Overwhelmed with the complexities of society, the Cynic took the easy rôle of over-simplification—disregard for dress, contempt for society, and a general attitude that whatever is is wrong. They called this the state of nature and actually taught that animals and savages were better off than man. According to the accounts, Diogenes in his personal habits was as shameless as a dog, while Antisthenes, the founder of the school, held that primitive man was a law unto himself.

There was little of this in the Stoics. They were not anti-social; they did not confuse a return to nature with a return to bestiality, nor did they follow the other extreme of Aristotle, who taught that man's highest aim is a life of leisure, spent in meditation, "thinking upon thought." The Stoic rôle was different; it was to be a man among men, whether in the common round, the daily task, or in the vexatious affairs of statecraft. Here, then, we find a wide range of representatives, from Epictetus, the slave, to Marcus Aurelius Antoninus, the emperor, the one standing for Stoicism in the cottage, the other for Stoicism on the throne.

The system was a livable system. In its second or Roman period it has come down to us not only in Epictetus's *Handbook*, and in Marcus Aurelius's *Meditations Addressed to Himself*, but in Cicero's work entitled *On Duties*, and Seneca's entitled *Of a Happy Life*. These works left their mark on the civilized world and many traces of them are to be found here and there. Thus Epictetus was recommended for the use of students by Thomas Jefferson and reprinted in his day in the original Greek at Philadelphia. The writings of

Marcus Aurelius and Seneca are still to be had in popular editions, while Tully's *Offices*, as Cicero's *De Officiis* was called, was often referred to by the Southern gentlemen of the old school.

This is part of the external history of the documents. The inner doctrines are the following: a belief in the goodness of the gods, in the moral government of the world, and in providence, and along with these a facing of the problem of evil and a final attitude of resignation and acquiescence in the course of events. The belief in the goodness of the gods was based on the conception of the world as a cosmos or orderly universe. Here the forerunners of Socrates were utilized by the earliest Stoics. They went as far back as Heraclitus, who taught that "this one order of things was created by none of the gods, nor yet by any of mankind, but it ever was, and is, and shall be, eternal fire—ignited by measure, and extinguished by measure." This order, in turn, is guaranteed by Logos, reason, which is everlasting although "men are unable to comprehend it before they have heard it or even after they have heard it for the first time." This primordial fire is divine and eternal, hence Zeno argues that man partakes of it, since human reason is a spark of the celestial flame. This doctrine, naturally, led to further inferences. The divine fire being the primitive substance from which all things derive, then those that possess it, especially man in his rational soul, are privileged by nature to hold communion with God. And so, concludes Marcus Aurelius, being united to Him in intercourse through reason, why may not a man then call himself a citizen of the world, why not a son of God?

The origins and inferences of Stoicism are consistent. But Zeno, the founder, drew from still other sources than Heraclitus. Socrates had discoursed at length on the wisdom and goodness of the gods toward the sons of men, while Plato, in his prose poem of creation, had put these words into the mouth of the imaginary philosopher Timæus: "We shall do well in believing on the testimony of wise men. God desired that all things should be good and nothing bad, so far as this was attainable." So, too, Aristotle, in opposing the anarchic atomists, believers in blind chance, had argued for an intelligent adaption of means to ends in the creation.

All this meant a purposive government of the world and such purposiveness was none other than providence. We Stoics, as you know, says Seneca, distinguish in nature cause and matter as conditions for all becoming. Matter is inert, indifferent to all determinations, and will remain in a state of rest unless it be moved. Cause or reason shapes matter and turns it at will in any direction, producing out of matter a variety of objects. In other words, that out of which all things are made must be distinct from that by which all things are made and this is what is meant by matter and cause. These are the positive points and are summed up in that single fragment of early Stoic doctrine that has come down to us unimpaired. This is the famous "Hymn to Zeus" by Cleänthes:

> O God most glorious, called by many a name,
> Nature's great King, through endless years the same;
> Omnipotence, who by thy just decree
> Controllest all, hail, Zeus, for unto thee
> Behoves thy creatures in all lands to call.
> We are thy children, we alone, of all
> On earth's broad ways that wander to and fro,
> Bearing thine image wheresoe'er we go.
> Wherefore with songs of praise thy power I will forth show.
> Lo! yonder heaven, that round the earth is wheeled,
> Follows thy guidance, still to thee doth yield
> Glad homage; thine unconquerable hand
> Such flaming minister, the levin-brand,
> Wieldeth, a sword two-edged, whose deathless might
> Pulsates through all that Nature brings to light;
> Vehicle of the universal Word, that flows
> Through all, and in the light celestial glows
> Of stars both great and small. O King of Kings
> Through ceaseless ages, God, whose purpose brings
> To birth whate'er on land or in the sea
> Is wrought, or in high heaven's immensity;
> Save what the sinner works infatuate.
> Nay, but thou knowest to make crooked straight:
> Chaos to thee is order: in thine eyes
> The unloved is lovely, who did'st harmonise
> Things evil with things good, that there should be
> One Word through all things everlastingly.
> One Word—whose voice alas! the wicked spurn;
> Insatiate for the good their spirits yearn:
> Yet seeing see not, neither hearing hear
> God's universal law, which those revere,
> By reason guided, happiness who win.
> The rest, unreasoning, diverse shapes of sin
> Self-prompted follow: for an idle name
> Vainly they wrestle in the lists of fame:
> Others inordinately Riches woo,
> Or dissolute, the joys of flesh pursue.
> Now here, now there they wander, fruitless still,
> For ever seeking good and finding ill.
> Zeus the all-bountiful, whom darkness shrouds,
> Whose lightning lightens in the thunder clouds;
> Thy children save from error's deadly sway:
> Turn thou the darkness from their souls away:

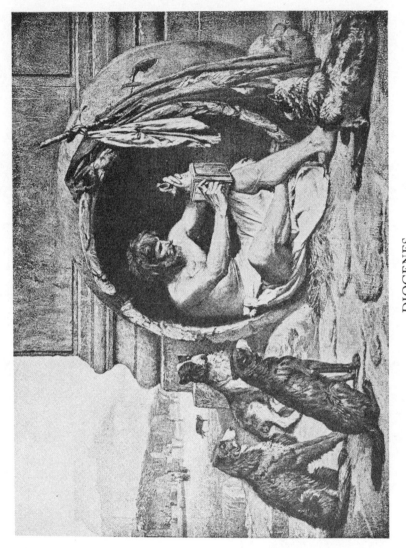

DIOGENES

In his tub—lighting his lantern to search out an honest man

Vouchsafe that unto knowledge they attain;
For thou by knowledge art made strong to reign
O'er all, and all things rulest righteously.
So by thee honoured, we will honour thee,
Praising thy works continually with songs,
As mortals should; nor higher meed belongs
E'en to the gods, than justly to adore
The universal law for evermore.

## THE GUIDE OF LIFE

"A brave man must expect to be taught, for he is to steer his course in the teeth of fortune, and to work against wind and weather. In the sufferings of torments, though there appear but one virtue, a man exercises many. That which is most eminent is patience (which is but a branch of fortitude); but there is prudence also in the choice of the action and in the bearing what we cannot avoid, and there is constancy in bearing it resolutely; and there is the same concurrence also of several virtues in other generous undertakings. When Leonidas was to carry his three hundred men into the straits of Thermopylæ, to put a stop to Xerxes's huge army—'Come, fellow-soldiers,' says he, 'eat your dinners here as if you were to sup in another world'; and they answered his resolution. How plain and imperious was that short speech of Calditius to his men upon a desperate action, and how glorious a mixture was there in it both of bravery and prudence! 'Soldiers,' says he, 'it is necessary for us to go, but it is not necessary for us to return.'"—*The Morals of Seneca*, Chapter XVI.

With their doctrines of the goodness of God and the moral government of the world and providence the Stoics sought a practical system. Their aim was to make men, and their motto, adopted by a later learned society, was: "Philosophy the Guide of Life." Already two rival schools had sought to solve the problem but this was in a negative way, by withdrawal from life. Thus Diogenes in disgust had rejected the very things which Greek civilization had gained, having little use for art, letters, and science. His was a kind of paradoxical bravery in trying to live like an animal without house or home, pleasures or possessions. Epicurus, in contrast, had lent himself to a certain cowardice; as the slave Epictetus later said: he disowned all manly offices, those of a father of a family, of a citizen, and of a friend.

Stoicism was opposed to both these attitudes. It sought not

only to guide the private life of the individual and the common life of the state, but to furnish consolation in times of trouble and distress. One great means toward this is for man to realize that he is part and parcel of the universe, that as such he partakes of its law and order. Here the Stoics compared life to a drama in which God has given each man his lines to learn, his part to play, whatever be the outcome. In this world he is not a mere puppet, a marionette pulled by the strings of an unseen fate. He is rather one who coöperates with the divine providence, for to him the world is rational and he, as portion of the world, partakes of its rationality. Zeno, the founder, called this living in conformity to nature. By this he meant not a return to the ways of the beasts but rather to "the ways of the stars." The thing sounds poetic; it was meant to be scientific. The age of Zeno was an age of new discoveries in astronomy, and of the formation of that system of regularly revolving orbs which led to the inference that order is heaven's first law. We men, then, as parts of the universal system, belong to a law-and-order league; as partakers of the divine fire we are of like nature with Zeus, the guide and governor of the universe. In this we are not blind instruments of a blind fate, but conscious agents coöperating with that "seeing force which runs things."

If there is order there is purpose, so reasoned the Stoics, and though this purpose may often be inscrutable to us, it nevertheless exists. As "God always geometrizes," though we may not know the final solution of the problem, so the divine playwright has a plot to be logically unfolded. The world's a stage in which we await our exits and our entrances. In these actions, of course, we may often miss our cues, but in whatever parts we have been cast we should do our best, just as those supernumeraries, the lower creatures, fulfil their proper functions. Nature is an unfolding process where the different orders have their destiny: the acorn grows into the oak, the foolish puppy into a faithful hound, the playing child into the earnest man. Nature then means orderly growth; the man with a natural capacity for virtue can fulfil his function in whatever state in his life it has pleased God to place him, whether as a slave or as an emperor.

This scheme is noble; at the same time there is in it a call to resignation. This is to be met by an appeal to reason and an appeal to duty. Thus Epictetus the slave says: "For this purpose God leads me hither and thither, shows me to men as poor, without authority, and sick, not because he does not care for me, but with a view of exercising me and of using me as a witness to others." So, too, Marcus Aurelius the emperor, speaking to himself of death, says:

"The day that you dread as though it were your last is the birthday of eternity." In this sublime utterance there is the implication that this life with its duties is a preparation for another life with even greater responsibilities. We start with certain disabilities such as leanings to ease and pleasure, but we are "God's athletes" and must undergo strict training, or, in even severer terms, we must be drastically cured of our moral ailings: "The philosopher's school, ye men, is a surgery; you ought not to go out of it pleased, but pained."

These are some of the more austere sayings of the Stoics called out by hard social or political conditions of a great slave or a great emperor. Such advices were utilized by a less commanding figure like Cicero, who as an eclectic found solace in Stoic doctrines. His *Tusculan Disputations* deal with the proper attitude in the face of sorrow, pain, and death. At one time he strives to comfort himself for the loss of his daughter, at another to brace himself at the threatened proscription of the Republican party. But in his treatise "On Duties" Cicero comes down to the level of ordinary affairs in which the Stoics were so effective. Such are the outward proprieties of speech and conversation, of domestic arrangements, of tact and behaviour, of honourable and dishonourable modes of life.

Another eclectic who utilized and applied the moral science of the Stoics was the historian Plutarch, who summarized the matter as follows: As exercise and medicine provide for the body's health and strength, so philosophy alone can cure the weakness or the sickness of the soul. By her help man learns to distinguish the noble from the base, the just from the unjust, the things worthy of our choice from those which we should shun; she teaches him how he ought to act in all the relations of his social life, warning him to fear the gods, honour his parents, respect old age, obey the laws, submit to governors, be loving to his friends, show self-control with womankind, tenderness with children, moderation with his slaves—above all, not to triumph overmuch in prosperous days, or to be cast down in adversity, not to be overmastered by pleasure, or brutalized by passion.

Stoicism was a livable system; it met the demands not only of the extremes in society, the slave or the emperor, but of the larger intermediate group of practical men of affairs. But this was the developed system after some of its difficulties had been smoothed down. These difficulties clustered about the baffling problem of evil. The founders of the school, in order to encourage themselves in times of trouble and adversity, had erected a great scheme of optimism.

Zeno began his lectures in the Stoa at Athens in the very year in which the city was besieged by the Macedonians and suffered from a consuming famine. In this there was an ironical contrast between the place where the philosopher taught and the conditions which he faced. While the Stoa was an artistic pantheon of war with its famous painting of the Greek victory at Marathon, the outlook for the city was anything but hopeful, for Athens itself now lay at the mercy of a military despot.

Furthermore, by this time the traditional religions of the Greek states had nearly collapsed. In the opinion of the wise, Homer had been "whipped out of the lists," and the old gods had gone. There was then a need to meet this double loss, political and religious. This need was met not only by the Stoic's confidence in his being a cosmopolite, a citizen of the world, but by his worship of nature. To him the cosmos, as an orderly universe, became the embodiment of reason, man being a part inherent in the greater whole. So to the Stoic, as a thoroughgoing pantheist, all were but parts of one stupendous whole, "whose body nature is and God the soul." This soul of the world may be variously called God, providence, destiny, fate, the seminal ether, and especially fire, the most subtle of all substances, which is diffused throughout matter as water through a sponge.

This is the first and greatest paradox. The Stoics were materialists, yet fervently religious; insistent on destiny and fate, yet ever appealing to man's free will, and all the time high optimists. To them the world, and all that therein is, is the product of divine power, is itself divine and therefore necessarily perfect. The Deity is active reason, manipulates matter and fashions all things to His end: "All that thou seest," says Lucan, "yea, all that moves, is God." This is the natural theology of the Stoics which was later accommodated to the popular mythology, since the universe, being God, the one supreme being, may be addressed as Zeus. Moreover, being divine in its totality, it is divine in its parts; hence the heavenly bodies may be worshipped as gods, also men of rare achievements are worshipful—heroes like Heracles and Odysseus; and, in the last stages of Stoicism, the very founders of the older school, Zeno, Cleanthes, and Chrysippus are worthy of worship. This deification of the Stoic sage, as the supremely wise man, approached perilously near to the later historic conceit—the worship of humanity. To a certain degree this was inevitable. To a man without a country, who had likewise lost his reverence for the gods of his people, there must be something to fill the void. So a system of morality embodied in the lives of men conspicuously good was a substitute for a lost land and a lost religion.

Under a despot like Demetrius, the spoiler of cities, or under a madman like Nero, it was proper to look on character as something fundamental, admirable, and worthy of worship. Man may become divine provided his ideal is divine. As Seneca puts the rule of life: So live among men, as if the eye of God were upon you; and so address yourself to God, as if men heard your prayer.

This is a high ideal, yet according to the Stoics it was not impossible of fulfilment. One significant line declares: "God is at home in the human body." This followed from a confidence in the will of God as revealed in the heart and conscience of those who seek to know that will. In other words, we are living in a cosmos, in a system of order, coherence, and reason, so in living according to nature we follow reason—and the end of reason is virtue. Man as a rational animal is therefore to carry on the work of the world. That which began as fire mist had implicit within it the divine reason. At the other end of the scale of being, in this later age of cosmic development, emerges man as a rational being, who must endeavour to steer a straight course. To rational man, then, philosophy becomes the art of living, just as navigation is the art of sailing.

## THE ART OF LIVING

"For my part I think the old man should be sitting here, not to devise how ye may have no mean thoughts, nor speak no mean nor ignoble things about yourselves, but to watch that there arise not among us youths of such a mind, that when they have perceived their kinship with the Gods, and how the flesh and its possessions are laid upon us like bonds, and how many necessities for the management of life are by them brought upon us, they may desire to fling these things away for abhorred and intolerable burthens, and depart unto their kin. And this is what your master and teacher—if, in sooth, ye had any such—should have to contend with in you—that ye should come to him and say, 'Epictetus, we can endure no longer being bound to this body, giving it food and drink, and resting it and cleansing it, and going about to court one man after another for its sake. Are not such things indifferent and nothing to us? And is not death no evil? Are we not in some way kinsmen of God, and did we not come from Him? Let us depart to whence we came; let us be delivered at last from these bonds wherewith we are bound and burthened! Here are robbers, and thieves, and law courts, and those that are called tyrants, which through the body and its possessions seem as if they had some power over us. Let us show them that they have no power over any man!' And to this it should be my part to say, 'My friends, wait upon God. When He Himself shall give the signal and release you from this service, then are ye released unto Him. But for the present, bear to dwell in this place, wherein He has set you. Short, indeed, is this time of your sojourn, and easy to bear for those that are so minded. For what tyrant or what thief is there any longer, or what court of law is terrible to one who thus makes nothing of the body and the possessions of it? Remain, then, and depart not without a reason.' Some such part as this should the teacher have to play toward the well-natured among his disciples."—*The Teachings of Epictetus*, Chapter IX.

The Stoics compared man to an apprentice who strives to imitate the master pilot, reason. But the waters of life are troubled and it is hard to steer a straight course. So like good navigators they sought guiding beacons and definite range lights. It was one thing to have a vague hope that all would come out well; it was another to know exactly what to seek and what to avoid. These, then, were their sailing directions: Follow the four cardinal virtues—prudence, manly courage, temperance, and justice; avoid the four primary passions—delight, desire, grief, and fear. Now while delight and desire have to do with good, and grief and fear with evil, yet it was the business of philosophy to avoid even things considered by many to be good. There were certain pleasures of eating and drinking which might seem harmless, but the Stoics' chief rivals, the Epicureans, in their search for pleasure had released a fatal formula when they spoke approvingly of the "sweetness of life." As the pursuit of pleasant things may lead to excess, it is better to stop our ears to them as did Odysseus to the Sirens. Much more did the Stoics steer clear of the opposites of delight and desire, namely grief and fear. These were denounced as furies which infest the life of fools; to give way to these emotions is the mark of a weakling; in grief there is selfish indulgence and in fear a sure sign that man has lost his presence of mind.

Curiously enough in these latter admonitions the Stoics had borrowed from their rivals. Epicurus himself had advised his followers not to give way to grief, not to torture themselves with unnecessary terrors; in short, to fear no evil either from gods or men. Here common conditions brought common advice; the refugee founder of Epicureanism, whose family was pursued by the Thracians, resembled the expatriate Stoics who advised undisturbedness even in physical torment. Thus Posidonius on his sick couch exclaimed: "You are making no impression, pain! Although you are hard to bear, I will never admit that you are an evil." Such advice came down the ages. It was this hard endurance that led the American colonists to call the silent Indian chief, tortured at the stake, a stoical savage. But the virtue of apathy, in turn, had its defects. It was what the poet called "virtue fix'd as in a front." At times it sounded downright cold-blooded. Apathy wiped out sympathy, as when the Stoic defined pity as "the vice of a petty spirit." The Roman senator Seneca, high in office, may have believed this, but the slave Epictetus corrected it. To him man was not to be emotionless like a statue. Those, too, were wrong who advised against marriage and the bringing up of children because of the anxiety such relations might entail. To such Epictetus declared that, while man should be a Stoic, a Stoic should be a man and should take up the duties of husband and citizen. This advice is directed against the extremists of the school, rigorous Stoics who laid themselves open to ridicule. With the latter apathy ranged from an indifference to pleasure to an indifference to country. For all this there were certain extenuating circumstances. The early Stoic was in close contact with the Cynic and like the later Thoreau, who glorified the life of single blessedness, eschewed the cares of family and preferred solitude to society. Moreover, the first founders of the school, Zeno, Cleanthes, and Chrysippus, being resident foreigners at Athens, could not be citizens and so made a virtue out of a necessity.

Hence arose the Stoic paradoxes—that the good things of life are matters of indifference; that the wise man is absolutely perfect, lord of himself and master of the world; that the sage is a citizen of the world; that local and national ties are not binding, and that even life itself may be thrown off when insult and injury make life intolerable.

The doctrine of things indifferent was a curious compromise. The Stoics declared that only that which is absolutely good, or virtue, can be considered a good; and only that which is absolutely bad, or vice, can be considered an evil. All other things, however great their influence may be on our state, belong to a class of things neither good nor evil, but indifferent. Neither health, nor riches, nor honour, not even life itself, is a good; and just as little are the opposite states—poverty, sickness, disgrace, and death—evils. Such are in themselves indifferent, materials which may be employed either for good or else for evil. Put in another way, some things are to be preferred, others to be avoided, while between the two lies the indeterminate class of things whose value lies in the use made of them. Theoretically the talk of things indifferent implies an attitude of scorn to both the goods and evils of this world, but when utility is brought in there arises a decided compromise with common sense. Consequently not only does a later Stoic like Seneca defend external possessions as aids to virtue, but even Chrysippus allows that it is silly not to desire health, wealth, and freedom from pain.

This admission has been called an anticipation of pragmatism, where the good is defined as the expedient. At any rate, it modifies the doctrine of apathy and runs counter to the second paradox, that the wise man is absolutely perfect. The ordinary Stoic, with his beggar's robe and cropped hair, drew ridicule upon himself when he claimed to be the perfect sage because he was indifferent to the comforts of life. But even the masters were hard put to it to find examples of the perfect sage. Heroes of the mythical Golden Age, like Heracles and Odysseus, hardly fitted the Stoic pattern, while even Socrates was acknowledged to be only a traveller toward virtue.

That the sage was a citizen of the world contained a large measure of truth since theory and practice were congruous. The Stoics were convinced of the solidarity of the race because of the solidarity of the universe. In this great city of the universe, says Epictetus, there is a governor and overseer who orders each and all to fulfil their tasks— the sun to run his course, Agamemnon to lead his army, and all good men to be trained and exercised by God. Now as in Greece all the tribes were called to the Olympian games, so in the greater game of life all contestants enter on an equality and there is no distinction between barbarian and Greek, bond and free.

At this point Epictetus solves these paradoxes in a half-disguised bit of autobiography: "How is it possible that one can live prosperously who hath nothing; a naked, homeless, hearthless, beggarly man, without servants, without a country? Lo, God hath sent you a man to show you in very deed that it is possible. Behold me, that I have neither country, nor house, nor possessions, nor servants; I sleep on the ground; nor is a wife mine, nor children, nor domicile, but only earth and heaven, and a single cloak. And what is lacking to me? do ever I grieve? do I fear? am I not free?"

The lame slave feels himself a citizen of the world, a partaker of universal privileges. His conviction is shared by the aristocratic Seneca, who asserts that birth is of no importance because all are sprung from the gods. So, he argues, the door of virtue is shut to no

ZENO: Founder of Stoicism
DUTY, DEVOTION, SELF-DENIAL

man: it is open to all, admits all, invites all—free men, freedmen, slaves, kings, and exiles. Its election is not of family or fortune; it is content with the bare man.

Such is the system of the Stoics, a doctrine of liberty and equality which is in marked contrast to the teachings of Plato and Aristotle. In the former the most virtuous man is at the top as governor; in the latter the highest virtue consists in solitary contemplation possible only for the man of means. But in this new morality the poor slave could call himself king provided he was ruler of himself. Others have no power over him. When the tyrant says: "I will show you that I am master," the Stoic can reply to him and his guards with their sharp swords: "You may bind the leg and take away the head, but you cannot bind, you cannot take away the will."

This is defiant democracy, based not on conceit but on reason. The Stoic calls himself a servant, but at the same time a sharer in the rule of Zeus. He is thus enabled to draw up this charter of liberty which Epictetus entitles: "How We Should Think as God's Offspring": If those things are true which are said by philosophers concerning the kinship of God and men, what else remains for men to do than after Socrates's way, who never, when men inquired of him what was his native country, replied Athens or Corinth, but the universe. For why wilt thou say thou art an Athenian, and not rather name thyself from that nook alone into which thy wretched body was cast at birth? Is it not plainly from the lordlier place, and that which contains not only that nook and all thy household, but also the whole land whence the race of thy ancestors has come down even to thee, that thou callest thyself Athenian or Corinthian? Whoso, therefore, hath watched the governance of the universe, and hath learned that the greatest and mightiest and amplest of all societies is that which is composed of mankind and of God; and that from Him have descended the seeds not only to my father alone, nor to my grandfather, but to all creatures that are conceived and born upon the earth (but especially to reasoning beings, since to these alone hath nature given it to have communion and intercourse with God, being linked with Him through Reason)—wherefore should such a one not name himself a citizen of the universe? wherefore not a son of God? wherefore shall he fear anything that may come to pass among men? And shall kinship with Cæsar, or with some other of those that are mighty at Rome, be enough to let us live in safety and undespised and fearing nothing at all; but to have God for our maker and father and guardian, shall this not avail to deliver us from griefs and fears?

## THE DIFFICULTIES OF THE DOCTRINE

"Some are of opinion that death gives a man courage to support pain, and that pain fortifies a man against death; but I say, rather, that a wise man depends upon himself against both, and that he does not either suffer with patience in hopes of death, or die willingly because he is weary of life, but he bears the one and waits for the other, and carries a divine mind through all the accidents of human life. He looks upon faith and honesty as the most sacred good of mankind, and neither to be forced by necessity nor corrupted by reward. Kill, burn, tear him in pieces, he will be true to his trust; and the more any man labours to make him discover a secret, the deeper he will hide it. Resolution is the inexpugnable defense of human weakness, and it is a wonderful providence that attends it. Horatius Cocles opposed his single body to the whole army, until the bridge was cut down behind him, and then leaped into the river, with his sword in his hand, and came off safe to his party. He is the happy man that is the master of himself, and triumphs over the fear of death, which has overcome the conquerors of the world."
—SENECA, "Of a Happy Life," edited by Walter Clode.

The Stoic is a sharer in the rule of Zeus, a citizen of the universe, but this universe in its lower mundane sphere is by no means one of undiluted happiness. That which stared the Stoic in the face was the misery engendered by military conquests. Even Aristotle with his doctrine of contemplative withdrawal was said to have shown a certain "failure of nerve" when he saw the fall of the independent Greek cities. With the spread of the Macedonian Empire matters grew worse, for the quarrels between Alexander's successors rendered all things insecure; exile, slavery, violent death were possibilities which every man must face. Against these possibilities the philosophers formed a mental security league. The different schools after Aristotle may have been rivals, just as the Greek city-states had been, but they had a common policy against the eventualities of evil. This policy was one of inward peace of mind—in the case of Epicurus through a liberation of man's will from nature's law, in that of Zeno in submission to that law, and in the case of the Eclectics by a utilizing first of one then of another of these doctrines as expediency should demand.

Of these three schools the Stoics were the most successful because the most tough-minded. They alone faced the hardest of practical moral problems, the problem of evil. So against the darts and arrows of outrageous fortune they put on the armour of apathy. Thus they declared that pain was not an evil, because not morally bad, and it was manly to endure it, while they sometimes went so far as to call diseases mere annoyances. However, they were not such foolish illusionists as to deny the existence of evil, as a mere error of mortal mind. Zeno never taught that pain was not painful, while Epictetus compared it to the hardships endured by the athlete: "Thou art about to enter thy name for the Olympic games, O man; no cold and paltry contest. Nor canst thou then be merely overcome and then depart; but first thou must be shamed in the sight of all the world; and not alone of the Athenians, or Lacedemonians, or Nicopolitans. And then if thou hast too rashly entered upon the contest thou must be thrashed, and before being thrashed must suffer thirst and scorching heat, and swallow much dust."

The heat and labour of the day make men tough; hardships are a help to manly virtue. In this way the Stoics sought to explain physical evil, that is, pain and suffering, as a stimulus to fortitude. This is the very spirit of sportsmanship instilled into the Boy Scout and college athlete. "Grin and bear it" is then a Stoic motto illustrated by many an anecdote. Thus Epictetus had his leg broken by his master and simply retorted: "Now you have done it"; while Seneca declared that amid all the extremities of fire and rack men have been found never to groan, never beg for mercy—men who never answered a question, and indeed laughed heartily.

Such instances concern human doings. What of nature's? We may be brave when men use us despitefully, but what shall be our attitude under the vicissitudes of fortune? To this Marcus Aurelius gives an answer: We talk of doctors' orders and say: Æsculapius has prescribed horse exercise, or cold baths, or walking barefoot. It is the same with nature's orders, when she prescribes disease, mutilation, amputation, or some other form of disablement. Just as doctors' orders mean such and such treatment, ordered as specific for such and such state of health, so every individual has circumstances ordered for him specifically in the way of destiny.

This is drifting into the doctrine of necessity. Much pain and suffering, ranging from that of the athlete to that of the ambitious man, come under the caption of "things in our power," and, as such, allow for the play of free will. But there are things not in our power and here free will seems abrogated. Not so, replies the Stoic; our attitude is under our control and if we accept calamities with resignation we are still free. The rational man can thus act because he can see good in apparent evil. If nature prescribes disease and disablement, continues Marcus Aurelius, let us accept such orders as we do the orders of our Æsculapius. They are rough oftentimes, yet we welcome them in hope of health. Try to think of the execution and consummation of nature's good pleasure as you do of bodily good health. Welcome all that comes, perverse though it may seem, for it leads you to the goal, the health of the world order, the welfare and well-being of Zeus. He would not bring this on the individual were it not for the good of the whole.

This is a familiar argument, but it has its flaws. Resignation to calamity is a form of apathy, but while apathy to oneself leads to a rational fortitude, apathy to the sufferings of others leads to emotional callousness. The Stoics are here driven into a corner from which they find it hard to escape; they return to the analogy of the athlete in a curious form. Thus Epictetus gives as an example Socrates before his judges. Socrates, he says, knew how to play ball: and what was the ball that was there thrown about among them? Life, chains, exile, a draught of poison, to be torn from a wife, to leave his children orphans. These were the things among them that they played withal; yet none the less did he play, and flung the ball with proper grace and measure. And so should we do also, having the carefulness of the most zealous players, and yet indifference, as if it were merely about a ball.

This is a poor example and does not present the human spirit of Socrates's apology. He was torn from wife and children, but while the sharp-tongued Xanthippe may not have missed him, his sons did. In other words, the Stoic was often too self-regarding. The general misery might offer him a stage to exhibit his indifference, but that did not obviate the misery of others. The cosmic good must have been cold comfort to orphans.

It was the fault of Stoicism that it made too little of pain. Yet over against this fault must be put the fact that when driven into a narrow pass the Stoic generally exhibited high courage against overwhelming odds. Epictetus's defiance of the tyrant included even the defiance of the great tyrant, Death. In this the Stoics carried to its last issue the double distinction between things to be preferred and avoided and things in our power and not in our power, and sought to solve the problem of man's end by a double paradox. That which most men considered the worst of evils they said should be preferred, and that which men said was not in our power they declared was in our power. By this they meant that arbitrary death at the hands of a tyrant and inevitable death by disease or accident should be scorned, while death by one's own hand should, under certain circumstances, be considered allowable.

In plain language, they justified suicide and called it "reasonable departure from life." The wise man, they said, may take his "free departure" because of a call to sacrifice himself for his country, or because of a tyrant's doing him violence, or because disease hinders the use of the body. But in spite of fair words and an appearance of rationality the Stoics were hard pressed to find cases which justified this dreadful doctrine. They cited the cases of Socrates who drank the hemlock voluntarily and of the younger Cato who fell on his own sword after the defeat at Pharsalia by Cæsar, when the ruin of the commonwealth stared him in the face.

In both these cases the self-immolated victims discoursed on immortality, and were considered models of nobility. But in other cases the Stoics descended to absurdity, as when they cited the case of Zeno, who hanged himself because he had broken his finger, and the case of the aged Cleanthes, who at the command of his physician abstained from food for two days, and then persisted in a course of starvation, saying that it was a pity to retrace his steps as he was now so far upon the road.

The last two cases may be apocryphal, concocted by the enemies of Stoicism. At any rate, they came from a later period of decadence, when suicide became an obsession. However, even in the reign of Nero, a time of violence, cruelty, and lust, Seneca condemned the doctrine of "free departure" as a social disease pointing to morbidity of soul rather than to healthy resolution. Seneca himself was forced to cut his veins because the waiting soldiers saw to it that the orders of the infamous emperor were carried out; but his own view in no way justified the subterfuge of "reasonable departure." He rather took the older Stoic position when he said: "Let every man make the best of life. How terrible is death to one man, which to another appears the greatest providence in nature, even toward all ages and conditions! It is the wish of some, the relief of many, and the end of all. It sets the slave at liberty, carries the banished man home, and places all mortals upon the same level: insomuch that life itself were punishment without it. When I see tyrants, tortures, violences, the prospect of death is a consolation to me, and the only remedy against the injuries of life."

The general attitude of Stoicism is one of courage. Here the models to be imitated are those of the warrior, the athlete, and the gladiator—life is a camp and living soldiers' work; life is a race and the messenger from Marathon will run till he drops dead; life is an arena where men face mortal combat with joy. This is the dominant note, and because of it many a young Stoic, when the new religion from the East came in, was converted to the manly gospel of St. Paul, who had fought the good fight, had run the race, and contended with beasts at Ephesus. In the great apostle they found a Stoic unconscious of his Stoicism, and in the Christian martyr who "met the lion's gory mane," the ideal of Stoic courage.

## THE SUPREME PROBLEMS

"For the consciences of the young revolted. Trained at home and in school to believe in providence, in duty, and in patient endurance of evil, they instinctively recognized the Socratic force and example not in the magistrate seated in his curule chair, nor in the rustic priest occupied in his obsolete ritual, but in the teacher on the cross and the martyr on the rack. In ever increasing numbers men, who had from their Stoic education imbibed the principles of the unity of the Deity and the freedom of the will, came over to the new society which professed the one without reservation, and displayed the other without flinching. With them they brought in large measure their philosophic habits of thought, and (in far more particulars than is generally recognized) the definite tenets which the Porch had always inculcated. Stoicism began a new history, which is not yet ended, within the Christian church; and we must now attempt to give some account of this after-growth of the philosophy."—E. VERNON ARNOLD, *Roman Stoicism*.

"Friends," said Epictetus, "wait for God; when he shall give you the signal then go to him." In this advice the Stoic raises the supreme problem of providence, or the moral guidance of the universe, in its relations to the alternative solutions of fate and of fortune. What does philosophy profit you, asks Seneca, if God is the ruler? What, if chance rules? What if all is fated? This last query was based on the solution first offered by the Stoics. Their physics, or philosophy of nature, began with determinism, according to which every event is but a link in an adamantine chain of cause and effect. They start with the apparently meaningless statement that "the universe is." But this is expanded into "Whatever is, is," and the inference drawn is that whatever is cannot be helped. Fate is here contrary to free will and leads to what is called the lazy argument. The classic example is that of sickness. One says to the sick person, "If it is your fate to recover then you will recover whether you call in the physician or not; and if it is your fate not to recover then you will not recover in either case. But it is your fate either to recover or not to recover; therefore it will be useless to call in the physician." This is pure fatalism and the confusion was worse confounded by the answer of Chrysippus that in case of sickness it may be determined by fate that you should both call in a physician and recover.

If, as the early Stoics declared, all these things are equally predestined and go together as links in a chain, the universe may be described as a cobweb of causation in which the movement of a single strand affects the entire web. But the talk of chains and cobwebs may be wrong for it makes the universe mechanical and impersonal. According to the majority of Stoics it was not that; it was dynamic and even personal, and as one all-embracing whole included all mental and spiritual characteristics. It started with the fire of Heraclitus, but that fire is at the same time reason, since the nimble flame is not only a symbol of the alert intelligence, but in its steady fixity is itself reason. Hence the primordial fire mist, permeating all things, is both mental and material, and the universe, after the analogy of man who is both mind and body, may be called person.

Such is the Stoic pantheism where nature is identified with God, who is defined as the fashioner of the ordered frame of the universe. This definition disposes of that second alternative offered by Seneca, the alternative of chance. Here the rival school of Epicurus was wont to say that nothing happens by design, but all by chance; that good fortune arises from a lucky throw of nature's dice and bad from an unlucky throw. All events are uncertain because all are due to a fortuitous concourse of atoms; everything occurs at random and nothing according to reason; there is no purpose or fixed end in the universe.

These conclusions are wrong, retorts the Stoic. Chance combinations of atoms explain nothing; there are rhyme and reason in the universe. Atomism would no more account for the designs of providence than alphabets thrown on the ground would account for the composition of the Iliad. Chance is thus disposed of, but another dilemma arises. Are events to be explained as due to blind fate or to seeing providence? The choice makes a great difference and some of the Stoics choose one alternative and others another. Fate, says Zeno, is a power which stirs matter by the same laws and in the same way; it may equally well be called "providence" or "nature." The essence of fate, says Chrysippus, is a spiritual force, duly ordering the universe; it is the Logos or reason of the universe; it is the law of events providentially ordered in the universe; finally, it is the

law by which things that have been, have been; that are, are; that
will be, will be.

Thus reason two of the early teachers of the school, but a third,
Cleänthes, midway in time between the two, takes a mediating
position. This compromiser is for a general providence and in his
famous hymn addresses Zeus as "ruler of nature, that governest
all things." But the facts of evil remain and Cleänthes cannot hold
providence responsible for it. Hence he makes his great exception:
"Nor is aught due upon the earth without thee, O God, save the
works that evil men do in their folly." To this Stoic leader there is a
general providence only in name, for fate is a wider force back of
providence, just as in Homer's day it was back of the ruler of Olympus. There was evidently a split in the school, but most of the Stoics
followed Chrysippus and believed in a universal, benign providence.
To them the universe is a thing of beauty. The heavens are "Time's
fair embroidery." Even the terrors of the universe are admirable;
storms and lightnings, deluges and earthquakes, call forth awe and
wonder. The universe is not only a thing of beauty but a universe
of utility. God hath builded thee a great palace, declares Seneca,
whose foundations are everlasting, the roof whereof shineth after
one sort by day and after another by night . . . and doth not God
bestow all benefits upon us? From whence have we so many trees,
bearing sundry sorts of savoury fruits; so many wholesome herbs for
the maintenance of our healths; such variety of meats answering
unto the seasons of the whole year?

All this verges toward a belief in a particular providence, yet
the Roman statesman warns us that man is apt to swell himself too
greatly, as if the world were made for him. As a matter of fact, he
points out, only a small part of the world is fit for man to dwell in,
while the seasons would roll around even if no man observed them.
But other Stoics were not so cautious and the argument sometimes
descends from the sublime to the ridiculous. Thus Chrysippus is
alleged to have reasoned that horses assist men in fighting, dogs in
hunting; lions and leopards provide a discipline in courage; the sow
is convenient for sacrifices to the gods, who have given her a soul
to serve as salt, and keep the flesh from rotting; the peacock is
created for his tail, and the peahen accompanies him for symmetry's
sake; the flea is useful to wake us out of sleep, and the mouse to prevent us from being careless in leaving cheese about.

These absurd arguments are attributed to one of the founders of
Stoicism, but it may be that such attributions were the work of jealous enemies. However, more dignified difficulties as to the benefi-

cence of nature remain. If all things work together for good, how explain the death of Socrates by poison, the burning alive of Pythagoras, the suicide of Zeno? If the gods care for all men, argues Cicero, it follows logically that they care for each single man. It is but a feeble answer to respond that the gods, who have great things in their charge, must sometimes overlook small matters, just as a good housekeeper is not to be blamed for the loss of some grains of wheat. But what of the wholesale destruction of men and cataclysms such as pestilence and famine, earthquake and conflagration? Here the Stoic at times had recourse to the feeble argument that evil is good in disguise, that pestilence and famine are needed to punish men for their misdeeds, and earthquakes and conflagrations to purify the world from wickedness.

There are echoes of this doctrine of cleansing conflagration in the words of St. Paul, who speaks of the last great day when men shall be purified as by fire, and when the elements shall be melted in a fervent heat. Now Paul the apostle had once been Saul of Tarsus, a city infiltrated with Stoicism. Furthermore, this special doctrine of the moral uses of conflagration has a longer history. It went back to Zeno's authority, Heraclitus, who declares that "fire shall one day come and judge all things." Moreover, to the Stoics God was not only the all-encircling sea of fire called ether, not only the creative rational substance from which the whole universe issues, but a cleansing force which leads to a new creation. In other words, the universe which began as fire shall end as fire. However, this implies construction as well as destruction; there shall be a new heaven and a new earth; the human soul is an emanation from Deity and the warm vital breath shows that it partakes of the supreme soul substance, fire, and is thus penetrated by divinity. Finally, this leads to the assurance that the wise man who has purged his body of the grosser elements shall survive.

Such is the moralized materialism of the Stoics which paradoxically leads to the blessed hope of immortality. And this doctrine of the restitution of all things had still further implications of happiness. As the universe moves in vast cycles, from fire back to fire, so this particular world shall circle back to better times. Though this present age is one of iron, of chain, of dungeon, and of sword, a happier age shall return, the golden age of youth and innocence. The Latin poet Vergil sang of this in his prophecy of the return of the hero when another Jason shall embark in quest of the Golden Fleece, a note reëchoed by the English poet Shelley in his superb lines: "A brighter Hellas rears its mountains from waves serener far."

The Stoic doctrine of the restitution of all things is bound up with the theory of recurrent cycles in which history repeats itself and what once was shall be again. Plato had once derided this doctrine when he put into the mouth of a certain Pythagorean this statement: "I with this little rod in my hands shall some day once again be addressing you, my class, sitting around me precisely as you sit now, and everything else in like manner will recur precisely as before."

This quaint notion was concocted by the Pythagoreans to uphold their doctrine of the transmigration of souls. A similar speculation is also in use among the Epicureans who with their infinite number of atoms, infinite time, and infinite space argue as did their poet Lucretius that the same combination of circumstances can recur again and again. But with these views the Stoics would have nothing to do; they came from rival schools as did the doctrine of the Aristotelians, who held that the existing order of things is fixed forever as it is. No, the doctrines of the great conflagration and of the eternal return go back to Heraclitus, the philosopher of fire and flux and of the guiding reason. The Stoic founder caught his spirit and his followers moralized it. Whatever, then, befall us, whatever the vicissitudes of fortune, we shall trust in providence, play our part, and quit ourselves like men.

## II. EPICUREANISM

". . . For Epicurus the purpose of retirement was primarily the desire to escape so far as possible the incursions of society, with no thought of fitting himself for citizenship in another world. To this end political life was to be utterly eschewed; for how, indeed, could the philosopher maintain his precious calm of soul, while suffering the anxieties of ambition or the envies of office? To the same end marriage and the cares of a family were to be avoided, though not so rigorously as political entanglements. In one respect Epicurus was better than his creed. It is notorious that his school made much of friendship, theoretically and practically; and their kindly comradeship, even their readiness to sacrifice ease and possessions for a friend, threw something like a glow of romance over their otherwise unlovely profession of egotism. No doubt Epicurus could find logical excuses for this human weakness in the mutual protection offered by such unions, but in fact some inextinguishable nobility of mind carried him here quite beyond the bounds of his boasted principles. His hedonism might leave a place open for friendship as the greatest felicity which wisdom procures for the whole of life, but he was surely forgetting the claims of the flesh when he added that it was of more account to know with whom we were to eat and drink than what we were to eat and drink. And his rejection of the Pythagorean community of goods (which had been so alluring to Plato), because it shows some lack of confidence in the generosity of friendship, is one of the finest and, in the French sense of the word, most *spirituel* of ancient maxims.

"Such was the social ideal of Epicurus, and his rules for private conduct were of a piece with it—they were directed as completely, considering the place of friendship in his social scheme even more completely, toward the attainment of that outer and inner security on which the continuous state of pleasure must depend. To this end morality of a sort is necessary: 'It is not possible to live pleasantly without living wisely and fairly and justly, nor to live wisely and fairly and justly without living pleasantly.'"—PAUL ELMER MORE, *Hellenistic Philosophies*.

## THE SCHOOL OF DELIVERANCE

In contrast to Stoicism with its doctrine of duty comes Epicureanism with its doctrine of pleasure. Both sought to discover the chief end of life; the Stoic drew up a scheme which in the main is plain and practical; the Epicurean is more subtle. To achieve a perfect equilibrium between pleasure and pain, so that a state of undisturbedness shall result, is more difficult than to count pleasure as but dust in the balance. To the Stoic the good things of life could be disregarded as of no account; to his rival the pleasurable quality was the thing to be considered. By a strange paradox the simple things might give the finest sensation—if hunger is the best sauce, bread and water is a feast.

The goal of both movements was the simple life, but the roads by which they sought their goal were different; the one being that of renunciation, the other that of calculation. The Stoic made it his rule "to do without," and let life go at that; his rival considered what he should do without and for what reason. His was a studied effort so to pick and choose that he might achieve the pleasantest sensation. The limit of pleasure, says Epicurus, is obtained by calculating the pleasures themselves and the contrary pains.

The Epicureans' method of calculation is in marked contrast to that of the Stoics. The latter sought to solve the problem of life by erasing pleasures; the former by pondering over their uses. If you reject absolutely any single sensation without stopping to discriminate, they explained, you will throw into confusion even the rest of your sensations by your groundless belief, so as to reject the truth altogether. Truth, then, lies in considering all factors, and the search for the right sensation resembles the construction of one of those magic squares where the final identical sums are obtained only after the most careful placing of the digits. There is a certain fascination in the Epicurean scheme because of its very subtlety. Whatever way you look at it the results are consistent. It works not only positively but negatively. If life is the summation of sensations, death is their subtraction. Hence arises the paradox of the privative, as when Epicurus boldly asserts: "Death is nothing to us; for the body, when it has been resolved into its elements, has no feeling, and that which has no feeling is nothing to us."

This is one of the "golden" maxims of the founder of the school of pleasure and offers a challenge to the founder of the school of duty, for where Zeno made death a call to courage, Epicurus made it a matter of no account. All this moral arithmetic sounds cold-blooded, but it serves to correct the popular conception that the Epicurean doctrine was one of fleshly indulgence. Calculation is mental, and as a criterion to pleasure served to show that mere animal pleasures are not to be desired. Consider the voluptuary. Epicurus does not censure him but only analyzes him: If the objects which are productive of pleasure to profligate persons really free them from fears of the mind—the fear of death, the fear of pain—we should not have any reason to censure such persons. But do the latter consider these consequences? No, says Epicurus, the flesh assumes the limits of pleasure to be infinite, and only infinite time would satisfy it. But the mind, grasping in thought what the end and limit of the flesh is, and banishing the terrors of futurity, procures a complete and perfect life and has no longer any need of infinite time. However, continues this mathematical moralist, let us not accuse the flesh as the cause of great evil, neither let us attribute our distresses to outward things. Let us rather seek the causes of this distress within our own souls, and let us cut off every vain craving and hope for things which are fleeting, and let us become only masters of ourselves.

The musings of Epicurus take the form of an inner dialogue between the mind and the flesh and exhibit a spirit of detachment which is the strength of his system. In fact, his cool and calculating attitude caused a certain feverish irritation in his rivals. The man who addresses his warring members as if they were litigants in a law-suit is a judge, and judges are formidable opponents. The jury may be moved by sentimental appeals; not so Epicurus. Thus he pro-pounds this case: Public speaking abounds in heart throbs and in anxiety whether you can carry conviction. Why, then, pursue an object like this, which is at the disposal of others?

With all his talk about feelings Epicurus is no vapid sentimental-ist. He is a calculating rationalist who scrutinizes the false beliefs of his fellow-men. One of his aims, therefore, is to free poor humanity of its delusions. Legend has it that as a boy he used to accompany his mother when she went about the small cottages, performing the purifications, and that he used to read the magic formula. However, when he grew up he strove to remove such vulgar superstitions. Men, he declared, "live in dread of what the legends tell us, fears, I mean, inspired by celestial and atmospheric phenomena, the fear of death, the fear of pain. . . . There would be no advantage in pro-viding security against our fellow-men so long as we were alarmed by occurrences over our heads or beneath the earth, or in general by whatever happens in the infinite void."

In these strictures Epicurus had an end in view which he achieved with such success that the poet Menander sings his fame as one who "freed his country from foolishness." But the legends he attacked were not so much the old discredited mythology as the new super-stitions filtering in from the East. The chief of these was astrology. The great Persian king had long since been defeated, but there now arose a Persian or Chaldean worship of the gods—"bright poten-tates, shining in the fire of heaven." Aristotle's successor, Theo-phrastus, was reported to have said that the most extraordinary thing of his age was the lore of the Chaldeans, who foretold not only events of public interest but even the lives and deaths of individuals.

These wise men of the East did not seem so wise to Epicurus. No stars in their courses ever fought for him, nor did comets and eclipses trouble his tranquillity. Besides the fears inspired by celestial and atmospheric phenomena he mentions the fear of death and the fear of pain. He asserts that these may be obviated. Death he has already said "is nothing to us," and pain, he adds, even if ex-treme, is present a very short time. For these reasons, he argues, men should drop their apprehensions; fears are foolish and a foolish life is restless and disagreeable; it is wholly engrossed with the future.

Properly interpreted, these are significant statements. Fears, in the original Greek, were phobias, and the cure of phobias suggests the modern psychiatrist or physician of the soul. In other words,

Epicurus was not so much the founder of a philosophy of pleasure as the founder of a school of mental hygiene. So the constant use of the phrase "the health of the soul" makes Epicurus an early advocate of mental medicine. The ancient conditions were of course in many ways different from the modern. Astrology and mythology are obsolete, but there remain countless worries over religious problems and over the hazards of life and over business and public affairs. All these psychic tensions are mentioned by Epicurus and also means for their relief. There is the baffling problem of religious pathology from the fear of dying to the fear of committing the unpardonable sin. Fragments of the teachings of Epicurus suggest his treatment of the anxious soul: "Learn betimes to die, or if you like it better, to pass over to the gods. . . . The knowledge of sin is the beginning of salvation." These religious anxieties, he continues, are based on certain fundamental phobias which must first be removed. Here the study of nature shows that the fear of death, the fear of the gods, the fear of divine retribution are all alike chimerical; they are false apprehensions based on ignorance. The utterances of the multitude about the gods are not true preconceptions but false assumptions. . . . Verily there are gods, but they are not such as the multitude believe.

This is negative advice and tends to remove fear; positive advice follows and fear is supplanted by hope and that in turn by a most modern device, "the will to believe." "Those things which without ceasing I have declared unto thee, those do and exercise thyself therein, holding them to be the elements of right life. First, believe that God is a being blessed and immortal, according to the notion of a God commonly held amongst men; and so believing, thou shalt not affirm of him aught that is contrary to immortality or that agrees not with blessedness, but shalt believe about him whatsoever may uphold both his blessedness and his immortality."

Suppressed complexes due to religion are thus treated by a thinker falsely charged with atheism. But there are more subtle problems remaining. These concern not the fear of death but the fear of life itself. Here Epicurus first excludes that class of men who argue in laboured fashion that life is not worth living and that all is vanity; these are the professional pessimists who extract a certain amount of pleasure from constructing their sombre systems. They are really tough-minded. But there is a larger class of ordinary people, the tender-minded, "the sick souls," who are afraid of living itself and suffer from constant anxieties and apprehensions over their daily tasks. They are afflicted in varying degrees with the inferiority complex; they are the social snails who draw into their shells, the timid souls who were born bashful and prefer solitude to society. Virtually Epicurus says to these: "Come into my garden, memorize my maxims, repeat them daily, and your worries will disappear." Actually he defines philosophy as "a daily business of speech and thought to secure a happy life." Thus he begins his letter to his disciple Menœceus: "Let no one be slow to seek wisdom when he is young nor weary in the search thereof when he is grown old. For no age is too early or too late for the health of the soul. And to say that the season for philosophy has not yet come, or that it is passed and gone, is like saying that the season for happiness is not yet or that it is now no more. Therefore, both old and young ought to seek wisdom, that so a man as age comes over him may be young in good things, because of the grace of what has been, and while he is young may likewise be old, because he has no fear of the things which are to come. So we must exercise ourselves in the things which bring happiness, since, if that be present, we have everything and, if that be absent, all our actions are directed toward attaining it."

This letter is extraordinarily modern in spirit and so is a later inscription which was but recently discovered. A certain Diogenes of Cappadocia, an Epicurean teacher in an obscure town of Asia Minor in the century of Marcus Aurelius, wished to leave the teachings of Epicurus in a permanent form and caused an inscription to be made. This runs in part as follows: "This writing shall speak for me as if I were present, striving to prove that nature's good, namely tranquillity of mind, is the same for one and all. . . . Since the vast majority of men suffer from the plague of false opinions the number of victims increases—for in mutual emulation they catch the contagion one from another like sheep—I wish to make use of this portico to exhibit in a public place the remedy which brings salvation. For thus I banish the vain terrors which hold us in subjection, eradicating some pains altogether and confining such as are due to nature within very moderate bounds and reducing them to the smallest dimensions."

The system of Epicurus which his enemies denounced as atheistic and immoral turns out to be an ancient combination of religion and mental medicine. Calumny represents the Master's garden in Athens as a place of luxury and gilded vice, but the inscription placed at the entrance of the garden does not bear this out. It runs as follows: "The hospitable keeper of this mansion, where you will find pleasure the highest good, will present you liberally with barley cakes and water fresh from the spring. The gardens will not provoke your appetite by artificial dainties, but satisfy it with natural supplies. Will you not be well entertained?"

What Epicurus really taught was the art of life for those who found life difficult, first by removing false notions gained in youth and then, if needs be, by withdrawing from society according to the maxim "Live concealed." The efficacy of the system lies in the first of these measures, but only in the second if it be taken figuratively. Few of his followers could live with the Master in his garden, yet all of his successors could erect a mental wall against the outside world. Here they had his own advice: Do everything as if Epicurus had his eye upon you. Retire into yourself chiefly at that time when you are compelled to be in a crowd.

## MENTAL HYGIENE

Epicurus has been criticized for advocating a flight from society. He assuredly makes too broad a generalization when he declares that man is not by nature adapted for living in civic communities and in civilization. However, there remains the not inconsiderable class of people who find life difficult. For these the simple life is the thing and it is for these that Epicurus added the maxim: "The wise man will be fond of living in the country." This is also a counsel of perfection, hence for the city dweller some substitute must be offered. This substitute is mental freedom and its corollaries. The whole matter is summed up in this remarkable saying: The most precious fruit of independence and plain living is freedom.

There are many implications in this advice. Plain living is obvious; the twin brother of the strong mind is the strong body; no cure of mental trouble, great or small, can be effected without a careful regimen. The need for health is obvious; that for independence is more subtle for it offers a real defense mechanism against the mental complex. Or as Epicurus puts it in a better way: Let us become wholly masters of ourselves by seeking the causes of distress within our souls.

To cultivate the feeling of independence is the first advice of this physician of souls. It is in very childhood, he explains, that we have gained those fears engendered by false notions of the universe. Old Homer was a fabricator of myths, but much worse is he who says that it were good not to be born, but when once one is born to pass with all haste through the gates of Hades. Who this false adviser, who this pessimist was Epicurus does not say, but he asks sarcastically: If he in truth believes this, why does he not depart from life?

EPICURUS
A Misunderstood Philosopher

This reference may be to the Cynics; more obvious are the references to the Stoics, who so often confused providence, chance, and fortune. To them the Epicurean makes this reply: Destiny, which some introduce as sovereign over all things, the wise man laughs to scorn, affirming that certain things happen of necessity, others by chance, others through our own agency. For he sees that necessity destroys responsibility and that chance or fortune is inconstant; whereas our own actions are free. This call to intellectual freedom is a dominant note in the teachings of Epicurus and he concludes his letter to Menœceus with these words: "Exercise thyself in these and kindred precepts day and night, both by thyself and with him who is like unto thee; then never, either in waking or in dream, wilt thou be disturbed but wilt live as a god amongst men."

It is surprising to see how closely the Epicurean rules for the health of the soul fit into the most recent schemes of mental hygiene. It is for this reason that we may interpret his call to mental independence as a defense mechanism against an inferiority complex. The Stoics implied as much, without the use of the modern scientific jargon, when they charged the "Garden Philosophers" with being weak and effeminate, unable to face the hazards of life. The charge is partly true. Epicurus advised his followers to live the hidden life, to avoid society and civic duties, "unless something extraordinary should occur." This timidity and aloofness may be explained by the poor health of the founder. As a boy, according to one account, he had to be lifted down from his chair and had so sensitive a skin that he could not bear any clothing heavier than a tunic. Another account states that he was in so pitiable a state of health that he could not for many years arise from his couch. Further and fully authentic details have come down to us in a final letter to his disciple Idomeneus: "On this last, yet blessed, day of my life, I write to you. Pains and tortures of body I have to the full, but there is set over against these the joy of my heart at the memory of our happy conversations in the past."

Adding to his invalidism the fact that Epicurus lived when very difficult times oppressed Greece, we have an explanation of his advice to his followers to live the hidden life and to avoid society and public affairs. This advice substantiates the charge of the Stoics that the Epicureans neglected civic duties, yet what the latter lacked in practical activity they made up in intellectual agility. The type is familiar. The Epicureans were social egotists, ancient representatives of that modern intelligentsia who exercise their brains in criticizing the structure of society. They may be afraid of much, but they are not afraid of expressing their opinions. They are not utter pessimists, for they take an unholy pleasure in hitting the heads of the conventional. They may be called pacifists who are afraid of the firing line, but they are certainly not afraid of the consequences of their criticism.

This is the modern type, familiar in the Great War. The ancient type was not unlike it. We have at least two records of Epicureans being banished by the authorities, and banishment in those days was no light thing. To say the least, the Epicureans, with all their words about not meddling with other people's affairs in order to avoid pain, did a good deal of meddling. They attacked the current conventions not only in religion but in politics, and criticism of the latter in classic days brought severer penalties than the former. There was as yet no Holy Roman Empire, but the state itself was counted holy. For criticizing it the entire body of philosophers— Epicureans, Stoics, and Eclectics—were at one time banished from Rome by the emperor Domitian. Here we may well expect that the Epicureans were the chief trouble makers, for when the Stoics advised participation in the activities of the state the Epicureans cast doubts upon the very foundations of the state itself.

Thus the Stoic charge of their opponents' timidity falls flat when applied to the intellectual sphere. Epicurus showed himself a radical in political science when he made these bold statements as to jurisprudence. There never was an absolute justice, runs one of the golden sentences, but only a convention made in mutual intercourse, in whatever region, from time to time, providing against the infliction or suffering of harm.

The conservative upholder of eternal justice would consider this a highly subversive sentiment, but more of the same kind is to follow: Natural justice is a contract of expediency. . . . Whatever in conventional law is attested to be expedient in the needs arising out of mutual intercourse, this law is by its nature just. . . . But where the conventional laws, when judged by their consequences, were seen not to correspond with the notion of justice, such laws were not really just.

Put in more recent language, this is radically pragmatic. The law as such is to be considered artificial, conventional, and expedient, "so long as we do not trouble ourselves about empty terms, but look broadly at the facts." For these statements Epicurus has been called practical, realistic, and modern, a radical whose views ran counter to the pagan notion of the omnipotent state. As such he was the anticipator in political science of Hobbes in his doctrine of natural law as mutual agreement, of Hume in his government based on the common consent of mankind, and of Rousseau in his social contract. Epicurus was bold in theory but not in practice. The Epicureans, declares Plutarch, shun politics as the ruin and confusion of true happiness. Now happiness is the sum of tranquillity, and tranquillity Epicurus pronounced to be "the alpha and omega of a perfect life." From this definition, then, there logically follows this advice of the master: When safety on the side of man has been tolerably secured, it is by quiet and by withdrawing from the multitude that the most complete tranquillity is to be found.

This is a fatal admission of surrender, yet it is characteristic of that type of verbal reformers who are not real reformers—armchair critics who while denouncing the law take advantage of the law whenever their rights of personal liberty and free speech are threatened. The Epicureans have been excused for not engaging in rough-and-tumble politics because such avoidance is the common practice of mankind in a period of despotism. It is true that the Greek provinces under Roman rule were no Elysian fields of freedom, but we know of no case where any Epicurean followed even this exceptional case mentioned by the Master: A wise man will not enter upon political life unless something extraordinary should occur.

With such advice we may speculate as to the number of followers of Epicurus. The system rightly understood was so subtle that it probably had but few genuine adherents. The Stoics could cite among their number those who, like Epictetus the slave, taught civic duty and others, like Seneca the statesman and Marcus Aurelius the emperor, who carried on in all the cares and perplexities of state. But Epicurus had no such following. The most famous exponent of his doctrine was the Roman Lucretius, who in his speculative poem, *On the Nature of Things*, gave an extraordinary picture of the rise of mankind from savagery to civilization and took as his dominant motive the freeing of the mind from superstitious fears. In portraying "man's life upon earth in base dismay," he exclaims, "So great are the evils wrought by religion." Besides a radical attack on conventional statecraft, the freeing of man from the religious complex appears to be a fundamental aim of Epicurus. The whole matter is summed up with incisive brevity in the portico inscription of the ancient Diogenes of Cappadocia: Nothing to fear in God: Nothing to feel in death: Good can be attained: Evil can be endured.

So much for the last of the pagan schools. In contrast to this doctrine of surrender we turn to the Christian philosopher St.

Augustine, whose great work, *On the City of God,* may be summarized in this fourfold opposite statement: Everything to hope in God: Everything to feel after death: Good cannot be attained in this life: Evil cannot be endured—except for the grace of God and the blessed hope of immortality.

# PART FIVE
## ECCLESIASTICAL MORALS

# I. ST. AUGUSTINE (354–430 A. D.)

"THE representative and promoter of this retrograde movement in the moral domain was the African bishop St. Augustine. His *City of God*, viewed from one side, is altogether like unto the old city of man. It is simply the ancient classical city in its early period of aristocratic pride and exclusiveness before it had felt the broadening influence of a thousand years of varied experience and growing culture. Only a few can acquire citizenship in the new city. Its privileges are only for 'the elect.' A great multitude, the non-elect, are left outside the city gates. Thus, in the words of Wedgwood, 'all the arrogance, all the exclusiveness, all the love of privilege, for which the city of man no longer afforded any escape, found a refuge in the *City of God*.

"The narrowing and hampering influence upon the moral development of the European peoples of this unethical system of Augustinian theology and metaphysics it would be difficult to exaggerate."—P. V. N. MYERS, *History as Past Ethics*.

Aurelius Augustinus, greatest of the Latin fathers, is best known for his extraordinary work the *City of God*. At the time when Rome was in conflict with the barbarians he led the literary attack on the "Great Babylon" of his day by prophesying that the end of this world was at hand, but that another world would recompense the faithful for their sufferings. This prophetic work is usually explained as due to political and economic causes, since it holds out the hope of better times coming after hard times, and offers a kind of promissory note that there will ultimately be a balance of happiness for those now bankrupt of happiness. Such messages of a speedy coming of the kingdom arise periodically during times of financial or political depression, as instanced in the prophets at the close of the Thirty Years' War in Germany and the Millennial movement accompanying the Panic of 1837 in America.

This is the usual explanation of the religious apocalypse, or unfolding of the future, but a more particular explanation is also needed. By a strange oversight the critics have failed to connect Augustine's *City of God* with his *Confessions*, and have thereby lost the light which his past life could throw on his future prophecies. In describing the saint they have forgotten the sinner and thus missed the clue to this piece of compensation literature, for such, in its last analysis, is the explanation of these bitter attacks on the wickedness of the world. Subconsciously aware of his lurid past, Augustine now makes this present "adulterous generation" the surrogate for himself, the scapegoat for his own sins.

A certain apologist for the African churchman declares that "while Augustine relates the sins of his youth with a plainness which the factitious modesty of an inwardly impure mind has sometimes condemned, it is always with the most genuine and unaffected sorrow and abhorrence." This sounds very fine, but it is only half the story. What we want to know is how this lurid past explains the latter lurid description of a Roman world threatened with "the wrath to come." The key is to be found in the parallel case of Jean-Jacques Rousseau, whose equally frank confession of sex transgressions was followed by an attack on the French society of his day which he condemned as utterly depraved and deserving a revolutionary upturning.

At this junction a curious situation arises. The Augustinian apologist, without knowing it, actually suggests the solution of the riddle. He goes on to say that the only work, in any language, that bears any comparison with this of the North African Father is that in which Rousseau pours out his life of evil concupiscence, but that while Augustine's confession is really such—an acknowledgment to God—Rousseau's merely followed that impulse of a burdened soul which necessitates self-utterance, that law of both mind and matter which absolutely forbids the perpetual suppression of struggling powers and forces.

This conventional critic has inadvertently hit the nail on the head but has neglected to drive it in. He has almost formulated the principle of the suppressed complex but he has failed to utilize it in the case of his own subject. Augustine did know that confession is good for the soul and that putting the past on paper made him feel better. The object of this book, he declares, is "to call to mind my past foulness and the carnal corruptions of my soul . . . thus soul-sick was I, and tormented, accusing myself much more severely than my wont, rolling and turning me in my chain till that were wholly broken."

Augustine here uses the exact phrases of the modern psychologist in describing the perturbations of the "sick soul," and like a latter specimen of morbidity, John Bunyan, employs the kindred language of Vanity Fair, "Behold with what companions I walked the streets of Babylon and wallowed in the mire thereof . . . the very toys of toys, the vanities of vanities, my ancient mistresses still held me." At this point the connection between the *Confessions* and the *City of God* becomes evident. The latter is distorted history in proportion as the former is distorted autobiography, and both are the products of an abnormal personality. What healthy-minded man could write as does Augustine that as a little boy he was a "great sinner" because he stole some pears; that the enjoyment of stage plays is "miserable madness"; that rhetoric is "damnable"; that the chair of rhetoric is a "chair of lies"; and that Rome is filled with people in love with a lying life.

Because John Bunyan called down the wrath of God on merry England, as Vanity Fair, he has been described as a half-mad enthusiast; why was there not an equal pathological strain in this other author of an older Pilgrim's Progress, who prophesied the judgment of damnation on pagan Rome and foretold the fate of unbaptized infants as that of crawling forever on the floors of hell?

If there is manifest distortion in Augustine's views of humanity it must be traced back to the immorality of his earlier career. A certain editor of the *Confessions* has declared that its tone of intensity is due to the fact that Augustine's tropical North African nature immersed itself in the sensuality of his clime and his race. This is description, not explanation. Augustine was born in North Africa and as bishop of Hippo died there, but his mental perturbations did not begin until certain matrimonial complications arose in Italy. While a student of rhetoric in Milan he had taken to himself a concubine. Meanwhile his mother had arranged a marriage for him upon which there arose a conflict between contentment and ambition, and Augustine, who had little of the Stoic in his nature, describes the crisis as follows: "Meanwhile my sins were multiplied, and my concubine being torn from my side as hindrance to my marriage, my heart, which clave unto her, was torn and wounded and bleeding. And she returned to Africa, vowing unto Thee never to know any other man, leaving with me my son by her. But unhappy I, who could not imitate a very woman, impatient because not till after two years was I to obtain my wife, and not being so much a lover of marriage as a slave to lust, procured another concubine. Nor was my wound cured, which had been made by the previous incision, but after inflammation and most acute pain, it mortified, and then my pains became less acute, but more desperate."

Augustine makes out that he was a sick soul; he was also a weak soul, for the *Confessions* are almost incredible in their naïveté. Having abandoned one mistress, only to take another, he excuses himself on the ground that celibacy is a painful course; "for" as he adds, "I thought I should be too miserable, unless folded in female arms." Then follows his famous prayer-with-a-proviso: "Lord, make me pure and chaste—but not quite yet." Rousseau at his frankest moment never went quite so far as this, but it must be admitted that Augustine did at last break away from the "defilements of the flesh." A pathological experience turned the scale; one day while "weeping in the most bitter contrition" he thought he heard a voice, the light of serenity was infused into his soul, and "all darkness of doubt vanished away."

Augustine's conversion follows one of the familiar types in the varieties of religious experience; hallucinations of sound and sight bring about a radical change in conduct and an attempt is made to rationalize this change. He can no longer enjoy worldly pleasures; he therefore vents his spleen on the world. His own terrible self-accusations are now turned upon his former associates, and while they are to be punished, he is to be saved. To use two titles of John Bunyan, they represent "Mr. Bad Man," he represents "Grace Abounding." Thus do the *Confessions* prepare the way for the *City of God* and a strange story of a single life furnish the plot for a stranger story of mankind.

## THE CITY OF GOD

Augustine's *City of God* was written at a crisis. In 410 A. D., three years before this dramatic work was started, Alaric the Goth had captured and sacked Rome. With the fall of the Eternal City men awoke from their fancied security to the realization that the empire itself was in danger. They had been sure that the power of Rome was keeping the outer ramparts safe; Ostrogoths and Visigoths, Huns and Allemanni, Vandals and Moors, had been pressing in vain against the borders, but now the very citadel had fallen.

A similar state of uncertainty had arisen in the religious world. Paganism and Christianity had been in conflict, with Christianity apparently in supremacy since the conversion of Constantine the Great. At this juncture the pagans turned on the Christians as responsible for the fall of Rome because of their neglect of the ancient protective gods, while the Christians in turn began so to lose faith in the efficacy of their system as to believe that the end of the world was at hand.

With these things in mind the Christian bishop begins his monumental work. His aim is twofold—to attack the pagans and encourage the Christians. He first seeks to prove that even if the old gods are neglected that makes no difference, because the Roman pantheon is but a collection of impotent images. He next seeks to cheer his fellow religionists with the assurance that the kingdom to which they belong is superior to any existing kingdom. It is not an earthly paradise but a spiritual realm in which the true believer is safe against all harm, a realm which contains in itself the promise of future glory when the church militant shall become the church triumphant, when the City of Men shall be superseded by the City of God. This is the promise; the plan is equally ambitious. The *City of God* has been called a monumental work. It merits the term, for it was a vast edifice constructed with materials from all quarters. As with the stones that Rome was built with, so here. The process of building is like that in the construction of a palace of the Cæsars. First the foundations are laid in massive blocks of ancient myths, crude beliefs borrowed from Persians and Jews. This part is primitive, but the superstructure partakes more of the classical patterns, the well-ordered city-state of Plato and Aristotle and the Stoics. Finally, overlaying all, like shining mosaic and marble, is the transcendant finish, the glittering promise held out to Christian believers: The house of the New Testament, says Augustine, is of another lustre, the workmanship being more glorious and the stones being more precious.

In constructing his ideal city Augustine had to use the materials at hand. There are, of course, traces of the aristocratic ideals of Plato and Aristotle where the wise men rule, but now the saints take the place of the sages. There are also traces of the cosmopolitan spirit of the Stoics, who welcomed disciples from all nationalities. But the chief pattern is that of the Jewish messianic kingdom, the notion of an oppressed people whose hopes lie in the future, the new Jerusalem—"a city which hath foundations, whose builder and maker is God."

There are then two cities, the City of Men and the City of God. Rome typifies the one, the church the other. It is granted that the earthly city has its excellencies—the Pax Romana, the Roman peace, guaranteed law and order—but this is bound to pass away with the growth of the City of God. The earthly city is but temporary; the saints are in it but not of it; they are pilgrims and strangers on this earth; they look forward to a better city of eternal peace and eternal felicity.

Such is the attitude of Augustine. It is also that of many of his predecessors, for to praise the Christian ideal was to criticize the pagan actuality—relentless Rome, its rulers and its gods. All this serves in part to explain the persecutions of the new religionists. Even to the good emperor Marcus Aurelius, Christianity was a disturbing novelty and the growing church threatened to become a state within the state. Hence arose the charges of atheism and anarchy brought against the Christians. Technically they were atheists in rejecting the old gods and refusing to worship the divinity of the emperor; technically also they were anarchists in refusing army service or the duties of public office. Justin Martyr had already argued against these charges by declaring that the popular gods were demons unworthy of worship. So had Origen in his controversy with the Platonist Celsus. Continuing this argument, Augustine now contends that the loss of the old gods was a gain, not a loss. Rome had fallen in spite of the gods and the emperor, for the Roman state religion guaranteed neither strength, virtue, nor the assurance of a happy future life.

However, Augustine does not utterly reject the state. He declares that there are grounds of concord as well as of discord between the two hierarchies: This celestial society, while it is here on earth, does not break, but observes the temporal laws in diverse nations, if they oppose not the adoration of the one and only God. So that you see the heavenly city observes and respects its temporal peace here on earth and the coherence of men's will in honest morality, as far as it may with a safe conscience; yea, and so far deserves it, making use of it for the attainment of the peace eternal.

This is a clever compromise, the defense of an astute utilitarian in a difficult situation. Nevertheless, proceeds Augustine, the members of the City of God must not forget that while they are in this world they are not of it. In spite of this sympathy, our city lives not in the present, but as it were in captivity. This is because there are really two hierarchies, the City of Men and the City of God, and this because there were two contrary courses taken from the human race from the beginning, for mankind is divided into two sorts—such as live according to man, and such as live according to God. These we mystically call "two cities" or societies, the one predestinated eternally to reign in God, the other condemned to perpetual torment with the devil.

It is at this point that Augustine propounds his fundamental doctrine of the dualism of mankind. Before his conversion to Christianity the African father had been a follower of Manicheism, a curious Third Century cult made up of elements from Zoroastrianism, Buddhism, Judaism, and Christianity. In this amalgam the first source is the most significant. The founder Mani, or Manes, an Arab born in Persia, based his system on the old Persian dualism of Zoroaster. This was really a primitive form of fire worship, for over against the power of fire or light was set the opposite power of darkness. Two gods, then, contended in the world—the god of good and the god of evil. Now the Jews, in the course of their long history, were affected by this doctrine of their neighbours, and we have the familiar Old Testament antithesis, deity and devil, Jehovah and Satan.

To this ancient scheme, which was in fact an old mystery religion of the Orient, Augustine attaches his philosophy of history which forms the very basis of his system of morality. In his famous thirteenth book he portrays the two contrary courses taken by the human race in the beginning. Adam, tempted by Satan in the form of a serpent, fell and through this first rebellion of the parents of mankind against God sin and death came into the world. This is the initial step. The next occurred in the death of Cain and Abel. Here Cain is the first begotten and he belongs to the City of Man; Abel was the later and he belongs to the City of God. So in the first propagation of mankind the course of the two cities is made manifest; the carnal citizen was born first, and the pilgrim on earth, or heavenly citizen, afterward, being by grace predestinated, and by grace elected; by grace a pilgrim upon earth, and by grace a citizen in heaven. For as for his birth, it was out of the same corrupted mass that was condemned from the beginning; but God like a potter out of the same lump made "one vessel to honour and another to reproach." Thus, concludes the author, we find this earthly city in two forms: the one presenting itself, and the other prefiguring the city celestial.

The dualism does not stop here. The contrary courses taken by the human race persist. Our nature, explains Augustine, corrupted by sin, produces citizens of earth; and grace, freeing us from the sin of nature, makes us citizens of heaven: the first are called the vessels of wrath; the last, of mercy. And this was signified in the two sons of Abraham: the one born of the bondwoman was called Ishmael, being the son of the flesh: the other, the freewoman's, Isaac, the son of promise. Both were Abraham's sons, but natural custom begot the first and gracious promise the latter. In the first was a demonstration of man's use, in the second was a commendation of God's goodness.

In constructing this scheme Augustine declares that these things are an allegory, a shadow and prophetical image of the holy city. In other words, he has infected his system with that allegorical method which had influenced even the system of the Stoics in their fanciful treatment of the classical mythology—Prometheus and his fire standing for wisdom, Heracles for strength, Circe for carnal temptation, and so on. So when the Latin father with his logical mind employs mental imagery he does not shrink from its moral implications. Summing up the origin of the two states—the holy city, the city celestial, the free city, and the carnal city, the city terrestrial, the city of bondage—he concludes as follows: Thus the two cities are described to be seated: the one in worldly possession, the other in heavenly hope, both coming out at the common gate of mortality, which was opened in Adam, out of whose condemned race, as out of a putrefied lump, God elected some vessels of mercy and some of wrath: giving due pains unto the one and undue grace unto the other, that the citizens of God upon earth may take this lesson from those vessels of wrath, never to rely on their own election but hope to call upon the name of the Lord: because the natural will which God made (but yet here the unchangeable made it not changeless) may both decline from him that is good, and from all good, to do evil, and that by freedom of will; and from evil also to do good, but that not without God's assistance.

Such is Augustine's system, based on a dualism which is at once one of the easiest and one of the most difficult forms of philosophizing. It is an obvious law of thought that when the mind thinks of one thing it is apt to think of another; such are the ancient tables of opposites: light and darkness, good and evil, deity and devil. But to carry out this way of thinking and apply it strictly to such a medley and confusion as the history of the human race is an impossible task. Recorded events, whether fabulous or real, hardly arrange themselves into parallel columns. Nevertheless, Augustine essayed this Herculean labour. He had treated of Adam and his two sons, the one a wanderer, the other a pilgrim; of Abraham and his two sons, the one a vessel of reproach, the other a vessel of honour. He now proceeds to interpret the history of Rome. As the strife of Cain and Abel, he explains, shows the opposition of the City of Men and the City of God, so the strife of Romulus and Remus shows a division of the earthly city in itself. In other words, the act of the first founder of the earthly city was paralleled by the builder of Rome: This earthly city's foundation was laid by a murderer of his own brother, whom he slew through envy, and who was an earthly pilgrim of the heavenly city. Whereupon it is no wonder if the founder of that city which was to become the world's chief, and the queen of the nations, followed this his first example or archetype in the same fashion. . . . Such was Rome's foundation, and such was Romulus's murder of his brother Remus, as their histories relate; only this difference there is, these brethren were both citizens of the earthly city and propagators of the glory of Rome, for whose institution they contended.

Augustine has now reached the point at which he can draw up his grand moral contrasts. From the beginning of time there has been a fundamental conflict between good and evil. Since the first rebellion against God two cities have been formed by two loves: the earthly by love of self, even to the contempt of God; the heavenly by the love of God, even to the contempt of self. This is a double contrast and great moral difficulties arise. Why should man have no love and only contempt for himself? Because of the first rebellion, for when Adam yielded to temptation he infected all his descendants, through ordinary generation, with the stain, the taint, of sin. In other words, to use the brief but effective language of *The New England Primer:* In Adam's Fall We sinnèd All. This, in fine, was the dark side of Augustine's system already implied in its references to Adam's corrupted nature and to Cain's being born of the same currupted mass that was condemned from the beginning.

## ORIGINAL SIN

Such is the doctrine of the fall of man and of the dogma of hereditary guilt, of the inherited vitiation of human nature—a debt, a mortgage which could never be paid off except by miraculous means. Logically, ancestral sin means total depravity, but at this point Augustine relents. There is a saving clause in this dread document; a small minority is to be saved and that minority is the body of Christians whom persecutions have purified as by fire. In the cruel days from the evil Nero to the good Marcus Aurelius, and on through the tenth persecution under Diocletian, a little band has stood steadfast, waiting for the coming of the kingdom and counting on the grace of God. Their faith shall save them; they alone of all have not depended on the numerous heathen gods but only on that sole sovereign of heaven, the one true God almighty to save.

Such is the promise held out by the father of the church. In the midst of a wicked world the Christians alone are offered the magic gift of grace. Relying upon this, they shall escape out of this "great

Babylon of the West," the imperial city. The onslaught of the barbarians is proof that the ancient gods are powerless to save, but the "horrible persecutions" endured by the faithful and the "ever-conquered tortures of the martyrs" prove that God is going on with his miracles.

Such is Augustine's philosophy of history which "yields great comfort to the devout soul." Therefore, he concludes, in these malignant days not only from Christ and his apostles' time, but even from holy Abel whom his wicked brother slew, so along unto the world's end does the church travel on her pilgrimage, now suffering worldly persecutions, and now receiving divine consolation. Yet the present is by no means perfect, as the word "malignant" implies. The church's increase is uncertain because of the commingling of the righteous and the wicked in this world. In these mischievous days many reprobates live among the elect. The gospel may be preached and gloriously confirmed by the blood of the preacher, but the devil seeing his temples empty set heretics on foot to subvert Christ, in a Christian mask, as if there were that allowance for them in the heavenly Jerusalem which there was for contrariety of philosophers in the devil's Babylon.

There is a double reference here: one is to the heretics whom Augustine had already fought—the "tender" Christians like the followers of Pelagius who had been unwilling to condemn the majority of mankind to eternal torment—the other is to the pagan philosophers whom Augustine now proceeds to demolish. Of the real Plato and Aristotle he knew but little; their complete works were not available to him; but of the later classical moralists he knew enough to be able to hold them up to derision. So he asks: Were not the Epicureans in great account at Athens, holding that God has naught to do with man? And were not the Stoics, their opponents, that held that gods be directors of all things, even as gracious as they? These are the queries of a hostile critic, not of one who seeks a constructive understanding. So by emphasizing the differences of the schools Augustine seeks a mutual cancellation of all pagan systems. In a series of rhetorical questions he attempts to prove that for a happy life secular wisdom is of no avail: Did not everyone defend his opinion in public, in the town gallery, in schools, in gardens, and likewise in all public places? One held one world, another a thousand; some hold that one created, some not created; some hold it eternal, some not eternal; some say it is ruled by the power of God, others by chance. Some say the souls are immortal, others mortal; some transfuse them into beasts, others deny it; some of those that make them

ST. AUGUSTINE

"Lord, make me pure and chaste—but not quite yet"

mortal say they die presently after the body; others say they live longer, yet not forever; some place the chiefest good in the body, some in the soul, some in both; some draw the external goods to the soul and the body; some say the senses go always true, some say but sometimes, some say never. These and millions more of dissensions do the philosophers bandy; and what people, state, kingdom, or city of all the diabolical society has ever brought them to the test, or rejected these and received the other, but has given nourishment to all confusion in their very bosoms, and upheld the rabble of curious janglers, not about lands, or cases in law, but upon main points of misery and bliss? Wherein if they spake true, they had as good leave to speak false, so fully and so fitly sorted their society to the name of Babylon, which (as we said) signifies "confusion." Nor cares their king, the devil, how much they jangle, it procures him the larger harvest of variable impiety.

These forensic flourishes certainly sound like special pleadings and point back to the time when Augustine, before his conversion, had prepared himself by classical studies for the office of teacher of rhetoric. He could not but know that these "janglers" with all their "inundations of arguments" had attained some truth. Nevertheless, he proceeds as follows: For what truth soever the philosophers attained and disputed of amidst their falsehood, as, namely, "That God framed the world, and governed it most excellently, of the honesty of virtue, the love of our country, the faith of friendship, just dealing," and all the things belonging to good manners: they knew not to what end the whole was to be referred.

This is but the beginning of the attack in which the Christian father makes use of the arguments of a pagan opponent of the schools. How sages have rambled about the end of life, says Augustine. As Varro has observed, there are two hundred and eighty-eight sects of the philosophers in their question of the perfection of goodness. To take the Augustinian summary: There are four things which everyone desires—either sensible pleasure, or "nature's first positives," as in the body health and strength, and in the mind sharpness of wit and soundness of judgment. Now these four may each be tripled: "I will show it in one and that will make it apparent in all the rest. Bodily pleasure being either set under virtue, above it, or equal with it, gives life to three different opinions. Now add but one difference, to wit, society of life, and the whole number is doubled. . . . Now bring in but your new Academics and these twenty-four sets become forty-eight, for every one of these positions may be either maintained Stoically to be certain, or Academically as uncertain. Again, each of these positions may be defended either in the habit of any other philosopher, or of a Cynic, and this of forty-eight makes the whole of ninety-six and thus the whole matter may be carried on to the grand total."

This is a dangerous method. Turn the tables and the critics of Augustine's own doctrines might show how churchmen also have wrangled about the end of life and how the various schools of the fathers have differed widely from one another. There was, for instance, Augustine's great rival, the British monk Pelagius, who argued in the Stoic fashion that man is able by his nature to accomplish good, as against the Augustinian doctrine of the total inability of corrupted human nature. There was Pelagius's follower, the Irishman Cœlestius, who held that the sin of Adam injured himself alone and not the whole human race. Besides these Pelagians came the later semi-Pelagians. There was the scholarly Jerome of Dalmatia, who ascribed to the human race a share in conversion. There was John Cassianus of Gaul, who held that the will always remains free in man, and it can either neglect or delight in the grace of God. There was the French monk Vincent, who rejected Augustine's essential doctrines of predestination and irresistible grace. There was finally Faustus, Bishop of Riez, who held that grace is not an inward transforming power but a divine promise and warning which inclines the weakened but free will to choose the right.

The method of elimination through differences is a dangerous one; the tables may be turned and the system of Augustine may be shown to have bred a multitude of sects differing in varying degrees from one another. But Augustine had a one-track mind. Unlike his greater successor Thomas Aquinas, who sought to reconcile the Augustinian scheme with the ancient schools, he would have none of the latter. Returning to the philosophers of the reprobate city, he proceeds to knock the props out one by one from beneath their speculative structures. As for the Stoics, suicide proves their failure for it contradicts their maxim of endurance: "Was it patience that made Cato kill himself?" As for the Epicureans, there can be no truce of tranquillity between flesh and spirit because of the inbred vices that are inherent in our own bosoms so that you cannot do what you would. As for those who make so much of friendship, from Plato to Cicero, proceeds Augustine, we do not reject social life, yet is there no bliss therein, whether in the family, the city, or the world at large. What man is he that can recount all the miseries incident unto the society of mortals? Hear what the comedian Terence says: "I married a wife. Oh, what misery wanted I then! I begat children, so there's one care more." So, then, if a man's own private house afford him no shelter from these incursions, what shall the city do, which, as it is larger, so is it fuller of brabbles, and suits, and quarrels and accusations, even if we grant the absence of seditions and civil contentions, which are too often present.

After the city follows the whole world, wherein the third kind of human society is resident, the first being in the house, and the second in the city. Now the world is as a flood of waters, the greater the more dangerous. How much hinders the brotherhood of mankind! The great Western Babylon endeavours to procure a fuller society, that is true, but how many lives has this cost! And suppose that done, the worst is not past: for although she never wanted stranger nations against whom to lead her forces, yet this large extension of her empire procured greater wars than those, named civil and confederate wars, and these were they that troubled the souls of mankind both in their heat, with desire to see them extinct, and in their pacification, with fear to see them renewed. "If I should stop to recite the massacres, and the extreme effects hereof, as I might (though I cannot do it as I should) the discourse would be infinite."

At this point Augustine has completed his philosophy of history from the fall of Adam to the fall of Rome. It is a dreary drama whose theme is the hopelessness of life upon this earth. And yet it is not a tragedy, for the last great act has not yet been completed. The world is full of evil, but evil, continues Augustine, does not disturb the order and beauty of the universe. As a painting with dark colours rightly distributed is beautiful, so also is the sum of things beautiful for him who has power to view all at one glance. The Christian has this power—his eagle eye can pierce beyond the grave. Our hope, then, looks for life eternal and the vision of peace, the beatitude of eternal rest, that true perfection wherein the saints are installed. And so, concludes Augustine, in a final outburst of faith: "In the City of God there shall be eternal felicity. How great shall that felicity be, where there shall be no evil thing, where no good thing shall lie hidden, there we shall have leisure to utter forth the praises of God which shall be all things in all. This, then, is the Sabbath of rest which fitly closes the world's ages."

With this peroration there is a call to a final evaluation of this remarkable document. Augustine's system may be explained as a dramatic device; the blacker he painted the present, the brighter would be the future. In this way the philosophy of the *City of God* became a philosophy of compensation; for all the ills that are suffered in this earthly life recompense will be offered in the heavenly life. In turn this final dualism may be explained by Augustine's earlier experiences. His mental patterns were set early in life. Long before he became Bishop of Hippo in Africa he had been a Manichean, and although he subsequently repudiated that sect, he evidently never got over its way of looking at the world. So, given the postulate of original sin and the doctrine of divine grace, out of these he constructed the system of moral dualism whose opposing elements were arranged as symmetrically as the stones in the opposite sides of an arch. But the theory of original sin led to a libel on humanity. Man is utterly corrupt, his morality specious. Hence the virtues of the pagan philosopher were but "splendid vices." An earlier generation of Christians which had been closer to the founder had caught more of his spirit of charity; they compared the martyrdom of Socrates to that of Jesus; they referred to Plato as a Christian unconscious of his Christianity, and as a schoolmaster to bring us to Christ. These were the views of the scholars of the Patristic age, like Clement and Origen. Augustine was of a different nature, relentless in condemnation because he followed a relentless postulate. Not only were the sages of Greece and Rome to be relegated to everlasting flames, but unbaptized were left "to crawl on the floors of Hell." An American historian has described this system, as revived by Calvin and adopted by the Puritans, as one which "blasted the morality of the universe and damned the character of God."

From another and opposite side this scheme has been lightly cast aside as an epic, as if it were so much harmless fiction, a mere poetic artifice regarding an ancient King of Heaven and his descendants.[1] It may be artificial but it is not harmless, from the moral point of view. It led to an arbitrary division of mankind into good and bad, into saved and lost, with only a species of magic to determine which was which. The criterion was not works but faith, not conduct but conformity. To believe in a creed became the touchstone of virtue, and those who did not happen to believe, or were unable to believe, were declared reprobate. The scheme was worse than the Roman device of decimating a mutinous legion where every tenth soldier had to step out for execution, for Augustine thought that the bulk of mankind was doomed to destruction.

No such wholesale condemnation as this was known among the pagan philosophers. They spoke of the wise man, the sage, the contemplative thinker as good, but they did not say that those who

---

[1]George Santayana, *The Life of Reason.*

did not agree with their systems were bad. They made them less good than the best, but nonconformity was no crime. Yet while Augustine was cruel, he was consistent. He made certain grudging admissions, but always with some proviso, as that the pagan philosophers saw, though obscurely, the eternal fatherland, but that they missed their way and were lost. The admissions of Augustine are always followed with retractions, for logic forces him to go back to his first postulate, the greatness of Adam's sin inflicting eternal punishment upon all that are out of the state of grace.

It is hardly necessary to contrast this iron, this rigid, this cruel system with the genuine teachings of Christ. To Jesus the Kingdom of Heaven was both present and future, for evil as well as good, for the publican, the harlot, the thief on the cross, as well as for the fisherman John, the beloved physician Luke, and others not yet of the fold. Such are the defects of Augustine's *City of God*, that drama of compensation in a time when men's souls were tried and when Rome, the world's conqueror, had fallen. It remained, then, for a later and a greater thinker to attempt a reconciliation of the three systems—that of the founder of Christianity, that of the classical moralist, and that of Augustine himself.

## II. ST. THOMAS AQUINAS (1227–1274)

IN CONTRAST to Augustine, greatest of the church fathers, Thomas Aquinas, greatest of Scholastics, was one of the most sane and strong-minded of men. In spite of his family's opposition to his becoming a monk he joined the Dominicans, who sent him to study at their school at Cologne, presided over by Albertus, called the Great because of his scholarship. Here Aquinas, because of his plodding silence, received the nickname of the Dumb Ox; at this his master is said to have prophesied that this ox would one day fill the world with his bellowing. This may be a legendary afterthought, still the fact remains that the fame of Aquinas did fill the mediæval world. As an ambitious systematizer his task was to do for the thought of his day what the Holy Roman Empire did for the body politic, and the Holy Catholic Church for the souls of men. Aquinas by birth was related to emperors, by intellect he made himself head of an empire of thought. His final aim was to embrace in one science all the knowledge of his time and of previous times. He attempted that in his *Summary of Theology*, for theology, according to the conception of the Middle Ages, was counted the science of sciences.

Aquinas was the Aristotle of his day and like the pagan philosopher took all knowledge to be his province. Because of his immense scholarship and his eminent goodness he was given various titles—Universal Doctor, Angelic Doctor, Prince of Scholastics, and finally Doctor of the Church. The last epithet is the most precise, because it was church doctrine embellished with ancient learning that was presented in his various works, especially the *Summary*. The latter is divided into two parts, the first discussing more than one hundred questions as to the nature, attributes, and relations of God, and the second speaking of man in all his relations, especially as regards the end or aim of life. It was from this part, which deals mainly with ethics, that Aquinas gains the title of Father of Moral Philosophy. In spite of the dry form in which it is put—questions and answers, objections and replies—the Aquinian moral system is profoundly interesting. It is a veritable road map for the journey of life, a true itinerary for the pilgrim in his progress toward heaven, for it is significant that from his first published work to his last Aquinas dealt mainly with the moral problems that trouble all classes and conditions of men. So because of his great learning and his practical good sense he became not only adviser of popes and teachers in the cloisters of his order, but guide, philosopher, and friend to many a troubled soul in the ordinary walks of life.

Historically considered, the system of Aquinas is a great system, but in it there was latent this weakness: it was a closed system. Its final admonitions were meant for Catholics, not for those outside the fold of St. Peter. Thus the very title of the treatise *Against the Gentiles* implies that the faithful alone are assured of salvation. Like the splendid heathen of classic times, the gentiles may possess the light of reason, but this is not sufficient. More important than the truths of human experience are the mysteries of faith given by revelation. Since, then, the church claimed to possess the keys to these mysteries all those without the pale were in a parlous state; their light was too feeble to guide them on the road of life, and at the last they were virtually the blind leading the blind. Therefore, being a hindrance and not a help in the propagation of the faith, they should be "compelled to come in," and, if compulsion failed, they should be cut off.

Such was the relentless conclusion drawn by the Angelic Doctor from a mere distinction between faith and reason, and it is an instance of the irony of history that the failure to draw this distinction on the part of another great Dominican, Giordano Bruno, cost the latter his life.

## MEDIÆVAL MORALS

Eight hundred and fifty years after Augustine had finished his *City of God* Thomas Aquinas, most famous of the schoolmen, began his *Summary of Theology*. The Thirteenth Century has been called the greatest of the centuries largely because of the building of the cathedrals. Those were structures of stone; Scholasticism was an equally imposing structure of thought rearing its towers of speculation toward the heavens. Like the Gothic architect with his pillars, buttresses, and vaulting, Aquinas had intricate logical problems of stress and strain to solve. But in order to reach his highest point, the last end of man in general, the vision of the divine essence, he had first to look to his foundations. For these he accepted the corner stone which other builders had rejected and that corner stone was the system of Aristotle. Moreover, to erect a Christian structure he had to have a ground plan. Here Augustine had already provided the rough draught with his doctrines of creation, original sin, and the division of mankind into elect and non-elect. The sketch was effective because of its very boldness, but it needed the finishing touches of a master to tone down its crudity. Too much was left out; pagan morality had been virtually omitted, with the result that, from the critical point of view, the whole effect was wrong. The great defect was the disregard of nature, as if physical bodies, made of matter, were the very embodiment of evil and represented a rival power over against the spiritual. This flaw was in a way excusable, since Augustine's fear of the tremendous force of fleshly sin was but a vestigial remain of his early theory of opposites.

Aquinas started from a different angle. In his conception of nature he followed Aristotle, whose works had been translated into Latin at his suggestion. To him nature was a vast hierarchy, a series of creative steps from the least perfect and the most shapeless to the most complete and finished creature—man, a social and religious "animal." This much was taken from the greatest of Greek systematizers, but in this otherwise orderly scheme Aquinas now made a division. Nature was separated into two great kingdoms, that of necessity and that of grace. The distinction was obviously borrowed from Augustine and might appear to justify the African father's propensity to put all things on the opposing side of a black line of division, as if the works of nature were unquestionably bad and the works of grace unquestionably good. But Aquinas ameliorates and softens such a harsh position. To him the world of humanity as well as the world of nature are the works not only of the power but of the goodness of God. It is by love that he created us and we must render him love for love. This nature does involuntarily by obedience to his law, and this we must do by obedience to his commandments. Yet this is not sheer optimism, for Thomas adds this qualification: There is in things more or less goodness, more or less truth. Hence a distinction must be made. By his general will God desires man to be saved; but by his particular will, he wishes the sinner to be punished. Here arises the conflict between the divine providence and human free will which may be put in the form of a dilemma: if God foresees our actions, we are not free; if, free, we act contrary to his provisions, then he is not all-powerful. This conflict and this dilemma Aquinas seeks to resolve as follows: There is not prevision, there is vision, because we are in time, whereas God is in eternity. He sees at one glance and instantaneously all the past, present, and future. Therefore, he does not foresee but sees, and this vision does not hinder human freedom any more than being seen acting prevents one from acting. Because God knows our deeds after they are done, no one can plead that that prevents our full liberty to do them; if he knew them before it is the same as knowing them after, because for him past, present, and future are all the same moment.

Aquinas is more subtle than Augustine; he is also more liberal. He does not cast aside the human virtues of the pagan philosophers —courage, wisdom, temperance, justice—for these lead to happiness upon earth. But to these he superadds the divine virtues— faith, hope, and charity—inspired in man by God and leading to eternal happiness. These are the more difficult virtues, especially charity, which would make us love our neighbours as ourselves, and even our enemies. So our own powers are not enough, our liberty and our will are not sufficient; it is therefore necessary for God to help us, and that help is due to divine grace.

This sounds less harsh and repellent than the statements of Augustine. Aquinas grants that the ancient philosophers accomplished much; that they discovered in man a power for good which urges us to virtue. Their work was preliminary; that of the church is final; revelation and dogma show the need of superadded power which will enable the weak will to go forward. In short, "infused grace" is necessary to practise the Christian or "theological" virtues.

Aquinas defends this position in his discussion of the cause of the virtues. The problem is this: Is virtue in us by nature? Some have laid it down that the virtues are totally from within, others that they are partially so, and still others that they are totally from without. Thus Plato held that the virtues preëxist in the soul and that discipline and exercise remove the obstacles as when iron is polished by filing. Next Aristotle held that the virtues are in us by nature in aptitude, but not in perfection. Thus one man has a natural aptitude for knowledge, another for fortitude, another for temperance. And in these ways the virtues, intellectual as well as moral, are in us by nature to the extent of a certain rudimentary aptitude, but not in their perfect completeness: the reason being that nature is limited to one fixed course of action, whereas the perfection of the said virtues does not lead to one fixed course of action, but is varied according to the diversity of matters wherein the virtues operate, and the diversity of circumstances. It appears, then, that virtues are in us by nature, in aptitude, and in a rudimentary phase, but not in their perfection—except the theological virtues, which are wholly from without.

By being "wholly from without" Aquinas means that a theological virtue is a sort of faculty of supernatural action infused by divine power. He is obliged to bring in this outside force by the demands of dogma which required complete salvation. He grants that Aristotle's habit of virtue is enough to keep a man from evil acts for the most part, and especially from those that are very much opposed to reason, as drunkenness in respect to temperance. But there are, nevertheless, some mortal sins that man can nowise avoid without grace; to wit, the sins that are directly contrary to the theological virtues which are in us by the gift of grace.

In this typical treatment of the virtues Scholasticism shows itself to be an amalgam of the classical and the ecclesiastical materials. There was the pagan tradition which appeals to the reason of Aquinas; there was the Christian canon which he accepts as the faith once delivered to the saints. So there was presented to Scholasticism the immense task of reconciling the two discrepant elements. This was effected by a kind of theological alchemy. If Aristotle was referred to as "the philosopher," his logic might be called the philosopher's stone which had power to transmute all speculative substances. The first experiments were not entirely successful. The earlier theologians who utilized Aristotle did not possess his doctrines in their purity; only defective translations of his works were available. So we find Albertus Magnus falling back on allegory. Thus he explains the dogma of the Trinity, of the three in one and the one in three, by comparing it to the Nile, which is still the Nile, whether it be stream, river, or ocean. But Aristotle and allegory did not mix. So Albert's pupil Aquinas succeeded better in comparing the compatibility of Trinity and Unity, of three persons in one Godhead, to the trinitarian structure of the human mind with its three aspects—appetitive, sensitive, and rational.

In other words, Aquinas was a past master in the ingenuity of his method and in his ability to throw an air of plausibility about the most difficult of subjects. His chief work, the *Summa Theologica*, is a mixture of subtlety and simplicity, of acute logic and common sense, and possesses the same ingenuous and disarming manner throughout, whether it is dealing with the doctrine of original sin or of the usefulness of sports, whether with the subject of divine omnipotence or matters of the toilet and modesty in dress. The work in its entirety is a veritable encyclopædia; it ranges from metaphysics to morality, from problems of the cosmos to problems of cosmetics, from a proof of how the world is created out of nothing to a piece of fatherly advice to women to adorn their persons in order to please their husbands.

These more trivial examples are taken from the "Ethics" or part two of the *Summa*. They show its author to be not only a scholar in the cloister but a man of the world, not only a professor of sacred theology at Paris, but a citizen familiar with the ways of fashion in that Athens of the Middle Ages.

With this wide range of subjects, sacred and profane, one can understand what a powerful weapon the *Summa* became. It helped more than any other single mediæval work to fulfil the aim of Scholasticism, namely to make the world serviceable to clerical interests. It served not only the professor in his chair, but the priest in his confessional and the pope on his throne. It enabled the theologian to answer objections to all dogmas; the confessor to give spiritual advice on an alphabet of perilous topics, from adultery to stratagems, and the holy father to bring subjects to a state of penitence and rulers to their knees.

What a work! It was not only a book of sacred knowledge, but a book of discipline; not only a book of etiquette, but a book of statecraft. Aquinas's "Ethics" has been called dry. Yes, but like dry food, when properly masticated it gave strength and sustenance. On it the Middle Ages built up its moral bones and flesh and for a full half millennium it served to nourish the body spiritual and even the body politic. From it may be drawn vindications of beliefs as far apart as the celestial vision and popular sovereignty, although many have found in it justifications for the tortures of heretics and the divine right of kings. The last perhaps explains its fearful potency in the hands of those who quoted the Angelic Doctor in the days of the Inquisition and the troublous times of shady pretenders to the throne. This is as it may be. But without the first set of vindications it is hard to explain how by the Thomistic arguments mystics were spurred on to the vision of God, and rulers prevented from disregarding the rights of the people. The *Summa* is a great historic document, and the second part, the "Ethics," is anything but of secondary importance. Properly used it kept as many people on the straight path as any pilgrim's itinerary planned by a single directing intelligence. Yet it was not a mere Pilgrim's Progress such as that imagined by the inspired tinker of Bedford jail. Aquinas was no John Bunyan; he partook too much of the nature of Mr. Worldly-Wise-Man and in the long run gave the better advice for that. Aquinas never referred to this world as a mere Vanity Fair; he evidently thought it an interesting place to live in, for he passed his days not only in Cologne and Paris but in Rome, Bologna, and Naples. Bunyan talks like a country bumpkin, Aquinas like a cosmopolitan. He was well acquainted with the polite society both of his day and of antiquity and approved of the ideals held by Athenian gentlemen, cardinal virtues which he found in no way incompatible with the Christian virtues.

All this makes the "Ethics" a book of ready reference on casuistry in the proper sense of the term. Once master its plan and one can turn to this or that section and settle cases of conscience. There are the four cardinal virtues determined by the golden mean, and the three theological virtues not so determined. Over against these are the seven capital sins from vainglory and gluttony to covetousness and envy, fitly called "capital" because out of them other vices spring and all leave a stain in the soul. But besides the capital or mortal sins there are the venial sins, a distinction which must have saved a deal of worry in those fearful of having committed the unpardonable sin.

Finally there are the monastic virtues—poverty, chastity, and obedience. The Angelic Doctor was no ascetic, yet he said that these virtues are not to be despised; they are of high value; they are advisable for the few, not for the many, for if all practised them there would be no public wealth, no population, and no progress, especially in political affairs. In short, in a vast range of ethical problems and in spite of the distinction between the natural and the theological virtues, between ordinary and "religious" men, Aquinas exhibits a sanity and common sense quite equal to his dialectical subtlety. In other words, he is the master-builder where the stresses and strains of life are so well thought out that his conclusions are perennially useful. Take the problems of sex. Here Aquinas is no prude in the sense of "a person with a nasty mind." With his Latin temperament he is frank and he is logical. First he goes beyond the easy acquiescence of the Greeks and condemns unnatural vices in unqualified terms. As for the "natural" vices, adultery and fornication, he does not blink their existence, but points out their fatal consequences—of the former because it breaks up marriage, of the latter because the offspring of such illicit union are generally deprived of a father's care. There is nothing of the "scarlet letter" about this as applied to ordinary citizens, outside of holy orders, but only an appeal to reason and to natural right. The moralist might here have based his strictures on the ground of the sanctity of marriage being one of the seven sacraments. Aquinas prefers to use logic and to point out results, especially as regards helpless children.

In this survey of the "Ethics" one topic has been left out, namely, that of law, whether eternal, natural, or human. This may be left till later since ethics, as Aristotle says, properly passes over into statecraft, and since this subject opens up the burning historical question of the uses and abuses of the Thomistic system on the part of a church which started as an integral part of the Roman Empire and finally sought to dominate men's minds not only in ethics but in politics. To return then to the first division of the "Ethics," with its hundreds and hundreds of questions and subquestions. The fundamental problem is the last end of man in general and the object in which man's happiness consists. Does it consist in riches, honour, fame and glory, power, good of the body, pleasure, or any created good? To all these queries a single answer is given and that is, No. The first four objects, which Aristotle calls "goods of fortune," may be helpful but are not absolutely necessary to happiness. Like the last three, they have the fatal defects of being but temporary and bound to pass away; at the best they furnish the means and not the end. Thus a captain does not intend as a last end the preservation of the ship intrusted to him, because the ship is referred to something else as its end, namely, navigation. So we come to the final problem which sums up the rest: Does man's happiness consist in any created good? By no means, since nothing can set the will of man at rest but universal good, which is not found in anything created, but in God alone. Hence God alone can fill the heart of man.

This reminds us of Augustine's poignant passage in his *Confessions:* "Our hearts are restless till they rest in Thee." And just as

Augustine inferred from this that man's final goal is the beatific vision, so does Aquinas. He continues on the same quest and asks: Does man's happiness consist in the vision of the Divine Essence? Yes, he responds, the last and perfect happiness of man cannot be otherwise than in the vision of the Divine Essence. In evidence of this statement two points are to be considered: first, that man is not perfectly happy so long as there remains anything for him to desire and seek; secondly, that the perfection of every power is determined by the nature of its object. Now the object of the intellect is the essence of a thing: hence the intellect attains to perfection so far as it knows the essence of what is before it. And therefore, when a man knows an effect, and knows that it has a cause, there is in him an outstanding natural desire to know the essence of the cause. If, therefore, a human intellect knows the essence of a created effect without knowing aught of God beyond the fact of his existence, the perfection of that intellect does not yet adequately reach the First Cause, but the intellect has an outstanding natural desire to search into the said Cause: hence it is not yet perfectly happy. For perfect happiness, therefore, it is necessary that the intellect shall reach as far as the very essence of the First Cause.

This conclusion may seem dogmatic and arbitrary, for it answers in the affirmative the questions as to happiness. This is defined as uncreated, an activity of pure intellect and not of sense, an activity of understanding and not of will, an activity of the speculative and not of the practical understanding. But lest this seem a question-begging procedure, which suggests the answer in the query itself, Thomas goes over the ground again and makes certain qualifications. In happiness, though it deals with the uncreated, namely, the Divine Essence, there is something of sense, namely, delight; something of will, namely, rectitude; and going back to the first set of "natural goods," even perfection of the body is requisite for happiness. Here Aquinas differs with some previous authorities, especially with Augustine, who quotes some words of Porphyry to this effect: That in order that the soul may be happy everything corporeal must be avoided. To Thomas this is unreasonable, for as it is natural to the soul to be united to a body it cannot be that the perfection of the soul excludes this, its natural perfection. Here Aquinas follows out his comparison of the Christian to a sea captain who cannot fulfil his purpose, which is navigation, in a leaky boat.

In these conclusions the scholastic is opposing the ascetic with his extreme claim that those who crucify the flesh gain salvation thereby. Indeed, he has no liking for "saints" such as Simon Stylites, the Christian Diogenes who sought sanctity in the neglect of the body. Although a member of the Dominican order, Aquinas is no cloistered monk who would buffet the body. In other words, bodily good, though not the object of happiness, may yet be some ornament or complement of happiness.

## ORTHODOXY AND INTOLERANCE

Aquinas furnishes a fine example of the weighing and balancing of arguments in his discussion as to the last end of man in general. But that end is complicated by the problem of free will. Is there anything voluntary in human acts? Yes, he answers, provided the beginning of the acts is from within. Yet, he adds, it is not against the essence of a voluntary act for that internal beginning to be caused or started by some external principle. This qualification seems harmless, because it may refer to motives, external aims such as philanthropy or altruism which move the will. Such is the conclusion reached by a Puritan divine of America when he spoke of the will being moved by "the last dictate of the understanding." But such is not the full meaning of the mediæval moralist. The voluntary act may be from within, but the motive power is from without and this power is superhuman. The reason for this is that God is more powerful than the human will, even that of a ruler, or as the text has it: "The heart of the king is in the hand of the Lord; whithersoever he will he shall turn it." This means that the human will, in order to be a good will, is bound to be conformable to the divine will. Of course the will, as an intention, may be perfect and complete, but it stops short of action for want of power to act.

Does this grant ultimate moral freedom to man? By no means. Aquinas returns to the old Augustinian doctrine of moral inability and tries to defend the doctrine of the theologian by an appeal to "the philosopher." According to Aristotle, the original stuff out of which the world was made was set in motion by the prime mover, God. Now God, adds Thomas, is not only governor and ruler of the whole universe but of the whole community of the universe and especially of rational creatures. Hence all that man is and can be and has must be referred to God.

Morality is here resolved into metaphysics, and because of the character of the metaphysics borrowed from Augustine the nominal freedom of man is resolved into a far-reaching fatalism, since the scheme accounts for the state of the evil as well as of the good. Here Aquinas is in a terrible quandary from which he escapes by a mere verbal solution. There may be salvation for those bound in the straight and narrow road toward the beatific vision, but how about those on the broad road to destruction? This is the great scholastic solution: God does not will the damnation of anyone under the precise view of damnation, nor the death of anyone inasmuch as it is death, because he "wisheth all men to be saved"; but he wishes those things under the aspect of justice. Hence it is enough with regard to such cases that a man wishes the justice of God and the order of nature to be upheld.

Now what is this "aspect of justice?" What is the criterion whereby God wills some to salvation and some to destruction? To this Augustine gives but a lame answer: "It is a customary saying that a man's will is conformable to the divine will in this, that he wills what God wishes him to will." But this raises a further question: What does God wish men to will? Thomas again replies: Whoever wills anything under any aspect of goodness has a will conformable to the divine will in point of the thing willed. But we do not know what God wills in particular.

In its final issue Augustine's "Ethics" ends in a note of agnosticism. As a later partial follower, the Jewish moralist Spinoza, put it: "Our refuge is the sanctuary of Nescience." This conclusion has led many to interpret the system of Aquinas as a system of despair, as if pessimism, to use a mediæval figure of speech, were a "daughter" of agnosticism. But such a conclusion is unwarranted. A thinker's temperament and a thinker's times determine the tone of a philosophy. The *City of God* of Augustine is much blacker than the *Summa* of Aquinas. The former lived in a period of lost power and of hope; the latter in an age of fresh power and high aspiration, the age of the cathedral builders, whose structures were the embodiment of strength and beauty, two qualities that ever evince the energies of men.

Hence we find Aquinas going around the discouraged disciple of dualism and going back to the Greeks with their manly virtues derived from the age of the pioneers. For these qualities Aquinas with his robust temperament had a decided liking. His nickname as a young scholar in Paris was the Ox, and there always remained in him a kind of placid strength which carried him on through all difficulties.

And there was another Hellenic influence. Aristotle, who had once been anathema to the church, now became to Aquinas the paramount philosopher. Moreover, Aristotle's prime motive of philosophy, curiosity, became that of his followers. Curiosity asks questions

and the Thomistic ethics is a game not of twenty questions but of
twenty hundred. Take but one of these, and that perfectly Aristotelian: As regards the science of morals are speculative habits of intellect virtuous? Yes, answers Aquinas. Man has the ability to con-
template a truth in the matters on which his science turns. But his
using the science that he has comes of the motion of his will, and
therefore a virtue which perfects the will, as charity or justice, also
causes one to make good use of speculative habits.

This is a pregnant passage. It shows Aquinas not as a champion
of dogma but as an advocate of the rule of reason. In putting charity
and justice on a par Aquinas really breaks down the conventional
distinction between the secular and the sacred virtues, the latter
being those which orthodoxy had already claimed to be due solely to
infused grace.

Take another natural or pagan virtue, prudence. This Thomas
defines as a right method of conduct, apt to give advice on points
that appertain to the whole life of man and to the last end of human
life. Now as the last end of human life was at the very start defined,
as a quest of the Divine Essence, prudence or wisdom would logically
become a means of attaining that end. Thus vanishes a fundamental
distinction between the virtues human and divine, secular and
sacred, cardinal and theological.

Aquinas's habit of asking questions in the true Aristotelian fashion
leads to a softening of his system. In contrast to what has been called
the "literary hysteria" of Augustine, he exhibits a temper of sanity
well in accord with the ancient golden mean. Man is not as black as
his predecessor had painted him. Thomas insists that there is a
fundamental inclination toward good abiding in the depths of
human conscience which can be darkened but not extinguished.
In the worst men human nature remains good and retains the in-
delible imprint of the eternal law.

This is one side of the picture; the other is not so favourable.
Aquinas's followers picked out the darker aspects of his thought.
His doctrine of human nature was tied up with the doctrine of last
things. Man may be inclined toward good, but lest he fall into sin in
this life, the terrors of the future life must be held over him. So we
find his successors in their distrust of human nature putting their
trust in threats. Most of them found it easier to be severe than to
be moderate, easier to be moral policemen with a club than philosophers with an appeal to conscience.

Aquinas may be defended, as he often is in modern times, as an
advocate of the worth of the individual, of the royal rule of reason,

*From a painting by Carpaccio*

ST. THOMAS AQUINAS
"The Dumb Ox" that filled the world with his bellowing

and of moderation in all things. But in his day and long after political exigencies came in, and the thunders of theology were used to keep the people in line and to make the Papacy, as a temporal power, supreme. Here recourse was had to the Thomistic division of sin into three kinds and sinners into three classes: he who sins against God, as does the heretic, the sacrilegious, and the blasphemer; he who sins against self, as does the glutton, the debauchee, and the spendthrift; and he who sins against his neighbour, as does the thief and the murderer. Of these three classes the first is the worst. The heretic must be punished not only in the future life, but destroyed root and branch in this life. He who strikes at the foundations of the faith strikes at the foundations of the state, whether secular and sacred, whether of the Holy Roman Empire or of the Holy See.

This opens up the vast subject of intolerance and its terrible instrument, the Inquisition, which, by a kind of historical irony, was dominated by Aquinas's own order, the Dominican. As to the other classes of sinners—the glutton, the debauchee, and the spendthrift, the thief, and even the murderer—greater leniency may be shown. Theirs in many cases are sins of the flesh, not of the spirit; sins venial, not mortal; sins to be atoned for by penance and works of restitution and, in that corrupt period just before the Reformation, by the purchase of indulgences. For many of these also in the future life purgatory becomes an intermediate means of escape, a post-mortem penitentiary whose term was not eternal. But for the heretic and for those other sinners whose hearts remained obdurate Hell and eternal torment lay waiting. Thus out of the harsher side of the Aquinian system Dante constructed his vast fantastic and lurid pictures of Purgatorio and Inferno, the *Divine Comedy* where those in Paradise could laugh at the tortures of the damned. It seems incredible that the mediæval mind could so depart from the original doctrine of love, the Christian ethics of charity. But the Middle Ages were in a way not more culpable than the modern. Over against the Catholic Inquisition and the Catholic dogma can be put the Protestant treatment of heretics and the Protestant teachings as to original sin, total depravity, and the damnation of unbaptized infants. The church of the Middle Ages and of the counter-Reformation has had a blacker reputation because of the many layers of sombre pigments upon the historical canvas. This is a quantitative judgment. The Protestants' reputation seems just as bad in quality. Over against the horrors of the Albigensian Crusades, when slaughtered heretics were ploughed into the soil as fertilizer, over against

the terrible autos-de-fe can be put the cases of Calvin's burning of
his rival Servetus and the ruthless campaign of Cromwell in Ireland, the whole forming a terrible indictment of man's inhumanity
to man. The excuse for these deeds and for the mutual persecutions
of Catholics and Protestants is that theological morality logically
leads to the ethics of persecution. Thus Thomas Aquinas, along
with other theologians, argued that if the death penalty could be
rightly inflicted on thieves and forgers, who rob us only of worldly
goods, how much more righteously could it be inflicted on those
who cheat us out of supernatural good, out of faith, the sacraments,
and the life of the soul.

This depressing outcome of mediæval morals still has an echo in
modern times in the social ostracism and educational repression of
modernists on the part of the so-called fundamentalists. For the
latter are not really fundamental; they stop in the halfway house of
mediævalism and fail to go back to the teachings of the Founder of
Christianity.

And so to summarize the morality of the Middle Ages. The
Aquinian scheme is ultimately based on right opinion, the Christian
on right living; the former virtually denies the liberty of the creature
in attaining the higher virtues of faith, hope, and charity; the latter,
as in the Sermon on the Mount, implies that man has a free choice
to follow the better life. The conflict between the two systems' points
of view is based on the old, the fatal, dualism of Augustine, which in
the last and most important issue, that of salvation, makes man
impotent in the pursuit of virtue. In fine, the whole difference lies
in that between autonomy and authority, between self-rule and
supernatural rule, between free will and infused will, whereas the
Gospel account has it that the disciples of Christ followed the law
of love gladly, willingly, and without compulsion.

# PART SIX
## THE RENAISSANCE

## I. NICCOLÒ MACHIAVELLI (1469–1527)

"THE greatest of the Florentines has likened worldly fame to the breath of the wind that blows now one way and now another way, and changes name as it changes quarter. From every quarter, and all the points of the historical compass, the veering gusts of public judgment have carried incessantly along, from country to country and from generation to generation, with countless mutations of aspect and of innuendo, the sinister renown of Machiavelli. Before he had been dead fifty years his name had become a byword and a proverb. From Thomas Cromwell and Elizabeth; from the massacre of St. Bartholomew, through League and Fronde, through Louis XIV, Revolution, and Empire, down to the Third Napoleon and the days of December; from the Lutheran Reformation down to the blood and iron of Prince Bismarck; from Ferdinand the Catholic down to Don Carlos; from the Sack of Rome down to Gioberti, Mazzini, and Cavour; in all the great countries all over the West, this singular shade is seen haunting men's minds, exciting, frightening, provoking, perplexing them, like some unholy necromancer, bewildering reason and conscience by riddles and paradox. So far from withering or fading, his repute and his writings seem to attract deeper consideration as time goes on, and they have never been objects of more copious attention all over Europe than in the half-century that is now closing."—JOHN MORLEY, The Romanes Lecture, 1897.

The life of Machiavelli, both of whose parents were of the old Florentine nobility, falls into three periods. His youth was spent under the sway of Lorenzo de' Medici, whose title, The Magnificent, reflected the greatness of Florence. This was also the period when Savonarola attempted a rival rule over the city, but Machiavelli preferred the patron of arts and literature to the advocate of Puritanic austerity. This preference was later shown in Machiavelli's writings, which used as examples of worldly success not the mediæval ideals of abnegation and resignation, but the Roman ideals of conquest through force.

In his second period, that of diplomacy, Machiavelli gained that practical experience which he was later to embellish by references to the Latin historians. Thus from his mission to France, which sought to obtain terms from Louis XII for keeping up the war of Florence against Pisa, he was able to point out that this monarch was guilty of the five mistakes in statecraft later summarized in his chief book *The Prince*. This work is a strange mixture. To the school of the diplomat it adds the school of the soldier; on the one side it advocates suavity and trickery, on the other blood and iron. In all this Machiavelli's preaching was more successful than his practice. He urged upon others a combination of duplicity and bravery, while he himself was overreached by rival diplomacies, and the mercenaries he hired were conspicuous for their cowardice. So through his own failures Machiavelli was able to understand the failures and weak points even in the case of the so-called hero of *The Prince*, Cesare Borgia, Duke Valentino, son of Pope Alexander VI. Although he called Valentino a basilisk and hydra, he nevertheless had a sneaking admiration for his adroit cunning and force. This admiration is expressed in that extraordinary chapter whose subtitle might be "Murder as a Fine Art." This is the "Description of the Methods Adopted by the Duke Valentino When Murdering Vitellozzo Vitelli, Oliverotto Da Fermo, the Signor Pagolo and the Duke Di Gravini Orsini."

As no man is a hero to his valet, so no ruler is a perfect prince to a diplomat behind the scenes. Hence the Duke is presented as the type of a man who rises on the fortunes of others and falls with them; who takes every course that might be expected from a prudent man but the course which will save him. The course which the Duke should have taken, comments Machiavelli, was to prevent the election of Julius II, but in allowing himself to be cheated in this choice he made the fatal mistake of thinking that new favours will cause great personages to forget old injuries. But Julius II had much reason to fear the Duke, therefore he did not rest until he had ruined him. Machiavelli's sage advice does not stop here. The son of one pope had been undermined by another pope and the latter succeeded because he was impetuous. In other words, reasons this strange moralizer, Julius II succeeded because he treated fortune like a woman, for it is the bold rather than the cautious who will win and hold them both.

Machiavelli's portraits do not constitute a mere rogues' gallery. He also presents characters who are a mixture of good and evil. Duke Valentino was an unmitigated rascal; he employed a certain Ramiro d'Orco "a swift and cruel man," to be governor of the Romagna, but finally caused him to be executed and left on the piazza with the block and the bloody knife at his side and thereby "caused the people to be at once satisfied and dismayed." Episodes like this have led many to call *The Prince* a mere manual for tyrants. But alongside of such bloody descriptions we have the moral, drawn from the conduct and fate of Caterina Sforza, that it is far better to earn the confidence of the people than to rely on fortresses. In this connection Machiavelli writes with enthusiasm of the national militia of Switzerland, which appeared to him the model of the nations, because it depended on the arms of the populance and not of mercenaries. All these opinions are put down in his well-known work, *The Prince*, and in the *Discourses of Livy* and the *History of Florence*, which were the products of his third period, that of enforced leisure. With the return of the Medici, Machiavelli lost his position as secretary of the republican government of Florence, was suspected of plotting against the new rulers, "put to the question," which meant put on the rack, declared innocent, but forced into political inactivity on his meagre estate near Florence. Here he evolved those maxims of mingled force and subtlety which have given the word "Machiavellian" its sinister significance. This reputation is not wholly deserved. Machiavelli was not strong on piety except as a screen, but he was a genuine patriot, dismayed at the ruin which threatened Italy and willing to justify any means to attain the end of emancipation.

## POLITICS WITHOUT ETHICS

The mediæval moral system had thousands of adherents who tried their best to practise its virtues and avoid its vices. It also had its opponents, and of these we take two contrasting types of the Renaissance—Niccolò Machiavelli and Giordano Bruno. One was a cool and calculating thinker who considered the virtues to be overrated, the other an ardent and impulsive soul who thought them to be underrated. Machiavelli, the Florentine diplomatist, whose very name has a sinister significance, might be called submoral. He declares, for example, that this or that act is not a crime but a stupidity. On the other hand, Bruno, the martyred monk, whose burning at the stake was a torch that lighted Europe, was perhaps supermoral. He divides men into two classes, the vulgar and the heroic, the former following the lower principle of sense and sensual passion, the latter the higher principle of intellect and reason. For these "the soul struggling with passions and vices within and vicious enemies without must aspire and rise, and pass, in one breath over this mountain of difficulty."

Here were two men of the Renaissance, one of northern Italy, the other of southern, who were wide apart in their opinions yet each in his own mind a faithful son of the church. Here the resemblance ceases. To Machiavelli both religion and morality were means and not ends. Thus he praises Ferdinand of Aragon as one who accomplished great things under the cloak of religion, but who in reality had no mercy, faith, humanity, or integrity. He also puts forward as one who has accomplished great deeds in the world a certain Castruccio Castracani. It was this adventurer who for his further security raised a fortress in Lucca with the stones of the towers of those whom he had killed or hunted out of the state, and when made a Roman senator, clothed himself in a brocaded toga, which had the following words embroidered on its front: "I am what God wills."

This is but one of many pictures in Machiavelli's portrait gallery of moral opportunists, and this has given him not only a bad name personally but the historical reputation of being "an unholy necromancer." However, it may be said in extenuation that his ethics were those of his contemporaries among the ruling classes of Italy, men like Lorenzo the Magnificent, to whom he dedicates his book entitled *The Prince*, and men like Cesare Borgia, the Duke Valentino, whom he offers as a pattern of a prince, successful because unscrupulous. Here, says Machiavelli: "I believe also that he will be successful who directs his actions according to the spirit of the times, and that he whose actions do not accord with the times will not be successful. . . . For my part I consider that it is better to be adventurous than cautious, because fortune is a woman, and if you wish to keep her under it is necessary to beat and ill-use her; and it is seen that she allows herself to be mastered by the adventurous rather than by those who go to work more coldly. She is, therefore, always, womanlike, a lover of young men, because they are less cautious, more violent, and with more audacity command her."

The age of Machiavelli, adviser of the Medici, has been considered a moral interregnum where might was right and every man's hand was against his neighbour. The Renaissance was hardly that, but rather an age when anarchy was tempered with culture, force combined with subtlety, the iron hand hidden in the velvet glove. Under these circumstances political guile became a matter of learning and Machiavelli, with his knowledge of classical antiquity, employed those of its tenets which he found useful. Like the duellist of his day, he fights now with the rapier, now with the poniard, and now with both. When the cloak of religion will serve him he uses it to catch his opponents' thrusts; when the ancient morality is applicable he draws from it as from an armoury of weapons. Of the old Roman virtues he rejects honesty and justice, but selects gravity, fortitude, and prudence. The ancient's self-control, the iron will—cold, calculating, cruel—these appeal to him. He speaks even of the enemies of Rome with admiration—Hannibal, who crossed the frosty Alps and preserved discipline in his motley horde by means of "inhuman cruelty." The Spartans, also, are to be admired; like the Romans they stood "armed and free."

But Machiavelli's system is not so much the morals of militarism as the morals of opportunism. Force must be combined with astuteness. The Romans in the countries which they annexed kept down the greater powers and did not allow any strong foreign princes to gain authority, while they sent colonies and maintained friendly relations with the minor powers. In other words, although in politics there are no perfectly safe courses, prudence consists in choosing the least dangerous ones. Here the wise man ought always to follow the paths beaten by great men, and to imitate those who have been supreme, so that if his ability does not equal theirs, at least it will savour of it. Moses, Cyrus, Romulus, Theseus, and such like are most excellent examples. And although one may not discuss Moses, he having been a mere executor of the will of God, yet Cyrus and others who have acquired or founded kingdoms, if their particular deeds and conduct shall be considered, will not be found inferior to Moses, although he had such a great preceptor. And in examining their actions and lives one cannot see that they owed anything to fortune beyond opportunity which brought them the material to mould into the form which seemed best to them.

In this description Machiavelli shows that his principles are plastic; if morality will not serve try militarism of the right kind. But in advocating variant means to attain one's aim Machiavelli does not lose sight of his own great aim. That aim was the purpose of a patriot who, like Cavour in later days, sought to wipe out the stain of Italy unredeemed. Italy must be redeemed, declares Machiavelli, and by its own soldiers. It has been ruled many years by mercenaries. Nevertheless, you must understand that the empire has recently come to be repudiated in Italy, that the pope has acquired more temporal power, and that Italy has been divided up into more states for the reason that many of the great cities took up arms against their nobles, who, formerly favoured by the emperor, were oppressing them, whilst the church was favouring them so as to gain authority in temporal power: in many others their citizens became princes. From this it came to pass that Italy fell partly into the hands of the church and of republics, and the church consisting of priests and the republic of citizens unaccustomed to arms, both commenced to enlist foreigners. The first who gave renown to this soldiery was Albergio da Conio, the Romagnian. From the school of this man sprang, among others, Braccio and Sforza, who in their time were the arbiters of Italy. After these came all the other captains who till now have directed the arms of Italy; and the end of all their valour has been that she has been overrun by Charles, robbed by Louis, ravaged by Ferdinand, and insulted by the Switzers.

Historical conditions, the spirit of the times, explain the motive of Machiavelli's book. To him mere morality cannot save a state. Military force must be used and that of the right kind. Hence the author concludes with this exhortation to liberate the peninsula from the barbarians: "It appears to me that so many things concur to favour a new prince that I never knew a time more fit than the present. And if, as I said, it was necessary that the people of Israel should be captive so as to make manifest the ability of Moses; that the Persians should be oppressed by the Medes so as to discover the greatness of the soul of Cyrus; and that the Athenians should be dispersed to illustrate the capabilities of Theseus: then at the present time, in order to discover the virtue of an Italian spirit, it was necessary that Italy should be reduced to the extremity she is now in, that she should be more enslaved than the Hebrews, more oppressed than the Persians, more scattered than the Athenians; without head, without order, beaten, despoiled, torn, overrun; and to have endured every kind of desolation. . . . So that Italy, left as without life, waits for him who shall yet heal her wounds and put an end to the ravaging and plundering of Lombardy, to the swindling and taxing of the kingdom and of Tuscany, and cleanse those sores that for long have festered. It is seen how she entreats God to send someone who shall deliver her from these wrongs and barbarous insolences. It is seen also that she is ready and willing to follow a banner if only someone will raise it."

All this explains why *The Prince* is dedicated to the grandson of Lorenzo de' Medici, the Magnificent, whose powerful and unscrupulous rule had so impressed Machiavelli. Material force then seemed more effective to Machiavelli than moral force. Thus the reforming priest who in Machiavelli's younger days was for a time the spiritual dictator of Florence did not appeal to him, judging by this comparison: "If Moses, Cyrus, Theseus, and Romulus had been unarmed they could not have enforced their constitutions for long—as happened in our time to Fra Girolamo Savonarola, who was ruined with his new order of things immediately the multitude believed in him no longer, and he had no means of keeping steadfast those who believed or of making the unbelievers to believe."

To Machiavelli morals are weaker than arms and the mere reformer cannot depend on the populace. He cites as a trite proverb, "He who builds on the people builds on mud," and adds that the private citizen deceives himself who makes a foundation there and persuades himself that the people will free him, when he is oppressed by his enemies and by the magistrates. There may, of course, be the rare case where by happy shrewdness a leading citizen becomes the prince of his country, because the people do not wish to be ruled or oppressed by the nobles, but in general force must be added to astuteness. Here the author directs his Prince to consider the way to govern cities or principalities which lived under their own laws before they were annexed. Three courses are opened: the first is to ruin them, the next is to reside in them in person, the third is to permit them to live under their own laws, drawing a tribute, and establishing within each an oligarchy which will keep it friendly to you. Of these three courses the first would be morally the worst, but the means must be judged by the result, for nothing succeeds like success. Consider the ancients. The Spartans held Athens and Thebes by establishing there an oligarchy; nevertheless, they lost it. The Romans wished to hold Greece as the Spartans held it, making it free and permitting it laws, and did not succeed. But in order to hold Capua, Carthage, and Numantia they dismantled them and did not lose them. Men of old succeeded best by the first course. In modern times the Prince can choose between ruin and residence especially in cities accustomed to freedom. In republics there are more vitality, greater hatred, and more desire for vengeance, which will never permit them to allow the memory of their former liberty to rest; so that the safest way is to destroy them or to reside there.

Machiavelli advises his Prince not as a moralist, but as a moral duellist. He balances motives in his mind as a swordsman balances the proffered weapon in his hand. The choice of arms is important. Look attentively at the duels and hand-to-hand combats, he says, how superior the Italians are in strength, dexterity, and subtlety. Now subtlety in statecraft may employ any means. The way to govern cities may be either ruin or residence. It may be also force or fraud, or both. Here appears the famous Machiavellian chapter, "Concerning Those Who Have Obtained a Principality by Wickedness." In this is presented for imitation the ancient example of one who by nefarious ways ascended to the principality. Agathocles, the Sicilian, became king of Syracuse in the following way: One morning he assembled the people and senate of Syracuse, as if he had to discuss with them things relating to the Republic, and at a given signal the soldiers killed all the senators and the richest of the people; these dead, he seized and held the princedom of that city without any civil commotion.

In citing this character as an exemplar for his Prince has Machiavelli any moral scruples? Hardly. It is merely a question of choice between immediate success and subsequent reputation. If the courage of Agathocles in extricating himself from danger be considered, together with his greatness of mind in enduring and overcoming hardships, it cannot be seen why he should be esteemed less than the most notable captain. Nevertheless, his barbarous cruelty and inhumanity with infinite wickednesses do not permit him to be celebrated among the most excellent men, and it cannot be called talent to slay fellow citizens, to deceive friends, to be without faith, without mercy, without religion; such methods may gain empire but not glory.

A further distinction must be made. There is a decided difference between severities badly used and severities properly used. In our own times, continues the narrator, Oliverotto da Fermo gave a solemn banquet to his own uncle, Giovanni Fogliani, and the chiefs of Fermo. No sooner were they seated than soldiers issued from secret places and slaughtered Giovanni and the rest. Oliverotto also killed all the malcontents who were able to injure him, and his destruction would have been as difficult as that of Agathocles, if he had not allowed himself to be overreached by Cesare Borgia, by whom he was strangled. Now Agathocles was no such fool. He used severities properly, for these may be called properly used, if of evil it is lawful to speak well, that are applied at one blow and are necessary to one's security. Hence it is to be remarked that, in seizing a state, the usurper ought to examine closely into all those injuries which it is necessary for him to inflict, and to do them all at one stroke so as not to have to repeat them daily. . . . He who does otherwise, either from timidity or evil advice, is always compelled to keep the knife in his hand.

## MORALS WITHOUT SCRUPLES

Machiavelli evidently has no moral scruples in the choice of methods, for he advocates the cloak of religion and employs subtle theological distinctions to cover up his tracks. He has just advocated instantaneous cruelty in preference to lingering timidity. And those, he adds, who practise the first system are able, by aid of God or man, to mitigate to some degree their rule, as Agathocles did. But here another distinction arises. The aid of God must supplement the aid of man. Thus in exhorting the Prince to liberate Italy Machiavelli declares that a war which is necessary is just, and that arms are hallowed when there is no other hope but in them. So the difficulties cannot be great, he continues, "if you will only follow those men to whom I have directed your attention. Take the case of Moses: "He trusted in God, he also trusted in himself, how extraordinarily the ways of God have been manifested: the sea is divided, a cloud has led the way, the rock has poured forth water, it has rained manna, everything has contributed to your greatness; you ought to do the rest. God is not willing to do everything, and thus take away our free will and that share of glory which belongs to us."

As a true son of the church Machiavelli has utilized the appeal to providence as one method of success. But as a son of the Renaissance, influenced by the revived pagan notions, he now adds both the appeal to free will and the appeal to fortune, according as the one or the other may meet the case. He grants that ecclesiastical principalities may be sustained by the ancient ordinances of religion, no matter how their princes behave and live; but as temporal principalities they cannot be successful without the aid of men and of fortune. Thus before Charles, King of France, passed into Italy, the enemies of the pope in order to keep him down made use of the barons of Rome, who, being divided into two factions, Orsini and Colonnesi, had always a pretext for disorder, and, standing with arms in their hands under the eyes of the pontiff, kept the pontificate weak and powerless. And although there might arise sometimes a courageous pope, such as Sixtus, yet neither fortune nor wisdom could rid him of these annoyances.

Again, in his chapter on "What Fortune Can Effect," Machiavelli goes back to the ancient fatalism, but meets its problems in the spirit different from that of old. It is not by resignation but by shrewdness that the viscissitudes of chance can be met. Fortune is the arbiter of one half of our actions, but she still leaves us to direct the other half. Sometimes we can only repair the damage after the damage is done, as in canalizing a stream whose floods have carried all before it. But it is better to prepare than repair. We must be ready for any eventualities and alter our methods to meet fortune's fickle mood. Consequently it is necessary for the Prince to have a

mind ready to turn itself accordingly as the winds and variations
of fortune force it; not to diverge from the good if he can avoid
doing so, but, if compelled, then to know how to set about it; to appear merciful, faithful, humane, religious, upright, and to be so, but
with a mind so framed that should you require not to be so, you may
be able to know how to change to the opposite. So a prince is often
forced, in order to maintain his state, to act contrary to fidelity,
friendship, humanity, and religion.

This sounds thoroughly unscrupulous. Such advice has led the
critics of Machiavelli to call him a moral weathercock, advocate of
a double standard of morality—one for the individual and another
for the state. He has also been charged with being a corrupter of
political ethics whose book has had the most baneful influence on
European history.

Such is the attack, now for the defense, or rather for an explanation of such a code of immoralism. It may be said that Machiavelli
is mentally honest. He is frankly realistic; he simply describes
things as he saw them about him. In the words of another realist,
Francis Bacon, Lord Verulam, the Machiavellian system was a
presentation of things as they are, and not a "philosophy as one
would." So in *The Prince* we have simply a codification of the practices in vogue. In accordance with the "spirit of the times" to which
Machiavelli appealed, a moral code binding on the subject is not
binding on the ruler. As Lord Morley has put it: Machiavelli follows
up the divorce of politics from theology by a divorce of politics from
ethics. He was laying down certain maxims of government as an
art; the end of that art is the security and permanence of the ruling
power; and the fundamental principle from which he silently
started, without shadow of doubt or misgiving as to its soundness,
was that the application of moral standards to this business is as
little to the point as it would be to the navigation of a ship.

This comparison may be carried further in the way of defense.
If Machiavelli were alive now he might say that the ship of state is
guided better by a skilled pilot than by a sky pilot. There may be
talk about making the world safe for democracy, but success is on
the side of the strongest batteries. Militarism is not moral nor
politics pious. Stratagems, intrigues, and cruelties are justified
by results. The powers that first employed poison gas were denounced, but the other powers came round to its use. Propaganda
in the way of camouflaging the real aims of the war was also employed by both sides and now look at the impasse reached among
those who said this was "a war to end wars." The two most powerful

nations, closest in ties of language and of blood, talk about a scheme of naval reduction but end with a programme of naval enlargement. Again, if Machiavelli were now alive he might also point out that both sides used religion for a cloak. One said that "God is with us" and fell back on the help of an ancient tribal deity emerging from the Northern woods. The other appealed to the god of peace on earth, but at present possess the strongest military and naval forces. In fine, the modern "Prince" is not the prince of peace.

But to return to Machiavelli's own age. It was his task to point out with brutal frankness the difference between the pretended and the actual, and to show that ideal politics was quite different from real politics. While St. Augustine may have fancied that the City of God was the church, Machiavelli knew the meaning of the temporal power of the pope under the Borgias. The author of *The Prince* was no believer in ideal commonwealths, although the Renaissance revival of Platonism had brought forward a host of imitators of the *Republic*. Thus contemporary with Machiavelli was Sir Thomas More with his *Utopia*. This was a frank attack on militarism, for the author speaks of the ruin wrought by standing armies as in France, a country full of "a pestiferous sort of people— soldiers," who are still kept up in time of peace. Now Machiavelli had this sort of book in mind when he declared that many had pictured republics and principalities which in fact have never been known or seen, because how one lives is so far distant from how one ought to live that he who neglects what is done for what ought to be done sooner effects his ruin than his preservation.

In a later generation Machiavelli was attacked for such stark unmoral realism. His fellow countryman Campanella, author of *The City of the Sun*, called Machiavellianism triumphant atheism and regarded its author as the representative of the devil. Machiavelli had certainly drifted far from the mediæval ideal of the vision of God and of blessedness in the world to come, but he defends himself here by pointing out the poor results obtained by a religion of contemplation, humility, and self-denial. This scheme, he declares, has made men weak and given over the world to reckless and violent men who have discovered that most men are inclined, in the hope of paradise, rather to endure than to resent offenses. How much better were the ancients who loved honour, greatness of mind, physical strength and health; how much better the ancient religions which invested the mortals who had gained renown as great generals, heroes, or lawgivers with divine authority.

To Machiavelli, then, mediæval morality had failed. It was

especially ineffective in practical politics and a useless instrument for the ambitious patriot. He therefore gives this final advice: When the entire safety of one country is at stake, no consideration of what is just or unjust, merciful or cruel, praiseworthy or shameful, must intervene. On the contrary, every other consideration being set aside, that course alone must be taken which preserves the existence of the country and maintains its liberty.

## II. GIORDANO BRUNO (1548-1600)

"THE fundamental principle lay in the doctrine that salvation is to be found exclusively in the Christian Church. The profound conviction that those who did not believe in its doctrines would be damned eternally, and that God punishes theological error as if it were the most heinous of crimes, led naturally to persecution. It was a duty to impose on men the only true doctrine, seeing that their own eternal interests were at stake, and to hinder errors from spreading. Heretics were more than ordinary criminals and the pains that man could inflict on them were as nothing to the tortures awaiting them in hell. To rid the earth of men who, however virtuous, were, through their religious errors, enemies of the Almighty, was a plain duty. Their virtues were no excuse. We must remember that, according to the humane doctrine of the Christians, pagan, that is, merely human, virtues were vices, and infants who died unbaptized passed the rest of time in creeping on the floor of hell. The intolerance arising from such views could not but differ in kind and intensity from anything that the world had yet witnessed."—J. B. BURY, *A History of Freedom of Thought.*

When Florence of the Medici and Machiavelli lost its liberty for the second time free intellectual life in Italy received its death blow. It was then that the Inquisition was reorganized in an attempt to check the growth of the Reformation. In this counter-Reformation exile and martyrdom became the fate of those who essayed innovations in science or religion. Here Giordano Bruno was a conspicuous example. By the irony of fate the Dominican order which directed the machinery of the Inquisition received Bruno into its fold, and the very cloister of the greatest of the Dominicans, Thomas Aquinas, nourished the greatest rebel against his system. Bruno later confessed that when he assumed the habit of St. Dominic he made a fatal mistake. As he put it in a homely way, when the first button is wrong, all are wrong. He also recalled that his monastic life opened in the midst of sinister scenes. The year before his taking orders more than four-score victims of the Waldensian persecutions had been butchered with the same knife, and their bodies quartered and distributed along the road to Calabria. This was merely in accordance with the decision of the Council of Trent, "to erase with fire and sword the least traces of heresy."

With such a warning before him Bruno nevertheless read the writings of the ironical Dutch critic Erasmus, aroused the suspicions of his superiors, and was forced to flee. He thereupon began his unhappy wanderings. Driven from Rome, he first sought refuge in Geneva, but even there found little intellectual liberty, for Calvin's successors argued that it was lawful "to coerce heretics by the sword." It must be granted that Bruno was indiscreet in criticizing the local Swiss scholars, just as he was subsequently indiscreet in Paris when he attacked the "divine" Aristotle. At any rate, he next sought refuge in England, renowned for its tolerance under Queen Elizabeth. There he wrote his two chief ethical works and dedicated them to his patron, Sir Philip Sidney. In his *Expulsion of the Triumphant Beast* he was again indiscreet, for the title of the book was twisted by his enemies into an attack on the pope. However, in his *Enthusiasms of the Noble* he presented his best side, declaring man's highest aim to be an ecstatic unity with the divine life, in which all the miseries and misfortunes of the merely earthly life disappear.

But Bruno was not content to remain long in Elizabethan England, whose queen he praised as "among the nobles no one more heroic, among the councillors no one more wise." His restless spirit drove him back to France and then across the Rhine into Germany, where his evil genius of exaggeration pursued him. Then in a funeral oration over the Duke of Brunswick he tells how the university which the Duke had founded was free to all lovers of the Muses, even to strangers such as Bruno himself was—an exile from his Italian fatherland for honourable reasons and zeal for the truth, here he had received the freedom of the university: in Italy he was exposed to the greedy maw of the Roman wolf—here he was in safety: there he had been chained to a superstitious and absurd cult —here he was exhorted to more reformed rites.

Bruno was certainly rash. In this oration he attacks the church and "the violent tyranny of the Tiberine beast," yet three years later he returns to Italy and falls into the power of the pope. Some have suspected that the Inquisition laid a trap for the excommuni-

cated monk when he received a flattering offer as tutor to a young
Venetian patrician. At any rate, this Mocenigo, who had been one
of the assessors of the Inquisition board in Venice, denounced his
teacher to the Holy Office, charging among other things that Bruno
had said that the Friars were asses and the doctrines of the church
asses' beliefs. While the charge as a whole was a travesty, yet one of
Bruno's favourite ironical themes was that the "holy ass," which
was found in Noah's ark, was still to be found in that ark of safety
to the church among those who accepted its doctrines on faith and
upheld them by pedantry. In his first examination before the
tribunal of inquisitors Bruno was further charged by his former
pupil with declaring that the Catholics did not act on the model of
the apostles, who taught by example and good deed, converting
through love, and not force, and that while he preferred the Catholic
religion to others, it also stood in great need of reform.

This was sufficient; to advocate reformation before upholders of
the counter-Reformation was fatal. Yet it must be confessed that at
this juncture Bruno employed in the way of defense a distinction
which amounted to subterfuge. This was the famous doctrine of the
twofold truth. Speaking "catholically" he might say one thing;
speaking "rationally" he might mean another. Now, often as they
disavowed it, the scholars of the church had utilized this distinction.
Even the "divine" Aristotle could not be taken "literally" according to reason, but had to be interpreted "spiritually" according to
faith. But this distinction was of no avail. Bruno was in danger not
because of the fantastic charges of his pupil, not because of his
praises of "heretical" rulers such as Queen Elizabeth or Henry of
Navarre and religious leaders such as Luther, but because his judges
were astute enough to see that his personal belief was based on the
new scientific discoveries. There were the new astronomical conquests
of Copernicus and Galileo which taught that there were more worlds
than one, that the universe was not finite but infinite, from which
might be deduced the doctrines that providence was universal and
not particular, and its aim the perfection of all souls and not the
condemnation of the great bulk of mankind.

These discoveries and these deductions were highly significant.
Upon them was based the personal creed which Bruno now avowed
upon cross-examination: I believe in an infinite universe, the effect
of the infinite divine potency, because it has seemed to me unworthy
of the divine goodness and power to create a finite world, when able
to produce besides it another and others infinite: so that I have de-

clared that there are endless particular worlds similar to this of the earth; with Pythagoras I regard it as a star, and similar to it are the moon, the planets, and other stars, which are infinite, and all these bodies are worlds, and without number, constituting the infinite all in an infinite space; while the latter is called the infinite universe, in which are innumerable worlds; so that there are two kinds of infinity, one in the magnitude of the universe, the other in the multitude of worlds, by which indirectly the truth according to the faith may be impugned. In this universe I place a universal providence, in virtue of which everything lives, grows, moves, and comes to and abides in its perfection. It is present in two fashions: the one is that in which the spirit is present in the body, wholly in the whole, and wholly in any part of the whole, and that I call nature, the shadow, the footprint of divinity; the other is the ineffable way in which God by essence, presence, and power is in all and above all, not as part, not as spirit or life, but in an inexplicable way.

This was a noble avowal; it was nevertheless followed by an ignoble abnegation. Upon further examination in the prison house Bruno solemnly recanted all the heresies which he had embraced and all the doubts which he had harboured concerning Catholic doctrines. This was a blot upon his character, but the stain was wiped out at his second trial. The Venetian procurator had reported that the prisoner's faults were extremely grave in respect to heresy, but in other respects he was one of the most excellent and rarest of natures and of exquisite learning and knowledge. This was borne out by Bruno's conduct before the Sacred Congregation of the Supreme Tribunal of the Holy Office. Surrendered by Venice for political reasons, he was brought to Rome. There he was charged with eight heretical propositions by the Reverend Fathers Commissario and Bellarmino. Now Bellarmino was that Jesuit who had decided that the system of Copernicus was heretical, and who was later to play a part in the trial of Galileo, who had defended Copernicus. So Galileo, as is well known, was forced to recant his opinion that the world moves and that the sun is the centre of the universe and to accept the Aristotelian teaching that the world is the proper centre of the universe and the sun revolves about it.

But Bruno made no such final recantation and showed no fear before his judges at his last trial. After six years of imprisonment he was degraded and handed over to the Governor of Rome with the technical formula used by the church that he be punished "with as

great clemency as possible, and without the effusion of blood."
Bruno knew that this meant burning at the stake, but he boldly
answered, "Ye who pass judgment over me feel maybe greater fear
than I upon whom it is passed."

## THE PASSIONATE PILGRIM

The execution of the "apostate friar of Nola" is said to have
passed unnoticed in the great year of jubilee. But together with the
condemnation of Copernicus and of Galileo it furnished a triple
warning against those who would try to upset the orthodox arrangements. The latter made the world in which men dwelt a limited
liability company under the absolute control of its board of governors. As this globe was the centre of the universe, so was Italy of
Europe, and Rome of Italy, while the cardinals and pope formed
the final board of arbitrament in matters both secular and sacred.
This was the scheme which went so far as to distribute the dividends
of discovery between Spain with its intrepid Columbus and Portugal
with its circumnavigator Magellan. How foolish, then, were the
actions of single stockholders like Copernicus, or Galileo, or Bruno
in attempting to disturb this water-tight system! But though the
Inquisition had power to put on the Index Expurgatorius the books
of all three heretics, to reprimand Copernicus, confine Galileo in
his Florentine tower, and burn Bruno and scatter his ashes to the
winds, it could not prevent the establishment and extension of the
rival world system. By the new knowledge, declares Bruno, we are
loosened from the chains of a most narrow dungeon and set at
liberty to rove in a most august empire.

In this statement Bruno was in sympathy with the spirit of the
times and may be compared to the patriot Machiavelli, the diplomat
of Florence. As the author of *The Prince* strove for the enlargement
of Italy, so the author of *The Cause, the Principle and the One*,
sought for the enlargement of the universe. And as Machiavelli
was against a disunited country with a division of power between
church and state, so Bruno was for a united universe and a single
vital principle therein. In other words, one thinker was for a political
monarchy, the other for a philosophic monism, and both hostile to
any dualism. In Bruno's case the fight against the church doctrine,
backed by the authority of Aristotle, was for the time being hopeless. The church system was not only well established but highly
workable. The Holy See, holding the keys of St. Peter, was the sole
custodian of matters celestial and matters terrestrial; it proclaimed

jurisdiction over the two opposed realms—heavenly and earthly, sacred and profane, supersensuous and sensuous. In the language of the Aristotelian Schoolmen, these were the opposed realms of the empyrean or upper ether, where angels and higher spirits dwell, and of the sublunary sphere where things mortal are in a state of flux and uncertainty.

This cosmic dualism led further to a moral dualism, the familiar division of mankind into good and bad, saved and lost, elect and non-elect. And this moral dualism was in turn dependent upon a theological dualism as men were respectively relegated by an inscrutable providence to this or that governance: the kingdom of this world or that of the church; the City of Men or the City of God; and in the future the kingdom of glory or the kingdom of the prince of darkness. Finally this dualism was reflected in the social sphere. Feudalism lent itself to the system, or was itself based on it, in its divisions of men into ruler and subject, prince and peasant, master and serf.

Reënforced as it was by the iron bars of fixed mental patterns, Bruno had a well-nigh impossible task to break down this logical dividing wall. But he attempts that task in the most significant of his works, *The Cause, the Principle, and the One*. To him the unity and uniformity of nature, being once postulated, destroy the cosmic dualism, bring heaven to earth, and make the entire universe divine. Yet this was no baseless theory; it was backed by the discoveries of the heretical Copernicus. When this bold astronomer imagined himself as an observer from the sun as a centre, watching the earth and the other planets revolving about him, he exploded the delusion that the earth is the motionless centre of the universe and the most important point in space. This conjecture of Copernicus, in his great work *On the Motions of the Heavenly Bodies*, punctured the fallacy of the ancient astronomy of Aristotle and Ptolemy and made this earth on which men dwell to be merely one of the countless heavenly bodies.

Bruno knew this book of Copernicus's and declared that there is more understanding in two of its chapters than in the whole natural philosophy of Aristotle. This was because the followers of the ancient thinker considered the earth as the centre of the universe and the most important point in space, man the monarch of all he surveys and the end and purpose of all salvation. But to the men of the new age these new-time notions are untenable. The earth is not the centre of the universe but one of its humblest members, and humanity not the goal but only perfection itself.

### THE WAY TO PERFECTION

Here arises a paradox. Bruno seemingly degrades man, but this is really in order to elevate him. The individual has no longer to wait in fear and trembling for infused grace, a supernatural gift from without, to help him on his arduous way. Man is rather a passionate pilgrim, finding within himself stores of divine energy. As part of nature he shares in its divinity; he also has before him that common end, perfection. Here the eternal source is the divine mind: "As all things flow from, so all things tend to return to God."

To Bruno's opponents this came as presumptuous: it flies in the face of the church's teaching; it means self-help and not salvation from without. But to Bruno this claim has rational grounds; man is a creature of reason and reason approximates more and more closely to the divine mind, just as a polygon, when the number of its sides is increased, approaches more and more to the shape of a circle. Of course finite man can never be infinite, yet he can strive toward infinity. And this is as it should be; the flying goal calls out more effort than does mere passive waiting for a supernatural gift. This is the theory; the practical application is equally notable. Activity and not passivity, courage and not fear, form the moral message of Bruno. He sounds at times over-optimistic, but he had sense enough to see that all men could not employ his system as a rule of living. There are therefore two classes of men, the heroic and the vulgar, just as there are two principles, the higher intellect or reason, and the lower sense or sensual passion. This, then, is the Brunonian challenge: "Difficulty is ordained to check poltroons. Things ordinary and easy are for the vulgar, for ordinary people. But rare, heroic, divine men pass along this way of difficulty, that necessity may be constrained to yield them the palm of immortality. Although it may not be possible to come so far as to gain the prize, run your race nevertheless, do your hardest in what is of so great importance, strive to your last breath. It is not only he who arrives at the goal that is praised, but also whoever dies no coward's or poltroon's death; he casts the fault of his loss and of his death upon the back of fate, and shows the world that he has come to such an end by no defect of himself, but by error of fortune."

This inspiring passage, echoing the finest spirit of Stoic endurance, was written in England and as such was a prophecy and an epitome of Bruno's own career. So is his practical advice, again in the Stoic vein, as to the things the brave man ought not to fear: hunger, nakedness, thirst, pain, poverty, solitude, persecution, death.

This advice sounds Stoic and may be taken as Bruno's reaction to a degenerate form of Epicureanism brought in by the Renaissance revival of the classical system. But there is a more modern note in all this. Just as his cosmic speculations are said to rely on the present-day acceptance of the unity and uniformity of nature, so his ethical spirit has been called that of the strenuous life. This spirit was doubtless fostered by Bruno's sojourn in the Northern islands whence sailed the gentlemen adventurers like Drake and Frobisher and Sir Walter Raleigh. At any rate, while in England Bruno wrote in his book dedicated to Sir Philip Sidney these notable lines: "Even if the goal aimed at is never reached, even though the soul be consumed by the violence of its strivings, yet it is enough that such a noble fire should have been kindled in it."

Bruno's ardent nature has been fancifully explained as due to his birth near Mount Vesuvius. But it was no accident of birth, but rather harsh experience, that accounts for the substance of his doctrine that man has within him a spark of the divine fire, as a guide and beacon of life. The soul or spirit, he observes, tends toward that with which it has the greatest affinity, as the flower tends toward the sun. First of all, then, it is needful for the soul to present the light of intelligence to its eyes and thus to regain its lost virtue, to strengthen its sinews, and to put to rout its enemies. This is allegorical, for by enemies are meant the sense feelings and passions, those fears or phobias which keep man in darkness, whereas man's true destiny is to cherish the divinity within that impels him to love God in reality.

This sounds impossibly idealistic, yet it is not meant to be fanciful, for Bruno holds that it is not grace infused from without, but the divine energy within, that impels man to the final goal, "to become one with God." This needs explanation. The sunflower that turns toward the sun, or the moth to the candle, as he also explains it, are poetic expressions or tropisms—inevitable reactions to given stimuli, to put it in later scientific terms. But this turning toward the light, this approach of the soul toward its source, according to Bruno, is not necessitated. Man has free will as to his actions and is not bound to mere mechanical reflexes. Base natures may give way to carnal temptations, but heroic natures spurn them. There are two kinds of "furor" or inspiration. In some there is only blindness, stupidity, unreasoning impulse; others consist in a certain divine abstraction by which some men become better in fact than

ordinary men. This is a fine description but the problem of temperament is not solved thereby. Bruno does not explain why some are
fit to receive the higher inspiration and some to receive only the
lower. For example, we can only wonder, in retrospect, why Copernicus did not dare to publish his great astronomical work until the last
days of his life; why Galileo protested, and then recanted, and lived
alone in his tower a prisoner of the Vatican; why at first Bruno recanted, and in spite of imprisonment and torture faced the flames.

We have here no explanation of the mystery of free will, we have
only the documents in the case, and these show that Bruno was
no ordinary soul, and his morals no ordinary morals. His is the
categorical imperative, the supreme self-given command that "the
soul must come to the point when it no longer regards but despises
fatigue, the contest of passions, the struggle with vicious enemies,
but must aspire, and rise and pass over this mountain of difficulties."

While Bruno was called an apostate in the church, he was at the
same time a product of the church. Just as there were fighting
bishops, there were militant monks. He was one of these in the moral
campaign, a leader whose order of the day was struggle and his
password "aspiration." Some have considered this dangerous advice
because aspiration leads to absorption and man, in passing the lines
of the ordinary moral life, becomes lost in a no-man's land of
speculation. This was true in an early phase of Bruno's philosophy.
Then the strenuous life of activity seemingly ended in the blessed
life of passivity, as when Plato advocated the soul's ascent to the
ecstatic vision. Moreover, in his middle period Bruno seems to lean
toward a mere impersonal immortality, a pure pantheism implying
persistence but no personality. In that case the individual human
and animal souls would be merely modes or expressions of the
earth-soul, just as the different "star-souls" would be merely modes
of the soul of the universe, "the first and highest emanations of
divinity."

This is the flower of Platonism run to seed in neo-Platonism,
that exotic system which flourished in ancient Alexandria and
whose fancies hung like an obscuring haze in the sky of speculation.
Such teaching is not only fantastic but fatal to a practical doctrine
of immortality. Absorption of the finite into the infinite, like a drop
of water merging into the ocean, may appeal to the resigned pessimist; it does not appeal to the ardent optimist. So Bruno's earlier
notion of persistence without personality is succeeded by his final
doctrine of persistence plus personality. The first form of immortality is that of reabsorption, but no continuity of consciousness;

the last that of the conscious pursuit of an infinite object. All this is justified by the vast potentiality of the human mind, a potentiality in turn based upon the conviction that man is part and parcel of the divine. By this final conviction, Bruno escapes the pitfall of the transmigration of souls, and embraces the doctrine of transformism. Here he speaks not only to himself but to all other heroic men when he gives this stirring message: "The wise soul does not fear death, sometimes desires it, and goes to meet it. Before every substance lies eternity for duration, necessity for place, omniformity for realization."

After these final inspiring words of Bruno's philosophy it would seem an anticlimax to point out the defects in his thought. But it must be done. In a way his system is a melodramatic play and his explanations a play on words. In spite of his faults of temperament, his conceit, his arrogance, his indiscreet criticisms of his various hosts, his attempted use of the double standard of truth, his temporary lapse into retraction of his views—in spite of all this the Nolan monk was a genuine hero. Nevertheless, this paradox remains. Though the hero may conquer through his very death, yet virtue is not wholly triumphant. The problem of evil persists. In spite of his leanings toward pantheism Bruno avoided some of its weak solutions, but not all. Evil to him was not an illusion—he knew too well the meaning of excommunication, flight, poverty, the dungeon, and torture. Nor was evil to him mere negation or privation, as when the Sophists declared that cowardice is lack of courage. So while Bruno did not hold that evil is an illusion or a mere negation, yet he did hold that it is partial. In spite of the preponderance of suffering in his life, he considered evil to be a mere fraction of the whole. He, as a later poetic pantheist, held that "partial evil makes the general good." Everything is good and tends toward good, he declares; the contrary is only apparent when we refuse to look beyond the present as the beauty of a building is not manifest to one who sees only a part of it—a stone, a piece of cement, a partition wall—but is clearest to one who can see the whole and is able to compare part with part.

As evil is not only partial, it is also relative. It depends on the point of view. Thus Bruno recalls that when as a child he looked from Cicala toward Mount Vesuvius, he thought it dark, gloomy, bare of trees and flowers; but when he approached it, he found it fairer than Cicala itself, while now the latter was bare and dark. However, this specious relative view, that things are often not as bad as they look, is not emphasized. In general, when Bruno had any commerce with the evil of life he used it as a positive means to accomplish his end. As the Stoics taught that men are God's athletes willing to endure hard training, so it was with Bruno. Difficulty, he repeats, is ordained to check poltroons, heroic men constrain necessity to yield them the palm of immortality. In other words, Bruno insistently followed the spirit of his earlier work, written in England, the *Heroic Enthusiasms*, which teaches us that the noble soul can struggle through all difficulties toward union with the divine source of all things.

Such is the message of Bruno's positive optimism. It starts as an antidote to the fear of death, death that "empoisons all that is sweetest in our lives," and ends with a will to believe in the actuality of immortality and in the beauty, harmony, and permanence of nature.

PART SEVEN

THE ENLIGHTENMENT

# I. BENEDICT DE SPINOZA (1632-1677)

"AFTER experience had taught me that all things which frequently take place in ordinary life are vain and futile, when I saw that all the things I feared and which feared me had nothing good or bad in them save in so far as the mind was affected by them, I determined at last to inquire whether there might be anything which might be truly good and able to communicate its goodness, and by which the mind might be affected to the exclusion of all other things: I determined, I say, to inquire whether I might discover and acquire the faculty of enjoying throughout eternity continual supreme happiness.

"I say 'I determined at last,' for at the first sight it seemed ill advised to lose what was certain in the hope of attaining what was uncertain. I could see the many advantages acquired from honour and riches, and that I should be debarred from acquiring these things if I wished seriously to investigate a new matter, and if perchance supreme happiness was in one of these I should lose it; if, on the other hand, it were not placed in them and I gave them the whole of my attention, then also I should be wanting in it.

"I therefore turned over in my mind whether it might be possible to arrive at this new principle, or at least at the certainty of its existence, without changing the order and common plan of my life: a thing which I had often attempted in vain. For the things which most often happen in life and are esteemed as the greatest good of all, as may be gathered from their works, can be reduced to these three headings: to wit, Riches, Fame, and Pleasure. With these three the mind is so engrossed that it can scarcely think of any other good. As for pleasure, the mind is so engrossed in it that it remains in a state of quiescence as if it had attained supreme good, and this prevents it from thinking of anything else. But after that enjoyment follows pain, which, if it does not hold the mind suspended, disturbs and dulls it. The pursuit of fame and riches also distracts the mind not a little, more especially when they are sought for their own sake, inasmuch as they are thought to be the greatest good. By fame the mind is far more distracted, for it is supposed to be always good in itself, and as an ultimate aim to which all things must be directed.

Again, there is not in these, as there is in pleasure, repentance subsequently, but the more one possesses of either of them, the more
the pleasure is increased and consequently the more one is en-
couraged to increase them; but, on the other hand, if at any time
our hope is frustrated, then there arises in us the deepest pain.
Fame has also this great drawback that if we pursue it we must
direct our lives in such a way as to please the fancy of men, avoiding
what they dislike and seeking what is pleasing to them."—Szinopa,
*Ethics*, Everyman Edition.

Benedict de Spinoza's parents were Spanish Jews who had been
driven from that peninsula of persecution by the Inquisition. They
had found refuge in Holland, which in turn had driven out the
Spanish inquisitors in that war of liberation which brought about
the rise of the Dutch republic. Spinoza received his early education
in the Jewish academy in Amsterdam, and from the Old Testament
and the Talmud derived his basic belief in God as the one infinite
being. But the synagogue could not hold him. He came under the
influence of a Dutch physician who had the reputation of being a
freethinker, and in this "school of Satan," as his enemies called it,
studying the new physics and influenced by the new medicine, he
became dissatisfied with the traditional Jewish philosophy. From a
prospective rabbi he turned into a radical, at least in the eyes of his
co-religionists. They feared his defection, tried to buy him off
with a pension, are reported to have connived at his attempted
assassination, and were finally forced to excommunicate him. The
Protestant clergy also counted him a dangerous thinker and had him
banished from Amsterdam. Fortunately, in accordance with the
rabbinical tradition he had been taught a trade—that of grinding
optical glasses. By this he was permitted to live in meagre independence and to devote himself to meditation, for the understanding, he
declares, makes for itself its intellectual instruments wherewith it
acquires further strength for other intellectual works, and with these
makes others again and the power of investigating still further,
and so gradually proceeds until it attains the summit of wisdom.
Spinoza received scant justice, either in his life or in the generations following. He was literally anathematized by the Jews, was
considered dangerous by the Protestants, except for such liberals as
the brothers De Witt, and by the Catholics he was counted a
Sophist who had twisted the most precious definitions of the church
into a gross pantheism, where God and nature, spirit and matter,
were fatally fused. His contemporaries did not appreciate him nor

did his immediate successors. He was called atheistic and infamous; his system was referred to as a "hideous hypothesis." So it remained for a later age and for the period of romanticism to have him called a "God-intoxicated man," or for a less exaggerated and truer description of him: "the purest of Stoics, living well-nigh on nothing."

There is one influence here that throws light on Spinoza's character. For seven years he lived with a minor Protestant sect known as Collegiants, a small body of believers in the inner life with whom William Penn later came in contact. With the "innocent simplicity" which marked this obscure little body of believers Spinoza was in natural sympathy. In both there was the same sweetness of temper, the same contentment with the simple life, and the same abhorrence of strife. This new spirit had crept down the Rhine, through the regions devastated by the Thirty Years' War. It was a product of the persecutions undergone by the Germanic mystics at the hands of both orthodox Catholics and orthodox Protestants. Such were the Collegiants, a branch of the Brethren of the Common Life, whose later and more remote offshoots called themselves Friends. Their teachings must have been a healing balm to Spinoza, with all his pride of race and with a mind conscious of its great powers. The ethics of Spinoza is the ethics of a strong and self-reliant spirit. This is why he refused all pensions, even one at the hands of the great Louis XIV, why he refused the flattering offer of a professorship at Heidelberg, fearing lest his intellectual freedom be curtailed, since Germany was less liberal than Holland, and why he lived out his life in poverty and independence.

## MORAL RESIGNATION

The death of Bruno, the optimist, and the virtual suppression of Galileo, the scientist, were two signs that the Italian intellect was in chains. The torch of knowledge is now transferred to the north of Europe and the Netherlands becomes the beacon of free thought. It was in the hermitage of Holland that Descartes, the great French philosopher and mathematician, sought liberty to speculate. There, too, Benedict de Spinoza, the Jewish pantheist, found freedom to erect his vast system of which the chief part was the work on morals written in the form of a geometry.

This ethical Euclid, this mathematical moralist, starts with a definition of substance as the cause of itself, that which is in itself, and is conceived through itself. Here "substance" means literally that which stands beneath and logically that beneath which nothing else stands. From this follows the first axiom of thought, that all things which are, are in themselves or in other things. After such a definition and such an axiom there come propositions of like nature, for example: One substance cannot be produced by another; existence appertains to the nature of substance; all substance is necessarily infinite; the more reality or being a thing has, the more attributes will it have.

What now is that entity which can fulfil all these conditions? It is none other than God—"a being absolutely infinite, that is, a substance consisting of infinite attributes, each of which expresses eternal and infinite essence." With this initial definition of Deity, Spinoza proceeds to further propositions: Except God, no substance can be granted or conceived; whatever is, is in God, and nothing can exist or be conceived without God.

Whence did Spinoza derive these notions? From Scholasticism. They are modern in form but mediæval in content. Spinoza the Jew uses the very language of the Christian Schoolman Aquinas, and especially of his predecessor Anselm, "the new St. Augustine." It was he who put forward the well-known definitions of Deity as the sum of all things which are, or than which nothing greater can be conceived. These concepts are then used in the famous "proof" of the existence of God, namely, that which is in being as well as in thought is greater than that which is in thought alone; therefore God exists.

Such is the famous Anse mic argument, for it should be called that and not a "proof," since many doubted its validity even before Descartes revived it and gave it the great weight of his authority. Thus Erasmus, the Dutch skeptic in the century before the Frenchman, had written his ironical *Defense of the Fool*—the fool who "hath said in his heart there is no God."

These doubts may be left till later. It is with positive affirmations that we have to do and the practical use made of such affirmations. Spinoza has been called a utilitarian as well as a mystic. He has a veritable vision of all things in God. At times his actual use of geometrical diagrams appears to be a mere study in perspective, but in this study there is no vanishing point. Like Anselm in his "Monologue," like Descartes in his *Meditations*, so Spinoza in his solitary quarters in The Hague put before himself a goal toward which all things tend.

The key to Spinoza's life may be found in his remarks on the power of the intellect. Having treated of the strength of the emotions, he passes to that part of his work which concerns the way which leads to liberty. Mental liberty or blessedness, he explains, is mental satisfaction, and mental satisfaction consists in intellectual love toward God. For from this kind of knowledge arises pleasure, in so far as we understand God as eternal. In this, then, consists our salvation, blessedness, or liberty, since intellectual love toward God is the very love of God with which God loves himself, not in so far as he is infinite, but in so far as he can be expressed "under the species of eternity"; that is, mental intellectual love toward God is part of the infinite love with which God loves himself.

This famous passage has been described as the coldest abstraction ever put forward in Western ethics. The strange phrase "under the species of eternity" has been also translated "under the aspect of eternity" and interpreted to mean as looked at from the divine standpoint. In other words, just as Copernicus revolutionized astronomy by transferring his point of imagined observation to the sun, so would Spinoza revolutionize ethics by transferring himself to the centre of all being. It is an almost presumptuous imperative for man to act as if he had the point of view of the divine mind, yet in a way Spinoza is not as arrogant as he seems. Like Plato, the divine love draws him on, and like Aristotle, it is only in our highest moments that we obtain a glimpse of the divine mentality. Spinoza has defined pleasure as consisting in a transition to a greater state of perfection; in other words, man, being in this state of transition, is imperfect. Nevertheless, inasmuch as the essence of our mind consists of knowledge alone, the beginning and basis of which is God, there is nothing in nature which is contrary to this intellectual love for God, or which can remove it. The proof of this is that this intellectual love follows necessarily from the nature of the mind in so far as it is considered as an eternal truth to the nature of God.

In these various statements as to the intellectual love toward God there would seem to be little moral inspiration. They are bald and forbidding in style, and both the original proposition and the subsequent truth contain the dangerous phrase "in so far as." It may be a mere hypothesis to suggest that the mind of God and the mind of man are of the same essence. Spinoza with his rigid honesty acacknowledges that logically that doubt is possible. So he says: Although we did not know that our mind is eternal, we should hold before all things piety and religion, and absolutely all things which we have shown before to have reference to courage and nobility. Consequently, even without regard to the eternity of the mind, he concludes that the first and only basis of virtue or a system of right living is the seeking of what is useful to oneself.

Spinoza has been called mystic and utilitarian and here is the evidence for that peculiar combination of qualities. That combination has been considered impossible, as if Spinoza were trying to look at two things at once, the divine and the human, the supernatural and the natural. But in a way the problem is no more paradoxical than bifocal vision; as a matter of fact, we see differently with our two eyes, but our vision becomes fused by experience. This, then, is the moral adjustment which Spinoza would make. Considered under the aspect of eternity, all objects fall into line. The divine ideal may exist in the human mind, for the human mind is of like essence with the Deity. This might be called an optical adjustment of two different points of view, but with this qualification—it is not easy and instinctive and common to all mankind as in the case of ordinary vision, but, as Spinoza himself concludes, it is one of those exceptional things as difficult as it is rare. To gain the road to blessedness, to freedom of mind, he insists, is very difficult, yet it can be discovered. An ignorant man, besides being agitated in many ways by external causes, never enjoys one true satisfaction of the mind, but the wise man, in so far as he is considered as such, is scarcely moved in spirit; he is conscious of himself, of God, and of things by a certain eternal necessity, he never ceases to be, and he always enjoys satisfaction of mind.

## MYSTICAL MORALS

In this final note, appended to the *Ethics*, Spinoza has brought to one focus the most divergent rays of speculation, and like a sounding board his mind catches remote echoes of the past. Blessedness, beatitude, the vision of all things in God, form the dominant note of the Middle Ages; the control of the emotions and passions that of the Stoics; satisfaction of mind in the sense of undisturbedness that of the Epicureans. But these notes, dissonant in themselves, are now resolved into a higher harmony. The Middle Ages put the celestial vision in the after life, Spinoza put it here and now; the Stoics, as he specifically declares, were of opinion that the emotions depend absolutely on our free will and that we have absolute command over them, but as the Roman poet confessed, though one may approve of the better, one follows the worse. As for the Epicureans, Spinoza has certain curious affinities with them, but rises far above them. They had a veritable mental hygiene, so had he; but where they were selfish, he was social; where they hesitated over what to take and what to reject as if it were the choice of viands at a feast, he preferred the regimen of privation. Thus he deprived himself not only of a pension but of the luxury of criticizing others. Epicurus had a biting tongue, as when he called one of his teachers, who lacked backbone, a mollusc. But Spinoza showed quite a different attitude toward the teachings of his contemporaries. Thus Descartes, in order to explain the power of the mind over the body, locates the "seat of the soul" in a small gland suspended in the middle of the brain. As to this Spinoza simply remarks: "I cannot sufficiently wonder that a philosophic man who so many times reproved the schoolmen for wishing to explain obscure things by means of occult qualities, should take an hypothesis far more occult than all the occult qualities."

Spinoza disagrees with Descartes as to the power of the mind over the body in moving the pineal gland and thus controlling further hypothetical forces, the animal spirits. This to him is too mechanical; it is too much like opening or shutting a sluice gate in a Dutch canal. He therefore seeks some deeper and less mechanical means of control. In a word, his explanation is not a form of mental hydrostatics but of mental hygiene, in which ideas are controlled by ideas. Descartes had the clue, but he did not use it. His favourite phrase is "clear and distinct idea," but in placing ideas virtually in the brain he brought obscurity instead of clarity. To Spinoza the mind is its own place, inviolate and not to be invaded by outside forces. So, he argues, if we remove disturbance of mind or emotion from the thought of an external cause and unite it to other thoughts, then love or hatred toward the external cause, as well as waverings of the mind which arise from these emotions, are destroyed. Now that which constitutes the form of love or hatred is pleasure or pain accompanied by the idea of an external cause. When this, then, is removed, the form of love or hatred is also removed, and therefore these emotions and those which arise from them are removed. In other words, the emotion which is a passion ceases to be a passion as soon as we form a clear and distinct idea of it.

This is highly interesting. Like the doctrine of Epicurus, it is an anticipation of the mental clinic with its exploration of suppressed complexes and its claim that the exploration is often the cure. But Spinoza goes further and is more precise than the classical thinker. He lived in Holland at a time when the foundations of modern medicine were being laid, and while sojourning in Amsterdam most of his young friends were medical students. Now, as Rembrandt pictured the lesson in anatomy in a bodily sense, so did Spinoza in a mental. Yet his is no anatomy of melancholy but rather of beatitude.

He is acquainted with the dark vapours of depression, but he claims that it may be brought about that "they constitute the least possible part of the mind by a love toward the thing immutable and eternal. This is the way of health, this is the way of salvation—to avoid the love of wrong things, to seek the love of right."

Here, then, are his "remedies for the emotions." First the mind must be "diagnosed" in regard to its inadequate ideas. . . . These unhealthy states of mind and misfortunes owe their origin for the most part to excessive love for a thing that is liable to many variations, and of which we may never seize the mastery. For no one is anxious or cares about anything that he does not love, nor do injuries, suspicions, enmities arise from anything else than love toward a thing of which no one is truly master. From this we can easily conceive what a clear and distinct knowledge, principally that third kind of knowledge, whose basis is the knowledge of God, can do with the emotions, namely, that if it does not remove them entirely in so far as they are passions, at least it brings it about that they constitute the least possible part of the mind. Moreover, it gives rise to a love toward a thing immutable and eternal, and of which we are in truth masters, and which cannot be polluted by any evils which are in common love, but which can become more and more powerful and occupy the greatest part of the mind and deeply affect it.

At this point, observes Spinoza, he has done with all that regards his present life! It is already time that I should pass to those points which appertain to the duration of the mind without relation to the body. This is the problem of the future life, of immortality. The human mind cannot be absolutely destroyed with the human body, but there is some part of it that remains eternal. We feel and we know that we are eternal, for the eyes of the mind by which it sees things and observes them are proofs. In other words, the mind has to be eternal to understand the eternal One, and this understanding under the aspect of eternity, as has already been said, makes us partakers of the Divine Essence.

In this conclusion Spinoza has returned to the point at which he started. To many it has seemed reasoning in a circle, a long spun-out argument based on the very first definition in the first part of the *Ethics* entitled "Concerning God," namely, that the cause of itself is that whose essence involves existence. Though Spinoza may beg the question by starting with a dubious definition, his logic and his life were consistent. In that bit of autobiography, the *Correction of the Understanding*, he declares that after experience had taught him that all things which take place in human life are vain and futile, he determined to inquire whether he might discover and acquire the faculty of enjoying throughout eternity continual supreme happiness. In this determination, made as a private programme of conduct, he ran counter to much that was commonly taught. The general notion of the public, he observes, seems to be quite the contrary. They hope to receive a reward for their servitude, that is, their piety and religion. Not by this hope alone, but also, and even principally, by the fear of suffering dreadful punishments after death, are they induced to live as far as their feebleness and weakmindedness allow them according to the divine laws.

This was a criticism of institutional religion, and explains the obloquy cast on Spinoza by both Protestants and Catholics. Yet it is not said in a spirit of bitterness, but only to prove that disinterested motives are the best motives. To those who would follow his way, and he had many who followed it in later generations, the lonely thinker uttered this warning: Blessedness is not the reward of virtue, but virtue itself: nor should we rejoice in it for that we restrain our lusts, but, on the contrary, because we rejoice therein we can restrain our lusts.

Intellectual happiness is thus the aim and end of the wise man. For this he should be willing to give up the popular idea of freedom. Belief in free will is an illusion and a folly. Here Spinoza in certain letters to his friend Oldenburg declares that St. Paul was right when he said that men are in God's power as clay in the hands of the potter. No man can bring complaint against God for having given him a weak nature or an infirm body. A circle might as well complain to God of not being endowed with the properties of a sphere, as a man of feeble spirit complain because God has denied to him fortitude and the true knowledge and love of the Deity. This is a hard saying, but once choose the royal road of necessity and the journey is easy. Man should identify himself with the universal necessity; God and nature are one and the same, human nature is part of universal nature, therefore man should acquiesce in the divine order.

It seems strange that Spinoza should come to such a blank denial of freedom in a land where liberty of conscience was counted the right of all citizens. But he exercised this very privilege in choosing the doctrine of necessity in preference to that of the more popular doctrine of free will. To him will and intellect were one and the same thing. This he proves to his own satisfaction by the argument of the infinite regress: There is no mind absolute or free will, but the mind is determined by willing this or that by a cause which is determined in its turn by another cause, and this one again by another, and so on through infinity. This means that in the moral life actions are determined by motives, and motives are ideas. Or, as Spinoza puts it: There is in mind no volition, or affirmation and negation, save that which the idea, in so far as it is an idea, involves. In proof of this, he continues, let us conceive any individual volition, namely, the mode of thinking, whereby the mind affirms that three angles of a triangle are equal to two right angles. It can be said of this volition (for it was selected at random) what can be said of any other voli- tion, namely, that it is nothing but an idea. However, most people think that ideas are fabrications which we invent by our own free will; they therefore regard ideas as "lifeless pictures on a board."

This is mathematical morality with a vengeance. Ideas are not mere diagrams on a blackboard, but motives which move. As we have to say such and such a thing about a triangle when the idea of a triangle is presented to us, so we have to act according to that idea which contains more reality or perfection than another. In other words, men are mistaken in thinking themselves free; they are con- scious of their actions but ignorant of the causes by which they are determined. Their idea of liberty is that they should know no cause of their actions; they utter meaningless words when they say that human actions depend on the will, for none of them know what is will and how it moves the body.

In these statements Spinoza has extended mathematics into mechanics. Just as he has treated the passions as if they were paral- lelograms, in the same cold-blooded way he treats actions as if they could be calculated by a parallelogram of forces, when the resultant simply expresses the preponderance of one force over another. But in all this he is simply following the method of his day. The French- man Descartes had already declared that man was a machine and the Englishman Hobbes that our ideas are merely "apparitions" or appearances caused by the perpetual propagation of pressures upon the brain. Spinoza goes even further. In treating of the correction of the understanding and of the way in which it may be directed toward a true knowledge of things he makes such statements as these: Sensation is nothing else than sensation of impressions on the brain; the soul acts according to certain laws and resembles a spiritual automaton.

We have now reached the explanation of the Dutch philosopher's attack on the doctrine of liberty in the land of liberty. He has al- ready said that the human mind should be a part of the infinite intellect of God; now he goes further. Man is not only a machine but a part of the infinite world machine. As mind and matter are but two attributes or aspects of the divine reality, called indifferently God or nature, so our minds and our bodies are but minor aspects of the same stupendous totality. This was the grand conception that staggered the imagination of Spinoza's day and generation; they could not understand it, so they attacked it, and as it would be absurd to consider Spinoza a mere weak defendant, because he was perfectly able to defend himself, all they could do was to abuse the plaintiff, calling him variously atheist, fatalist, and underminer of morals because he found no purpose or design in the workings of the world, therefore no compelling motive.

The first charge was false. Spinoza contrasts fictitious ideas with eternal truths, but he declares that the first and eternal truth is "God is." The next charge is true. Spinoza was a fatalist, but so were the very authorities in whom his adversaries trusted. He quotes St. Paul as to man's being clay in the hands of the potter; he resembles St. Augustine and St. Thomas in arguing that, God being the immanent cause of all reality, all events come to pass because of the necessity of his nature. As for the denial of purposiveness, he is more consistent than the apostle of old, or the fathers of the church. He argues that God does not act with an end in view because that would imply something unattained and therefore imperfect, but God is perfect. In fine, purposiveness is a figment of the human imagination; there are no final ends to the universe; things are because they are; when we try to discover reasons why events happen we must resort to the sanctuary of nescience, the asylum of ignorance, and put them in the will of God.

## II.   THOMAS HOBBES (1588–1679)

"THE question who is the better man has no place in the condition of mere nature; where, as has been shown before, all men are equal. The inequality that now is, has been introduced by the laws civil. I know that Aristotle in the first book of his *Politics*, for a foundation of his doctrine, maketh men by nature, some more worthy to command, meaning the wiser sort, such as he thought himself to be for his philosophy; others to serve, meaning those that had strong bodies, but were not philosophers as he; as if master and servant were not introduced by consent of men, but by difference of wit; which is not only against reason, but also against experience. For there are very few so foolish, that had not rather govern themselves, than be governed by others: nor when the wise in their own conceit, contend by force, with them who distrust their own wisdom, do they always, or often, or almost at any time, get the victory. If nature therefore have made them equal, that equality is to be acknowledged: or if nature have made men unequal; yet because men that think themselves equal will not enter into conditions of peace, but upon equal terms, such equality must be admitted. And therefore for the ninth law of nature, I put this, *that every man acknowledge another for his equal by nature*. The breach of this precept is *pride*.

"On this law dependeth another, *that at the entrance into conditions of peace, no man require to reserve to himself any right, which he is not content should be reserved to every one of the rest*. As it is necessary for all men that seek peace, to lay down certain rights of nature; that is to say, not to have liberty to do all they list: so is it necessary for man's life, to retain some, as right to govern their own bodies; enjoy air, water, motion, ways to go from place to place; and all things else, without which a man cannot live, or not live well."—HOBBES: *Leviathan*. Ed. Molesworth, Chapter XV.

The life of Hobbes is given us in a quaint contemporary account: His father, Vicar of Charlton and Westport, was one of the "ignorant Sir Johns of Queen Elizabeth's time," who could only read the prayers and homilies of the church and valued not learning. So the son was educated by an uncle at a local school whence at the age of fourteen, with precocious skill in Latin verse, he was sent to Oxford. Here, to his mind, the scholastic logic furnished nourishment fit only for worms and geometry was counted a black art. Because of this latter obstruction it was not until the age of forty that Hobbes "fell in love with geometry" on meeting with the works of Euclid. Reading the forty-seventh proposition of the first book, "By God," he exclaimed, "this is impossible," but referring back to other positions he was at last demonstratively convinced of that truth.

This meeting with a famous book was significant, but meeting with a famous man was more so. In the continental tour which Hobbes took as tutor with the third Earl of Cavendish he visited the great Galileo, then confined in his tower outside of Florence by the Inquisition. Through him an interest in physics was added to an interest in geometry and Hobbes from now on started to build up a mechanical philosophy of life. Through this philosophy the actions of politicians could be explained as clearly as the actions of planets, and moral motives reduced themselves to veritable motions starting the very springs of conduct. From that mighty atom—the state—

## NICCOLO MACHIAVELLI
"Morals are weaker than arms"

down to those tiny atoms—men—the whole of society can be seen to be nothing but a mechanism whose stresses and strains, actions and reactions, furnish sufficient reason for the behaviour of the highest statesman as well as of the lowest yokel.

This sounds like the crudest kind of behaviourism, but traces of it are still to be found on all sides: in statecraft as the study of the balance of power between rival nations; in political science as the study of the political machine where the executive, legislative, and judicial powers are looked upon as so many weights and counter-weights, and finally in morality as the pulling and hauling of conflicting motives. These views may be crude as explanations, but they are serviceable as descriptions. Nowadays men still speak of wars as due to unfavourable trade balances, of elections being won by an overwhelming weight of public opinion, and of crimes being committed because of suppressed complexes or to relieve pent-up emotions. In short, statesmen, politicians, and psychologists still talk respectively in terms of mechanics, physics, and hydrostatics and in so far as they do this belong to the school of Hobbes.

Another influence on Hobbes—sometimes denied but wrongly so —was that of Francis Bacon, for Hobbes's biographer particularly says: "The Lord Chancellor loved to converse with him and his lordship would often say that he better liked Mr. Hobbes's taking his thoughts than any of the others." Following his master, who advocated the advancement of learning, his secretary contended that it is not through metaphysics that advancement is made, but through mathematics and mechanics. Here, then, in the England of revolutionary days, when the King and Cromwell were at swords' points, there were laid the foundations of a political ethics which had great influence on modern civilization. Hobbes's system, which began with the doctrine of the social contract—agreed upon by primitive men in woods and deserts to prevent "a war of all against all"—was not only revolutionary in itself, but contained the seeds of future revolutions. In England it led to a study of the respective rights of king and people, in France to the watchwords of liberty, equality, and fraternity, and in America it was at the bottom of that terse advice of Benjamin Franklin to his fellow colonials, then in rebellion against the crown, "Unless we all hang together we shall all hang separately."

Hobbes's influence was perhaps greater on his successors than on his contemporaries. This was because of his constitutional timidity, which made him a man of peace at any price. His biographer calls him "an harmonicall soule," which being interpreted means a compromiser. He was never, says the account, habitually a good fellow, for to drink every day with company spoils the brain, still I have heard him say that he has been drunk in his life a hundred times, which, considering his great age, did not amount to above once a year.

Hobbes's compromising spirit, which lay at the bottom of his principles such as the social compact, also extended to his practices. When his chief work, *Leviathan*, was counted suspect by a crown committee for the suppression of atheism and profanity he is reputed to have made a show of conformity to the established creed. And when some of the bigots made a motion to have the good old gentleman burned for a heretic he, says his biographer, fearing that his papers might be searched by their order, told me that he had burned part of them. But Charles II was a friend of Hobbes and the Merry Monarch, in spite of his other weaknesses, stood by his friend. When the wits of the court were wont to bait the old philosopher, the King would say, "Here comes the bear to be baited." And Hobbes would be "marvellous happy and ready in his replies." So Hobbes lived on, for as his biographer again relates, "he had a good eye which was full of life and spirit even to his last."

## MORALS AND THE STATE

Spinoza is a significant figure standing at the crossroads of two divergent lines of thought, the mediæval and the modern. The former for the time being is blocked, for it ends in the barrier of agnosticism. The latter must now be tried, for it promises a certain advancement in learning. At this juncture men are urged to abandon the high *a priori* road of speculation and be content with the low road of experience, where "by painful steps and slow" some progress may be made. Francis Bacon, Lord Chancellor of England, advocated this. Thomas Hobbes, his secretary, now puts it in practice. It is not by metaphysics that advancement is made, but by mathematics and mechanics. As Bacon had said, the mediæval doctrines of substance and essence were but barren virgins; what science demands is not fancies but fruits. Reason has been too rash, the mind needs weights and not wings. Unconsciously influenced by his master, Hobbes followed these precepts. First he avoided the supernatural. He considers it unprofitable to discuss entities that are "refined enough to escape the sense," such as angels and spirits. To him substances without bodies are a contradiction and books that contain nothing about matter and motion are so much waste paper.

We must therefore switch from the theological to the rational, leave things unattainable by speculation, and seek for those which may be known by the senses.

This is no mean project. It may abandon the hope of heaven and eternal peace, but consider what it will do: Were the nature of human actions as distinctly known as the nature of quantity in geometrical figures, reasons Hobbes, the strength of avarice and ambition, which is sustained by the erroneous opinions of the vulgar as touching the nature of right and wrong, would presently faint and languish, and mankind enjoy such an immortality of peace that (unless it were for habitation, on supposition that the earth should grow too narrow for her inhabitants) there would hardly be left any pretense for war.

This is an ambitious programme; it is a universai mechanical philosophy of life. The theologians had tried their hand, let the rationalists now try theirs. There are three concepts to be considered —nature, man, the state. The physical world is a vast contrivance consisting of nothing but matter and motion, atoms and aggregations of atoms acting according to the laws of mathematics. Man is likewise a contrivance, a machine; as in all animals there are two sorts of motion peculiar to him. One is called vital; it is begun in generation and continued without interruption throughout his whole life; such are the course of the blood, the pulse, breathing, nutrition, excretion. The other is animal motion, otherwise called voluntary; as to go, to speak, to move any of our limbs in such manner as is first fancied in our minds. Now these small beginnings of motion, within the body of man, before they begin in walking, speaking, striking, and other visible actions, are commonly called endeavour. So, although unstudied men do not conceive any motion at all to be there when the thing moved is invisible, there really exists back of the screen of the mind brain movements, or the fine movements of atoms in the nerves.

All this is clear and concise, perhaps too much so. It is a great temptation to simplify the mind and its activities into a machine, for a machine can be understood fairly easily. So Hobbes goes on and insists that what happens back of the scenes has its counterpart on the stage of consciousness. Brain movements and mental states are really one and the same. There are those small beginnings of motion before they appear in visible action, as Hobbes has already said; hence our ideas are but "apparitions" of those movements and we have no knowledge of aught save our brain state.

This is highly modern; it is the doctrine of the subjectivity of sense perceptions; it means that objects are not in themselves hot or cold, red or blue, but only appear to us to be such. The mind is an interpreting machine; external bodies are presented to it through the brain as an intermediary and through "the perpetual propagation of pressures"—such as heat waves, light waves, and the like. Their qualities are called hot or cold, red or blue.

Now apply this to morals. Take the objects of any man's appetite or desire. These objects are of two kinds: those which by some apparent sign promise good, and those which by some apparent sign promise evil. These again may be subdivided into three kinds: good in the promise, that is fair or beautiful; good in effect, as the end desired, which is called delightful; and good as the means, which is called profitable. Corresponding to these there are as many kinds of evil: evil in promise, that is base or ugly; evil in effect, as the end not desired, which is called unpleasant, troublesome; and evil in the means, which is called hurtful, unprofitable.

Hobbes is here translating various Latin terms in order to obtain the meaning of the words "good" and "evil." In the case of the good the emphasis is upon the profitable or useful, which has led some to call him the founder of the utilitarian school. At any rate, the practise of morals with him consists in the employment of means conducive to man's chief end, which is self-preservation. Just as the system of physical nature is held together by the attraction of gravitation, so is the system of human nature or society held together by the social compact. However, in a way, this is not a law of nature, but an artifice whereby mankind in ages long past has kept itself from going to pieces. As the original state of physical nature was a clash of atoms, so the original state of mankind was "a war of all against all." Authorities like Aristotle and the Dutch jurist Grotius have called man a peculiarly social animal, and the ancient poets have imagined an original golden age when brethren dwelt together in unity. This is false. As Lucretius, the Epicurean atomist, has more properly said, "Man is a wolf to man." This does not mean that he was by nature corrupt, but that he was a mere animal before he was a social animal. He was selfish because of the harsh struggle for existence, but this could not last; instead of self-preservation there would be mutual destruction; hence the exigencies of self-preservation itself demanded a step forward; consequently there arose the social compact.

This line of argument is not only realistic but familiar. It may show a certain ignorance of the prehistoric, for we are now pretty well convinced that as man's remotest ancestors hunted in packs, so did primitive man exist in tribes. Cave men were not so many Robinson Crusoes, but groups who had somehow agreed not to disagree. Pre-history contradicts the theory of Hobbes, but history corroborates it. His notion of the social compact was quite familiar in the statements: "In union there is strength," "United we stand, divided we fall."

Like conditions bring about like opinions. Hobbes lived in a time of civic dissension and social unrest. The results of the dreadful Thirty Years' War lay palpable before him. There was anything but a social compact between the contending forces, Catholic and Protestant. Spinoza had sought refuge from this state of affairs by solitary meditation. His correspondent, Leibnitz, the German optimist, with the same war in mind, was to seek another solution by imagining that this was the best possible world. But Hobbes was neither a contemplater of abstract essences nor a builder of ingenious card houses of hope. He lived in England at a time when the court was a palace of selfish pleasure and the Puritans were doing all they could to take the joy out of life, when Charles I was dallying with his mistresses and Cromwell sharpening the ax. But before the King was executed and before England was living under the Lord Protector and the Commonwealth, Hobbes put his finger on the pulse of this feverish state of affairs. As he wrote to his young patron, the Earl of Devonshire, in 1641: "The dispute for precedence between the civil and the spiritual power has of late, more than any other thing in the world, been the cause of civil wars in all parts of Christendom."

What, then, is the cure for these unhappy conditions? Machiavelli, in his cynical picture of a prince without scruples, advocated a politics without ethics; Hobbes advocates a politics with ethics; not an imagined perfect ruler, but a ruler with power based on reason. But here Hobbes is in a quandary. In whom shall the sovereign power reside, in the king, or the people, or in both? He had seen Britain under a "mixed monarchy"—on one hand the crown, on the other the Parliament—and this arrangement he considered chiefly to blame for the civil wars, red with the burning of cathedrals and the blood of Charles the Martyr.

In all this Hobbes had a veiled contempt for the Parliament "as an aristocracy of orators." He preferred a strong man of action like Cromwell to a set of talkers like Praise-God Barebones. But these are two extremes, therefore in his chief work, the *Leviathan*, he observes that it is hard to pass unwounded in a way beset with those that contend on the one side for too great liberty, and on the other for too much authority. His solution is a compromise between these two, which correspond to the first and second natural laws. In preserving his life against his enemies, every man has a right to everything, even to another's body. But from this fundamental law of nature is derived this second law: that a man be willing, when others are so, too, to lay down this right to all things, and be contented with so much liberty against other men as he would allow other men against himself, for so long as every man holdeth this right of doing anything he liketh, so long are all men in a condition of war. This is that law of the Gospel: Whatsoever you require that others should do to you, that do ye to them; and this is that law of all men: Whatsoever you do not wish should be done unto you, that do ye not unto another.

By means of the negative Golden Rule, Hobbes seeks to attain the golden mean between too much liberty and too much authority. But here he insists we must not confound *jus* and *lex*, right and law; right consisting in liberty to do, while law or obligation determines and binds. Now the right of every man to do anything leads nowhere, for unless a man is protected in his rights he runs the risk of losing them. Hence from that law of nature, by which we are obliged to transfer to another such rights, there follows a third which is this: that men perform their covenants. In this law consisteth the fountain and original of justice. If every man has right to do everything, no action can be unjust. But when a covenant of mutual trust is made, then to break it is unjust. Therefore, before the names of just and unjust can have place there must be some coercive power to compel men equally to the performance of their covenant, by the terror of some punishment, greater than the benefit they expect by the breach of their covenant.

## MORALITY AND MONARCHY

So far Hobbes is highly consistent. As the mind is an aggregate of sensations following the mechanical law of the association of ideas, so the state is an aggregate of men following the mechanical law of association of interests. In other words, the fundamental law of self-preservation develops into enlightened self-interest. Civil society is a prudential society bound together for mutual benefit. While this is enlightened selfishness, it is still selfishness. From it follows the fourth law, that of gratitude, where no man giveth but with intention of good to himself; the fifth law, that of complaisance, where every man strives to accommodate himself to the rest, just as stones of diverse nature are brought together for building an edifice.

Such is the first half of the Hobbite ten commandments. Here more briefly are the rest: that upon caution of the future time a man ought to pardon the offenses past of them that repent; that in revenge, that is retribution of evil for evil, men look not at the greatness of the evil past, but the greatness of the good to follow; that no man by deed, word, countenance, or gesture declare hatred or contempt of another; that every man acknowledge another for his equal by nature; and lastly, the tenth law of nature, that at the entrance into the conditions of peace, no man require to reserve for himself any right which he is not content should be reserved to every one of the rest. As it is necessary for all men that seek peace to lay down certain rights of nature—that is to say, not to have liberty to do all they list—so is it necessary for man's life to retain some, as right to govern their own bodies, enjoy air, water, motion, ways to go from place to place, and all things else, without which a man cannot live, or not live well.

The decalogue of Hobbes is an extraordinary document. It rings with the echoes of familiar phrases—the life, liberty, and pursuit of happiness of the American Revolution and the liberty, equality, and fraternity of the French. But alongside these catchwords of the revolutionaries, these glittering generalities of political enthusiasts, lay the more sober phrases of conservative and constructive men— teachings concerning solemn covenants and mutual trusts, natural rights and reserved rights, which furnished the very fabric of constitutional government. These are the laws of nature, continues Hobbes, dictating peace, for the means of the conservation of men in multitudes; they are immutable and eternal, for injustice, ingratitude, arrogance, pride, iniquity, contempt of persons, and the rest which the law of nature hath forbidden can never be made lawful. For it can never be that war shall preserve life, and peace destroy it.

Judging from the familiarity of its phrases, Hobbes's system had a vast influence on political ethics. Like the "diverse stones brought together for the building of an edifice," it furnished a veritable quarry of varied doctrines utilized by the radical and revolutionary, by the conservative and constructive, and even by the reactionary and ultraconservative. In this last class Hobbes finally put himself for reasons both personal and political. The personal reasons are curious. Following the occult thinking of his day, he sought even prenatal influences to explain his own character. In an autobiographic poem he tells the reader that he was prematurely born through his mother's terror at the coming of the Spanish Armada, and that she bore as twins "himself and fear." As for the political reasons, he confessed that when civil rebellion threatened he was the first that fled to France. There in his eleven years of exile he wrote the *Leviathan*, which brought further apprehensions. In this work he made two statements that offended two parties—the Roman Catholics because he asserted that no religion is infallible, the Royalists because he suggested that when a commonwealth is unable to protect its citizens in peace, a new sovereign commonwealth should be formed.

Suspected of both heresy and treason, Hobbes proceeded warily. The church had sent out its warnings and Hobbes knew, as did all men, what had happened to Giordano Bruno and what had happened to Galileo shut up in his tower of imprisonment near Florence. It was such common knowledge that made Hobbes flee from Paris lest the Roman Catholics should murder him for his remarks on religion. But when the refugee returned to England in 1651 further difficulties awaited him. Two years before Charles I had been executed, the country was living under a commonwealth with the Cavaliers routed and the Roundheads in power. The Puritan "saints" called themselves "a peculiar people," and Hobbes probably agreed with them, but while acquiescing in the rule of Cromwell and while defining "Leviathan" as the power of a commonwealth, Hobbes was at heart a monarchy man. He did not advocate the divine right of kings, but basing his notions of government on natural law and the original covenant, he substituted thereby a stronger foundation for autocracy.

Early editions of the *Leviathan* have a quaint title page with the figure of the ruler as a monstrous man made up of little men. This allegory is carried out in the proposition that the covenant between man and man originally created "that great Leviathan called the Commonwealth or State, which is but an artificial man, though of greater stature and strength than the natural, for whose protection and defense it was defended."

Hobbes here reminds one of Bunyan's Mr. Facing-Both-Ways. At first he was all for natural rights and the liberty of the creature; now he is for the surrender of those rights and for royal despotism. Theoretically he seemed to offer an ideal commonwealth where liberty should not run into license because checked by law, and law should not turn into tyranny because checked by liberty. But practically in a mixed monarchy, such as the author was acquainted with, there is no perfect balance between the two powers—that of the people and that of the king. Furthermore, judging from the civil war and the execution of the King, the Parliament had usurped the power of the sovereign. It had confounded the two fundamental laws of nature, and in turning its natural rights into national laws democracy had gone too far. So Hobbes asks the reader these questions: How many kings (and those good men, too) has this one error, that a tyrant king might lawfully be put to death, been the slaughter of? How many throats has this false position cut, that a prince for some causes may by some certain men be deposed? And what bloodshed has not this erroneous doctrine caused, that kings are not superiors to but administrators for the multitude? Lastly, how many rebellions has this opinion been the cause of, which teaches that the knowledge whether the commands of kings be just or unjust belongs to private men, and that, before they yield obedience, they not only may but ought to dispute them?

This seems a surrender of Hobbes's original principles, and such it was. He had made a distinction between liberty and obligation, between right and law, between *jus* and *lex*. He had condemned those who had confounded that distinction, but now he is himself guilty of confusion worse confounded. Natural right by the consent of the governed had been crystallized into law. The Puritan Parliament had emphasized the freedom of that consent. Consequently, as one of the great defenders of Parliament had implied in the very title of his book, *Lex Rex*, law is king. To Hobbes this would never do. Frightened by civil war and horrified by the beheading of the monarch, he would reverse this title. Hence the meaning of the *Leviathan* becomes "the king is law," and its final message is that the power once lodged in the royal hands is inalienable, that is, never again to be transferred back into the hands of the people.

It remained for a later political moralist to modify these extreme results. John Locke, as did Hobbes, derived political authority from the just consent of the governed and adopted the commonweal as the end of government. But though he lived in the time of the Restoration, when the Stuarts returned to the throne, Locke made no timid conclusions that the powers of the people once lodged in the crown were inalienable. He taught the rights of resistance and the responsibility of the prince for that which he held in trust, and insisted that in case of misuse the rights of royalty were not irrevocable but might be recalled by the people.

Hobbes had no such courageous outlook. According to his own account, fear pursued him from the cradle onward through life.

He declared, it may be recalled, that at his birth "myself and fear were twins." After the Restoration, when Charles II returned to the throne, he records that he considered the great fire of London to be a divine warning against the impurity of the English court. This persistent note of timidity is also to be found in his emphasis upon complaisance and caution as among the laws of nature and in his definition of Leviathan as "that mortal God who hath the use of so much power and strength conferred upon him, that by terror thereof he is enabled to perform the wills of them all." In other words, Hobbes's political ethics, which began with an insistence on natural rights and the equality of all men, degenerated into an instrument of peace at any price through non-resistance and passive obedience. So at least it was taken to be by the monarchy men and the advocates of the absolute power of the sovereign.

This is paradoxical. Hobbes's great work is utilized by some as a document of reaction; by others as a charter of liberty. The latter use of it was made by the American colonists in their struggle against the arbitrary power of the British crown. Thus Jonathan Mayhew, a colleague of James Otis, delivered certain "Discourses Concerning Unlimited Submission and Non-resistance to the Higher Powers—With Some Reflections on the Resistance Made to Charles I." Similar views were expressed by William Livingstone, just twenty years before the Declaration of Independence, in his remarks on "the divine rights of royal roguery. . . .'Twas a damnable sin to resist the cutting of throats and no virtue more Christian and refulgent than that of a passive submission to butchery and slaughter. To propagate such fustian in America argues a disposition prone to senility. . . . But there are two species of monarch. In absolute monarchies a vindication of the natural rights of mankind is treason, but in limited governments there are inherent rights and fundamental reservations. Therefore the right of self-defense is not a donation of law but a primitive right prior to all political institutions, resulting from the nature of man and inhering in the people till expressly alienated and transferred, if it be not in its nature inalienable."

Hobbes's system opens up two great vistas, one into the future and one into the past. In the latter case it exhibits the break with ecclesiastical ethics by going back to the original rights of mankind prior to revelation. Here the Dutch jurist Grotius, upon whom Hobbes partly depends, had expressed a view that natural law is a dictate of right reason, and that man's peculiar "appetite" for tranquil association with his fellows is as unalterable, even by God himself, as the truths of mathematics. This law, discoverable by the light of nature, apart from revelation, was acknowledged even by Thomas Aquinas, who in turn received it from Cicero by way of Augustine. Cicero finally received it from his master, the Stoic Posidonius, who believed in an original state of nature, social in part, but not yet political, a state in which individuals or single families had lived side by side under natural laws prohibiting mutual injury and mutual interference with each other's use of the goods that were common to all.

Views like these, embodied in the *Leviathan*, awakened suspicions of Hobbes's loyalty to the throne. He had been mathematical tutor to Charles II during the latter's exile in France. He now expressed a hope that the *Leviathan* would fall into the hands of a sovereign who would consider it himself without the help of any interested or envious interpreter, and by the exercise of entire sovereignty, in protecting the public teaching of it, convert this truth of speculation into the utility of practice.

But the Merry Monarch was not interested in the fiction of the original social contract, nor in the additional fiction that, in order to obtain "the conservation of men in multitudes," the people had virtually made a second contract by which their rights were perpetually vested in the person of the king. With customary official stupidity the book was burned by the common hangman and all that Hobbes could do was to derive a certain sardonic satisfaction, to judge from his quiet observation that the book's price had gone up from six to thirty shillings.

PART EIGHT

MORALS OF REVOLT

# I. VOLTAIRE (1694–1778)

"He is usually praised as a satirist, and satire is indeed a true description of these innumerable pamphlets; but it is not a vituperative or gross satire. Sarcasm, raillery, irony, wit, are the Voltairean weapons; he rarely breaks into serious denunciation and reproof, and still more rarely loses his temper, though when he does either his satire loses its force and skill. The mood of Voltairean satire is complex, and is expressed metaphorically in the traditional Voltairean smile of Houdon's statue. That smile is malicious but humorous, sarcastic but not unkindly; it is that of a tolerant and witty man whose intelligence is prodigiously alert. And these are the qualities of Voltaire's prose satire. Human beings alternately aroused his pity and his mirth; their crimes and follies exasperated him, but he thought men could more easily be laughed and mocked than reproved and denounced out of them. At times the imbecilities of human conduct and of human systems left him aghast; but he took pity on us—poor ignorant creatures seduced by priests, crowned fools, stupid ideals, and mad prejudices—and laboured ceaselessly to enlighten us with the truths of '*la saine philosophie*' though with no great hope of permanently reforming us. 'In the name of common sense, act a little reasonably and learn to face facts' is the burden of these numberless diatribes. On the whole, the Voltairean satire is an encouragement not to look at things and life too solemnly and lugubriously. Let us be reasonable, but let us make life endurable; we may not be immortal, the world may be and probably is a mass of ills, sufferings, and stupidities, but for God's sake let us crack a jest when we may. Let us, in fact, model ourselves upon the sage of Ferney; let us be active, industrious, sober, witty, ironic, philanthropic, Deistic, well-informed, and cheerful Rationalists; the deuce take the Pope and Rousseau, the Jesuits and the Jansenists, Leibnitz and Calvin, all the fanatics and the excessive, gloomy misanthropy and absurd optimism; let us mind our own business and cultivate our own gardens. Ithuriel, the guardian genius of the earth, having received Babouc's report, 'resolved to allow the world to go its way; for said he, if all is not well, it is all tolerable.' This is the 'lesson' of many of these brilliant little pieces; it is madness to hope for the earthly paradise, fantastic to assert that all is well with the world, idiotic to be gloomy about it; make the best of what you have."— RICHARD ALDINGTON, *Voltaire*.

François Marie Arouet was the real name of the writer who by an ingenious anagram derived therefrom the better known name of Voltaire. His father was a notary, his mother of noble extraction; from the former he obtained a fortune and from the latter an entrance into polite society. These two factors guaranteed this precocious youth an exceptional education at the College of Louis-le-Grand, which was under the management of the Jesuits. The latter, following the traditions of the Renaissance, made much of writing and acting, and this served to determine not only Voltaire's devotion to the stage but his prolific output of plays. His life matched his writings; it was a dramatic career marked by successive theatrical effects. At first Voltaire was but a fashionable trifler, but suspicion of his being the author of a libel against the Regent brought about his arrest and imprisonment in the Bastille. It was there that he changed his name, but not the free use of his sharp tongue. For an alleged insult to the Chevalier Rohan he was again sent to the Bastille by this unchivalric noble, but within a fortnight was shipped off to England. This was the turning point in his life. As the result of his visit and of his defense of the British principles of religious toleration, of freedom of speech and the press, his reputation was changed from that of a vain scoffer to that of a philosopher fighting for the natural rights of man in civilized society.

In all this he may be compared with another advocate of the same principles who went but halfway. Hobbes started with the principle of liberty in the making of the social compact, but surrendered that principle in matters civil, legal, and religious to an absolute monarch. With the Frenchman there was no surrender, but a life-long struggle for liberty of the person as against arbitrary arrest, for liberty of speech and writing as against censorship, and for liberty of opinion as against forced acquiescence in dogma. Because of his timid temperament, Hobbes had come to advocate peace at any price; Voltaire was of an opposite temperament and with subtle wit and irony opposed to the last the oppressive measures of a political tyranny buttressed by the spiritual powers of the church.

This naturally got him into more trouble. His *Letters on the English* were burned by the common hangman, he himself was pursued by the authorities, and found refuge in the independent Duchy of Lorraine in the château of Madame du Châtelet, a distinguished bluestocking. There he increased his fame as chief European critic of established ideas, and from that retreat, by a strange irony of fate, was invited by Frederick the Great, King of Prussia, to be his guest at Potsdam. An inevitable split arose between these rival dictators, one in the realm of literature, the other in politics. Upon this Voltaire, now a wealthy man, for he was astute in financial speculations as in dramatic satire, withdrew to Switzerland where at his estate at Ferney he became, in his own words, the "Innkeeper of Europe." This meant that he entertained a perfect host of the distinguished people of his day, people who were attracted to this old satirist whose bright eyes peered out of his strange wig, and whose tongue was ready to castigate any wrong that came to his notice in those famous letters which were read all over the Continent.

His reputation now becoming as immense as his correspondence, Voltaire was invited back to France. He was received with the greatest enthusiasm in Paris, was crowned with laurel at the performance of his latest play, and as a final triumph, was acclaimed at the Academy along with Benjamin Franklin, who in compliment was called "that other Voltaire" from across the seas.

## THE FIGHTING PHILOSOPHER

Living in the reign of the successor of that monarch who had said "I am the state," Voltaire had bitter personal experience of the Bastille which imprisoned enemies of the court, of police power which burned unwelcome books, and of the Inquisition which broke heretics on the wheel.

These were the conditions faced by Voltaire in the France of Louis XV. His exile to England was a blessing in disguise. By the time of Queen Anne and Horace Walpole the old restraints of the Stuarts had largely disappeared, and Voltaire there found in practice what he advocated in theory. There was the principle of toleration propounded by Locke in his great essay on that subject; there was freedom of the press which allowed criticism of the government; and there was the fine old British maxim that just as every man's house is his castle, so every man's mind is his own preserve of private opinions into which no outsider may intrude.

The fruits of Voltaire's enforced exile were his *Letters on the English*. By the decree of the Parliament of Paris these were publicly burned as scandalous and contrary alike to good manners and the respect due to principalities and powers. The real reason for this suppression lay in the series of ironical contrasts made between the two rival countries. England, says the author, has thirty kinds of religion but only one kind of soup; its bill of fare may be meagre but its bill of rights is ample. If there were one religion in England, they would have to fear its despotism; if there were only two, they would cut one another's throats; but there are thirty; so they live peaceably and happily together. In England, continues Voltaire, people have had two eyes for more than two hundred years. The French are starting to open one eye, but sometimes there are men in power who do not want to have even this one eye open. In England, still further, people do not believe that we are born with innate ideas any more than we are born with beards.

And so this telling contrast goes on with an irony that simply infuriated the authorities. That was exactly what Voltaire wanted. He knew that though his book might be burned, its ashes would fertilize the soil of free thought. The state and the church might try to suppress it, but the truth would keep on growing. Take the case of a sect that would never have been allowed to take root in France, namely the Society of Friends. When even the English derided the Quakers in giving them that nickname Voltaire praised them for the simplicity of their life, their repudiation of ritual, and their abhorrence of war. In this he made an implicit contrast with the state of affairs on the continent. To-day, he says, one half of Europe thinks that the other half has long been and still is superstitious. The Protestants regard the relics, the indulgences, the mortifications, the prayers for the dead, the holy water, and almost all the rites of the Roman Church, as a superstitious dementia. Superstition, according to them, consists in taking useless practices for necessary practices. Among the Roman Catholics there are some more enlightened than their ancestors. But even they excuse these usages by saying they are matters of indifference and cannot be evil.

In his *Letters on the English* Voltaire may appear to be merely destructive, to aim at cancellation by contrast. There is another side to the matter and that is his purpose to build up a system of morality without mystery, metaphysics, or revelation. In this he acknowledges help from three different sources. From John Locke he gained the conviction that it was not miraculous innate ideas but hard knocks that give knowledge. Even the Golden Rule needs proof, for as Locke argues, when propounded to the novice he might well ask why "one should do as he should be done unto." So, ashamed of having sought so many truths and found so many chimæras, says Voltaire, I returned like a prodigal son to his father and threw myself into the arms of that modest man who never pretends to know what he does not know.

Voltaire also acknowledges his indebtedness to another Englishman. It was from Sir Isaac Newton, whose system he popularized in France, that he derived his ideas of the workings of nature as due not to miracle and divine interference but to the orderly processes of matter and motion. But it was from the deists or freethinkers, and especially from Lord Bolingbroke, in whose London house he first sought refuge, that Voltaire obtained the very bones of that natural religion which he would substitute for supernatural religion. Now the deists were charged by their adversaries with atheism, and so was Voltaire, but this charge he refutes in a single sentence: "It is very presumptuous to define God; but, if God did not exist, it would be necessary that we invent him." While there must be a great first cause to account for the existence of the world, yet this does not mean that the great cause is an interfering providence or one who has his favourites: "I thank him for the benefits I enjoy, and even for the ills with which he tries me; but I take good care not to ask him for anything; he knows better than us what we need, and besides, I am afraid to ask him for good weather when my neighbour is asking for rain."

In his exile in England Voltaire received not only political ideals but philosophical ideas concerning experience as the basis of ethics, the uniformity of the laws of nature, and a notion of natural religion as common to all rational beings. It was Locke who began his system of morals with an attack on innate ideas, which was the doctrine of Descartes and the fashionable philosophy of Voltaire's day. The mind at birth, Locke contended, is not stamped with the maxims of morality any more than the infant knows the axioms of mathematics or the precepts of religion. The mind is rather a blank tablet upon which experience inscribes the principles of morality, education the principles of mathematics, and revelation the principles of religion. The negative proof of this is that infants, idiots, and savages, prior to experience, have no knowledge of goodness, of geometry, or of God. But though the mind is blank at birth, like an erased wax tablet, it has a capacity for knowledge, and in all these fields it is the finger of experience that traces truth.

All this teaching suited the temper of Voltaire's mind, which was practical and averse to mystery and miracle. The doctrine of innate ideas was to him too idealistic and too optimistic; it was too good to be true that all men are born with the Ten Commandments stamped on their brains. No, the English have fine ideals, like liberty of the press and liberty of thought, but they are not speculative ideals. The Schoolmen may have their insubstantial substances but the English do not. Of course, says Voltaire, one must start by a sincere submission to the incontrovertible dogmas of the church. The body of the entire church has decided that the soul is immaterial. But the modest Locke conjectures that it is not much more remote from our comprehension to conceive that God can, if he pleases, superadd to matter a faculty of thinking than that he should superadd to it another substance with a faculty of thinking.

John Locke was one Englishman from whom Voltaire gained ideas radically at variance with the orthodox philosophy of France. Another was Newton, from whom he largely derived his concept of the world as a machine. Previous scientists like Kepler and Galileo had investigated the workings of certain parts; the Englishman now discovered how the entire contrivance was held together by the force of gravity. But this "wonderful conjunction" cannot be explained according to mere mechanical laws. So Newton argues that, the world machine having a design, there must therefore be a designer of the harmonious whole. Science thus reënforces an ancient argument which Voltaire takes over in his attack on atheism. We are intelligent beings, he reasons; intelligent beings cannot have been formed by a crude, blind, insensible being. Newton's intelligence therefore came from another intelligence. When we see a beautiful machine we say that there is a good engineer, and that this engineer has excellent judgment. The world is assuredly an admirable intelligence, wherever it may be. This argument is old, and none the worse for that.

These words are from Voltaire's famous *Philosophical Dictionary*, a book that was attacked in orthodox circles in England and America as the handbook of atheism. It was anything but that, for the argument just given is expressly directed against atheists and furnishes the reasons of "the worshippers of God," of whom Voltaire counts himself one. He continues in the same strain: I meditated last night; I was absorbed in the contemplation of nature; I admired the immensity, the course, the harmony of these infinite globes which the vulgar do not know how to admire. I admired still more the intelligence which directs these vast forces. I said to myself: "One must be blind not to be dazzled by this spectacle; one must be stupid not to recognize the author of it; one must be mad not to worship him." These arguments are again from the *Philosophical Dictionary*. They were uttered in behalf of what was called naturalism as contrasted with supernaturalism. Now for a hundred years and more the English deists had been preaching a religion common to all mankind as a rational substitute for that which theology offered. This way of thinking explained that paradox in Voltaire's life—that while he attacked the church he built himself a private chapel. Just inside the gateway of his country estate at Ferney, on the lake of Geneva, may still be seen this building with the inscription "Voltaire erected this to God."

Besides Locke and Newton, English deism furnished the third great influence in Voltaire's thinking. Because of Locke he did not believe in innate ideas, in the sense, for example, of clear and distinct conceptions of God; because of Newton's *Principles*, known as the "Bible of Science," he did not believe in Scripture but in nature as the real book of revelations. As President John Adams, a great reader of Voltaire, once described it, the deist had for his creed: "Allegiance to the Creator and Governor and the Milky-Way and the Nebulæ, and Benevolence to all his Creatures." In other words, deism, or, as Voltaire more properly calls it, theism, was an attempt to reduce religion to ethics, revelation to a spiritual law in the natural world. It was this revelation, freed from mystery and miracle, that Voltaire used in his life-long struggle against the established church of France, backed as it was by the Bastille, censorship, and the Inquisition.

Voltaire's religion was the religion of humanity and his moral system humanitarianism. From this standpoint, then, he drew his great contrast between the intellectual atmosphere of France and that of England. In the latter country, as he wrote to a friend from London, it is possible to use one's mind freely and nobly, without fear and cringing. Now this liberty of philosophizing was in large measure due to the great deistic controversy which had been going on for over a century. Through John Toland's book, *Christianity Not Mysterious*, the word "freethinker" had first appeared in English literature. As the author says in the preface of this work, which Voltaire read: "For being educated from my cradle in the grossest superstition and idolatry, God was pleased to make my own reason and such as made use of theirs the happy instrument of my conversion." But even before Toland's day the attempt was made to free religion and ethics from revelation. Lord Herbert of Cherbury had declared that faith is not higher than knowledge, but that through the light of reason there have been gained certain propositions valid among all men. These are: There is one highest divine

Being; this Being is to be worshipped; the most important part of his worship consists of virtue together with piety; blasphemy and crime must be atoned for by repentance; punishment and reward follow after this life.

These are the famous five points common to all religions which Benjamin Franklin, known in France as "another Voltaire," declared that he never doubted. This was constructive deism, but there was also a destructive side which influenced Voltaire. During his stay in London he read the Collins' attack on prophecy and Woollston's on miracles, and later Tindal's strictures against revelation, Morgan's against the Old Testament, and Chubb's against Christian morality. From this apostolic succession of freethinkers Voltaire gained much of his material, while from Lord Bolingbroke he took his tone. The latter's infidelity was aristocratic; it was infidelity for the upper classes. This was the class to which François Marie Arouet de Voltaire belonged and which he tried to stir into action with darts of wit and irony. He did not accept the English lord's optimism, and yet like him he sought a philosophy and morality which should be entirely human, without revelation, or mystery, or miracle, and to tell the truth, without much metaphysics. Thus Voltaire's *Letters on the English* show where he derived many of his ideas, his *Discourse on Man* how he polished them up, and his philosophical tales like *Zadig* and *Candide* how the bland belief that all is for the best in this best possible of all worlds can be "withered with a grin."

## THE MORALIST IN ACTION

Now began the systematic attack on the status quo, on things as they were in a country whose monarch believed he was the state and whose church assumed itself to be the state of mind proper to all thinking beings. This was the Infamy against which Voltaire fought, this the doubleheaded monster of political oppression and intellectual tyranny which he went forth to cripple if not to slay. It was not a case of St. George and the dragon, for Voltaire was anything but saintly, nor was it a case of David and Goliath, for Voltaire was no pious stripling. It was rather another fable of Æsop where the blustering wind was less effective than the hot and steady light of the sun that made the traveller strip off his garments of prejudice. As the French critic, Émile Faguet, has said, Voltaire never really knew what he wanted, but he knew well enough what he did not want. He wanted neither religion, nor metaphysics, nor religious wars, nor philosophical disputes, nor spiritual power separated from temporal

power, nor persecution of heresy of faith or thought, nor an independent magistracy attempting to form a state within a state.[1]

This negative programme had been formed early in England by
what Voltaire saw there in the way of positive achievement. The
English had beheaded one king, exiled another, and achieved a
constitutional form of government with guarantees for the liberty
of the press and liberty of private opinions. In the days of Horace
Walpole there was, of course, enough of social inequality and
political corruption, the Reform Bill was some way off, but for social
oppression and intellectual tyranny there was no comparison with
France. Of this Voltaire had personal experience. He was twice
prisoner in the Bastille, once on a false charge of criticizing the
government, again through the cowardly act of a nobleman who on
account of his rank escaped the challenge to a duel on the part of the
young Voltaire. This was but the beginning. Besides physical duress
there were many attempts at intellectual suppression. His *Letters on
the English* were burned and also his *Philosophical Dictionary*, along
with the body of the unfortunate De la Barre. It was this volume,
a portable dictionary written in a popular style, that contained the
most telling criticisms of the established church and the established
social order. Thus at the start, under the caption "Authority," Voltaire reviews the absurdity of intellectual suppression. The Holy
Office, he says, condemned Galileo, and had the master of thought
in Italy thrown into prison at the age of seventy; and they pronounced a sentence in favour of the categories of Aristotle although
his books were previously burned by two councils. Further on a
faculty, which had not great faculties, issued a decree against innate
ideas, and later a decree for innate ideas, without the said faculty
being informed by its beadles what an idea is. In the neighbouring
schools judicial proceedings were instituted against the circulation of
the blood. An action was started against inoculation, and parties
have been subpœnaed.

For a contrast to this, turn to the article "Democracy." Voltaire
was an aristocrat at heart, but he had this to say in favour of republics: "Democracy seems suitable only to a very little country,
and further it must be happily situated. Small though it be, it will
make many mistakes, because it will be composed of men. Discord
will reign there as in a monastery; but there will be no St. Bartholomew, no Irish massacres, no Sicilian vespers, no Inquisition, no
condemnation to the galleys for having taken some water from the

---

[1] *A Literary History of France*, p. 492,

sea without paying for it, unless one supposes this republic composed of devils in a corner of hell."

These criticisms were directed against large and powerful autocracies, not merely that of Louis XIV but that of Cromwell, protector of England and persecutor of Ireland. In other words, the Infamy which Voltaire attacked was intolerance and superstition in any form, whether due to rulers Catholic or Protestant, whether to religions of the West or the East. Thus under the head of "Expiation" he satirizes Catholic penitences. In the early days of the church, he recounts, it cost two hundred sous of that time for killing a priest and four hundred for killing a bishop; so that a bishop was worth precisely two priests. Having thus compounded with men, one compounded with God, when confession was generally established. Finally Pope John XXII, who made money out of everything, prepared a tariff of sins: the absolution of an incest, four turonenses for a layman, for a man and woman who have committed incest eighteen turonenses; this is not just; if one person pays only four turonenses, the two owed only eight turonenses. So much for the West, now for the East. As soon as religions were established, there were expiations; the ceremonies accompanying them were ridiculous: for what connection between the water of the Ganges and a murder? How could a man repair a homicide by bathing himself? We have already remarked this excess of aberration and absurdity, of imagining that he who washes his body washes his soul, and wipes away the stains of bad actions.

Such were the ironical means by which Voltaire reached the public through his portable dictionary. His method, as he explains, was one of audacity, more audacity, always audacity, while his end and aim were the undermining of intolerance and superstition, whether of the Catholic with his surplice, the Protestant with his neckbands, or the Oriental with his turban. What is tolerance? Voltaire asks. It is the consequence of humanity. We are all formed of frailty and error; let us pardon reciprocally each other's folly— that is the first law of nature. It is clear that the individual who persecutes a man, his brother, because he is not of the same opinion, is a monster. That admits of no difficulty. But the government! but the magistrates! but the princes! How do they treat those who have another worship than theirs?

The answer was the case of the Calas, the case of the Sirvens, and the case of De la Barre and Mombailly. These were the famous miscarriages of judgment which made Voltaire a hero among the common people and which led the leaders of the Revolution to inscribe on his catafalque: "He prepared us to become free." But here Voltaire was no revolutionary in the sense of condoning such offenses as were committed later in the Terror. He was rather what he describes himself to be—"an advocate of lost causes." The first and most famous of these episodes was the Calas case, where a Protestant father had been executed on the charge of killing his son to prevent the latter from turning Catholic. The details are given by Voltaire as follows:

"You would like to know how this European protest against the judicial murder of the unhappy Calas, broken on the wheel at Toulouse, managed to reach a little unknown corner of the world, between the Alps and the Jura, a hundred miles from the scene of the fearful event.

"Nothing more clearly reveals the existence of that imperceptible chain which links all the events of this miserable world.

"At the end of March, 1762, a traveller, who had come through Languedoc and arrived in my little retreat two miles from Geneva, told me of the sacrifice of Calas, and assured me that he was innocent. I answered him that the crime was not a probable one, but that it was still more improbable that Calas's judges should, without any motive, break an innocent man on the wheel.

"I heard the next day that one of the children of this unfortunate man had taken refuge in Switzerland, fairly near my cottage. His flight made me presume the guilt of the family. However, I reflected that the father had been condemned to death for having, by himself, assassinated his son on account of his religion, and that, at the time of his death, his father was sixty-nine years old. I never remember to have read of any old man being possessed by so horrible a fanaticism.

"I had young Calas to my house. I expected to find him a religious enthusiast, such as his country has sometimes produced. I found a simple and ingenuous youth, with a gentle and very interesting countenance, who, as he talked to me, made vain efforts to restrain his tears. He told me that he was at Nîmes, apprenticed to a manufacturer, when he heard that his whole family was about to be condemned to death at Toulouse, and that almost all Languedoc believe them guilty. He added that, to escape so fearful a disgrace, he had come to Switzerland to hide himself.

"I gathered fresh information from two merchants of Geneva, of proven honesty, who had lodged at the Calas' house in Toulouse. They confirmed me in my opinion. Far from believing the Calas family to be fanatics and parricides, I thought I saw that it was the fanatics who had accused and ruined them. I had long known of what party spirit and calumny are capable."[1]

This was the beginning of Voltaire's inquiry. For three years he fought for this family, paid three lawyers to defend them, persuaded others to contribute to the cause, wrote memoirs and declarations and also his famous "Treatise on Tolerance," until, just a week after this letter was written, the innocence of Calas and his family was publicly declared by forty judges of the Council of Paris.

The Sirven case concerned a young Protestant girl who was torn from her family, put in a convent, went mad, and threw herself into a well. Again a whole family was accused, but, as Voltaire said, this was less dramatic than the Calas case because "it lacked a scaffold." This was due to Voltaire's personal efforts. Again he gave freely of his time and money to save "four sheep accused by the butcher of devouring a lamb." He had received this family of refugees at his estate in Switzerland, but it was not until 1771 that the Council of Toulouse exculpated the accused, having taken, as Voltaire remarked, "two hours to defend innocence, and nine years to give it justice."

In both these cases—famous throughout Europe—Voltaire was but carrying out his definition of the end of morality as not speculation but action. He concludes his letter: "I have only done in the fearful cases of the Calas and the Sirvens what all men do: I have followed my bent. A philosopher's is not to pity the unhappy —it is to be of use to them." This was no pious platitude, but was meant seriously. During the time he was fighting for the Calas Voltaire remarks, "Not a smile escaped me without my reproaching myself for it as for a crime." But still another miscarriage of justice engaged his attention. This concerned the young chevalier De la Barre who was charged with mutilating crucifixes, insulting a religious procession, and uttering blasphemies in Abbeville. For this he and also his friend d'Etallonde, and Moisnel, a boy of eighteen, were condemned to death after having their tongues cut out and their hands cut off. A public appeal was made and the case retried at Paris, but the sentence was confirmed. To Voltaire's horror De la Barre, not yet twenty years of age, was put to the torture and died at the stake "with the firmness of Socrates." With a ghastly irony, along with the victim's body was burned the first volume of the *Philosophical Dictionary*. This was a threat to Voltaire, who fled to Switzerland, whence he wrote that he did not conceive how thinking

---

[1] S. G. Tallentyre, translator: *Voltaire in His Letters*, pp. 189-191.

beings can live in a land of apes, who so often turn into tigers, and that for his part he was ashamed to be even on the frontier.

Voltaire was not only shocked at this horror but his feeling of patriotism was outraged at this additional sign of the degradation of his own country. Here, on the one hand, he writes, is Calas broken on the wheel, on the other Sirven hanged; a little farther from home a lieutenant general gagged; and a fortnight later five young men condemned to be burned for follies which deserved Saint-Lazare. . . . Is this the land of gaiety and philosophy? It is rather that of the massacre of St. Bartholomew.

But Voltaire did not stop with vain remonstrances and regrets. He wrote a terrible tract, "The Death of the Chevalier de la Barre," which, as he said, "frightened the carnivorous beasts off the others." This meant the dropping of the charge against the boy Moisnel, who deserved not death but only Saint-Lazare, the house of correction for juvenile offenders. So in defense of d'Etallonde, who had escaped to Prussia, Voltaire obtained protection from Frederick the Great, and from France final restitution of the Chevalier's civil rights through a pamphlet entitled, "The Cry of Innocent Blood." Yet even this did not end the calendar of judicial crimes with which the patriarch of Ferney was engaged. There was the case of Martin, executed for a murder which, as it turned out, another had committed. This poor agriculturist, Voltaire relates, when he was stretched out on St. Andrew's cross, asked permission of the sheriff's officer and the executioner to raise his arms to call heaven to witness to his innocence, as he could not make himself heard by the crowd. . . . "I can only lift my hands to heaven, like Martin, and take God to witness all the horrors which happen in his Work of Creation. I have enough to do with the Sirven family—the daughters are still in my neighbourhood. I have sent the father to Toulouse: his innocence is as clearly demonstrated as a proposition of Euclid. The crass ignorance of a village doctor, and the still grosser ignorance of a subordinate judge, added to the grossness of fanaticism, has ruined a whole family, made them wanderers for six years, destitute, and begging their bread. Finally, I trust that the Parliament of Toulouse will make it its honour and duty to show Europe that it is not always led away by appearances, and is worthy of the work it has to do. This affair gives me more trouble and anxiety than an old invalid can well bear: but I shall never slacken my grip till I am dead—I am so pigheaded."[1]

---

[1] Voltaire's *Letters*, p. 227.

This letter was prophetic. The last miscarriage of justice with which Voltaire was engaged was that of General Lally, executed on a false charge of treason. For weeks Voltaire sought to have the old soldier's memory vindicated; he succeeded, and four days before his own death wrote this, his last letter, to the General's son: "The dying man returns to life on hearing this great news: he tenderly embraces M. de Lally: he sees that the King is the defender of justice: and he dies content."

## CONTRADICTIONS IN CHARACTER

Voltaire as a moralist seems an anomaly and as a reformer a paradox. In character he was vain and deceitful and in private life anything but puritanical. He brought about reform but the historic reformer he detested, and he had the most biting things to say about such a dour Scotchman as John Knox, while as for John Calvin and his followers, he took a malicious delight in plaguing them. Thus he had one estate in gloomy Geneva which he ironically called Les Delices and had many a tilt with the city fathers over his private theatricals. In fact, he put forward a project for a state-supported theatre there which was about equivalent to proposing a ballet for Boston in the days of Governor Endicott. When things grew too hot for him he withdrew to his other estate, Ferney, just over the French border. He avoided trouble, as he said, by having his fore-feet in Switzerland and his hind feet in France.

Voltaire was an opportunist. He took the goods the gods provided, such as bequests from his father and brother, pensions from the crown, and lucky investments of his own. Of the evils of life some he took tolerantly and others not. He was not averse to lying about the authorship of his works when the lieutenant of police made trouble for him. He was not averse to female society, as in his liaisons with Madame de Châtelet and other attractive bluestockings. Such things were done in polite society and he followed the current of convention. Brought up by the Jesuits, he distinguished between venial and mortal sins, but he made his own list of the virtues. The theological did not appeal to him. As to poverty, he avoided it by astute investments of his capital and by subtle schemes in advertising his literary wares. As for chastity, he neither practised it nor respected it and coolly pointed out that monks and nuns who obeyed its mandates were a check on the population of France. As for obedience, the word is not in his dictionary. He is talking with his tongue in his cheek when he says that all the articles of the nature of metaphysics must start with a sincere submission to the incontrovertible dogmas of the church, for he proceeds to describe the soul as material, and men as frail automatons moved by the invisible hand which directs us on this stage of the world.

Voltaire had contempt for the theological virtues but no aversion to the venial sins. The mortal sins, or what he considered mortal, were in a different category. The first of these is intolerance, because tolerance is "the first law of nature." He has already defined this and asked certain uncomfortable questions: "It is clear that the individual who persecutes a man, his brother, because he is not of the same opinion, is a monster. That admits of no difficulty. But the government! but the magistrates! but the princes! how do they treat those who have another worship than theirs?" It was religious intolerance based on matters of worship that led the governments and magistrates to perpetrate atrocities on the Calas, the Sirvens, and De la Barre and his youthful companions, though a more kindly king quashed the charges against General Lally.

Voltaire was no enemy of the crown as such. He utilized monarchs as he did other men. When things grew too hot for him in France he went to Germany, where Frederick the Great had long sought him as an ornament to his court and where Voltaire finally became the royal guest at Potsdam. Of course they quarrelled, as two autocrats would, but it was not on questions of rank and privilege. With the system of government in Germany Voltaire had no direct concern, though he satirized this system in his *Candide*. But with the system of France he did concern himself. He called himself the innkeeper of Europe, but he lived like a prince on his Ferney estate and was proud of the seignorial rights that went with his purchase. But these rights he did not abuse. Touched by the condition of the poor on his land, he started a colony of watchmakers and weavers. Where he found fifty starving peasants, he left a self-supporting colony of five hundred. This was practical philanthropy. And so was his attack on the system of serfdom which he found to his horror still existed in the mountains back of his home. His letter on social conditions in 1760 points out how the real workers, behind the scenes, have hardly a modest subsistence, while certain selected personages flaunt on the stage: "It is sad to see—I confess it again—those who toil in poverty, and those who produce nothing, in luxury: great proprietors who claim the very birds that fly and the fish that swim: trembling vassals who do not dare to free their houses from the wild boar that devours them: fanatics who want to burn everyone who does not pray to God after their own fashion: violence in high places which engenders

violence in the people: might making right not only amongst nations but amongst individuals."

In this letter Voltaire acknowledged that he was not made to
govern. But there remained to him the rôle of critic of the powers
that be. It was the combination of intolerance and injustice that
Voltaire put at the bottom of the ills of his country. Is it unjust, he
sarcastically remarks, when those who do nothing should ask, Why
should we be taxed? Voltaire was no believer in communism, for
that system was too much like that of the early Christians to suit
him. He held that man had a right to property honestly acquired,
but he did not believe it right that social position or privilege should
mean exemption from taxation. In England, he pointed out, even
nobles and priests had to pay taxes.

Voltaire was no reformer in an extreme sense. As virtual president
of the republic of letters, he believed in liberty of thinking but not
in equality in property or in personality. It is certain, he remarks,
that a man who is well off will not leave his own land to come to till
yours. . . . All men have the right in the bottom of their hearts to
think themselves entirely equal to other men; it does not follow from
that that the cardinal's cook should order his master to prepare him
his dinner although he can say: "I am a man like my master; like
him I was born crying; like me he will die with the same pangs and
the same ceremonies." . . . As regards a man who is neither a cardinal's cook nor endowed with any other employment in the state;
as regards a private person who is connected with nothing, but who
is vexed at being received everywhere with an air of being patro-
nized or scorned, who sees quite clearly that many monsignors have
no more knowledge, wit, or virtue than he, and who at times is bored
at waiting in their antechambers, what should he decide to do? Why,
to take himself off.[1]

Voltaire has been called one of the precursors of the first revolution. He was, but in a limited sense. Seeing men as they were, he did
not believe in equality, nor by implication, in fraternity, but he was
ever for liberty. His ruling passion was for freedom of thinking in all
matters, from the time when he praised the English for having
thirty different ways of going to heaven to the time when on his
deathbed he blessed the young son of Benjamin Franklin with the
words, "God and Liberty." It was liberty of philosophizing, liberty
of thinking, for which he fought. It has been well said that his was
an immense and indefatigable propaganda, a bombardment of

---

[1] *Philosophical Dictionary*, article "Equality."

intelligence, unique in history. Letters and poems, sermons and dialogues, speeches, tales, and allegories all were directed to one end, the moral enlightenment of mankind, and all served to explain his remarkable prophecy: "Everything that I see appears the throwing broadcast of the seed of a revolution which must inevitably come one day, but which I shall not have the pleasure of witnessing. The French always come late to things, but they do come at last. Light extends so from neighbour to neighbour that there will be a splendid outburst on the first occasion, and then there will be a rare commotion."

## II. ROUSSEAU (1712–1788)

THERE is, however, much in the Rousseauistic view of life that militates against a complete moral honesty. "Of all the men I have known," says Rousseau, "he whose character derives most completely from his temperament alone is Jean-Jacques." The ugly things that have a way of happening when impulse is thus left uncontrolled do not, as we have seen, disturb the beautiful soul in his complacency. He can always point an accusing finger at something or somebody else. The faith in one's natural goodness is a constant encouragement to evade moral responsibility. To accept responsibility is to follow the line of maximum effort, whereas man's secret desire is to follow, if not the line of least, at all events the line of lesser, resistance. The endless twisting and dodging and proneness to look for scapegoats that results is surely the least reputable aspect of human nature. Rousseau writes to Madame de Francueil (April 20, 1751) that it was her class, the class of the rich, that was responsible for his having had to abandon his children. With responsibility thus shifted from oneself to the rich, the next step is inevitable, namely, to start a crusade against the members of a class which, without any warrant from "nature," oppresses its brothers, the members of other classes, and forces them into transgression. A man may thus dodge his duties as a father, and at the same time pose as a paladin of humanity. Rousseau is very close here to our most recent agitators. If a working girl falls from chastity, for example, do not blame her, blame her employer. She would have remained a model of purity if he had only added a dollar or two a week to her wage. With the progress of the new morality everyone has become familiar with the type of the perfect idealist who is ready to pass laws for the regulation of everybody and everything except himself, and who knows how to envelop in a mist of radiant words schemes the true driving power of which is the desire to confiscate property.[1]

The writings of Jean-Jacques Rousseau are to be explained largely by two factors—the place he was born in and the pathological strain in his own nature. From Geneva, he declares, he derived that "free and republican spirit, the indomitable and proud character which would not submit to the yoke of slavery, and which has tormented me all my life." This description suggests the favourable side of that famous city of theologians, politicians, and moralists which had such an influence on Protestants in Europe and America that we find even the Puritan Fathers of Massachusetts modelling their commonwealth on the Genevan plan. But as the Genevans had the defects of their qualities so had Rousseau. He was reserved and stiff, highly opinionated, always ready for controversy, intolerant of the beliefs of others, and critical of other forms of society, especially French society, against which he directed his very first treatise.

Born with a sentimental nature in this strait-laced environment Rousseau was a round peg in a square hole. "The only thing my parents bequeathed to me was a feeling heart," he exclaims. Consequently when he was apprenticed to a local engraver it was natural that he should lose his position when it was discovered that he spent most of his time daydreaming over sickly romances. Rousseau's father was perhaps responsible for feeding his son's fancies on such trash; at any rate, when the elder abandoned his family the younger followed suit, left the strict confines of Geneva where the authorities allowed no theatres and little dancing, and wandered into a more easy-going country, the adjoining Duchy of Savoy. Now begin those adventures so skilfully related in the *Confessions*. A certain Madame de Warens, who is later to play a large part in Rousseau's erotic and also his intellectual awakening, has him sent to Turin, where he is ostensibly converted to Catholicism, gains a few francs from that change of religion, but finally, in desperation, is forced to become a lackey in the household of a noble Italian family. The wearing of a servant's uniform was a bitter recollection which goes to explain the vehemence of his later attacks on aristocracy, just as his subsequent free-and-easy life as a begging vagabond goes to explain his praises of a "return to nature"—nature which provides food for the asking and a place to sleep under a bush.

---

[1] Irving Babbitt, *Rousseau and Romanticism*, pp. 155–156.

The *Confessions* disclose these things and more, too—how Rousseau falsely accused a fellow servant of theft, how he abandoned a travelling companion who fell in a fit on the road, how he stole wine and cakes from a patron. As the preface says: "I shall show my fellow creatures a man in all his nakedness—and that man is myself." But the *Confessions* do not tell all the truth, even to the author himself. He is unconscious of the implications of his own inconsistency. He accuses himself for his false accusation of theft but repents only on paper and not in deed; he abandons his companion on the road and preaches the beauties of universal benevolence in the style of the Savoyard vicar who trusts in a benevolent providence; he steals not only wine and cakes but ideas, and ruins his small reputation as a music master by playing another's melody as his own.

The *Confessions* form a curious double-faced document and so do the *Discourses, or Rousseau Judge of Jean-Jacques*. In this document he likewise deceives himself, for he is not the prosecuting judge the title would imply, but a sentimental and forgiving judge. But while he is lenient to himself, he is not to others. Here are some instances: When he commits his first theft in his apprentice days the blame is not for his own weakness, but for the brutality of his master, "a coarse and violent man, who in a very short time succeeded in casting a shadow over my radiant childhood and in dwarfing my gay and loving nature." Again when, with his rustic manners, he finds Parisian society cold and inhospitable, it is their fault that they have not discovered his genius. Finally, when recognition comes in 1750 through the publication of his first "Discourse" he uses that discourse for an attack on the arts and sciences—of which he had but slight knowledge—as being the cause for the present corruption in morals. The same attitude is shown in his break with his friends Diderot and D'Alembert, editors of the famous *Encyclopædia*, because they held that man's happiness is bound up with the progress of enlightenment. A similar discrepancy between practice and preaching is evident in Rousseau's other writings. When he abandons his children to the mother superior of a home for foundlings he describes the heroine of his *New Héloïse* as that superior mother who suckles and educates her own children.

Rousseau, who was anything but a saint, suffered from the same inferiority complex that afflicted St. Augustine. For Rome we must substitute Paris as the modern Babylon, centre of all the abominations of culture, yet the parallel still holds. Augustine would flee from this world to the next, Rousseau would overthrow this world and start afresh. His new ideal of humanity is a strange type, being a combination of the cave man and the Savoy vicar, of primitive simplicity and sentimental optimism. This type is summed up in the *Social Contract*, a book which on the testimony of Mallet du Pan had a hundred times more readers among the middle and lower classes than Voltaire, for Rousseau alone inoculated the French with the doctrine of the sovereignty of the people, and with its extremest consequences.

These consequences were certainly strange, for Marat, says the same witness, read and commented on this little volume in the public streets; the very principles of the revolution of 1889 were derived from its pages, and the Jacobin programme was based on its teaching. Robespierre, like Marat, knew it from cover to cover, and his famous report of 1794, on the ideals which should govern the National Convention in the administration of the internal affairs of the Republic, is simply Rousseau recast. Finally, even the Jacobin attempt to establish a civil religion, the formulary of which would open with the declaration that "the French people recognizes the Supreme Being and the immortality of the Soul," is once more unadulterated Rousseau.

## SENTIMENTAL MORALITY

The coming commotion which Voltaire prophesied was hastened by his younger contemporary, Jean-Jacques of Geneva. The two men have been called kings of the public mind who dominated public opinion. One was the intellectual leader, the other the sentimental; Voltaire stored up the materials for the explosion, Rousseau supplied the flame. But while the two men helped to bring about the common result, they started leagues apart. Rousseau attacked society as a whole, Voltaire only in part—the rotten part. He would not sweep away civilization as essentially bad, but enjoy the goods it offered. The artificialities of society were not anathema to him. Politeness, fine manners, the well-turned phrase, the subtle compliment, he used toward others and liked others to use toward him. On the fundamental question of wealth Voltaire was no communist. He saw that the privileged classes had indeed too much and that a fairer distribution of property would be desirable, but he fought not so much for material rights as for civil, for guarantees of mental freedom and for justice toward the oppressed. Save in the intellectual sphere he was a conservative.

Rousseau was of quite the opposite type of mind. What Voltaire liked he disliked. In his first "Discourse," which made him famous, he held that the arts and sciences had corrupted morals. In his "Discourse on Equality," as Voltaire sarcastically observed, he would so level us down as to put us on all fours. Finally, in his religious and educational work, *The New Héloïse* and the *Émile*, he would turn Voltaire's natural religion into an orthodoxy approaching that of his own birthplace, Geneva. His intellectual liberty turned out to be largely what the boy Émile was taught by his prig of a tutor, and that tutor was merely the author in disguise, who held that of all worlds this was the best possible world, despite the Lisbon earthquake.

Rousseau's first work that brought him fame was based on a paradox. It won the prize offered by the Academy of Dijon on the question: "Whether the restoration of the sciences and arts had contributed to purify manners." The answer is simple, declares Rousseau. Our morals are corrupted in proportion as our arts and sciences progress toward perfection. Before art had fashioned our manners and taught our passions to speak a borrowed language, our morals were rude but natural, but now convention has usurped the place of natural impulse; all is artificiality; no real friendships are possible. Under our fine manners we hide suspicion, fear, hatred, treachery, uncharity. As with the mind, so with the body: a rich man is known by his finery, an elegant man by his taste; but a powerful and healthy man has other characteristics; we find the powerful and healthy body beneath the peasant garb of the worker of the field, not beneath the gold lace of the courtier. And splendour and finery are no less foreign to virtue, which is the power and health of the soul. A good man is an athlete who likes to fight naked; he despises all these wretched decorations which hinder him in the use of his powers, and which, for the most part, were invented to hide some deformity. . . . If a stranger were to come to Europe and attempt to judge us from what he saw about him, from our science and art, the politeness of our manners, the pleasantness of our words, the good-will which we go about with from morning till night and pretend to show each other—the impression he would get of our morals would be exactly the opposite of what it should be.

This is most curious. How can it be explained? Partly as an inferiority complex, for Rousseau's was a pathological case; partly as a revolt of the democrat against the aristocrat; and partly as a reaction against Calvinistic Geneva, a city which John Calvin had turned into a society for the promotion of morals. These three factors may serve to explain the origin of Rousseau's paradoxes. They should be taken in the reverse order, for the Genevan doctrine was the earliest and the most fundamental. At the start there was a certain agreement between Geneva's two most famous citizens. Both believed in the fiction of man's primitive innocence. But where Calvin said that man was corrupted by the fall, Rousseau said he was corrupted by civilization. Man was once happy, he is now miserable, therefore we should undo all that has been done. Before art had fashioned our manners and taught our passions to speak a borrowed language, our morals were rude but natural. This does not mean that the most primitive state of nature was ideal, for in this point Rousseau largely agrees with Hobbes, who described the life of savage man as "solitary, poor, nasty, brutish, and short." It is in the second stage, that of dawning civilization, that Rousseau seeks his utopia, that stage before prosperity and privilege had arisen, and before religious doubt and fear had wiped out our original happy thoughtlessness. Here our models should be ancient Sparta with its plain manners and personal freedom, and early Rome with its manly virtues and outdoor life. These were the good old days when equality reigned and men were men.

This is, of course, bad history. Rousseau forgets or ignores what cruelties the Spartans perpetrated on the original inhabitants, the Helots, and how Rome was not built in a day because it took time to suppress its rivals. However, the "Discourse" proceeds to claim that as civilization continued to increase, corruption crept in, and that the cause of this was the cultivation of the arts and sciences. Arts brought luxury and the sciences vice; astronomy was born of superstition; eloquence of ambition, flattery, hatred, and lying; geometry of avarice; physics of idle curiosity; ethics, even, of pride. In other words, the beautiful simplicity of ancient times was destroyed by knowledge.

Why a discussion made up of statements like these should have won a prize is rather strange. The explanation may be found in the growing discontent in society as a whole. Rousseau held out to his sophisticated contemporaries the lure of the simple life. They lived in the age of reason and were weary of the strain imposed by the growing complexities of civilization. So the first "Discourse," like all Rousseau's works, was an invitation to return to paradise and beware of the forbidden fruit of knowledge. As if in the manner of La Fontaine it was the fable of the town mouse and the country mouse put in terms of philosophy. There was much false reasoning, but the message was there. Drop the cares of life; flee far from the madding crowd; be independent; be yourself; choose solitude in preference to society.

All this is familiar now; it was not then; it was a new note—the pipes of Pan luring to rustic quiet. The result was startling. Rousseau's first "Discourse" made its author famous and his doctrines fashionable. Some said he was a fool to prefer his Hermitage in the forest of Montmorency to the Faubourg St. Germain. To some it was an insult that he should leave his friends; to others it was an inspiration—this new statement that God made the country ·and man the town. Only within himself, argues Rousseau, can man find peace; only under the stars can he discover the Supreme Being who made the worlds.

While the doctrine of the return to nature and simplicity had its deeper side, it also had its shallower. As a fashionable novelty it was merely superficial, as when Louis XVI amused himself as a locksmith and Marie Antoinette played at being a milkmaid, while all the time the glittering palace of Versailles stood in the background. The court also followed suit, and excursions to the country became the mode. According to the illustrations in Rousseau's work, the idea of roughing it was a picnic, with the courtiers in wigs and lace and bottles of wine cooling in the stream. The return to nature also became a literary fad. It led to the reading of *Robinson Crusoe* and to the building of rustic retreats still bearing the alluring name of "Robinson." It also attached itself to the current admiration for the semi-civilized and the savage. When Rousseau held up to admiration the old Persians, Scythians, and Teutons, who were valiant because they were uncontaminated by art and science, his contemporaries matched them with the noble red man, the virtuous Natchez, the pious Peruvians; the Far East and Far West were drawn on for materials, and ignorance and distance lent enchantment to the view.

Such were some of the fads and fancies of the times. While they were superficial, they were yet symptoms of a real trouble. It was a critical period. In spite of appearances society was in a state of discontent, and boredom had become the disease of the century. Take, for example, the words of two women who were friends of Rousseau. Madame de Deffand declared that "All creatures seem to be equally unhappy, from the angel to the oyster," and Madame de Jully complained that there are very few things in the run of life that deserve to have any weight attached to them.

Such were the opinions of the fashionable world in which Rousseau lived, before the publication of his first "Discourse." It was a time when people played with social relations and religious beliefs as they did with everything else. Marriage was considered a matter of convenience and marital faithfulness plebeian. Love could not be represented by a simple equation of affection between man and wife, but became a series of shifting triangles of intrigue. As for religion, even the bare deism of Voltaire seemed veritable orthodoxy, and the salons took up with a radical materialist like Diderot who, as editor of the great *Encyclopædia*, propagated sheer atheism. Rousseau's reaction to these matters was curious. In his love affairs he was as free as the freest. His *Confessions* describe with amazing frankness his life-long affairs of the heart, from his *solitude à trois* with Madame de Warens to his last great passion for Madame de Houdetot. As for his relations with his common-law wife Thérèse le Vasseur, that was a matter of convenience, but not a marriage, unless one counts as such that belated and casual ceremony with which he sought to salve his conscience.

As for religion, that with Rousseau was a matter of emotion, and emotion was a luxury which he could never forego. Some have tried to make out that he effected a real intellectual compromise between traditional orthodoxy and materialistic radicalism. This is scarcely true. Born a Protestant in Geneva, he became a Catholic at the instigation of his first mistress. Then came his sojourn in Paris: when finally driven away he again turned to the Protestantism of his birthplace, but this was simply because he longed to regain some taste of the peace and quiet of his boyhood days. Switzerland, he exclaimed, thou protector of virtue! I praise thee! I touch a land of liberty! The Genevan fathers saw through this sentimental return of its prodigal son and, instead of falling on his neck, turned his books over to the public executioner to be burned.

Rousseau's religion was not an affair of the intellect but of the emotions. He was a sentimental deist and as such ran foul of the calculating atheism of Diderot and the hard-headed deism of Voltaire. Diderot he knew well but he did not think well of his doctrines. When Rousseau found himself at a dinner party where the Great First Cause was being discussed he declared that he would leave the room if another person denied the existence of a Supreme Being. So just before the appearance of the first "Discourse" he speaks of a thinking being as "the active principle behind everything," and of the Creation as the despair of disbelievers and the abyss in which philosophers have so often gone astray.

## THE CARD–HOUSE OF OPTIMISM

Rousseau's defense of religion explains his subsequent attacks on science. He thought that rationalism led to lack of religiousness, whereas his own lack of ability to reason made him an easy mark for the rationalists. He attacked the world of society as the worst possible but considered the world of nature the best possible. Now Voltaire had once been inclined to the dictum of the English poet that "whatever is, is right," but the Lisbon earthquake shook him out of this easy optimism. If Alexander Pope had been in Lisbon, he asks, would he have dared to say, "All is well"? And Voltaire asks another question in a poem of passionate remonstrance against those who would justify this disaster: "Would you say, in seeing that mass of victims, that God is avenged, that their death is the price of their crimes? What crime have these children committed who perished in blood on the breasts of their mothers? Lisbon, which exists no longer, has it more vices than London, than Paris, plunged in pleasures? Lisbon is destroyed, and they are dancing in Paris."

Rousseau received this poem and attempted to reply to it in his "Letter on Providence." He declared that God is perfect and this world is therefore perfect because it must be so. We blame God and nature for the destruction of Lisbon. Should we not rather blame ourselves? Nature did not build those twenty thousand houses, six or seven stories high. They were man's doing.

Voltaire did not reply directly to this document of apology but he did indirectly in the crushing rejoinder of that satirical romance *Candide*, which is at once a parody of Rousseau's character and an attack on his arguments for design. In the country of Westphalia, this novel begins, there lived a youth whom nature had endowed with a most sweet disposition. His face was the true index of his mind. He had a solid judgment joined to the most unaffected simplicity, and hence, I presume, he had his name of Candide. His preceptor was Master Pangloss, who taught the metaphysical-theologo-cosmolo-nigology. He could prove to admiration that there is no effect without a cause, and that this is the best of all possible worlds. "It is demonstrable," said he, "that things cannot be otherwise than they are; for as all things have been created for some end, they must necessarily be created for the best end. Observe, for instance, the nose is formed for spectacles; therefore we wear spectacles. The legs are visibly designed for stockings; accordingly we wear stockings." In the course of his travels after engaging in the war of the Bulgarians, when the bayonet was a sufficient reason for the deaths of several thousand, this young metaphysician, entirely ignorant of the world, together with Dr. Pangloss and another companion, James the Anabaptist, set sail together. Approaching Portugal they met with a tempest and James fell overboard. Candide was preparing to jump after him but was prevented by the philosopher Pangloss, who demonstrated to him that the coast of Lisbon had been made on purpose for the Anabaptist to be drowned there. . . . They escaped to shore and walked toward Lisbon, but scarcely had they set foot in the city when they perceived the earth to tremble under their feet, and the sea, swelling and foaming in the harbour, dash in pieces the vessels that were riding at anchor. Large sheets of flame and cinders covered the streets and public places. The houses tottered, and were tumbled topsy-turvy, even to their foundations, which were themselves destroyed; and thirty thousand inhabitants of both sexes, young and old, were buried beneath the ruins. . . . In the meantime, Candide, who had been wounded by some pieces of stone that fell from the houses, lay stretched in the street, almost covered with rubbish. "For God's sake," said he to Pangloss, "get me a little wine and oil; I am dying." "This concussion of the earth is no new thing," replied Pangloss; "the city of Lima in America experienced the same last year: the same cause, the same effect. . . . All this is for the very best end, for if there is a volcano at Lisbon, it could be in no other spot; for it is impossible but things should be as they are, for everything is for the best, for the fall of man, and the curse consequent thereupon, necessarily entered into the system of the best of worlds." So reasoned the philosopher Pangloss, but Candide, amazed, terrified, confounded, astonished, all bloody and trembling from head to foot, said to himself, "If this is the best of all possible worlds, what are the others?"

Such was the famous answer which Voltaire gave to Rousseau's attempted justification of a great natural disaster. Europe read it and laughed and at the same time realized that it was a terrific logical blow at the complacent optimism of the Eighteenth Century. It was a hit not only at Rousseau but at the Englishman Pope and at the German Leibnitz, who also sought to "justify the ways of God to man" by means of the principle of sufficient reason, of final ends, and of preëstablished harmony by which all things were arranged at creation to work together for good.

Rousseau claimed in his *Confessions* that he had never read *Candide*, but this is doubtful, since he was a fluent liar. At any rate, his later writings were so many attempted answers to Voltaire's crushing criticism. These writings show that Rousseau's mind was filled with a curious medley of the new sentimentalism and the old-fashioned theology. On Rousseau's own admission, that he felt before he thought, one can understand why he failed when he tried to

SPINOZA: Mystical Moralist

*From a painting by Hirszenbrg*

give a reason for his feeling. Let us transform our sensations into ideas! he exclaims. Let us see how the return to nature implies not only that man is by nature good, but that nature is itself a kindly nurse whose acts are all for the best. Thus his "Letter on Providence" implied that the great loss of life at Lisbon was man's own fault for living in high buildings, while his favourite work, *Émile*, repeats the same sentiment: God makes all things good; man meddles with them and they become evil. Upon this follows the "Creed of the Savoyard Vicar," the fine old priest who finds sermons in stones and good in everything.

This is the poetry of thought; it will not stand the prose of fact. Hence arose the fundamental contrast between the two rivals at Geneva. Rousseau stuck to his opinions and fell into the pathetic fallacy—that nature is ever in sympathy with man even in her corrective catastrophes. Voltaire changed his opinions and reached a distinction more in accordance with the evidence of the senses. To his mind nature bears signs of intelligence but not of feeling: "Men argue, nature acts"—and her acts are by no means always the best so far as man is concerned. This does not mean that Voltaire was a mere logic machine; he also had his feelings. He says of his estate in Switzerland that it would be an earthly paradise were it not for the gloomy spirit of Geneva. Now it was this gloomy spirit that explains not only the doctrine of catastrophes as punishment for sins, but of inevitable fate and the fear of persecution that haunted Rousseau to his last days.

The Savoyard priest begins his creed with the words: "I am no great philosopher." We can agree with him. His was not an appeal to reason but an appeal to feeling. It is at this point that Rousseau strikes his characteristic note. All his writings are drenched with sentimentalism, but after all is said, there is a certain fascination in the narrative, just as a song may be beautiful though the words be weak. Rousseau belongs to a special class of moralists. The Stoics had the epic quality with their adventures in the game of life; Bruno the dramatic in his heroic struggle against the trammels of tradition; Rousseau remains lyrical; his is an outburst of emotions, but he finds it hard to put these emotions in words for they are the emotions of a rebel. His successors considered him the precursor of the great revolution, though his character was but a distorted reflection of the revolutionary maxims. He was all for liberty, equality, and fraternity, provided these meant to do as he pleased, to denounce the nobility, and to consider all men brothers with a view to borrowing from them.

This picture is a fairly true representation of his life up to the time when fame came to him. Then he withdrew from the world and attempted a moral reform. Although this was by no means successful it was a valiant effort to put his principles into practice. In regard to this declaration of personal independence his enemies were critical and Voltaire was especially unfair. He called Rousseau an arch-fool for refusing a pension from the king and offers of advancement from his powerful friends. But, asks Rousseau, who was I to bring stern principles that I had adopted into harmony with the position with which they had nothing in common? And was it not rather easy to preach disinterestedness and poverty when one was cashier to a collector of state taxes? But Rousseau took the step and withdrew from society. As Spinoza ground optical glasses for a living, he copied music for four sous the page and thus managed to eke out an existence. Yet this was the final and not the first step. I began my reform, he recounts, with my dress; I discarded all gold embroidery and white stockings, adopted a little round wig, left off my sword and my gold watch, saying to myself with inconceivable joy: "Thank God I no longer need to know what time it is."

This last touch seems rather curious in the son of a watchmaker, and this whole professio nappeared so preposterous to his critics that they suspected that it was a mere scheme for advertising himself and his literary wares, just as Benjamin Franklin, emissary from America, called attention to his mission by the quaint simplicity of his dress. But while to wear an old fur cap and woollen stockings was but a calculated bit of acting on the part of that astute schemer from overseas, some of the critics of Rousseau treated his reform as a piece of clever calculation, others as mere foolish comedy. One of them says that Rousseau as a wild man, impolite, without sword or watch, and above all Rousseau as a music copier, turned the elegant Paris of the day upside down; all beautiful ladies wished to have music copied by his hands. Another critic, more severe, points out that the period of his moral reform occurred exactly in those years when he placed his third and fourth children in a foundling hospital. All this may be true, but Rousseau was but following his fundamental principle of simplicity in seeking to gain what he described as "the sweet feeling of existence, independent of all other sensations." As he wrote to one of his country correspondents: By living among slaves, I have learned to see to the depths what liberty means.

This one word "liberty" explains as well as any other the motives in the life of this unmoral moralist. He was not only a precursor of the coming revolution but the father of that new movement, romanticism, which has been described as the revolt of nature against civilization, simplicity against convention, the heart against the brain, liberty against tyranny. At this point the *Confessions* come to our aid. They are pathological, they are also pathetic. They offer the recurrent problem of a man overwhelmed by the complexities of civilization, of a man for whom the stress and strain of life were too much. In this situation simplicity is the antidote for complexity. Stripping oneself of fine clothes is the symbol of stripping oneself of cares and worries. This motive is found at work from Rousseau's early days to the end of his life. In the *Confessions* he declares that he acted on the maxim "to avoid situations which put our duties in opposition to our interests." In the first "Discourse" he would rid man of the arts and sciences; in the "Discourse on Inequality," of wealth; in the *New Héloïse* he urges that the babe should be freed of its swaddling clothes, and children of those stiff and starched garments which fashion prescribed. In his *Émile* he would empty the boy's head of the lumber of learning which conventional education demanded, and finally, in the *Social Contract*, he would go back to that age of pristine simplicity best described in the homely query of the English proverb: "When Adam delved and Eve span, who was then the gentleman?"

Rousseau as a physician of souls could give advice to others, he could not cure himself. He could live in a cottage, but he could not remove his mental furniture; prepossessions and obsessions remained. In his attack on luxury he betrayed the hatred of the workingman's son for wealth and privilege; in his assumption that vice is urban, virtue rustic, he exhibited the timidity of the country mouse; in his criticisms of the theatre he revived the spirit of his old Geneva, that "village called morality," where dancing was forbidden and comedy a crime.

The prepossessions of Rousseau s youth became the obsessions of his maturity, and here early environment played a preponderating part. As for his heredity as a dominant influence, we are on much less firm ground. Insanity has been found in his family just as in that of many another man of genius. But that explains little compared with the influence of early example. Rousseau's father was a vagabond watchmaker who abandoned his family and left his sons to shift for themselves. He seemed to follow the very maxim which Jean-Jacques summarized as "avoiding difficulties when they conflict with one's interest." He also put into the son's head specific and vicious ideas which the son soon put into practice. The books which this Genevan father read aloud to his impressionable offspring belong to that very class of spicy memoirs and adventurous amours which were frowned upon in the city of censorship.

This brings us to that work of Rousseau's by which he is best known. St. Augustine, according to his *Confessions*, was a sinner who became a saint; Rousseau, according to his *Confessions*, the devil a saint was he. The woman who perhaps knew him best, Madame d'Épinay, called him "a moral dwarf mounted on stilts." Rousseau certainly attempted to raise himself in the estimation of others, to appear better than he was, and at the same time the *Confessions* exhibit a certain moral advancement. In a way his life was an epitome of his own thesis that mankind, which began in innocency, was corrupted by civilization. Jean-Jacques was certainly innocent of the ways of the world when he began his wanderings, but speedily succumbed to the temptations of luxury, as in his sojourn with Madame de Warens. From that time he followed the primrose path. But strangely enough the fame which might have brought improvement in outward conditions was turned to effect a certain inward improvement. The unmoral stage of early youth and the immoral stage of manhood are succeeded by a genuine though pathetic attempt to be good. Conscience, which Rousseau now apostrophizes as the greatest thing in life, begins to sting, and the *Confessions* become an apology and a plea for absolution. This intimate journal is almost too intimate. As a book of adventure it is picaresque, at the same time it is pathetic. It offers a distressing picture of erotic excitements, of lies and subterfuges, of carefree idling and irresponsibility. To many Rousseau is a vagabond, but not a beloved vagabond; to so-called Anglo-Saxon critics he is the horrible example of Latin laxity. Yet certain Latin critics are more severe than English and American. Lassere, for example, holds up to derision the ideals of romantic morality, "idlers of genius, angelic female poisoners, sincere comedians, virtuous courtesans, metaphysical mountebanks, faithful adulterers." It is this class that Rousseau himself excuses in his absurd criticism of Madame de Warens as one whose "conduct was reprehensible, but her heart is pure." Rousseau has been called the advocate of false values, ever ready to discover beauty of soul in anyone under the reprobation of society. But by excusing himself he accuses himself, for the defense, by way of romantic sympathy, is achieved only at the expense of the great humanistic virtue—decorum, or the sense of proportion. To this, as a matter of fact, Rousseau never adjusted himself. In brief, his attitude toward life was "fundamentally bohemian."

Such is the revolt of common sense against the romantic ideal of "the sweet child of sickly fancy." But there is another side to the question. A deeper insight into the workings of Rousseau's mind was offered by his friend Diderot, who helped him put his first "Discourse" through the press. The latter explained its instant success in this striking way: "Do you wish to know in brief the tale of almost all our woe? There once existed a natural man; there has been introduced within this man an artificial man, and there has arisen in the cave a civil war which lasts throughout life." Rousseau's system, then, appears to be an unresolved conflict between two ideals. He was wrong in reversing the values of the primitive and the present, in making that which was early Elysian and that which was late corrupt. As a matter of fact, in the history of mankind the unmoral stage precedes the moral, but the conflict between the two persists. In the evolution of ethics there is a perpetual struggle in the cave, a struggle between the repressed complexes derived from man's brute ancestors and a decent respect for the opinions of civilized mankind.

## III. DAVID HUME (1711–1776)

"You must know then that from my earliest infancy I found always a strong inclination to books and letters. As our college education in Scotland, extending little further than the languages, ends commonly when we are about fourteen or fifteen years of age, I was after that left to my own choice in my reading, and found it incline me almost equally to books of reasoning and philosophy, and to poetry and the polite authors. Everyone who is acquainted either with the philosophers or critics knows that there is nothing yet established in either of these two sciences, and that they contain little more than endless disputes, even in the most fundamental articles. Upon examination of these, I found a certain boldness of temper growing on me, which was not inclined to submit to any authority in these subjects, but led me to seek out some new medium, by which truth might be established. After much study and reflection on this, at last, when I was about eighteen years of age, there seemed to be opened up to me a new scene of thought, which transported me beyond measure, and made me, with an ardour natural to young men, throw up every other pleasure or business to apply entirely to it. The law, which was the business I designed to follow, appeared nauseous to me, and I could think of no other way of pushing my fortune in the world, but that of a scholar and philosopher."—J. H. Burton, *Life of Hume*

Apparently David Hume was a born philosopher in the popular sense of the word an unpractical and introspective soul. A reputed saying of his mother's was that "Our Davie's a fine, good-natured crater, but uncommon wake-minded." This curious statement simply means that Hume had the outward manner of an absent-minded man, unconscious of much that was going on around him. It was a peculiarity which led him later to write to his touchy guest, Jean-Jacques Rousseau: "What! Because sometimes, when absent in thought, I have a fixed look or stare you expect me to be a traitor. . . . Are not most studious men subject to such reveries or fits of silence?"

Hume had a vacant look but not a vacant mind. Indeed he was precociously learned; at the age of twelve he was entered in the class of Greek in the University of Edinburgh; at sixteen he was quoting Vergil to a friend in defense of "this pastoral happiness I have in a great measure come at just now." This meant that he had left the university and gone back to study by himself at home, for his father, though a poor Scottish laird, had left a fine library. Within two years Hume had read so much philosophy that he had actually begun to doubt the reality of an external world. But since, in his own words, "a true skeptic will be diffident of his philosophic doubts," he decided to seek further experience. First he tried law, the profession for which his family had intended him; then commerce, but found neither to his liking. Hereupon, according to his autobiography, "I now went over to France with a view of prosecuting my studies in a country retreat, and there I laid the plan of life which I have steadily and successfully pursued. I resolved to make a very rigid frugality supply my deficiency of fortune, to maintain unimpaired my independence, and to regard every object as contemptible except the improvement of my talent in literature."

Devotion to literature, as is so often the case, did not pay in financial rewards, and what Hume's mother said of him may have been an afterthought based on his lack of worldly success. His first book was the *Treatise of Human Nature*, a book whose marvellous subtlety reflected the influence of the French Jesuits with whom Hume had studied for some three years. But this volume, since recognized as one of the great masterpieces of British thought, in Hume's frank words "fell deadborn from the press without reaching such a distinction as even to excite a murmur among the zealots."

In the latter statement Hume was mistaken, for when later he became candidate for the chair of ethics in Edinburgh university the
*Treatise* was brought up against him as teaching "heresy, deism,
skepticism, and atheism." These charges were exaggerated; what
Hume was after was to do away with an easy acceptance of conventional beliefs. Like Descartes, who had studied under the same school
of Jesuits as the Scotchman, Hume believed that there was a certain
duty to doubt, for only by testing one's beliefs could convictions be
said to be honestly arrived at. However, as Hume confessed to a
friend about his *Treatise*, his principles were so remote from all the
vulgar sentiments on the subjects that were they to take place
they would produce an almost total revolution in philosophy; "and
you know, revolutions of this kind are not easily brought about."

Hume, as a matter of fact, did bring about a revolution in thought;
it was he who later awoke Kant from his "dogmatic slumber" and
led the great German thinker to propound a fruitful doctrine that
beliefs, for example in God, freedom, and immortality, are not prov-
able by pure but by practical reasons, being over-beliefs or postulates by which man helps himself along in life. Hume was right in
holding that his first book would offend popular prejudices and
that the time was not ripe for his radical principles. Hence he published his second work, *Essays, Moral and Political*, which were written with such elegance of style that he attracted the attention of
what he called "good company." This led to his obtaining a "very
genteel" appointment as secretary to General Saint Clair which
ultimately led Hume not only to France, but to Holland, Germany,
and Italy. The Scotchman's experience as a diplomat brought him
both knowledge of the world and ultimately comparative riches,
since he kept those resolutions of rigid frugality which he had
made when a young man. After another sojourn in France, where he
was lionized by a society which loved a skeptic, Hume retired to his
native city. There, as he wrote to a friend, he lived a life of leisure
and happiness without the least regret of London or even Paris, for
now he had a chance to exhibit his "great talent in cookery," had
plenty of claret in which "nobody excels me," and best of all had
abundance of time to "cultivate friends and philosophers."

## SKEPTICAL MORALITY

David Hume, the skeptical moralist of Edinburgh, exhibits a
characteristic Scotch economy in his thought. Be cautious, he says,
do away with unnecessary and unknown causes: keep away from

complexity, for paucity of explanation is better than extravagant fancies. Begin, then, with freeing yourselves from the luxuries of supernaturalism and sentimentalism, for it is more sensible to live the simple life of caution than to dwell in the fairyland of occult agents, or in a supposititious paradise where all men are fancied to possess liberty and equality.

In this advice the canny Scotchman attacks by implication several well-known doctrines. Such are the mediæval notions of universal providence, the innate ideas of Descartes, the social compact of Rousseau. The first is pure supernaturalism, since its advocates assert that the Deity is the immediate cause of the union between soul and body, for it is not any energy in the will that produces locomotion in our members, it is God himself who is pleased to second our will, in itself impotent. According to these philosophers, everything is full of God. Not content with the principle that nothing exists but by his will, that nothing possesses any power but by his concession, they rob nature and all created beings of every power in order to render their dependence on the Deity still more sensible and immediate.

This is going too far, asserts Hume, because it would argue, surely, more power in the Deity to delegate a certain degree of power to inferior creatures than to produce everything by his own immediate volition. It argues more wisdom to contrive at first the fabric of the world with such perfect foresight that, of itself, and by its proper operation, it may serve all the purposes of providence, than if the great Creator were obliged every moment to adjust its parts, and animate by his breath all the wheels of that stupendous machine.

To employ the mediæval doctrine of universal providence in order to account for moral acts is therefore an extravagance of thought rather than an economy of thought. The same holds true of the Cartesian doctrine of innate ideas whereby man is supposed to have stamped on his mind at birth clear and distinct ideas of right and wrong. All such analogies are false. The mind is not a cabinet furnished with samples of the virtues and vices, but at birth is empty of any ideas, for ideas depend on impressions, and impressions on experience. Moral principles are not so many packages wrapped up and delivered to man's keeping, they are rather labels attached by man to actions which are found to be serviceable to society. Utility is therefore the criterion, and not assumed eternal truths.

In the same way we do not have to go back to a supposed age of innocency, as does Rousseau to a state of nature, when pure justice flourished. The observation of justice is not due to an original compact, but to a gradually attained convention similar in kind to that by which language and currency must be conceived to have come into existence.

Infused grace, innate ideas, social compacts are alluring fancies. Let us not be tempted by them, but come down to simple experience and find what that will do for us in explaining the derivation of morality. Here we have to be cautious and not dogmatic, because it is only the apparent interests and necessities of human society which determine moral codes, since these codes are not all alike in different ages and since at times good may be based on evil itself. Thus, if we trace government to its first origin in the woods and deserts, we must allow that nothing but their own consent could at first associate men together and subject multitudes to the command of one. But the present duty of allegiance to government cannot be derived from this ancient agreement of savages, for history shows that almost all historical governments have been founded originally either on usurpation or conquest, or both. In other words, concludes Hume, civic fidelity need not be derived from a supposed original compact, but to the everyday experience of man. In short, reflections on public interest and utility are the sole cause of the moral application paid to fidelity, justice, veracity, integrity.

As experience is the connective tissue which holds society together, so is it the binding principle which constitutes the mind. And as society is not a thing in itself but only a convention, so is the mind not a substance but only a name for that bundle of impressions and ideas which experience gives us. This being so, the moral code is also a construct, an artificial but useful scheme which has had no pattern in the empyrean, but has been slowly built up by the accumulated experiences of mankind. Moral truths are not eternal truths handed down to us, or injected into us, but instruments created by human experience.

In his attack on mediævalism, for such is this, Hume becomes highly modern. To make out that moral principles are not truths once delivered to mankind, but useful tools fashioned by man himself, is what is nowadays called "instrumentalism." Yet, as Hume admits, this is not "the easy philosophy," but one highly difficult to grasp. The common-sense view may be more obvious and engaging, but the profound philosophy endeavours to be more accurate and at the same time more abstruse. For this reason it is necessary to go more deeply into the metaphysics which underlies morality. This

"Inquiry Concerning Human Understanding" may be painful, but it is requisite to those who would describe with success the obvious and outward appearances of life and manners. Here analogy is in order.. The artist is better qualified to succeed in his undertaking who besides a delicate taste and quick apprehension possesses an accurate knowledge of the internal fabric. So, too, the anatomist, though he may present to the eye the most hideous and disagreeable objects, yet his science is useful to the painter in delineating even a Venus or a Helen. In like manner the philosophic moralist must possess an accurate knowledge of the internal fabric, the workings of the passions and the various species of sentiment, which discriminate vice and virtue.

It is thus that the Scotch moralist proceeds to attack not only the common-sense system of his fellow countrymen but also the more fundamental notion of mind as a substance, held by the majority of contemporary thinkers. It seemed a dangerous innovation, a profound revolution in thought that Hume projected, for without mind how could there be morals? His procedure is so subtle that the internal fabric that he speaks of seemed to many but an insubstantial fabric, of such stuff as dreams are made. But the defense is based on the principle of economy; it is directed against the multiplying of unnecessary causes, and would get rid of the mind in itself as a mere fifth wheel in the vehicle of thinking. To Hume the mind is not a substance, an entity, a thing in itself, a separate spiritual organ, but mental operations in the aggregate are sufficient to constitute a mind. They are the organic filaments which mysteriously spin themselves into what is called the self. Hence the mind resolves itself not into a reality but into a name, and the mediæval conception of mind-substance disappears like so much mist. and leaves not a wrack behind.

Critics have asked whether this philosopher, in arguing thus, has not virtually "lost his mind." Hume quietly replies that this may be true, if the mind be considered as a substance, but it is not proved, if a sufficient substitute be offered. In the same way that justice is not a celestial pattern, but a name for that complex of useful moral relations accepted among men, so with the human understanding. Now in all this David Hume is but going one step further than John Locke. When the cautious Englishman declares that there is nothing in the intellect which was not previously in the senses, the canny Scotchman argues that there is nothing in the concept of mind as such, since it is but a name for these impressions in series, this series in itself constituting all there is to the mind. What we

call mind, he concludes, is nothing but a heap or collection of different perceptions, united together by certain relations, and supposed,
though falsely, to be endowed with perfect simplicity and identity.

This is a subtle doctrine, revived in recent times under the phrase
"the stream of consciousness." It baffled Hume's contemporaries,
but it was part and parcel of his entire system which made even
moral principles to be but self-created tools. To many it seemed
that Hume was so sharp that he cut not only himself but the very
ground of rationality from beneath his feet. Hume is not troubled by
this, but proceeds in his analysis of the understanding, which he
describes as a mighty complicated machine. Take the problem of
causality. To the thinkers of his time cause was another thing in
itself, while effects were explained as due to an actual physical nexus
or bond between means and end. No, says Hume, cause is not a
nexus or knot tying events together, but only a relation of succes-
sions more or less invariably. There is no such thing as "a train of
causes, connected together by what we are pleased to call a physical
necessity."

Furthermore, causes and effects are discoverable not by reason
but by experience. No man imagines that the explosion of gun-
powder or the attraction of a lodestone would ever be [discovered
by arguments, *a priori*, that is, prior to experience. We only fancy
that, were we brought on a sudden into this world, we could at first
have inferred that one billiard ball would communicate motion to
another upon impulse, and that we needed not to have waited for
the event in order to pronounce with certainty concerning it.
When I see, for instance, a billiard ball moving in a straight line
toward another, even supposing motion in the second ball should
by accident be suggested to me as the result of their contact or
impulse, may I not conceive that a hundred different events might
as well follow from that cause? May not both these balls remain
at absolute rest? May not the first ball return in a straight line, or
leap off from the second in any line or direction? All these suppositions are consistent and conceivable. Why, then, should we give
the preference to one, which is no more consistent or conceivable
than the rest? All our reasonings *a priori* will never be able to show
us any foundation for this preference.

In a word, then, every effect is an event distinct from its cause,
and the first invention or conception of it must be entirely arbitrary.
Hence we may discover the reason why no philosopher, who is
rational and modest, has ever pretended to assign the ultimate cause
of any natural operation. Human reason may resolve the many

particular effects into a few general causes, such as elasticity, gravity, cohesion of parts, communication of motion by impulse, but as for the causes of these general causes, we should in vain attempt their discovery. The most perfect philosophy of the natural kind only staves off our ignorance a little longer, as perhaps the most perfect philosophy of the moral or metaphysical kind serves only to discover larger portions of it.

Hume's caution has landed him in a learned ignorance: his "mental geography" has ended with vast portions of the map labelled "unknown." But this is as it should be. Let us be content with the territory we know, and leave northwest passages to reckless explorers who lose their way in the end.

Here Hume reaches what he calls " the skeptical solution of these doubts." All inferences from experience are effects of custom, not of reasoning, and custom is the great guide of human life and with this we should be content. As nature has taught us the use of our limbs without giving us the knowledge of the muscles and nerves by which they are actuated, so she has implanted in us an instinct which carries forward the thought in a "corresponding course" to that which she has established among external objects, though we are ignorant of those powers and forces on which this regular course and succession of objects totally depend. By this "corresponding course" Hume means the fundamental principle of causality which he called a kind of preëstablished harmony between the course of nature and the succession of our ideas. This principle is not from the senses, for we cannot see, hear, or touch the nexus or bond between cause and effect; nor is it from the consciousness, such as the feeling of energy. While the motion of our body may follow from the command of our will, we simply know that it happens; we do not know how it happens. But though the means escape our attention, though there be no warrant in sense of reason, yet we can trust the fact without knowing the nature of the occurrence.

Hume thus reaches his academic or moderate skepticism. By this he would not destroy the trustworthiness of human reason, but only get rid of imaginary faculties like the causal. In other words, he gives this answer as to human knowledge: its origin is sensation; its extent is within the limits of experience; its certainty is probability or proximate certainty. It is in this last point that Hume exhibits his characteristic caution which finally did so much to upset the notions of his times. Nevertheless, all these views so subtle, so baffling, and ultimately so shattering to dogmatic philosophers, at the first, had no effect on his contemporaries. As a youth he had high hopes of putting forward a new "universe of thought," and at the age of five and twenty he published his first work, "*A Treatise of Human Nature*, being an attempt to introduce the experimental method of reasoning into moral subjects." But this great work, the fruit of months of meditation in a country retreat in France, when published in London in 1740 brought only bitter disappointment. But nine years later the persistent young Scot put his subjects into more popular form in his *Inquiry Concerning Human Understanding*. Now notice came to be taken of the bold thinker from over the border. The challenge of the book came in its very last passage. The main principle of Hume's system, as we have already noticed, is that custom based on experience is the guide of life. So then he asks: When we run over libraries, persuaded of these principles, what havoc must we make? If we take in our hand any volume of divinity or school metaphysics, for instance, let us ask, Does it contain any abstract reasoning concerning quantity or number? No. Does it contain any experimental reasoning concerning matter of fact and existence? No. Commit it then to the flames: for it can contain nothing but sophistry and illusion.

## THE CHALLENGE

This was the challenge issued to the whole army of thinkers who reason from assumptions prior to experience, assumptions which lie entirely beyond the reach of human capacity, such as those concerning the origin of worlds, or the region of spirits. Now the existence of any being, continues Hume, can only be proved by arguments from its cause or its effect, and these arguments are founded entirely on experience. If we reason *a priori*, or prior to experience, anything may appear able to produce anything—"the falling of a pebble may, for aught we know, extinguish the sun, or the wish of a man control the planets in their orbits." Away, then, with such reasoning and return to experience, which teaches us the nature and bounds of cause and effect, and enables us to infer the existence of one object from another.

Here we must make a qualification. When we come to morality we are at a disadvantage. Compared with other subjects, the chief obstacle to our improvement in the moral sciences is the obscurity of the ideas and ambiguity of the terms, whereas the great advantage of mathematical sciences above the moral consists in this, that the ideas of the former, being sensible, are always clear and determinate, the smallest distinction between them is immediately perceptible, and the same terms are still expressive of the same ideas, without ambiguity or variation. An oval is never mistaken for a circle, nor an hyperbola for an ellipsis.

Geometry is on one footing, the moral science on another. The latter has this fundamental disadvantage, that our authority over our sentiments and passions is much weaker than that over our ideas. Furthermore, our self-command is very different at different times. A man in health possesses more of it than one languishing with sickness. We are more master of our thoughts in the morning than in the evening; fasting, than after a full meal. Can we give any reason for these variations, except experience?

It may be that here, either in a spiritual or material substance or both, there is some secret mechanism upon which the effect depends, but to Hume this mechanism is unknown and incomprehensible. And yet the generality of mankind assume the existence of such a mechanism, just as they have recourse to some invincible intelligent principle as the immediate cause of extraordinary phenomena such as earthquakes, pestilences, and prodigies of any kind. Like the ancient theatre where "the god from the machine" extricated the players from their dilemmas, so men as a last resort are wont to appeal to a higher power even in common events. Instead of saying that one billiard ball moves another by a force which it has derived from the author of nature, it is the Deity himself, they say, who, by a particular volition, moves the second ball, being determined to this operation by the impulse of the first ball. As with the playwrights, so the philosophers have recourse to similar fancies when they try to explain human movement. In like manner, they say, it is not any energy in the will that produces local motion in our members: it is God himself who is pleased to second our will, in itself impotent, and to command that motion which we erroneously attribute to our own power and efficacy.

Thus the matter-of-fact Scotchman, who even as a youth showed no interest in the border ballads or tales of "the little people," warned his readers against getting into "fairyland," his name for that realm where supernatural suppositions and not natural experiences are relied upon for the explanation of events. However, just before his final advice to commit the great mass of books of divinity or school metaphysics to the flames, he makes this concession to current opinion: Divinity or theology, as it proves the existence of a Deity, and the immortality of souls, is composed partly of reasonings concerning particular, partly concerning general, facts. It has a foundation in reason, so far as it is supported by experience.

But its best and most solid foundation is faith and divine revelation.

When Hume wrote this, as a government servant, he perhaps had his tongue in his cheek. At any rate, the concession made with one hand is withdrawn by the other. Faith and revelation may be well for the majority, but not for the follower of academic or mitigated skepticism. John Locke, he notes, divided all arguments into demonstrative and probable; he himself would make a finer division into demonstrations, proofs, and probabilities—the first concerning mathematics, the second matters of experience, and both the second and third morals. Yet even as regards matters of experience, probability or uncertainty creeps in. Fire has always burned and water suffocated human creatures; but there are other causes, which have been found more irregular and uncertain; nor has rhubarb always proved a purge, or opium a soporific, to everyone who has taken these medicines.

Now apply this doctrine of probability to conduct and where is the universal standard of morals you talk of? This is the ethical inquiry which Hume now sums up in one of the most brilliant of his essays entitled simply, "A Dialogue." In this Hume is really describing himself in the person of his friend Palamedes, "who is as great a rambler in his principles as in his person, and who has run over, by study and travel, almost every region of the intellectual and material world." In all this Palamedes has found how great is the influence of different customs in engendering different moral ideas. A degree of luxury may be ruinous and pernicious in a native of Switzerland, which only fosters the arts, and encourages industry in a Frenchman or Englishman. We are not, therefore, to expect either the same sentiments or the same laws in Berne which prevail in London or Paris. But not only economic but also social customs engender different mental attitudes. For example, Greek manners were reserved and of an extreme purity, and as a consequence, except the fabulous stories of a Helen and a Clytemnestra, there scarcely is an instance of any event in the Greek history which proceeded from the intrigues of women. On the other hand, in modern times, particularly in a neighbouring nation, the females enter into all transactions and all management of church and state: and no man can expect success who takes not care to obtain their good graces. Henry III, by incurring the displeasure of the fair, endangered his crown and lost his life, as much as by his indulgence to heresy.

By his reference to "a neighbouring nation" Hume means France, where he had lived so many years and had met with so much hospitality as a member of the British embassy. Hence his aim is not to censure the French, but rather to point out the relativity of ideas and to show how under different skies there are different customs. Thus nothing can be more absurd and barbarous than the practice of duelling, but those who justify it say that it begets civility and good manners, and a duellist, you may observe, always values himself upon his courage, his sense of honour, his fidelity and friendships. Take another instance: Have the gods forbidden self-murder? An Athenian allows that it ought to be forborne. Has the Deity permitted it? A Frenchman allows that death is preferable to pain and infamy.

Here are three decided differences of opinion as to luxury, purity, and suicide. They show that chance has a great influence on national manners and that many events happen in society which are not to be accounted for by general rules. At this point Hume draws a distinction and by means of it furnishes a valuable generalization as to the flux and reflux of opinions. What we have just been talking about, he explains, is artificial lives and manners in which the changing fashions and systems of thought have shown the artificiality of those systems. Take the varying rôles of religion and philosophy. You know that religion had, in ancient times, very little influence on common life, and that, after men had performed their duty in sacrifices and prayers at the temple they thought that the gods left the rest of their conduct to themselves, and were little pleased or offended with those virtues or vices which only affected the peace and happiness of human society. In those ages it was the business of philosophy alone to regulate men's ordinary behaviour and deportment; and accordingly, we may observe that, this being the sole principle by which a man could elevate himself above his fellows, it acquired a mighty ascendant over many and produced great singularities of maxims and of conduct. At present, when philosophy has lost the allurement of novelty, it has no such extensive influence, but seems to confine itself mostly to speculations in the closet, in the same manner as the ancient religion was limited to sacrifices in the temple. Its place is now supplied by the modern religion, which inspects our whole conduct and prescribes a universal rule to our actions, to our words, to our very thoughts and inclinations; a rule so much the more austere, as it is guarded by infinite, though distant, rewards and punishments; and no infraction of it can ever be concealed or disguised.

In all this Hume runs true to type. Just as he practised rigid frugality in his life so did he in his beliefs. He is therefore attacking not so much philosophy and religion as extravagant philosophy and extravagant religion. Here Diogenes is the most celebrated example of the former and Pascal of the latter. The foundation of Diogenes's conduct was an endeavour to render himself as independent a being as possible, and to confine all his wants, and desires, and pleasures within himself and his own mind; the aim of Pascal was to keep a perpetual sense of his dependence before his eyes, and never to forget his numberless wants and infirmities. The ancient supported himself by magnanimity, ostentation, pride, and the idea of his own superiority above his fellow creatures. The modern made constant profession of humility and abasement, of the contempt and hatred of himself; and endeavoured to attain these supposed virtues as far as they are attainable.

In these contrasted portraits of the Athenian and the Frenchman Hume is but pointing out the relativity of results arising from varying points of view. Both these men, he declares, have met with general admiration in their different ages and have been proposed as models of imitation. Where, then, is the universal standard of morals which we talk of? The question is difficult but is not the final conclusion of the whole matter. Artificial systems give rise to artificial lives and manners, but erroneous conclusions can be corrected by sounder reasoning and larger experience. Though many ages have elapsed since the fall of Greece and Rome, though many changes have arrived in religion, language, laws, and customs, none of these revolutions has ever produced any considerable innovation in the primary sentiments of morals, more than in those of external beauty. But the Apollo and the Venus of antiquity are still our models for male and female beauty; in like manner as the character of Scipio continues our standard for the glory of heroes, and that of Cornelia for the honour of matrons.

This, then, is the key to Hume's system—"experience and the practice of the world readily correct any great extravagance on either side." Consider how this rule has already been applied in getting rid of imagined entities like the social contract, causation, and even the self as substance. Of these three the first was not an historical fact but an artifact, a name for that social consent which holds men together in multitudes. Next causation, supposed to be a physical nexus or knot which ties means and ends together, is but "the offspring of experience engendered on custom." Finally, the self as substance is but a fancy, for the mind is but falsely supposed to be endowed with perfect simplicity and identity. What we call mind, Hume explains, is a kind of theatre where several perceptions successively make their appearance, pass, repass, glide away, and mingle in an infinite variety of postures and situations.

If even the concept of mind is but a Baconian idol of the theatre, a glittering generality which has no particular existence, what of religious beliefs? The answer is brief. Hume would explain the rise of religion as due to fear and its continuance to priestcraft. Here the Scotchman again followed the naturalistic Lord Bacon, since fear is but an idol of the cave and priestcraft an idol of the tribe. Religion arose when men stood in awe before sickness and pestilence, tornado and earthquake; it continued when priests took advantage of these fears of invisible powers and agents and invented prayers and sacrifices, rites and ceremonies to appease these deities. On incessant fear there was built up that immense fabric of superstition, and it was ages before men left their first rude notions of religion. It seemed certain that, according to the natural progress of human thought, the ignorant multitude must first entertain some grovelling and familiar notion of superior powers before they stretch their conception to that perfect Being, who bestowed order in the whole frame of nature. We may as reasonably imagine that men inhabited palaces before huts and cottages, or studied geometry before agriculture, as assert that the Deity appeared to them a pure spirit, omniscient, omnipotent, and omnipresent, before he was apprehended to be a powerful though limited being, with human passions and appetites, limbs and organs.

Thus does Hume cast down another of the idols or false beliefs of his day—the notion of an original religion of mankind, pure and undefiled. Hume thus shows himself a consistent iconoclast, for his destructive views on natural religion merely follow out his previous procedure in rejecting current notions on the social contract, causality, and personal identity. As he had said before: "Let us chase our imagination to the heavens or to the utmost regions of the universe, we never really advance a step beyond ourselves, nor can we perceive any kind of existence but these perceptions which have appeared in that narrow compass."

Thus far Hume has shown himself perfectly consistent. As he started with "a very rigid frugality" in life, he pursued similar frugality in thought. His "plan of life" was the counterpart of his philosophy, whose central principle was that experience and the practice of the world readily correct any great extravagance. Nevertheless, Hume allows himself one extravagant theory and that is the doctrine of universal human sympathy. If he has been blamed for his shattering doubts because of his skeptical nature, why should he not be praised for his redeeming doctrine of sympathy because of his amiable disposition? In spite of his frugality of thought, Hume was a pattern of hospitality. Besides a cool head, he had a warm heart, as was shown by his treatment of Rousseau. Jean-Jacques as the author of unorthodox and revolutionary writings had been exiled from both France and England. When appealed to by Rousseau's friends, Hume harboured the refugee but got no thanks for the pains he took. He entertained Rousseau in his own house in London, obtained the promise of a pension from the king, and finally settled the Frenchman in a quiet country home. But the two men were incompatible in nature. Hume was subtle, cool, and placid, whereas Rousseau was the very opposite. Adding to this Rousseau's great limitation described as "an utter incapacity for establishing healthy relations with one single human being," an inevitable break arose. Rousseau charged Hume with persecuting him and with fomenting designs against his honour. Rousseau's pathological strain may excuse all this, for his persecutory hallucinations finally made him flee from England back to France. However, Hume comes out with credit in this sorry affair. At first he was outraged at the "wickedness and madness" of his guest, but he finally forgave him and exerted himself to protect the poor exile from the French government.

This affair showed that Hume practised what he preached. He sought to be frugal in most of his philosophy, but he allowed himself one extravagance and that was a belief in the principle of benevolent affection or "a feeling for the happiness of mankind" as the motive force of morality. It is impossible, he says, for such a creature as man to be wholly indifferent to the well- or ill-being of his fellow creatures, and not readily of himself to pronounce that what promotes their happiness is good, what tends to their misery is evil. As in strings equally wound up the motion of one communicates itself to the rest, so all the affections readily pass from one person to another and beget correspondent movements in every human creature.

In a way all this represents conflict and concession. There arose in Hume's mind a struggle between sense and sensibility. He leaned toward "the cool philosophy," but he had warm sympathies not only toward a man without a country like Rousseau but also toward the American colonists in their struggle for larger liberties. When it was pointed out to him that the crown had legal rights, Hume, in spite of his Tory leanings, was opposed to military coercion. Yet on the whole Hume's trend was cautious, conservative, and skeptical. Probability being the guide of life, even the assumption of social sympathy has to be modified, for he concludes that it is only probable that the final sentence depends on some internal sense or fear which nature has made universal in the whole species.

# PART NINE

## IDEALISM

# I. IMMANUEL KANT (1724–1804)

"KANT is a man of strong and constant purpose. He is a man who has made himself what he is by his strength of will. He governs his life according to principles, in moral as well as in economic and dietetic respects. He is the complete opposite of Rousseau, to whom he felt himself so irresistibly drawn. Rousseau is weakly, at the mercy of his temperament, a gypsy nature inclined to libertinism and vagrancy. Kant is, to the point of pedantry, a friend to order. Nothing is left to inclination, to the disposition of the moment. Reason is everything, nature nothing, nothing but the substratum for the activity of reason. Kant himself evidently sat as the model for his moral philosophy: the man of rational will, who acts according to principles, is the perfect man. All that takes place through natural genius, as well as the worship of the 'beautiful soul' (whose discoverer was Rousseau), was foreign to him. Perhaps we may say that there is an inner relationship between Kant's ethics and the Prussian nature. The conception of life as service, a disposition to order everything according to rule, a certain disbelief in human nature, and a kind of lack of the natural fullness of life, are traits common to both. It is a highly estimable type of human character which here meets us, but not a lovable one. It has something cold and severe about it that might well degenerate into external performance of duty and hard doctrinaire morality. The German people may well regard themselves as fortunate that there is room as well for another type of character in their nation; that is, the richer, warmer, more joyous type of the South, such as simultaneously found its embodiment and expression in the life and ideals of Goethe and Schiller.

"Kant has been often compared with Socrates. Herder, for example, in the passage already quoted, made this comparison, and it is not without justification. There is a real kinship of character and thought between the two men. In the case of both we may say that independence of disposition was the fundamental trait of their character. With their attention directed exclusively to what they considered essential, to the realization of their personal ideals, they were indifferent to external consequences. The personal mission was dominant; external position and influence were of little importance. This was true even of authorship: Socrates never attempted it, and Kant was nearly sixty years old before he attained influence as an author. And this came almost without his seeking; it is seldom that a book has been written with so little thought of the reader as the *Critique of Pure Reason*."—FRIEDRICH PAULSEN, *Immanuel Kant.*

In the life of Immanuel Kant the events of importance were the mental events which led up to what has been called that immortal masterpiece of philosophy, the *Critique of Pure Reason*. This work in turn prepared for its companion volume, the *Critique of Practical Reason*, that treatise on morality which had an immense effect both on Kant's own and on subsequent generations.

The early influence on Kant was pietism, from which is derived the derisive adjective pietistical, a word which implies a person who is narrow, puritanical, and too good to be true. Kant, of course, objected to the compulsory pietistical morality of his schooldays as making a hypocritical lot of boys, but as his parents belonged to that persuasion he wrote the following in the way of defense: "Say what you will of pietism, no one can deny the real worth of the characters which it formed; they possessed the highest that man can possess— a peace, a cheerfulness, an inner harmony with self which was disturbed by no passion."

In these words Kant described not only his parents but himself, for he led the most peaceful possible life in the little city of Königsberg in East Prussia, where the philosopher's were habits so regular that it was said that the town clock was set by his daily walk. In a way Kant was a mechanical metaphysician. When he had settled down to his old bachelor life, his manservant called him at five o'clock winter and summer and then started him off like an automaton to study two hours, to lecture another two at the university, to write at his desk, then to partake of his single meal of the day, to be followed by an hour's walk rain or shine, after which more work until nine or ten, "and so to bed."

Kant's life daily was a Pepys' Diary without any adventures, amorous or otherwise. His greatest excitement was an occasional trip to the country, where he visited his former pupils, sons of the Prussian squirearchy, such as the Counts Kayserling. But what he lacked in external events he sought to make up by learning of what other men were doing. He read travels voraciously, listened to the sea captains who dropped in at the port of Königsberg, though he himself never ventured on the sea, and was intensely interested in foreign affairs, especially in such history in the making as the revolt of the American colonies and the French Revolution. It was his sympathy with these uprisings of the people that got him into the only trouble of his life. This was an act of persecution on the part of the Prussian government when a narrow-minded monarch, Frederick William II, sought to suppress Kant's book on *Religion Within the Boundaries of Pure Reason*. Kant had been in favour with the former minister of the freethinking Frederick the Great, but this work, which would keep religion within the limits of reason alone, ran directly counter to the teachings of the state-supported Lutheran Church. The suppression of his book, the ripe fruit of almost two score years of thinking, deeply hurt Kant's feelings and also injured his health. With his naturally weak constitution, for his was a great mind in a feeble body, the philosopher had been obliged to eschew all excitement; but this cruel and stupid piece of persecution was too much for him. It was in 1794 that the College of Censors, consisting of three theologians, issued their interdict, and it was in that year that Kant withdrew from society—no small sacrifice, as Kant had many friends, and visitors often crowded into his favourite restaurant to see the famous philosopher. The next year he gave up his university classes, where he delivered highly interesting extemporaneous lectures, quite different from his dry-as-dust writings. Finally, he gave up his self-imposed Spartan regimen and consented to follow the advice of a physican.

In the meanwhile Kant's reputation had grown. The suppression of his work by a royal mandate expressing the royal displeasure as in the case of all literary suppressions only advertised the author's forbidden wares. Moreover, even the highly technical *Critique of Pure Reason* had so spread Kant's fame that in the dozen years after its publication it was expounded not only in Protestant but in Catholic universities. The reason for this was that the first *Critique* had actually effected in philosophy what Kant called a Copernican revolution. As he puts the matter: "Our suggestion is similar to that of Copernicus in astronomy, who finding it impossible to explain the movements of the heavenly bodies on the supposition that they turned round the spectator, tried whether he might not succeed better by supposing the spectator to revolve and the stars to remain at rest." Now apply this astronomical change in point of view to the realm of the mind and we find that, just as it is due to our position on the earth that the heavenly bodies appear to move about us, so it is due to the nature of our senses that we perceive events in terms, for example, of space and time. Carry this still farther into the moral realm, and just as the forms of our perceptive faculty determine our sense experience, so the forms, or postulates, of the moral faculty determine our ethical experience. In other words, we fit our lives into the frames we make for ourselves. All this, of course, makes morality subjective, but since men are built on the same pattern this leads to the hope of constructing a universal morality. How Kant tried to erect this tremendous temple of goodness which would house all humanity remains to be seen. Meanwhile, we have this picture of his personality drawn by his pupil Herder, a picture which discloses the fundamental goodness at the bottom of Kant's moral system: "I have had the good fortune to know a philosopher who was my teacher. In the vigour of life he had the same youthful gaiety of heart that now follows him I believe into old age. His open forehead, built for thought, was the seat of imperturbable cheerfulness and joy; the most pregnant discourse flowed from his lips; wit, humour, and raillery came to him at will, and his instructions had all the charm of an entertainment. . . . History in all its branches, natural science, physics, mathematics, and experience were the materials that gave interest to his lectures and his conversation; nothing worthy of study was to him indifferent; no faction or sect, no selfishness or vanity, had for him the least attraction, compared with the extension and elucidation of truth. He excited and pleasantly impelled us to mental independence; despotism was foreign to his nature. This man, whom I name with the deepest gratitude and respect, is Immanuel Kant; his image rises before me surrounded with pleasing recollections!"

## UNIVERSAL MORALITY

By those who can understand a speculative balance sheet Hume is said to have brought about the bankruptcy of Eighteenth Century philosophy. He practically declares that the notions of causality and personal identity are dubious, the soul as substance an airy nothing, and the belief in God, freedom, and immortality obsolete. He gives up religion as the source of morality, makes a certain concession as to social sympathy, but finally repudiates even that. Metaphysics may have been bankrupt under these conditions, but ethics as such was not. The Scotchman with his excessive caution may have well-nigh ruined the business, but it is a curious fact that a German philosopher of Scotch ancestry, acting as a receiver, found ethics to be a going concern. But first Kant had to take stock of the contents of his own mind and here he found that he had accepted as true those very concepts and beliefs which Hume's subtle criticism had found doubtful. It was at this juncture that he made his remarkable statements that Hume awoke him from his dogmatic slumber, by which was meant his trusting belief in the tenets of rationalism. However, the Humean rationalism was not the only subject which Kant had to handle. There was the whole movement of romanticism in which Rousseau stood as leader. The greatness of Kant's mind is shown in his ability to receive and assimilate this latter material which Hume had found so refractory. The cool Scotchman had an antipathy to what he called "enthusiasm." He might entertain Rousseau in person, but he could not entertain his ideas. But Kant sympathized with Rousseau. The latter's portrait was the only one that adorned the walls of his modest study and the day on which he received a copy of *Émile* was the only one on which he neglected to take his customary walk.

Thus Kant became the great reconciler of two opposite tendencies, rationalism and romanticism, sense and sensibility, or as he put it in new and rather clumsy terms, pure reason and practical reason. So first in his *Critique of Pure Reason*, the greatest of philosophical works since Aristotle, Kant attacked anew the problems which Hume had given up as insoluble. First came the problem of the self. To Hume the mind is but a bundle of conscious states the relations among which are mechanical and fortuitous. By the law of association one thing calls up another; this place reminds me of another, this chance odour recalls a forgotten scene of the past. In brief, the mind is but an association of ideas over which we have no control. To this Kant demurs. To him the mind is not a mere penny-in-the-slot machine which delivers ideas like so many postage stamps. The mind is not shut into sensations passively received, nor is it only mechanically acted upon by environing objects. No, the mind is active, it possesses an energy which conditions and almost creates knowledge as we shall have it. It is creative as well as critical, formative as well as formal.

In contrast to all this Hume had been reasoning in a circle. First he explained experience by the idea of causality which conjoins our impressions; next he explained causality by custom, and finally he explained custom by experience; in short, he explained experience by experience. This to Kant is not the road that leads to truth. Knowledge does not depend on sense experience alone: in knowledge there are two factors; there is, of course, one element supplied to the mind; there is also another supplied by the mind and here, as in the making of a marble statue, one element may be called the matter, the other the form. Knowledge, then, is the resultant of outward experience and inward activity; it is the laws of mind which make the reception of materials possible and without these laws there is no genuine knowledge. Imagine Newton and an idiot seated under the traditional apple tree; the fall of the apple on the head of the former—as the story goes—led to the discovery of the law of gravity; all the rest of the fruit might have fallen on the head of the idiot without any effect upon the advancement of learning.

In a way Hume makes man too simple-minded; he neglects certain complex laws of the mind which render the reception of materials possible. Such, in the terribly technical language of the German philosopher, are the pure perceptions of space and time, and the synthetic judgments *a priori*. By the former is meant the two lenses in our mental spectacles by which we look out upon the world; we would not have any experience at all unless we considered them in terms of space and time; for example, without deciding upon a place and a date we could never make a social engagement.

As for those fearful synthetic judgments, which stagger one in the first reading of Kant, they may be simplified into the statement that in certain spheres of knowledge the mind itself creates the objects with which it deals. This is especially true in mathematics; for example, the straight line, the triangle, the circle exist nowhere in nature in perfect form, yet they do exist as such in the mind. Thus the relation of the radius to the circumference of a circle cannot be measured by instruments of precision, but although incommensurable it is nevertheless a real relation. In a word, in geometry the understanding does not have to make a final appeal to experience in order to prove its propositions; it demonstrates them from the constructive principle furnished by the definition and it is this that makes geometrical principles universal and necessary.

Now credit must be given to Hume for having first clearly put forward these ideas as to what Kant calls "pure conceptual knowledge," by pure being meant that which transcends mere sense experience. Hume had already shown that in mathematics the understanding may be absolutely productive, but in morals he had reduced our knowledge of the maxims of living to mere experience. In the world of society we follow custom; when in Rome we do as the Romans do. With this conclusion Kant is not satisfied. He agrees with Hume as to mathematics; he goes beyond him in morals. Experience is a sorry guide to moral perfection; we may agree with social conventions in many ways, but we must supplement ordinary rules and regulations by the categorical imperative which manifests itself in each individual as the moral law and is formulated as follows: Act so that the maxim of thy conduct shall be a universal maxim.

In this way, continues Kant, we make the transition from popular moral philosophy to the metaphysics of morals. We must not draw our notion of duty from the common use of our practical reason, since the highest moral worth comes from a higher and purer sense. There have been, at all times, philosophers who have altogether denied that this disposition actually exists at all in human actions, and have ascribed everything to a more or less refined self-love. They spoke with sincere regret of the frailty and corruptness of human nature, but they did not attain to a noble enough idea of right to overcome these limitations. Indeed they attained only a medley of half-reasoned principles—at one time perfection, at another happiness, here moral sense, there fear of God, a little of this, and a little of that, in a marvellous mixture. It never occurred to them to ask whether the principles of morals are to be sought in the knowledge of human nature at all, and whether these principles are not to be found altogether *a priori*, free from everything empirical, just as pure mathematics are distinguished from applied.

Metaphysics of morals, then, calls for an absolute objective principle, obligatory on a will whose command is called an imperative. Now all imperatives command either hypothetically or categorically. The former may be called imperatives of skill. Here there is no question whether the end is rational and good, but only what one must do in order to attain it. The precepts for the physician to make his case thoroughly healthy and for a poisoner to insure certain death are of equal value in this respect, that each serves to effect its purpose perfectly.

But there is another imperative which commands a certain conduct immediately, without having as its conditions any other purpose to be attained by it. This imperative is categorical. It concerns not the matter of the action or its intended result, but its form and the principle of which it is itself a result; and what is essentially good in it consists in the mental disposition, let the consequence be what it may. This imperative may be called that of morality.[1]

This is highly abstract and apparently indefinite. But it is meant to be a general formula which has to be filled out by particular in-

---

[1] *Metaphysic of Morals*, Section II.

stances in order to become intelligible. The emphasis being on "the mental disposition" and not on "consequences" leads Kant to make a good will the first condition of morality and the consciousness of rectitude the final result. In other words, our motives must be perfectly pure and disinterested from start to finish and we must avoid such ends and aims as happiness, or pleasure, or utility. Take the first. Happiness leads to a doubtful search for a dubious good. The notion of happiness is so indefinite that although every man wishes to attain it, yet he never can say definitely and consistently what it is that he really wishes and wills. Does he will riches, how much anxiety, envy, and snares might he not thereby draw upon his shoulders? Does he will knowledge and discernment, perhaps it might prove to be only an eye so much the sharper to show him the evils that are now concealed from him. Would he have long life, who guarantees to him that it would not be a long misery? In short, he is unable to determine with certainty what would make him to live happy.

Take next the motive of pleasure. Reduced to its lowest terms, this means that man allows the animal in him to rule; reason is no longer the paramount rule in his life, but is subordinated to the impulses of sense. By this surrender to sense he degrades himself, abandons a higher order of things, gives up his rights as a citizen in the kingdom of rational beings, and exiles himself to the kingdom of animal nature, in short, renounces the "intelligible world" for the sake of the "sensible world."

Finally, take the motive of utility. In many cases this approaches perilously near to immorality. "White lies," for example, are supposed to be justified under certain conditions. If by a lie which is not found out I can obtain an advantage that is greater than any disadvantage for myself, why should I not lie? This sounds reasonable in particular cases, but suppose we try to make it a universal rule. We shall see that even a liar and deceiver wills that there shall not be lying and deceit, for he does not wish others to deceive him. Take a specific case. A man finds himself forced by necessity to borrow money. He knows that he will not be able to repay it, but sees also that nothing will be lent him unless he promises strictly to repay it at a definite time. He desires to make this promise but he still has so much conscience as to ask himself: How would it be if my maxim were a universal law? For supposing it to be a universal law that everyone when he thinks himself in a difficulty should be able to promise whatever he pleases, with the purpose of not keeping his promise, the promise itself would become impossible, as well as the

end that one might have in view in it, since no one would consider
that anything was promised to him, but would ridicule all such
statements as vain pretenses.

Another instance is of a man who is in prosperity while he sees
that others have to contend with great wretchedness. Suppose he
asks himself: What concern is it of mine? Let everyone be as happy
as heaven pleases, or as he can make himself; I will take nothing
from him nor even envy him, only I do not wish to contribute anything to his welfare or to his assistance in distress! Now no doubt if
such a mode of thinking were a universal law, the human race might
very well subsist. However, it is impossible to will that such a principle should have the universal validity of a law of nature. For a
will which resolved this would contradict itself, inasmuch as many
cases might occur in which one would have need of the love and
sympathy of others, and in which, by such a law of nature, sprung
from his own will, he would deprive himself of all hope of the aid
he desires.

It is unnecessary to go into other instances, such as the temptation
to suicide, where a man reduced to despair by a series of misfortunes
feels wearied of life, but is still so far in possession of his reason that
he can ask himself whether it would not be contrary to his duty to
himself to take his own life. Here the conclusion is even more
obvious than in the other cases, for we see at once that a system of
nature of which it should be a law to destroy life by means of the
very feeling whose special nature it is to impel to the improvement
of life would contradict itself, and therefore could not exist as a
system of nature; hence that maxim cannot possibly exist as a
universal law of nature, and consequently would be wholly inconsistent with the supreme principle of all duty.

By an application of the case system Kant thus builds up his
ethical jurisprudence. This he sums up in the principle that every
human will is a will which in all its maxims gives universal laws.
This, in short, is the basis of the categorical imperative which just
because of the idea of universal legislation is not based on any interest. Therefore it alone, among all possible imperatives, can be
called unconditional. So, looking back on all previous attempts to
discover the principle of morality, we need not wonder why they all
failed, for men never elicited duties, but only a necessity of acting
from a certain interest, such as happiness, or pleasure, or utility. In
other words, the categorical imperative is based upon the sublime
principle of the autonomy of the will; this means that, being self-
made and self-determined, it puts all men in a position of moral

sovereignty, in short in a kingdom of ends. By this is meant that all rational beings come under the law that each of them must treat itself and all others never merely as means, but in every case, at the same time, as ends in themselves.

Kant confesses at this point that this is "certainly an ideal," but in propounding this ideal his vision swept over a vast historical field from the system of Aristotle to the aspirations of the new American colonies. The ancient thinker was wrong when he spoke of slaves as living instruments; for that made men means and not ends. On the other hand, the new nation in the Western Hemisphere is in the right, for in its struggle for independence it is but applying the principle of the autonomy of the will; it will be no longer a means but an end, no longer a subject colony but a government of itself, by itself, and for itself.

### SELF–RULE

Kant, the lone thinker in the remote Prussian town of Königsberg, is declared by some to have been as important in history as the French Revolution itself. It is perhaps an exaggeration to compare a man to a movement, but at any rate the principle of autonomy was so much potential dynamite, both in the realm of ethics and in the realm of politics. In the coming romantic movement of the Nineteenth Century it made man the maker of his moral world and in the Twentieth furnished a philosophic basis for the principle of self-rule and the self-determination of nations. Thus the moral kingdom, argues Kant, is a kingdom of ends in which the autonomy of will is the supreme principle. Though this is the ideal, and not yet in actual existence, nevertheless every man should play his part as if it were real. This then is the law: Act according to the maxim of a member of a merely possible kingdom of ends legislating in it universally. The supreme principle of morality is the autonomy of the will whose end is the fitness of its maxims to be universal laws of its own dictation. But if this will goes out of itself and seeks this law in the character of any of its objects, then we have the source of all the previous principles of morality. Thus the principle of private happiness is false because experience contradicts the supposition that property is always proportional to good conduct. To say that it pays to be good contributes nothing to the establishment of morality, for such a maxim destroys the sublimity of morality, since it puts the motives to virtue and to vice in the same class, and only teaches us to make a better calculation, the specific difference between virtue and vice being entirely extinguished. Such moral arithmetic is on a low level; so is the police argument of future punishments where the awful conceptions of might and justice frighten some into obedience to conventional morality. This is an echo of the mediæval monarchic and despotic view, comparable to the mediæval theological view which derives morality from the divine, absolutely perfect will. This is specious because we have no intuition of the divine perfection. It also goes beyond the extreme limit of all moral inquiry. Here reason should be finally warned not to attempt the impossible lest it impotently flap its wings without being able to move in the empty space of transcendent concepts which we call the intelligible world, and so lose itself among chimæras.

Such is the substance of Kant's early views, which he called *Metaphysic of Morals*. It is only a preliminary sketch, a sort of architect's elevation in which is given a general view of the building. The exact plans and fuller details are to follow, and these are furnished in a highly technical form in the famous *Critique* or *Critical Examination of Pure Reason*, a work which has been the despair of countless students. As William James said, when we first read it we want to tear our hair; when we reread it we want to tear the author's hair. The work is elaborately divided into analytic and dialectic and subdivided into definitions and remarks, theorems and corollaries, the whole forming a jungle of subtle terms in which many have been lost. However, this book contains enough plain language and ordinary observation to enable us to catch its drift. Thus the practical principles are first divided into subjective principles, or maxims, when the condition is regarded by the subject as valid only for his own will, and objective or practical laws, when the condition is valid for the will of every rational being.

This distinction is fundamental, because by harmonizing the two Kant is able to reach his categorical imperative: Act so that the maxim of thy will can always at the same time hold good as a principle of universal legislation. This absolute moral command means that a private maxim, which shall become "valid for the will of every rational being," must be so sound that it shall be fit to be erected into universal moral legislation. Thus the principle that everyone may deny a deposit or loan of which no one can produce a proof, when brought as a law, would annihilate itself, because the result would be that there would be no deposits. This is a lofty ideal, but it may perhaps be reached by eliminating all selfish impurities and low motives. Imperatives, explains Kant, when they are conditional, are practical precepts and not laws. At the most they can be called only hypothetical imperatives, since they do not determine the will simply as will but only in respect to a desired effect. For example, tell a man that he must be industrious and thrifty in youth, in order that he may not want in old age, and this is a correct and important practical precept of the will. Now tell a man that he should never make a deceitful promise; this is a rule which only concerns his will. If now it is found that this rule is practically right, then it is a law, or a categorical imperative.

Practical laws that are quite pure, that is free from any taint of ulterior advantage, furnish the materials for constructing universal maxims. On the other hand, if with Epicurus we make virtue determine the will only by means of the pleasure it promises, such virtue is not of the highest. It is based on the principle of private happiness and its determining principles belong to the lower desires. The Epicurean system is really only a selfish moral arithmetic; it deals with the magnitudes of the feelings of agreeableness or disagreeableness. Thus a man may return unread an instructive book which he cannot again obtain in order not to miss a hunt; he may depart in the midst of a fine speech in order not to be late for dinner; he may leave a rational conversation, such as he otherwise values highly, to take his place at the gaming table; he may even repulse a poor man whom he would at other times take pleasure in benefiting, because he has only just enough money in his pocket to pay for his admission to the theatre.

The Epicurean, ancient or modern, is no seeker after pure rational principles of morality; he does not ask whether the ideas are of the understanding or of the senses, but only how much or how great pleasure they will give for the longest time. In the same way, to the man who wants money to spend, it is all the same whether the gold was dug out of the mountain or washed out of the sand, provided it is everywhere accepted at the same value. But the pure reason must be able to determine the will without any idea of the pleasant or unpleasant. Private happiness must not taint the purity of one's motive; the good will is the only thing that counts; even utility is no criterion of virtue, for outward results are secondary. Thus a man's volition may be frustrated by palsy; no matter, the mere intention is good in itself, good irrespective of success. Again the outward act, though meant for good, may be positively harmful, but if the will was good, conscience demands no more. In other words, the good will is good in itself, not for what it accomplishes, but for what it is. Here, of course, the mere pious wish is not the chief thing, but a man's conscious effort to do all he can.

Kant's aim in all this was to gain a universal law which pays no heed to the lower desires and has no regard to the self. This law is called an "imperative" because the good will is a command to itself, and "categorical" because it says: You *must* act thus and so. This has been considered by many as the high-water mark of morality. Whatever its practicality, at any rate, the rising tide of speculation wiped out the previous systems. Thus Kant himself drew up an elaborate table showing how his predecessors had failed to reach the true foundation of morality. This table is somewhat artificial, yet we may see how rival schemes do fit into its pigeonholes. Former practical principles are divided into subjective and objective, and these in turn are subdivided into external and internal. Thus subjective external principles are education as advocated by Plato and Aristotle and the civil constitution by Hobbes and Hume, while the corresponding internal principles are the physical feeling of Epicurus and the moral feeling of certain English and French thinkers. In the parallel columns of the objective we have as the internal principle the perfection of the Stoics, and as the external principle the will of God of theological moralists like Augustine and Aquinas.

This pretty well disposes of the great bulk of Kant's predecessors. But they on their part might turn upon him and make disparaging remarks: You call your categorical imperative the end and aim of practical reason; but how unpractical and how unreasonable it would be to expect moral advancement without external education to guide youth and civil government to keep men in the straight path. You repudiate physical feeling as a false internal principle, but does any man live who does disregard creature comforts and condemn himself for being a bit of an Epicurean? You even repudiate the moral feeling or moral sentiment, but did you not once have a great enthusiasm for Rousseau? His sentimentalism may have been overwrought and his character bad, but you yourself said that even in the case of Voltaire the badness of his character should not blind the true scholar to the greatness of his talents. As for the system of the Stoics, how does this differ so widely from your famous declaration: "Two things there are which the oftener and the more steadfastly we consider them, fill the mind with an ever new and rising admiration and reverence—the starry heaven above, the moral law within"? Finally, as for the will of God, consider how many thousands of devout believers in the principles of Augustine and Aquinas, of Calvin and Luther, have depended upon this external objective principle as the lodestar of their lives. You warn such believers against this exercise of supernatural faith, telling them that reason should not attempt to pass the extreme limit of moral inquiry lest it may impotently flap its wings in empty space. Really, now, do you not do the same thing when you declare that the categorical imperative should have no reference to self, no reference to utility, no reference to practical results?

In eliminating all previous principles of morality Kant reminds one of the pedagogue who goes to the blackboard, rubs out all he finds on it, and proceeds to put down his own solution as the final answer to the problem. For this erasure there was a certain justification. As a teacher in a state-supported institution, a teacher who was also interested in politics, Kant objected to certain Prussian policies. His pure morality was a counterfoil to such "real politics" as when the Prussia of Frederick the Great and his successors followed the precept of Machiavelli, that the end justifies the means. This was Kant's personal reaction to unmoral utilitarianism. His objection to external authority was also personal. Under the doctrine of the divine right of kings the ruler was the supposed interpreter of the "will of God." This hit Kant when he was reprimanded for publishing his *Religion Within the Bounds of Reason* and forbidden by the narrow-minded minister of Frederick William II to write further on any problems which might impinge on the state religion.

But a more profound motive drove Kant to reason as he did. He was a descendant of pietists, and his parents, from all accounts, were model members of that persuasion. Kant himself recalls the unselfishness of his mother and how his father, the saddler, even when overreached by his rivals never gave way to recriminations. There was a practical purity about his people which fundamentally influenced their son and led him, at least in theory, to reach out after a universal law which pays no heed to the lower desires, has no regard to the self, and makes the good will the supreme test. This may sound like a principle of self-abnegation, and Kant has been criticized as the advocate of a Quakerish doctrine of non-resistance. It is true that he temporarily gave in to the absurd demands of the Prussian private chancellor as to writing further on the rational limits of religion. This is the one act of moral weakness in his long life. But his fundamental principle of self-sufficiency, of individual reliance on a self-made categorical imperative, was not a principle of weakness but of strength to the coming generations. It furnished the very marrow of resistance in Fichte's addresses to the German people to throw off the yoke of Napoleon; it reappeared in the revolution of 1848 when the men who revolted against the tyranny of the crown demanded a constitution made by the people themselves and not by self-styled interpretors of "the will of God."

Thus Kant the philosopher of Königsberg, who never crossed the boundaries of East Prussia, was the spiritual creator of the new Fatherland, and while Machiavellians like Bismarck and his crew might claim the chief credit in guiding the ship of state, it was the people, inspired by the principle of autonomy, who furnished the driving power.

## II. ROMANTICISM

"SCHELLING was himself, always, even as philosopher, a creature of the moment. His moments were indeed often very great ones and might need each a whole volume to express itself. But Schelling is not, like Kant, a systematic and long-plotting thinker; nor yet, like Fichte, a man who, after many adventures, is completely overwhelmed and thenceforth possessed by a single idea. No, Schelling possesses directly the wavering passion of his romantic friends. His kaleidoscopic philosophy, which changed form with each new essay that he published, was like their whole scheme of life and of art. Trust your genius; follow your noble heart; change your doctrine whenever your heart changes, and change your heart often. Such is the practical creed of the romanticists. The world, you see, is after all the world of the inner life. Kant cut us off from things in themselves; Fichte showed us that it is the I, the self, that makes the world. Let us accept this lesson. The world is essentially what men of genius make it. Let us be men of genius, and make what we choose. We shall then be as gods, knowing good and evil.

"Herein, as you see, lies at once the great difference between the romantic school and Fichte. Fichte said: The world is the world as self-consciousness builds it; but the essence of self-consciousness is the moral will, the will to act dutifully, steadfastly, nobly, divinely; and therefore the world is duty solidified to our senses. The romantic spirit says from the very start: The world is indeed the world as self-consciousness builds it; but the true self is the self that men of genius, poets, constructive artists know; hence the real world is such as to satisfy the demands of the man of genius, the artist. Emotion, heart-experience, longings, divinations of the soul, are the best instruments for the philosopher. Dream out your world. It is after all but a dream of the inner life, this vast universe about us. The noblest dreamer will be the man to understand it the best."—JOSIAH ROYCE, *The Spirit of Modern Philosophy.*

## PERSONAL IDEALISM

Immanuel Kant left this as his message: Do not depend upon the senses or upon society, but depend upon yourself and your own spirit. The outcome of this advice was romanticism, or the cultivation of the inner life. This has been described as a movement in which the whole energy of spiritual forces was directed to the enlargement, enrichment, and independence of the ego, a movement where new powers and possibilities are added by one thinker or another until man is ready to acclaim his personal soul as a spark of the divine fire, a spirit free from the limitations of the body.[1]

Some have considered romanticism as a mere temperamental journey through life and the romanticist as a Don Quixote fighting verbal windmills and achieving no practical results. This is too severe a criticism. Romanticism was a new crusade; it awakened whole peoples to a fresh vision of life and spiritual adventure; in fact, it was what the earliest of the romanticists called "the way to the blessed life." This meant, in the language of an American romanticist, Josiah Royce, that the only real world is the world of conscious activity, and so of spiritual relationships, of society, of serious business, of friendship, of law, of natural existence—in a word, of work.

This description is largely true to the facts. Romanticism was the main highway from which there branched off roads traversed by philosophers like Fichte and Schelling, by poets and dramatists like Goethe and Schiller, by political writers like Moeser and Schubart, by educational reformers like Pestalozzi and Froebel, and by religious liberals like Novalis and Schleiermacher. It was the great movement of "Storm and Stress," the movement toward freedom from the bondage inspired by society, the stage, and the church, from fixed traditions, conventional canons, and rigid creeds. It was a modern movement which, beginning with Rousseau, fell back upon the original rights of man and upon his instincts and feelings; in brief, a valiant, and at times futile, effort of man to enlarge his spiritual sphere by giving back to him his birthrights.

In this alluring map of fresh fields and pastures new we can follow but one road, that of the moral philosophers. The path had already been traced by those who were tired of the dusty highroad of dogmatism. These were the rationalists of the so-called Illumina-

---

[1] R. M. Wernaer, *Romanticism and the Romantic School in Germany*, p. 134.

tion who had held that all things were fashioned according to fixed principles, as if providence were a Roman surveyor who carried the Via Rationalis straight over hill and dale, over crag and torrent until he reached his destination. But the romanticists did not think that nature was built in straight lines, nor the cosmos arranged in geometrical patterns. They revolted against this cut-and-dried way of looking at things. Leibnitz, for instance, had taught that this is the best possible world and that all is arranged according to pre-established harmony. Now Voltaire had declared that this is, after all, not such a well-ordered universe as is commonly supposed. Nevertheless, he, too, had had a touch of the romantic spring fever and had helped in the revolt against those who held that man should be guided by the strict regimen of custom and confined in the strait-jacket of tradition. Here to a certain degree he approached the position of his rival Rousseau, and the two French writers thus came to inflence profoundly the German mind, the one affecting the upper classes, the other the middle. Voltaire had liberalized the mind of Frederick the Great in regard to religious matters, and Rousseau had so moved Kant in matters concerning the morals of emotion that the day on which the latter received a copy of *Émile* was a red-letter day in his life.

The romantic movement, in other words, was no sudden outburst, no uncaused event. The summer of sentimentalism had been preceded by a long springtime of speculation. Here the apparently unemotional Kant had been stirred in turn by the apparently unemotional Hume, for the latter's *Dialogues on Natural Religion* were founded on feeling or natural sentiment rather than upon reason and demonstration. Skeptical of the achievements of reason, Hume had finally fallen back upon the principle of faith. These two phrases were repeated by Kant. In his *Pure Reason* he had come to the conclusion that man dwells on an island of phenomena, or appearances, where the fog bank of ignorance hides from his vision the noumena, or things-in-themselves. To pierce these mists of agnosticism which blanket the intelligible world he invented various devices such as the categorical imperative and the three postulates of practical reason. Thus he added to the home-made universal maxim of conduct the three great beliefs in God, freedom, and immortality, the first of which guarantees a moral order of the universe, the second the possibility of human activity, and the third a future life of happiness.

Schopenhauer, the pessimist, in a cynical mood called these postulates a series of tips to compensate the slave of duty for a life devoid of happiness here below. In this criticism he missed the spirit of the very first of the romanticists. It was Johann Gottlieb Fichte who insisted that the essence of morality is the joyous doing of right, and that life consists in working and hoping. Here the chief mark of German thought, from the mysticism of the Middle Ages onward, has been described as indomitable will and strong self-confidence without which the conviction of the everlasting supremacy of the inner over the outer cannot be asserted and maintained.

It was here that Fichte, son of a Saxon peasant, had to build himself an ideal world as compensation for what he lacked in actual opportunity. In this romantic scheme there was considerable conceit, but also considerable truth. In a way Fichte illustrates the saying that a self-made man is one who worships his own creator; but he also propounded the correct formula of creative idealism that "the outer world is the stuff, the material for our duty, made manifest for our senses." Without a projective imagination, which sets the goal of ambition in the future, man becomes an idle drifter, whereas the ambitious man is like the athlete who determines to break his record, who never gives up, and is never discouraged. This ideal Fichte exemplified in his own life of alternate struggle, defeat, and moral victory. When he first taught school he raised the standards so high that the parents of his pupils dismissed him. After that he betook himself to the Kantian doctrine and applied it to the philosophy of religion in his *Critique of Revelation*. By a curious chance Fichte's name was omitted from the title page, the work was attributed to Kant himself, and when the latter corrected the mistake the real author became famous and in spite of his youth was called to fill a professorship at Jena. Here he was falsely charged with atheism, the actual motive for the attack being Fichte's defense of the freedom of the press against the reaction engendered by the fear of the French Revolution. Dismissed from his professorship, he finally went to Berlin, where his romantic idealism, as applied to the political situation, had a magnificent vindication. Berlin at that time was garrisoned by the French and the rest of Germany lay under the iron heel of Napoleon. So in 1808 Fichte delivered his famous *Addresses to the German People*. In these the burning question is asked: "Where is the Fatherland?" The answer of the idealist is: "The Fatherland is within your hearts." This means that while the nation cannot yet control its external affairs, nothing can prevent its cherishing the secret desire for autonomy and independence. This message was carried far and wide, and when the war of liberation ensued Fichte, although not a combatant, fell a victim to the war.

*Boule's famous statue*

FRANCIS BACON: An Elizabethan moralist

Attacked by an infectious hospital fever, he died in 1814, a date whose meaning is symbolized in the symphony of Tchaikowsky, where the strains of the Marseillaise break through and stir the blood of every son of freedom.

The idealism of Fichte became, as it were, the intoxicating music of the soul. Kant had stood for the autonomy of the self, but the semi-feudalism of his day prevented him from defending such political liberty as the French advocated. But Fichte was all for personal freedom and for that liberty of philosophizing which entitles the thinker to project out of himself schemes not only for individual rule and for national independence, but even for man's domination over the world of nature. All this is portrayed in Fichte's *Vocation of Man*, whose message goes beyond that of Kant's *Practical Reason*. This work does not place happiness in a transcendent life but declares that it is possible to achieve it here and now: I *am* immortal, imperishable, eternal, declares Fichte, as soon as I form the resolution to obey the laws of reason; I do not need to *become* so, the supersensual world is no future world; it is now present; it can at no point of finite existence be more present than at another; not more present after an existence of myriads of lives than at this moment. My will, which is directed by no foreign agency in the order of the supersensual world, but by myself alone, is this source of true life, and of eternity.[1]

All this is consonant with the usual statements of personal idealism, but it does not lend itself to that curious form of so-called "new" thought, which implies an actual power of the animate soul over inanimate objects, as in those psychological fictions of thought transference by ether waves, or the levitation of tables by "will power." Fichte is an idealist but not an occultist. I am indeed compelled to believe, he explains, and consequently to act as if I thought, that by my mere volition my tongue, my hand, or my foot might be set in motion; but how a mere aspiration, an impress of intelligence upon itself, such as will is, can be the principle of motion to a heavy material mass—this I not only find it impossible to conceive, but the mere assertion is, before the tribunal of the understanding, a palpable absurdity; here the movement of matter even in myself can be explained only by the internal forces of matter itself.

With this distinction between the inner and the outer world Fichte proceeds to describe the second step in his thought. My view of the will, he continues, absolutely disregards all earthly objects,

---

[1] *The Vocation of Man*, Book III, Section III.

and generally all objects lying out of itself, and recognizes itself, for its own sake, as its own ultimate end. But by such a view of my will I am at once directed to a supersensual order of things, in which the will, by itself alone and without any instrument lying out of itself, becomes an efficient cause in a sphere which, like itself, is purely spiritual, and is thoroughly accessible to it.

From these two steps Fichte attains to faith in the supersensual, eternal world, and overcomes his blindness concerning spiritual things by being absorbed no longer by mere earthly objects. In this he goes further than Kant, who had said that man is confined to an island of sense phenomena where his vision into a world of things-in-themselves is blocked by the fog bank of human ignorance. To this Fichte demurs: My moral will, he asserts, shall certainly produce consequences, shall break through the magic circle of ignorance by conceiving of a law of the spiritual world, in which my pure will is one of the moving forces, as my hand is one of the moving forces of the material world. My own firm confidence in these results, and the conceptions of this law of the spiritual world, are one and the same— they are not two thoughts, one of which arises by means of the other, but they are entirely the same thought; just as the confidence with which I calculate on a certain motion in a material body, and the conception of a mechanical law of nature on which that motion depends, are one and the same. The conception of a law expresses nothing more than the firm, immovable confidence of reason in a principle, and the absolute impossibility of admitting its opposite.

Here the romanticist takes a bold step; the little ego of self-determination upon which Kant based his categorical imperative has given way to the great ego from which is derived a law of a spiritual world. This law, explains Fichte, is not given by my will nor by the will of any finite being, nor by the will of all finite beings taken together, but is a law analogous to the law of gravity in which each body partakes of the universal moving power of nature.[1] Just as in the physical world the ambitious athlete can set himself to lifting heavier and heavier weights, so in the spiritual world the ambitious youth can put before himself the goal of professional or business success. To gain an education as a doctor or a lawyer or a financial expert he will deny himself pleasures, work harder, and bend every effort to attain his object. In a way Fichte preaches the good side of the gospel of success as dependent upon the power of the will and of faith in oneself to move mountains of difficulty. But the

---

[1] *Vocation of Man*, Book III, Section IV.

function of the will here is not only negative but positive; it not only overcomes but creates. Like a track-laying machine it keeps projecting from itself the rails upon which it is soon to run.

The romanticist expresses this in more technical and also in more poetic forms. The ego posits itself, said Fichte, and its world is an eject of the ego; while his poetic followers compared it to a flying goal which, though never reached, lends the intoxication of movement, since in romanticism all is movement, all is tendency. This has been called a revival of the ancient philosophy of fluxility where all things flow. The world is a rushing metamorphosis, as Emerson said; it is a constantly changing stream whose charm is motion and novelty. This, of course, lends itself to a certain vagueness, a certain indefiniteness of goal, and at times to a certain spirit of melancholy. The symbols are strange and varied. The romantic quest becomes the "blue flower," ever sought, but never found; its banner bears "a strange device," and its bearer perishes in the Alpine cold of disappointment. This is the later and somewhat decadent phase of romanticism, the phase of the sorrows of Werther, who in the ironic language of the robust Thackeray, being rejected by his lady-love, went and "blew his silly brains out."

However, this morbid metaphysics, which eventuated in the pessimism of Schopenhauer, was not the metaphysics of Fichte. His was a personal idealism which looked on the bright side of life and was all for success. So, as the inspirer of Germany, his teaching has been called the "ethics of creative genius" and his rôle that of a liberator. Here a severe critic of the historical moral systems declares that even if German philosophy of the first half of the Nineteenth Century, like German society of that time, did not dare throw off the fetters of the feudal system, still it aided the sadly needed moral revival of Germany, inspiring the young generation toward a higher and more idealistic service to society. In all this Fichte is of particular importance and nearly approached some of the conclusions of rational, scientific ethics. The philosophy of Ancient Greece strove to become a guide in human life. The same aim was pursued by the moral philosophy of Fichte. His demands with respect to morality itself were very high, that is, he insisted upon complete disinterestedness of moral motives, rejecting all egoistic aims. He demanded complete and clear consciousness in human will, and he upheld the broadest and highest aims, which he defined as the supremacy of reason attained through human freedom and the eradication of human inertia. In other words, it may be said that morality, according to Fichte, consists in the triumph of the very essence of man, of the very basis of his thinking, over that which he passively assimilates from the environment. Furthermore, Fichte maintained that conscience should never be guided by authority. He whose actions are based on authority acts in a conscienceless manner. It can easily be imagined how elevating an influence such principles were to the German youth in the twenties and thirties of the Nineteenth Century.[1]

Fichte was but one figure in a great pageant which began with Luther and the Reformation, continued through the German struggle for liberty against the Napoleonic tyranny, and apparently ended with the abortive revolution of 1848 when those of its own household tore up the liberal constitution and repudiated the promised rights of free speech, a free press, and universal suffrage. On this historical canvas may be put romantic figures like the exiles of 1848 who escaped from the Fatherland, came to America as the promised land of freedom, and founded on the banks of the Mississippi a school of idealism which blended its currents with the transcendental movement of New England. In the latter Emerson, like Fichte, was the prophet of the "golden age" of American thought, and his essays on "Self-Reliance" and the "Over-Soul" reproduce in transatlantic form the message of courage and independence, of self-confidence and the importance of the inner life, which Fichte was advocating across the Rhine. Here Emerson was no copyist and his works no mechanical echo. As an independent Yankee he declared that the sentiments of the German idealist had long been in his own mind and only served to confirm what he had already thought himself. But like Fichte this native prophet of romanticism found a kindred soul and a common inspiration in Kant. Or, as Theodore Parker expressed it, there are to be found in the works of the philosopher of Königsberg three great primal principles, namely, the instinctive intuitions of the divine, of the just and right, and of the immortal, the last meaning a consciousness that the essential element of man, the principle of individuality, never dies. It is this principle that Fichte in part, and his successors more fully, seize as a central principle. But it must be said that as a personal idealist Fichte was inclined to exaggerate his discovery. Thus in the conclusion of the *Vocation of Man* he declares that there is no destructive principle in nature, for nature throughout is pure, unclouded life; it is not death which kills but the more living life, which, concealed behind the former, bursts forth into new developments.

---

[1] Prince Kropotkin, *Ethics: Origin and Development*, p. 225.

Death and birth are but the struggle of life with itself to assume a more glorious and congenial form. And *my* death—how can it be aught else, since I am not a mere show and semblance of life, but bear within me the one original, true, and essential life? It is impossible to conceive that nature should annihilate a life which does not proceed from her—the nature which exists for me, and not I for her.

This is a bit of colossal conceit, a fatal weakness in the Fichtean system left for correction by his successors. To make the world an eject of the ego, to say that when one expresses himself he expresses the universe, is to put in metaphysical terms the fable of the frog and the bull, for the romantic egotist literally bursts with his own self-importance. In the face of ridicule, then, the matter must be mended, and this is done by Friedrich Wilhelm von Schelling, who transforms or enlarges subjective idealism into objective idealism. By this conversion it is nature which becomes absolute reality. Here man is not the source, but the remote consequence. So while the idealist may participate in the infinite source of light, yet only broken rays reach his consciousness, or, as put in the inspired language of Shelley, "Life like a dome of many-coloured glass stains the white radiance of eternity."

## ROMANTIC MORALS

Published in the year 1800, Fichte's *Vocation of Man*, with its emphasis on egotism, pointed the inevitable way to a larger view of man's relation to the universe. Fichte himself in his later doctrine of religion enlarges his personal idealism to a cosmic idealism. The moral order no longer lies in man but in the divine Being, and supreme beatitude consists in the union of the soul with the absolute One. This thought, showing the influence of Spinoza, whose mystical morality had at last come into its own, is expressed by Fichte in highly poetic language. The divine existence is absolutely through itself, and, of necessity, light, namely, inward and spiritual light. This light, left to itself, separates and divides itself into an infinite multiplicity of individual rays; and in this way, in these individual rays, becomes estranged from itself and its original source. But this same light may also again concentrate itself from out this separation and conceive and comprehend itself as One, as that which it is in itself, the existence and revelation of God.[1]

---

[1] *Doctrine of Religion*, Lecture X.

Fichte, like Spinoza, urged a belief in the necessity of man's union with the divine, and also like Spinoza confessed that we are unable to conceive this relation. It therefore remained for his successors, the romanticists proper, to attempt to lead man out of this asylum of ignorance. It was Novalis who sang the praises of this new mystical morality. Philosophy, he explained, will not bake your bread, but she will give you God, freedom, and immortality. This explanation, printed on the title page of the earliest philosophical journal in America, was all very well for a motto, but sadly in need of vindication. Novalis could not furnish this, for he simply returned to the earliest egotism of Fichte when he said: "We seek the plan of nature in the outside world. We ourselves are this plan. Why need we traverse the difficult road through physical nature? The better and purer road lies within our own mind."

This is futile; it is reasoning in a circle, a mere return upon one's own tracks. It was therefore left for a greater romantic thinker to break out of this magic circle of conceit and to show that he who thinks that he is creating a world by the mere projection of his thoughts is already a part of that world, in short not a creator, but an exponent of the cosmic order. But though man may be but a fragment of the stupendous whole, his rôle is important. In the language of an earlier thinker, Francis Bacon, man is the interpreter of nature, while in the language of later evolution, which watches the moving hand of time, man is the latest product of the unrolling cosmic processes.

Romanticism, then, is a species of creative evolution. There is not only mind within, but mind without; the outer world order is not an eject of the ego, but man himself is the product of that world ego. His coming into being is late, but when at last he appears on the stage the part he plays is significant. Nature is intelligent but inarticulate, so it is for man to speak the prologue and tell what has taken place and what is preparing behind the curtain. So man becomes the interpreter and spokesman of nature; he tells its tale not as a drama whose beginning and end he fully grasps, but as an immense epic without proper beginning and definite end, a vast poem in which the ages are as cantos and single beings as single words, words which have no meaning separated, but only when considered as identified with the whole.

This is the fine interpretation of a recent American idealist: it is akin to the statement of Emerson, who defined nature as the present expositor of the divine mind whose serene order is inviolable to us. It can be imagined what an appeal this made to the poetic imagination of the times. Kant had said that we cannot know things-in-themselves; Fichte had made nature a sterile negation, a mere self-limitation, technically called the "not-me," which meant practically nothing. In contrast to all this Schelling now held that nature is a palpable emanation of the divine mind, and claimed that the romanticist has a direct and intuitive knowledge of this mind. This is not because of a magic insight, but because of essential kinship. Man understands nature because he is of its own household and in his epic wanderings longs to return to nature as did Odysseus to Ithaca. And as the hero of old grew wise by visiting many cities and meeting many men, so the race by its very vicissitudes enables the individual thinker to explain, at least in part, the meaning of history and the meaning of the unfolding of the divine plan. Thus in contemplating the ruins of empires and the rise and fall of peoples, the philosopher has gained a deep sympathy with the struggles of humanity because he finds in himself traces of these struggles.

Such notions as these led Schelling to translate the forbidden Marseillaise and to see in the French Revolution, despite the Terror, the very ferment of freedom, and as a philosopher, looking within, to discover an even wider and deeper meaning in the vast backward of the race. As with Rousseau, the return to nature signified to him a return to more primitive times, when men dwelt in innocency, simplicity, and morality. This to the opponent of romanticism has seemed a voyage to mere coasts of illusion, like Odysseus' journey into fairyland, to fair Calypso's isle and the land of the lotus eaters. But there was a modicum of truth in the matter. As Pestalozzi, the romantic pioneer in educational reform, put the matter, the growing child grows through the very stages which humanity once traversed and his years, from infancy through adolescence, recapitulate the hunting, nomadic, agricultural, and industrial ages of mankind.

This scheme of phylogeny, of the gradual genesis of the race, is a scheme which has again and again reappeared in the history of education from Froebel with his kindergarten to John Dewey with his experimental school at Chicago. It may be artificial and specious to a degree, for no child unfolds in this historic fashion, nor passes in set order through these precise stages. Still the romantic originators of this scheme, despite its faults, did seem to explain that restless change which affects every child of nature. It especially applied to the "Stormers and Stressers" of Schelling's day, the younger generation in revolt against conventional morality, a rigid social system, orthodox religion, and even the classical canons in the arts. To them no one was a true romanticist who had not undergone his year of wandering, or sought far and wide for the "blue flower" of romance.

Such was the poetic and symbolic language which more or less disguised the revolt of flaming youth. Nevertheless, these "beautiful days of hope and inspiration" had a sinister side. The strange actions of the Jena circle were enough to disturb even the Jovelike calm of Goethe, who, like the ruler of Olympus, had had his affairs of the heart, but had finally settled down. Nevertheless, the very outpourings of his genius furnished an excuse for all these romantic experiments, not so much his morbid *Sorrows of Werther*, or the insipid tale of *Hermann and Dorothea*, as the spirit of Faust, the taster of the joys of life and experimenter in the dangerous potions of passion. As the great genius acted and thought so did the lesses geniuses.

In all this the Jena circle has been compared to the Brook Farm experiment, which also sought to break with a puritanic past. But here the young American transcendentalists were almost monastic in comparison to the young German romanticists, for out of the threefold vows of poverty, chastity, and obedience the latter followed perforce only poverty. In this connection the matrimonial permutations that occurred between Schelling and the brothers Schlegel on the one side, and the sisters Dorothea and Caroline on the other, furnished a sorry example of the formula of "an unrestricted life according to nature" and did much to discredit the whole romantic movement. Caroline was responsible for the fatal phrase, "an easy-going way of dealing with things," while Dorothea, during her liaison with Friedrich Schlegel, illustrated the latter's romantic aim of establishing the free world of the spirit, not only in art but also in life. This new freedom, however, had good points as well as bad. Thus in Friedrich Schlegel's curious novel of sex, *Lucinde*, the doctrine of autonomy, of self-determination, was carried into relations of which the real author of this doctrine, the old bachelor Kant, never seemed to have thought. If Dorothea called the experiment a whirligig of speculation, it was also a matrimonial game. Under the guise of "elective affinities" its members exchanged wives as well as ideas, and that which began with free thought ended with free love. It was a strange situation. With Machiavelli the ends justified the means; with the later romanticists genius justified moral lapses, and the beautiful heart or a poetic disposition covered a multitude of sins.

Schelling's *Lucinda* was ahead of its times. It advocated a kind of companionate marriage where love came first and the ceremony afterward, if at all. One can imagine the tempest stirred by this sort of progressive polygamy in a respectable monogamous land like

Germany. So the word "romantic" was used loosely to denote loose living, and centres like Jena were considered centres of moral infection in the social body. But all this may be partly discounted, for the advocates of elective affinity were few in number. The hectic excitement of romantic love burned itself out and the broader romantic philosophy of nature took its place. The love of nature, the study of nature, came into its own and had a beneficial effect, for contact with the mind of outdoors has a way of cooling the human mind.

Although the nature philosophy of Schelling and his followers did much to assuage the earlier fervours, a certain weakness remained in their study of the external world. This world was not so much the fair apparition that shines about us as Emerson described it, not so much the quiet entity that asks, "Why so hot, little man?"— but rather the counterpart, the counterfoil, that vibrates in sympathy with all human emotions. Hence arose the pathetic fallacy, the notion that for every mood in man there is a corresponding mood in nature. Thus the sorrows of some wandering Werther are reflected in the "weeping" clouds, while even the successive acts in the play of *William Tell* are symbolized by the storm on the lake and the succeeding calm. For the drama and for the accompanying music all this might be legitimate, but stage thunder and pastoral pipings are hardly the proper accompaniments of real life. Nevertheless, a whole generation was entranced by what old Kant had called "the phantoms of the magic lantern," until a strange air of unreality hung about the whole movement. At this juncture Schopenhauer, the pessimist, appeared, turned his cynical eye upon these scenes, and argued that the romantic philosophy of nature was false. To him nature was not kind but cruel, not sympathetic but ruthless— in brief, relentless will hiding behind the phenomena of the cosmic unfolding.

## III.   ARTHUR SCHOPENHAUER (1788–1860)

"IT MAY come as a surprise to those who affect to hold Schopenhauer in abhorrence, without, perhaps, really knowing the nature of his views, that, in this theory of the essential evil of the human will— the common selfish idea of life—he is reflecting and indeed probably borrowing what he describes as the fundamental tenet of Christian theology, that 'the whole creation groaneth and travaileth in pain,' standing in need of redemption. Though Schopenhauer was no friend to Christian theology in its ordinary tendencies, he was very much in sympathy with some of the doctrines which have been connected with it. In his opinion the foremost truth which Christianity proclaimed to the world lay in its recognition of pessimism, its view that the world was essentially corrupt, and that the devil was its prince or ruler. It would be out of place here to inquire into the exact meaning of this statement, or to determine the precise form of compensation provided for the ills of life under any scheme of doctrine which passes for Christian: and even if it were in place, the task would be an extremely difficult one; for probably no system of belief has ever undergone, at various periods, more radical changes than Christianity. But whatever prospect of happiness it may have held out, at an early date of its history, it soon came to teach that the necessary preparation for happiness, as a positive spiritual state, is renunciation, resignation, a looking away from external life to the inner life of the soul—a kingdom not of this world. So far, at least, as concerns its view of the world there is nothing in the theory of pessimism which does not accord with that religion which is looked up to as the guide of life over a great part of the civilized world."— T. BAILEY SAUNDERS, *Essays of Arthur Schopenhauer.*

Schopenhauer was essentially selfish; circumstances to a certain extent made him so. His father, a rich merchant, left him a good income, while his mother practically told him that she preferred his room to his company. This callous act was perhaps an indirect means of revenge upon the son as surrogate or scapegoat for the father, for the latter was egotistical, cynical, and melancholy. Schopenhauer's antecedents were against him; whether the father's death by drowning was intentional or accidental is not known; at any rate, he left his son a sorry inheritance—the grandmother insane, one uncle insane, another idiotic, a third neurotic. This bad family history goes far to explain the life and system of Schopenhauer, from his cynical remark that the philosopher need be no saint to his final rejection of the virtue of lovingkindness on the ground that altruism is not the last step in life, for even acts of charity are scarcely worth while. The whole matter is summed up in these sombre words: He who sees through the individual and recognizes the real nature of the thing-in-itself, as world will, his will turns round, no longer asserts its own nature, but denies it; that is to say, it no longer suffices for such a man to love others as himself, but there arises within him a horror of the nature of which his own phenomenal existence is an expression.

It is the fashion to call Schopenhauer a degenerate, but the word is meaningless when one considers the brilliancy of his work and the fact that he preserved his faculties to the last days of a long life. He was cynical, selfish, emotional, neurotic—yes; degenerate—no. There is more than one factor to explain his system, factors external as well as internal. It is true that he was terrified by fears of robbery and assassination, morbid fears that made him keep a loaded pistol at his bedside; it is true that he fancied a conspiracy of silence on the part of the philosophers when his writings received but tardy recognition. But this was not the only factor that made him declare that "life is a ticklish business." He was also affected by outside influences. There were the abortive revolutions in Germany with the inconsequent killings of bystanders, the wrongs of the industrial system in England with its child workers in the factories, the cruelty of slavery in North America with its thousands of slaves driven by the lash. With these known facts in mind Schopenhauer's pessimism seems but a protective covering for his feelings; he suffered himself, he could not help suffering for others.

It is this unexpected humanitarian note on the part of the pessimist that later drew attention to his writings. From a different angle, but with a similar sympathy, he was like Elizabeth Barrett Browning in voicing the cry of the children, like Charles Dickens in denouncing the strict penitentiary system of Philadelphia which made solitary confinement, idleness, and ennui means of punishment, and like Samuel Taylor Coleridge in abhorring cruelty to animals. Here the Sacred Books of the East came in to reënforce his sentiments. Pitifulness, he exclaims, is the cardinal virtue, and the sense of organic solidarity, of the ultimate identity of all creatures great and small, is the basis of morality. This contact with the Oriental wisdom literature was highly significant; outwardly it was shown by a statue of Buddha in Schopenhauer's study, inwardly by the statement that the reading of the Upanishads had been the "consolation of his life, and would be the consolation of his death."

## PESSIMISTIC MORALITY

*The World as Will and Idea.* These words, which form the title of the chief work of the greatest modern pessimist, are taken from the very vocabulary of the romantic school. But what a difference in meaning is given them. The "will" so far has been interpreted as ranging from the good will to the free will, and the "idea" has been expanded into glittering hopes of human perfection and human happiness. The romantic school in thought had been like the contemporary sentimental school in art, where every picture had a burst of high lights, every figure was outlined in bright colours, and every face was fair. But Schopenhauer would have none of this. His pictures of the world and of humanity were more akin to the deeply bitten lines of Albert Dürer with their sombre subjects, Melancholy, and Death and the Knight. So while Schopenhauer takes the words out of the very mouths of the romanticists, he transvaluates their values. The will is the world will, relentless, implacable, caring nothing for man; the idea is no bright sun of hope shining in the sky, but only fond illusion, vanity of vanities, the Web of Maya.

In these phrases drawn from the skeptics, the Scriptures, and the Sacred Books of the East the foremost pessimist of the Western world rings the knell of romanticism. His words have the fascination and poignancy of a tolling bell when in the twilight of feeling eye and ear are lulled to rest. To judge from its numbers, the romantic optimism had a greater success, but the pessimism of Schopenhauer was more profound. Fichte had started by putting the pyramid of reality on its apex. He had conceived of the universe as an eject of the ego, as if total reality were a mere projection of man's mind. Schopenhauer reversed this romantic procedure. He put reality back on the solid base of nature, the world will being fundamental and man but the last expression of that will. The romanticist had said, "You are what you think you are." Schopenhauer retorted: "If you think that, you are wrong." The ground or sufficient reason lying behind reality is "a restless appetite toward being, life, and realization which sweeps through us, which we are and which is all things." In the language of Wordsworth, it is a "motion and a spirit that impels all thinking things, all objects, and all thoughts, and rolls through all things."

The cosmic will, then, is primary and essential; it is not an abstract idea, an empty conception, but a vital impulse and instinct. When we think we create this power we are mistaken; it creates us. The followers of pure reason, who thought they could pyramid their mental assets, brought on bankruptcy. They were no more successful in spinning real universes out of their inner consciousness than were the revolutionists of 1848 in their manufacture of paper constitutions. In other words, man is not the master, but the product, not a creative first cause, but the last manifestation of immense cosmic processes. And yet in all this vast sweep humanity's part is not petty. In man the world will is striving most fully to express itself; man represents the latest step in the scale of being. And

though man is at the top of the ladder of existence, he has no reason
to consider himself monarch of all he surveys, for he represents but a
fraction of the tremendous forces at work in the universe. Let us
look back, said Schopenhauer, to the beginnings. Starting with a universal, all-pervading will, the world ground objectifies itself first in
mere force. Like a blind and unconscious god it strives to express itself in rude efforts and impulses like gravitation and the cohesions
and repulsions of masses of brute matter. After this titanic stage
comes the vegetative, and the world will becomes the principle of
life and growth in plants. In animals it becomes more individualized
and, lastly, in man receives its highest manifestation as self-consciousness. Then the will at last knows itself and what it is.

But what is this will and what the value that nature puts upon
itself in its final efflorescence? In a similar vein and with a similar
plan the later romanticists, the so-called nature philosophers, had
come to the conclusion that man is not only the last but the most
valuable of nature's products, the finest flower of the cosmic processes. They looked into nature as into a mirror, and like Narcissus
were entranced at their own reflected image. What fools! exclaimed
Schopenhauer. The world will may strive endlessly to objectify itself, but only to find the futility of conscious striving. It begins as
a Titan and ends as a Sisyphus, for it has but vainly rolled the stone
to the top of the hill.

This is pessimism, the very opposite of the romantic optimism.
Both made much of the will and of the spirit of effort. Yet though
both have a common centre, their conclusions are diametrically
different. The romanticist begins with energy and ends with the joy
of living; Schopenhauer begins with energy and ends with ennui.
Vanity of vanities, all is vanity—again and again he echoes the
words of the preacher of old. The explanation of this reversal of
romanticism, this transvaluing of values, is perhaps pathological.
Yet at this critical point, the great divide where the optimist looked
into the happy valley and the pessimist into the valley of despair,
there is much that is valuable. The ethics of Schopenhauer may end
in self-abnegation, but it begins with self-assertion. In the course of
evolution man emerges on the scene full of appetites and desires.
The will to live, which means the will to self-preservation, is nature's first law. From the start man strives to satisfy his appetite.
The intellect, increasing, multiplies the impulses to be gratified.
Civilization enlarges the sphere of man's desires, it does not morally
improve him. But the desire to be happy clashes with others' happiness, hence society strives to curb it. Civil justice between man and

man arises, but this is merely a compromise, not a corrective. Society may put on the muzzle, it does not change the character. It gives an opiate, it does not eradicate the disease—selfishness. But besides society there is something stronger. This is the cosmic will, which now turns on man, as shown in remorse and the stings of conscience. This means that the world ground is striving to show us that our lives are petty in relation to the whole and that the things we strive for are really not worth while and that greater than the individual self is the self of humanity. In a word, ethics, which begins with self-assertion, ends with self-abnegation, and egoism turns to altruism.

This to many has seemed a strange conclusion. The majority in the Western world have held that pessimism leads to wickedness, that its essence is selfishness, that it even justifies suicide, when the individual finds that he has not obtained what he longed for in this life. The outcome of a proper idealism is optimism and the happiness of mankind, declares the romanticist. But that, retorts Schopenhauer, is a false interpretation. Kant turned men's thinking the wrong way when he held before them the glittering hopes of God, freedom, and immortality, and Fichte's ethics was "a magnifying glass for the errors of the Kantian ethics." The personal idealists were especially in error; they fancied that in making the world an eject of the ego they were creating a world of progress and prosperity, whereas they were only blowing iridescent soap bubbles to be pricked by the first touch of logic. It is not the individual who determines nature, but nature which determines the individual. The life and efforts of man may be "the most perfect manifestations of nature," but in interpreting these manifestations we must take care lest we put upon them a superficial polish which only hides the true character of the material beneath. In the words of Talleyrand, "man has received language in order to conceal his thoughts," and those thoughts, deep within his consciousness, are really thoughts of sorrow and sadness. Hence personal happiness must be given up, the great sacrifice of self must be made in order to obtain salvation. Lovingkindness, says Schopenhauer, is the real cardinal virtue, and it was reserved for Christianity to theoretically formulate and expressly advance it, not only as a virtue, but as the queen of all, and to extend it even to enemies. We are thinking only of Europe, he continues, for in Asia, a thousand years before, the boundless love of one's neighbour had been prescribed and taught as well as practised.

Nevertheless, altruism is not the last step, for even acts of charity are scarcely worth while. Beyond the positive is the negative step, the quietistic ethics of self-abnegation, where the assertion of the will gives place to the denial of the will. Here the individual learns that the happiness of the community is greater than that of the individual and also that relatively the community is little compared to the cosmos. If my happiness is a relative illusion, so is the service of the whole race, and the conclusion of the whole matter is this: All is vanity.

This is the very reversal of romanticism, the philosophy of personal idealism, of faith in progress and in the happiness of the race. It marks the reaction against the two European revolutions, that of 1789 in France, where the perfectibility of man was launched with high hopes, and that of 1848 in Germany, when dreams of freedom and self-determination soon vanished under the return of political reaction. This is the external side; what went on in Schopenhauer's own mind is more to the point. The optimistic pantheism of the nature philosophers seemed superficial to him, and the pathetic fallacy of nature's sympathy with man only maudlin sentimentalism. When the romanticists exclaimed: We are the poets, literally the makers of the universe, Schopenhauer retorted: Certainly you are poets, but your description of the shining goal in which the hero expects to find fulfilment is a mere idyll, while your ethics are very insignificant, being made up of trifling sorrows, trifling delights, and trifling efforts. In other words, the romanticist is a petty interpreter of nature, for nature is made up of the tremendous forces over which man has no control—the force through which the crystal is formed, that by which the magnet turns to the north pole, the force whose shock he experiences from the contact of two different kinds of metals, the force which appears in the elective affinities of matter as repulsion and attraction, decomposition and combination, and, lastly, even gravitation, which acts so powerfully throughout matter, draws the stone to the earth and the earth to the sun.

It there was one man who gave a staggering blow to romanticism is was Schopenhauer. Take as a test a comparison of what the optimist said on the final issues of life and what the pessimist. In the *Vocation of Man* Fichte thus soliloquizes: "And *my* death? . . . It is impossible to conceive that nature should annihilate a life which does not proceed from her;—the nature which exists for me, and not I for her." Put over against this the words of Schopenhauer in the *World as Will and Idea:* It is a weary longing and complaining, a dreamlike staggering through the four ages of life to death, accompanied by a series of trivial thoughts. Such men are like clockwork, which is wound up, and goes it knows not why; and every time a man is begotten and born the clock of human life is wound up anew, to repeat the same old piece it has played innumerable times before, passage after passage, measure after measure, with insignificant variations. Every individual, every human being and his course of life, is but another short dream of the endless spirit of nature, of the persistent will to live; is only another fleeting form, which it carelessly sketches on its infinite page, space and time; allows to remain for a time so short that it vanishes into nothing in comparison with these, and then obliterates to make new room. And yet, and here lies the serious side of life, every one of these fleeting forms, these empty fancies, must be paid for by the whole will to live, in all its activity, with many and deep sufferings, and finally with a bitter death, long feared and coming at last. This is why the sight of a corpse makes us suddenly so serious.

## THE REVERSAL OF ROMANTICISM

Why is there so diametrical a difference in the conclusions of the two philosophers, romantic and pessimistic? Their systems are like two streams starting from a common watershed, one diverging into a sparkling river of happiness, the other ending in a dead sea of despair. The critical point, the initial force that explains the ultimate diversions, is apparently temperamental. In the case of Fichte we have the born optimist bound to look on the bright side of life; in the case of Schopenhauer a born pessimist who at the time he became of age declared that "life is a ticklish business." Now while Schopenhauer was a precocious genius, this precocity has itself been declared pathological and signs of a progressive degeneration have been traced back to these early days. The problem is difficult. Schopenhauer's appalling picture of humanity, with its vain struggles and distressing sense of the illusion of life, has been declared the metaphysics of a madman and dismissed as futile and worthless. For all that the insight of his genius was not the less deep. Like his follower and successor Nietzsche, another pathological case, the clarity of his vision leads to a stark realism which is difficult to discount, for the romanticist, looking at life through rose-coloured spectacles, cannot be said to give a true picture of things as they really are. At the least the pessimist dared to look at the dark side of life and in doing so claimed that many of the greatest figures of history were of like mind with himself—Gautama Buddha, Christian saints from St. Francis of Assisi to Angelus Silesius, Meister Eckhart and Madame Guyon. But even this comparison does not settle the problem. The teachings and practises of ascetic saints have been declared the results of sheer morbidity and even of abnormal sexual conditions and the consequent mysticism with its doctrine of absorption into Nirvana, or the Divine Essence, as purely pathological.

Whether this be true or not, Schopenhauer praises these ascetics as beautiful souls, because they mortify not only the will itself, but also its visible form, its objectivity, the body, and because they practise fasting, chastisement, and self-inflicted torture in order to break down and destroy the will, and at last, when death comes, to welcome it and receive it gladly as a longed-for deliverance. Life, he concludes, is like a course or path through which we must unceasingly run—a path of red-hot coals, with a few cool places here and there. To escape this, then, the mystic must cease to will anything, to guard against attaching his will to anything, and seek to confirm in himself the greatest indifference to everything.

Schopenhauer had perhaps gained contact with Eastern thought through Friedrich Schlegel's *Language and Wisdom of the Old Hindus*, but he was the first of the Western philosophers to build up a system which ran counter to the spirit of his times. We Occidentals, he as much as says, in believing that force, energy, and will power and material success represent reality, go only halfway. The Orientals are more profound. The true sense of reality which is inward has been overlaid by the veneer of conventionality, the calls of ordinary life, the practices of civilization. The result is that we have fallen into the bad habit of looking upon ourselves in the same way we look upon other things. In the white light of reason everything appears isolated and independent. But feeling and intuition are deeper; they bring back the lost sense of cosmic solidarity. Everything, though apparently independent, has reference to something else, and cause and effect represent a sort of shadow thrown across from one thing to another by the unrecognized fundamental unity. Here the wisdom books of the East come in with their message. The Vedas and Puranas have no better simile than a dream for the whole knowledge of the actual world which they call the Web of Maya. . . . Perhaps I also may be allowed to express myself by a metaphor. Life and dreams are leaves of the same book. The systematic reading of this book is real life, but when the reading hours (that is, the day) are over, we often continue idly to turn over the leaves, and read a page here and there without method or connection: often one we have read before, sometimes one that is new to us, but always in the same book. . . . If, therefore, we consider the question from a point of view external to both, there is no distinct difference in their nature, and we are forced to concede to the poets that life is a long dream.

It is certainly strange that, starting with the world as will, as energy, as force, Schopenhauer should reach the conclusion of the world as an idea, or representation of unreality, a mere presentation, a vain apparition, in a word, illusion. Others had taken the doctrine of will and had made it optimistic and positive; Schopenhauer took the same doctrine and made it pessimistic and annihilistic. How explain this? When Schopenhauer declared that life was "a ticklish business" he suggested a solution; it was mere touch and go which way he would envision the universe. His manner of thinking seems like the optical illusion where, in gazing at a mosaic pavement, at one moment the white squares, at another the black, fall into pre-dominant patterns. In ordinary vision the images shift; in speculative vision one image or the other remains fixed and this fixation seems to be due to temperament. It appears that Schopenhauer was no voluntary pessimist, but that he could not help being one; he did not take the belief, the belief took him; he did not will to believe, he could not help believing. Periods of passivity, succeeding the over-strenuous life, left him in a state of exhaustion and disillusionment. Feeling devitalized, he no longer willed to live as an individual, but to leave the toils and troubles of the creature and sink into "the vast bosom of a peaceful Nirvana." It is as if he said to himself: I am so exhausted that nothing is worth while except to escape this exhaustion. In other words, it was nerve depletion that led him into the successive steps of quietism, pessimism, and philosophical nihilism, and to find satisfaction in the inscription on an Italian tomb, "Seek the eternal calm."

Yet this is not the whole of Schopenhauer. At one time he says that life swings like a pendulum backward and forward between pain and ennui. At another he admits that life is not all suffering and boredom; a more virile point of view is presented in his famous theories of æsthetics, whereby he seeks redemption, not by the ascetic life, but by the medium of art. In the quest for the platonic idea as the object of art he advocates pure knowing, free from will, as the only pure happiness, which is neither preceded by suffering or want nor necessarily followed by repentance, sorrow, emptiness, or satiety. . . . What we see in poetry we find again in music; in the melodies of which we have recognized the universal expression of the inmost history of the self-conscious will, the most secret life, long-ing, suffering, and delight; the ebb and flow of the human heart.

This is significant. We know that Schopenhauer was so highly strung that he was driven distracted by noise and that as an antidote to this he sought the solace of music. To him this was the highest of the arts, because it gives the ultimate essence of the life of will throughout the universe; its burden is the quintessence of all joy as well as of all sorrow. It best interprets the secrets of our very being; there is no such pleasure and no such sadness as are brought forth by its poignant strains.

But there are other realms or objects of art in which we may reach reality, for art as the offspring of genius beholds only eternal ideas, the essential and permanent lying behind the phenomena which are only shadows. It is the artist's aim to impart these ideas to others by expressing them in sensible form. In this way he bodies forth creations of beauty which exemplify the similar stages of the world will. Just as there is a higher grade in the plant than in the stone, and in the animal a higher grade than in the plant, so it is in the hierarchy or successive orders of the arts. First are the plastic arts, and at the bottom of the scale comes architecture, from the massive forms of pyramids to the flying buttresses of the cathedral, the series exhibiting the play and mechanical forces of resistance against gravity, the calculated balance between stresses and strains. In sculpture, as a plastic art, a higher stage is reached, for here the artist gives the general through the particular, as in Michael Angelo's recumbent figures of Night and Day. So, too, individual figures can open up the very secrets of life and death; such are Dürer's etching of Melancholia, and Rembrandt's "Hundred Guilder" print of Christ Healing the Sick. And the poetic arts go even higher, for they give ethical lessons. Through tragedy, especially, does Aristotle declare that our hearts are purified by pity and by fear. But music is the highest of the arts; it alone hales the soul out of the body; it alone frees us from the limitations of space and time and enables us so to forget ourselves as to be absorbed in another world, another realm of being.

All the arts, though in varying degrees, are satisfying, for all tend to the absorption of the subject into something higher; all tend to assuage the spirit distracted by the multiplicity of objects. With art the many are left behind and transcended by the one, the persistent form or type of the whole species of things. The beautiful object is now contemplated out of its uses and out of space and time. In the language of Emerson, it is a symbol of higher uses and higher meanings, since it opens up vistas of infinite suggestion. The beautiful object is sufficient in itself, its bare contemplation is its own reward.

In the frame of meditation the spectator is no longer an anxious, care-worn personality, seeking what he has not, craving rest and happiness and being constantly disappointed. Now, at last, in ecstatic contemplation, he no longer wills or wishes; he is absorbed in his object, identified with it, and gives up his individual being. Ethics, which began as self-assertion, ends in self-abnegation; man is now one with nature; he has pierced the veil of phenomena, he has reached the thing in itself, the ground or sufficient reason lying behind the world; he has identified himself with that will which disposes of all things in vital sympathy. In other words, he has attained the stage of empathy, of a sublimated sympathy, he feels himself part and parcel of the universe; he has passed beyond egoism and, in the strange formula of the Eastern wisdom literature, he can say not "I am I," but "I am Thou."

## IV. FRIEDRICH WILHELM NIETZSCHE (1844–1900)

"HERE we observe that Nietzsche advocated an aristocratic arrangement of society. A firm believer in tradition, law, and order, and, in spite of his opponents' accusations, an undaunted enemy of anarchy and *laisser aller*, he saw in socialism and democracy nothing more than two slave organizations for the raising of every individual to his highest power. Individuality made as general as possible, or, in other words, socialism and democracy, meant to Nietzsche the annihilation of all higher aims and hopes. It meant valuing all the weeds and noble plants alike, and with such a valuation, the noble plants, being in the minority, must necessarily suffer and ultimately die out. Where everybody is somebody, nobody is anybody. Socialism, i.e., organized individualism, seemed to Nietzsche merely the reflection in politics of the Christian principle that all men are alike before God. Grant immortality to every Tom, Dick, and Harry and, in the end, every Tom, Dick, or Harry will believe in equal rights before he can even hope to reach heaven. But to deny the privileges of rare men implies the proscription from life of all high trees with broad branches—those broad branches that protect the herd from the rain, but which also keep the sun from the envious and ambitious shrub—and thus it would mean that the world would gradually assume the appearance of those vast Scotch moors of gorse and heather where liberalism and mediocrity are rampant, but where all loftiness is dead."—A. M. LUDOVICI, *Nietzsche: His Life and Works.*

## BEYOND GOOD AND EVIL

Schopenhauer's system begins with self-assertion and ends with self-abnegation. With his acknowledged pupil, Nietzsche, self-assertion is reasserted, but in place of a gray twilight where the individual will is absorbed into the world will, there is presented a picture where "the strongest and highest will to life does not find expression in the miserable struggle for existence, but in a will to war, a will to power, a will to overcome."

These words were uttered by Nietzsche to his sister; they furnish a key to the philosophy of life of an invalid who declared that the year contained for him two hundred days of pure pain. As such they express not only a reaction against the current pessimism, but a declaration of independence on the part of an intensely emotional and nervous temperament, which sought to substitute a "gay philosophy" for a gloomy philosophy, a "joyful science" for world weariness. But the revolt went further than mere personal protest. Nietzsche the individualist sought to become a leader of other individualists, to hold up the banner of liberty of action for all free spirits. Modern Europe, he declared, is overspread with a dull gloomy seriousness, and modern civilization tends to engender mediocre men, while herd morality governs the masses who, like silly sheep, blindly follow the calls of the shepherd in church and state. The present age, in brief, is in a period of decadence. Slave morality rules and master morality is forgotten. Hence it is needful to take a wider view of history, to forget the present and look backward to the past and forward to the future. On the one hand, this means to prehistoric man who won all his virtues from the wildest, most courageous beasts, and on the other to the coming superman, engaging in vast hazardous enterprises "with a conscience of steel, and a heart of brass."

To put this in another way, the modern man, threatened with decadence, needs a sort of "flight and forgetfulness." He must erase the ethical ideas of the present, however popular and respectable they may be. He must see that democracy is the cult of incompetence and Christianity a morality for slaves. In their place he must put the doctrines that there is no law for the overlord, because he dwells in a realm "beyond good and evil," and no limit to "the will to power," because the soul has skill to pluck out of battle sweet and glorious truths.

From the very titles of Nietzsche's works one can construct his philosophy. In part it resembles that of Rousseau in the latter's return to nature and in his revolt against convention and the whole civilized environment in which he was brought up. But when the Frenchman sought by going back to primitive tribes to recover an Arcadian peace the German scorned the "placid happiness of the herd." For his ideal, then, he picked the lover of war and not the lover of peace as the type to be indicated. Let us here, he says, acknowledge without prejudice how every higher civilization hitherto has originated. Men with a still natural nature, barbarians in every terrible sense of the word, men of prey, still in possession of unbroken strength of will and desire for power, threw themselves upon weaker, more moral, more peaceful races (perhaps trading or cattle-rearing communities), or upon old mellow civilizations in which the final vital force was flickering out in brilliant fireworks of wit and depravity. At the commencement, the noble caste was always the barbarian caste: their superiority did not consist first of all in their physical, but in their psychical power—they were more complete men (which at every point also implies "more complete beasts").

Such, according to Nietzsche, is the origin of ethics, which arose, as it were, by creating a kind of moral vacuum, beyond good and evil, where the noble type of man disregards the petty distinctions of right and wrong existing among the weaker peoples and replaces them with other standards. Here the noble type, with a fine disdain for others, regards himself as a determiner of values; he does not require to be approved of, he himself passes the judgment. Saying to himself that that which is injurious to me is injurious in itself, he knows that it is only he himself who confers honour on things; in a word, he is a "creator of values."

Whether this account is historically true is dubious, yet biologically it has a certain plausibility. Since a living thing seeks above all to discharge its strength, since life itself is will to power, it follows that the conquering races represent the will to live, for in them there is the feeling of plenitude, of power, which seeks to overflow.

Lest this description be criticized as an over-simplification of history, Nietzsche hastens to add that there are many kinds of morals which have been invented by man. There are systems which are meant to justify their author in the eyes of other people; other systems of morals are meant to tranquillize him, and make him self-satisfied; with other systems he wants to crucify and humble himself; with others he wishes to take revenge; with others to conceal himself; with others to glorify himself and gain superiority and distinction—this system of morals helps its author to forget, that system makes him, or something of him, forgotten; many a moralist would like to exercise power and creative arbitrariness over mankind; many another, perhaps, Kant especially, gives us to understand by his morals that "what is estimable in me is that I know how to obey— and with you it shall not be otherwise than with me!" In short, a system of morals is only a sign language of the emotions.

Of all these systems it is the last which Nietzsche considers to have been the most potent, for it is the conquering races who have sought to exercise power and creative arbitrariness over mankind. In the longest period of human history—the prehistoric period— the value of an action was inferred from its consequences; this may be called the premoral period of mankind. But in the last ten thousand years, on certain large portions of the earth, it is no longer the consequences of an action but its origin which decides with regard to its worth, and that origin was the supremacy of the aristocratic values determined by the conquering races who unconsciously followed the biological urge. But when the modern bourgeois leaders in pacifism and democracy claim that morality consists in refraining mutually from injury, from violence, from exploitation, and in the attempt to put one's will on a par with that of others, they are wrong. This would make the fundamental principle of society a will to the denial of life, a principle of disillusion and decay. But here, insists Nietzsche, one must think profoundly to the very basis and resist all sentimental weakness: life itself is essentially appropriation, injury, conquest of the strange and weak, suppression, severity, obtrusion of its own forms, incorporation, and at the least, putting it mildest, exploitation.

However, continues Nietzsche, on no point is the ordinary consciousness of Europeans more unwilling to be corrected than on this matter; people now rave everywhere, even under the guise of science, about coming conditions of society in which "the exploiting character" is to be absent—that sounds to my ears as if they promised to invent a mode of life which should refrain from all organic functions. "Exploitation" does not belong to a depraved, or imperfect and primitive society: it belongs to the nature of the living being as a primary organic function; it is a consequence of the intrinsic will to power which is precisely the will to life.

In this diatribe there is manifest Nietzsche's contempt not only for what he called the "anæmic Christian ideals" but for the current socialistic movement with its abhorrence of exploitation, whether military or capitalistic. Yet in spite of the prevalent beliefs of his day Nietzsche stuck to his guns. Fascinated with his ideas of the origin of morals as due to the imposition of arbitrary aristocratic values, and reënforced by the evolutionary doctrine of the struggle for existence, he argued that humanity could proceed only in so far as it followed the lower orders of nature. The coming aristocracy, he explained, must have as its fundamental belief that society is not allowed to exist for its own sake, but only as a foundation and scaffolding, by means of which a select class of beings may be able to elevate themselves to their higher duties, and in general to a higher existence—like those sun-seeking climbing plants in Java which encircle an oak so long and so often with their arms, until at last, high above it, but supported by it, they can unfold their tops in the open light, and exhibit their happiness.

To a certain degree Nietzsche recognizes that this is a relapse into a more primitive state of mankind, for the coming ultramoral stage beyond good and evil resembles to a certain extent the prehistoric, premoral period of mankind. But there is this difference: The cave man was not bothered as to either the origin or the character of his actions; all he cared for was consequences. If irrational taboo or silly incantations brought certain results, that was all he was interested in. But with the modern man, after ten thousand years of specu-lation, the outlook is different. Bedevilled with doubts about remote origins, good intentions, categorical imperatives, and the like, he is not as well off as was the cave man who wanted only results. There is need, therefore, for an ultramoral stage, a surmounting of morality, a certain "extravagance and adventurous pluck," in short, severity and craft which furnish favourable conditions for the development of strong, independent spirits rather than gentle, refined, yielding good nature. In the present age men are not great enough, not hard enough, to be entitled as artists to take part in fashioning man; men, not sufficiently strong and far-sighted to allow, with sublime self-constraint, the obvious law of the thousandfold failures and perish-ings to prevail; men, not sufficiently noble to see the radically differ-ent grades of rank and intervals of rank that separate man from man—such men, with their "equality before God," have hitherto swayed the destiny of Europe; until at last a dwarfed, almost ludi-crous species has been produced, a gregarious animal, something obliging, sickly, mediocre, the European of the present day.

In painting this picture of his contemporaries Nietzsche was paint-ing a picture of himself, except that he was not mediocre. As an invalid he had much time to think, and suffering gave him an almost abnormal clarity of insight into the workings of the human mind. As he himself put it: "the enormous tension of the intellect bent on the mastery of pain shows everything in a new light." So like a wounded animal he watched those about him, and their slightest gestures had a meaning for him. Thus his remarkable classification of the different systems of morals as being based on self-justification, or tranquillization, or revenge, or concealment, or self-glorification, led him to describe any system of morals as only a sign language of the emotions.

Now what were the emotions that stirred him? From countless casual remarks in his own works, and from the inadvertent admission of his sister in her elaborate biography of her brother, we know that he who prided himself as being the "first immoralist" was quite the opposite. When he held up for admiration the inhuman superman "with a conscience of steel and a heart of brass," he himself, to borrow one of his own phrases, was "human all too human."

At this point Nietzsche has been pictured as a mere degenerate with a decadent body.[1] It is more accurate to say that he was a brilliant intellect striving to overcome years of suffering brought about by a series of unhappy mischances. In his schooldays he was strong, to judge from the amount of work he accomplished; but at the beginning of the Franco-Prussian War a fall from his horse brought on a suppuration, and camp diseases, which he contracted as a voluntary nurse, led to the use of strong medicines which ruined his digestion. So in the ensuing low state of vitality in which Nietzsche found himself he received such impressions of the horrors of war that he could never speak of them afterward. Impaired in health and yielding to use of chloral to assuage his insomnia, Nietzsche now did what others have done in like circumstances. He erected a defense mechanism and sought in a kind of waking dream to fashion the figure of a man who was everything that he himself was not. In other words, the supersensitive soul erected the figure of a superman, the invalid invented an ideal compounded of those very qualities which he himself lacked. The contrast between fact and fiction was striking. A retiring student, he nevertheless wrote: "Combat is the food which gives strength to the soul"; a model of obedience in school and army, he declared that he loved "him who is of a free spirit and a free heart."

This is the positive paradox; the negative is of like nature. "With the soul of a Christian knight," as his sister described him, Nietzsche

---

[1]According to Havelock Ellis there seems to be no trace of insanity or nervous disorder at any part in the family history, as far back as it is possible to go. The Nietzsches and Oehlers were simply very intelligent, very high-strung.

was forever denouncing "the anæmic Christian ideal"; "incredibly good," as a close friend insisted, he held up the coming man as one beyond good and evil. The contrast between fact and fiction can be carried still further. The son of a middle-class parson of Prussia and in his days of invalidism somewhat spoiled by a devoted sister, Nietzsche's admiration was all for the aristocracy, particularly the Prussian aristocracy, while his ideal of life was for "vast, hazardous enterprises," and for "throwing the dice with death." Some have considered these palpable discrepancies as marks of a self-deluded fool, and these flamboyant ideals as a symptom of an exaggerated egoism, verging on madness. It is true that Nietzsche finally became insane, but that was only after his work was done and only after years of suffering had led him to the use of dangerous drugs. How valiant was his will to overcome only he himself knew, for the conclusion of a previous passage shows that it was a strong and not a weak mind that could write such words as these: "The enormous tension of the intellect, bent on the mastery of pain, shows everything in a new light, and the unspeakable charm of every new light is often powerful enough to overcome all the allurements of suicide, and to make the continuance of life appear as most desirable to the sufferer."

Nietzsche has been counted among the weaklings. The truth seems to be that he should be counted among the heroic souls, portrayed by Giordano Bruno, who overcame mountains of difficulty. As a sympathetic French critic has well expressed it, he took from himself every prop and yet he did not bend; to complain, even in a passing manner, would be to avow defeat.[1]

Nietzsche put himself through a process of renunciation, issued to himself a series of self-denying ordinances. The son of a Christian minister, he denied himself the comforts of religion; born in a bourgeois family, he avoided the complacent morality of the middle classes. In short, he did what the Epicureans did, prepared himself for a life of revolt and solitude. His scheme may be called one of salvation through selfishness, but to judge from the state of his mind this was largely justified. A passage from his allegorical work *Thus Spake Zarathustra* is apparently a bit of his own biography: "I am too hot and burnt with mine own thoughts . . . then I must go into the open air and away from all dusty rooms." This, to repeat a former memorable phrase, was but "flight and forgetfulness," and explains another strange document, namely Nietzsche's negative

---

[1]Daniel Halévy, *The Life of Friedrich Nietzsche*, p. 218.

commandments. They run as follows: "You must neither love nor hate the people. You must in no way occupy yourself with politics. You must be neither rich nor poor. You must avoid the path of those who are illustrious and powerful. . . . You must accept none of the ceremonies of the church."

The ancient antipathy and indifference are here brought into modern life and serve as a cooling potion to one hot and burnt with his own thoughts. Impatient at "the secret hardship of his lot," Nietzsche well knew what he needed, and that was mental peace at any price. He had had certain warning experiences when his too active brain had almost run away with him. Upon first reading Schopenhauer he had undergone a period of nervous excitement and had scarcely slept for nearly two weeks, for, as he declared, his soul at last had found its truth. Again in regard to another master, in another realm, he had experienced still further alarm. Of Richard Wagner he said: "I try in vain to listen to his music in a cold and reserved frame of mind, but every nerve vibrates in me." The results of these two experiences led to a double reaction: in the case of Schopenhauer, an attempt to turn his pessimism into a philosophy of joy; in the case of Wagner, a state of melancholy that the genius of Bayreuth should have descended from the Dionysiac mood of freedom into the anæmic Christian mood of Parsifal.

When Nietzsche denounced the prejudices of philosophers he was all the time weaving an elaborate network of his own prejudices, a screen of likes and dislikes with which to hide the realities about him. Thus his admiration for the aristocracy was a counterfoil for his contempt for the masses. In the first place, in the War of 1866 he declared that his natural sympathies were for Prussia, although its action against Austria was by no means moral. Again in the later growth of the social democracy, when greater rights were demanded by the masses, he exclaimed: "The Devil and statistics take them." All this meant that Nietzsche was working away from the claims of conscience engendered in a pietistic family such as his, and toward the ideal of the unscrupulous superman. There is a strange note of envy in his description of the Prussian overlords as "free powers without ethics! How happy they are, how strong those pure wills which the mind has not troubled!" Upon this theme of the free spirits Nietzsche plays constant variations. There runs through his mind a kind of counterpoint. There are two voices which answer the one to the other. The advocate of equality of rights says: "Be like other men, become mediocre"; the advocate of inequality says: "Be different; do not seek security, safety, comfort, and the alleviation of life for everyone, but develop subtlety and daring, be ready for every adventure, be ready even to play the dice with death."

These are actual phrases taken from Nietzsche's description of the free spirits. It is not hard to see that these tempting possibilities were developed as a counterfoil to the commonplace actualities of the author's own life. They disclose what he describes as "a defensive attitude, a closing of windows, an inner denial of this or that." In a word, Nietzsche's creed is but another example of that specious and alluring "philosophy as one would" against which Francis Bacon, Lord Verulam, uttered his warning. We believe, says Nietzsche, that severity, violence, danger in the street and in the heart, that everything wicked, terrible, tyrannical, predatory, and serpentine in man serves as well for the elevation of the human species as its opposite.

What was this opposite? The answer is the thinker's own life and experiences, a life of common morality and constant suffering. The creed of Nietzsche, in short, was the creed of what he wanted to be in contrast to what he was not, for at this very juncture he follows his declaration of faith by an inadvertent declaration of fact. On the very page in which he calls himself a free spirit he unconsciously offers this picture of his own personality: Having been at home in many realms of the spirit, having escaped again and again from the nooks in which preferences and prejudices, youth, origin, and accidents of men and books, full of malice against the seductions of despondency, and grateful even for the stress and the vicissitudes of illness, he becomes ready for every adventure, owing to an excess of free spirit.

The spirit was willing, but the flesh was weak; the trite phrase describes the pathetic descrepancy between Nietzsche's actual life and his ideal of the superman who, despising "the green meadow happiness of the herd, the low level of the gregarious conscience, prefers the lofty independent spirituality, the will to stand alone."

## THE SUPERMAN

Nietzsche's sister, in a loyal but pathetic apology for her introspective brother, calls him "the lonely Nietzsche." If the matter stopped there the problem would be comparatively easy. We could leave Nietzsche as an ineffective recluse, one of those "weak men" whose fundamental desire, as he described it, is that the war in him should come to an end, one to whom happiness appears in the character of a soothing medicine, a mendacious, artful, and inscrutable animal, who has invented the good conscience in order finally to enjoy his soul as something simple. But this description Nietzsche would not apply to the "strong man." The very contrariety and conflicts in such natures operate as an additional incentive and stimulus to life, the recluse may sit day and night, from year's end to year's end, alone with his soul in familiar discord and discourse. But with the men of action, the matter is different. If, in addition to their powerful and irreconcilable instincts, they have also inherited and indoctrinated into them a proper mastery and subtlety for carrying on the conflict with themselves (that is to say, the faculty of self-control and self-deception), there then arise those marvellously incomprehensible and inexplicable beings, those enigmatical men, predestined for conquering and circumventing others, the finest examples of which are Alcibiades and Cæsar.

Here begins Nietzsche's historical vindication of the superman, men described as possessing strong and dangerous instincts, such as the love of enterprise, foolhardiness, revengefulness, astuteness, rapacity, and the love of power. This is unfortunately a generalization in which the particulars are lacking. In his examples from classical antiquity Nietzsche is decidedly at a loss. The Romans, especially, were not conspicuous for that subtlety which is a mark of the superman. He therefore had recourse to the Renaissance and to the Machiavellian Italians described as so lucid, so grasping, who had in them so little of the Christian; who lied to others, but were frank toward themselves, without sophistry. Thus in Genoa there were the Corsair merchants whose golden palaces testified to the glory of men "whose instincts were fettered by no scruples." So, too, in Venice the rule of the Doges was that of men thrown upon their own resources, who wanted to make their species prevail, chiefly because they must prevail, or else to run the terrible risk of being exterminated.

While the merchant adventurers of the age of discovery may furnish good biological examples in the sense of the survival of the fittest of tough and adaptable animals, Nietzsche does not stop with them. He declares that the beast of prey and the man of prey (for instance, Cesare Borgia) are fundamentally misunderstood, "nature" is misunderstood, so long as one seeks a "morbidness" in the constitution of these healthiest of all tropical monsters and growths, or even an innate "hell" in them—as almost all moralists have done hitherto. Does it not seem that there is a hatred of the virgin forest and of the tropics among moralists? And that the "tropical man" must be discredited at all costs, whether as disease and deterioration of mankind, or as his own hell and self-torture? And why? In favour of the "temperate zones"? In favour of the temperate men? the moral? the mediocre? If this be so, reasons Nietzsche, if the strong and unscrupulous be discredited, then we shall have to write the history of morality as the history of timidity, and falling back upon the mediæval scheme, take fear as "the mother of morals." Of course, he continues, one has to thank the hitherto paramount religions for invaluable services, but when they had given comfort to the sufferers, courage to the oppressed and despairing, a staff and support to the helpless, and when they had allured from society into convents and spiritual penitentiaries the broken-hearted and distracted, what else had they to do in order to work systematically in that fashion, and with a good conscience, for the preservation of all the sick and suffering, which means, in deed and in truth, to work for the deterioration of the European race? To reverse all estimates of value—that is what they had to do! And to shatter the strong, to spoil great hopes, to cast suspicion on the delight in beauty, to break down everything autonomous, manly, conquering and imperious—all instincts which are natural to the highest and most successful type of "man"—into uncertainty, distress of conscience, and self-destruction; forsooth, to invert all love of the earthly and of supremacy over the earth into hatred of the earth and earthly things—that is the task the church imposed on itself, and was obliged to impose.

This, then, is what ecclesiastical culture has done: in abandoning paganism it has abandoned the hope of biological progress in the sense of rearing a ruling race. The inherited morality of Europe may be useful to the herd, but it represents the last, the most degenerate, stage in the denaturalization of morality. What the age needs is new lords of the earth, great men who despise "the divine," cold, hard, free from the fear of public opinion, whose aims shall be in dealing with men to make something out of them. But the present condition of things in Europe is not particularly promising; the commanding class is infected with moral hypocrisy. They know no other way of protecting themselves from their bad conscience than by playing the rôle of executors of older and higher orders (of predecessors, of the constitution, of justice, of the law, of God himself), or they even justify themselves by maxims from the current opinions of the herd, as "first servants of their people," or "instruments of the public weal."

Nietzsche here projects upon the screen of public affairs the struggle going on within his own mind. The conflict between the

classes and the masses is but a magnification of the conflict that
waged in his own conscience between the principles of unscrupulous
success and the principles of a decent respect for the opinions of mankind. But how he envies those who are able to follow the former, and
how he pities those who succumb to the latter! Here is his picture
of the spirits who would be free: It is the business of the very few to
be independent; it is a privilege of the strong. And whoever attempts
it, even with the best right, but without being obliged to do so,
proves that he is probably not only strong, but also daring beyond
measure. He enters into a labyrinth, he multiplies a thousandfold
the dangers which life in itself already brings with it; not the least
of which is that no one can see how and where he loses his way, becomes isolated, and is torn piecemeal by some minotaur of conscience. Supposing such a one comes to grief, it is so far from the
comprehension of men that they neither feel it, nor sympathize with
it. And he cannot any longer go back! He cannot even go back again
to the sympathy of men!

This is not all. The conflict in Nietzsche's soul represents in min-
iature the larger conflict that was going on about him, the conflict,
namely, between recent romanticism and primitive paganism. To a
high degree he stands as a representative of his race which, at this
very time, found itself torn by the struggles of a dual nature. On the
one side there was the Germany of the days of Kant, Fichte, and
Schelling; on the other the Germany of Bismarck, Treitschke, and
the militarists. Nietzsche himself, in spite of his pietistic upbringing,
had been all but won over to the views of the war party. The doctrines of the good will and appeals to the beautiful soul appeared
thin and unreal when opposed to the stirring realities about him. At
the beginning of the hostilities of the Franco-Prussian War, although
Nietzsche could only pose as a soldier, as his photograph shows, he
was nevertheless enamoured of soldiering. Hence it was at this moment that Frau Förster-Nietzsche says that her brother gained his
first inkling of his characteristic doctrines. She recounts how on a
certain evening, at the close of a very heavy day with the wounded,
he suddenly heard a roaring noise of thunder, and a magnificent
cavalry regiment—gloriously expressive of the courage and the
exuberant strength of the people—flew by him like a luminous storm
cloud. "Then," Nietzsche confessed, "I felt for the first time, dear
sister, that the strongest and highest will to life does not find expression in the miserable struggle for existence, but in a will to war,
a will to power, a will to overcome."

The struggle for existence to which Nietzsche referred is evidently a struggle between two ideals. Put briefly, these were the principles of conscience and the principles of conquest, or what the hostile critics of Nietzsche would prefer to call the principles of Christian pacifism and the principles of Prussian militarism. But this antithesis is too simple to explain what was taking place either in Nietzsche's mind or in the minds of his compatriots. The romantic age, with its glittering generalities, had not added one acre to Germany's soil, nor given her what she deemed her rightful place in the sun. In fact, it was during this very age of introspective intoxication that Germany's rivals had been quietly extending their dominions. The romanticist might boast that while England ruled the sea and France the land, Germany ruled the sky—of speculation. But what of that? As Kant himself once said: "Those who dwell on lofty towers meet with much wind."

Speculation, however high and mighty, is futile and ineffective; mere morality gets one nowhere, and it was because of the realization of this, declares Nietzsche, that a new conception of the German spirit gradually established itself, in spite of all romanticism in music and philosophy. It is this new spirit that has awakened Europe out of its dogmatic slumber, and freed it of its former conception of the Germans as gentle, good-hearted, weak-willed, and poetical fools. Thus Nietzsche, the invalid and physical weakling, the scholar unable to be a soldier, sought to arouse his countrymen. Chance had set him on the track that he was now to travel. As early as his eighteenth year he had taken as a subject for his valedictory address at school the life of Theognis, the Greek moralist and aristocrat, so contemptuous of the will of the people. So, too, Nietzsche's later studies as a professor led him to prefer the rude and primitive centuries of the Homeric heroes to the days of Aristotle, whose system he considered so rational as to be anæmic. To him, speculating upon speculation was of no avail. Furthermore, Nietzsche had the same outlook upon German history. It was not the philosophers of the Fatherland who made men, but the Hohenzollerns. Thus the genius for war and conquest made its first entry into Germany in the person of Frederick the Great, and even the latter's crazy father had on one point the very knack and lucky grasp of the genius; he knew what was then lacking in Germany—men were lacking.

At this point Nietzsche, finding it as hard to find examples of his supermen in German history as he did in general history, has recourse to the prehistoric period and seeks in mythology a vindication of militarism. The noble man, he continues, is one who takes

*From Houdon's portrait-statue in the Théâtre Français, Paris*

THE FIGHTING PHILOSOPHER

pleasure in subjecting himself to severity and hardness, and has reverence for all that is severe and hard. "Wotan placed a hard heart in my breast," says an old Scandinavian saga: it is thus rightly expressed from the soul of a proud Viking. Such a type of man is even proud of not being made for sympathy; the hero of the saga therefore adds warningly: "He who has not a hard heart when young will never have one."

There is something strangely familiar in all this; it reminds one of the utterances of the chief of the Teutonic war lords who rattled his sabre and held up as an ideal to German youth the young Siegfried in shining armour. Still Nietzsche did not depend solely on a remote and fabled past to vindicate his views. The new warlike age on which we Europeans have evidently entered, he exclaims, may perhaps favour the growth of another and stronger kind of skepticism, the new German skepticism for all that is rapturous, idealistic, and feminine, and especially for those visionaries of fraternity calling themselves socialists, who with their programme of repudiating the notions of master and servant and with their hatred of suffering generally threaten Europe with a new Buddhism. Consequently, in place of these levellers, with their religion of sympathy, there is need of a new caste to rule over the continent, a caste with a persistent rule of its own that can set its aim thousands of years ahead. In fine, the time for petty politics is past; the next century will bring the struggle for dominion of the world and compulsion to great politics.

In this remarkable description, which begins with the remote past and projects itself into the distant future, Nietzsche in a measure substantiates his claim of being "a born psychologist and soul-diviner." As an advocate of the new German skepticism he shows himself not only an exponent of the ideals of his own generation, but an uncanny prophet of the coming World War, for his revival of paganism in its harshest aspects becomes the very programme of the Prussian militarist, and his fevered dreams the calculated plans of dominion emanating from Potsdam.

The matter did not stop there. What Nietzsche propounded Heinrich von Treitschke, the semi-official historian of Berlin, expounded, and what both held in theory the war lords put into practice. Some critics have held these two men largely responsible for the German military measures in the late war; they have talked of the embattled professorate—for both Nietzsche and Treitschke were professors—as furnishing the battle cries which did so much to make the German masses acquiesce in the measures of their leaders. Such accusations are overdrawn. Speculative writers like Nietzsche and Treitschke were mouthpieces and not masters, and their opinions not effective causes but significant symptoms of what might be called the common skepticism of Germany as to the ineffectiveness of ordinary morality. Romanticism, with its everlasting good wills and beautiful souls, had not increased the boundaries of the empire, but the military preparedness shown in the Franco-Prussian War had, and this, as it was argued, was because milk and water had been replaced by blood and iron, and the will to be good by the will to power.

It is easy to pick out parallels between the sentiments of Nietzsche and the sentiments of the militarists, not because one borrowed from the other, but because both drew from a common source. It was the new skepticism that drew Nietzsche to declare that "the coming of the great day" would bring strength and vigour in place of the slave morality of Christianity and the low ideals of democracy, and for Treitschke, in like manner, to inveigh against the "Sunday-afternoon preacher" on politics and to assert that socialism could not be convinced by reason but must be suppressed by forcible laws.

The new skepticism is only the negative side of the problem. The positive is that notion of the superman which in the hands of official historians became enlarged into the notion of the superstate. Nietzsche's vision of the coming superman may have been a projection of the exaggerated ego, and the matter might have been harmless, if it had stopped there. But this idol of the cave ultimately became the idol of the tribe, and the folly of grandeur, of which Treitschke accused Nietzsche, was a folly which he himself helped to foster.

The state is, itself, an object, like everything else; the state is an independent order which lives according to its own laws; there is no absolute limit to the state power—in these three statements Treitschke has but transformed into political morals the familiar phrases concerning the superman as the coming type, beyond good and evil, free to act as he sees fit. Now teach this doctrine under official sanction, as did Treitschke in the great hall of the University of Berlin, and megalomania is broadcast as by a megaphone, speculation becomes propaganda, and a docile democracy believes what it is told to believe. Here Treitschke may have nothing directly to do with Nietzsche, but the latter's first sketch of the superman appears a veritable blue print for the erection of that

Frankenstein monster, that gigantic entity, the superstate, whose body is a people in arms and whose brain a coldly calculating bureaucracy.

And just as the recluse sought to rationalize his conception of the superman by claiming that national success followed the unscrupulous exploits of Alexander the Great, Julius Cæsar, and Napoleon Bonaparte, so did the publicist. Emphasizing one aspect of the current doctrine of evolution, Treitschke argued that the generative importance of war lies in this, namely, that it causes selection, and thus becomes a biological necessity, an indispensable regulator without which there could be neither racial nor cultural progress.

But enough. In Nietzsche and Treitschke, the respective exponents of the superman and the superstate, we see how romanticism had not only run its course but had also run to seed. A movement which in its original purity was a help to the individual and an inspiration to a people had in the meanwhile made such an amazing alliance with materialistic science that the old watchwords acquired a sinister meaning.

The political side of romanticism was one thing, the practical another. Fichte was more or less justified in believing that the world was an eject of the ego when his own world was so narrow, cramped, and unhappy. Nor was the lonely Nietzsche to be blamed for dwelling on the ideal of a vigorous and aggressive superman as a substitute for his own state of low vitality and failure of nerve. But when these fond illusions were turned into formulas, to be taught as realities to the people, danger followed. Nietzsche himself acknowledged that there is a propensity of the spirit to let itself be deceived in the enjoyment of manifestations of power, yet he goes on to enlarge this private deception into a public policy. Rulers, he says, should propagate conserving illusions to insure the duration of the state; here patriotism is the most essential thing and every child of the Fatherland must be brought up in love of the king. The religious illusion must also be conserved, and with this double illusion the ordinary man can live a happy life.

"Conserving illusions"—Nietzsche in this fatal formula betrayed the weakness of his own system and the national disillusionment that was to follow. Beginning as the propounder of the joyous philosophy, he ends as a prophet of woe, and there emerges something positively foreboding as to the future in his final vision of the supermen. His phrases, in retrospect, have become strangely familiar: There shall be the coming of "The great day" when the vikings of the hard heart, with conscience of steel, shall undertake vast, hazardous enterprises. In that day the people shall be slaves and instruments, led on by a double illusion of patriotism and religion. But the life of the prince and his counsellors shall be a more dangerous thing; they propagate the illusions, they also judge them—life appears to them unveiled and they know how tragic it is!

# PART TEN

## MODERN SCHOOLS

# I. UTILITARIANISM

"This doctrine about the relation of legislation to morals corresponds closely with the doctrine about the relation of industry and legislation which was taught by Adam Smith and his followers. It is defended by many powerful arguments. It is urged that the judgment of the community about right and wrong is by no means infallibly correct; that the tendency of government to encroach upon the sphere of individual action and domestic life is an exceedingly dangerous one; that the limits which may be at first assigned to such interference will almost always eventually be overpassed, and that to place the private actions of men of ripe years under constant government supervision and control is the surest way to emasculate the character and to withdraw from it the power of moral resistance. To extend into manhood the restrictive system which is appropriate to childhood seldom fails to stunt and to enfeeble, and, as the sphere of government interference dilates, the robust, self-reliant elements and spontaneous energies of character naturally decline. Yet it is these qualities that are most essential to national freedom and to a masculine morality. Men seldom realize how much more important the indirect and distant consequences of their acts often are than those which are direct and immediate, and it is in its indirect and ultimate effects that excessive government regulation is especially pernicious. It is added that government interference constantly defeats its own ends. Compression produces reaction, which often goes much further than the original vice. Evil things driven from publicity and placed under the ban of the law take in secret more dangerous and insidious forms.

"Even when it is in the power of the government complete.y to suppress some habit or amusement which in itself produces more evil than good, it by no means follows that this suppression is a real or an unmixed gain. It will often be found that this habit, or amusement, springs from a craving for some strong excitement which is deeply planted in human nature, and which in some periods and with some classes has an altogether abnormal strength, and the extirpation of one more or less vicious excitement is often followed by the growth of another. The real cure for the vices of society must go to their roots, and is to be found in moral and intellectual changes affecting habits, interests, and tastes, which the hand of power can never produce."—W. E. H. LECKY, *Democracy and Liberty*.

## THE GREATEST HAPPINESS PRINCIPLE

With the last fevered dreams of German romanticism in mind there is a certain relief in turning back to a system built up by a succession of cool and practical thinkers. In contrast to master morality and privileged supermen, the British utilitarians and their predecessors had, for almost two centuries, been constructing an ethics based on democracy and aiming toward the equal rights of all. The movement which came to flower in the mid-Victorian period had its roots in a more remote past. As far back as the time of Richard Cumberland, contemporary of Charles II, the common good was regarded as the end of all moral actions. This thesis was put forward in opposition to Thomas Hobbes, who confounded the common good with the compulsion exerted by "that great beast Leviathan," or the state with autocratic powers. It will be recalled that Hobbes had sought to locate this power in the person of the king, but that the Merry Monarch made but a sorry superman. However, the theory, reënforced by the mediæval notion of the divine right of rulers, still hung on and political egoism, when Louis XIV could say, "I am the state," was rendered more or less plausible by the successes of the greatest of the centralized powers of Europe.

Englishmen opposed this theory and sought to balance the powers of the monarch by demanding increased powers for the people. While in this familiar struggle between king and Parliament the politicians were ever in the historical foreground the moralists were working no less successfully in the background. Here it has been claimed that the long labours of the utilitarians were not in vain and that their various ideals from "the joint felicity" of Cumberland to "the greatest happiness" of Hutcheson at last bore fruit in the Reform Bill of 1832; in short, that that which the theorist pled for, the crown at last was forced to grant.

In general, the controversy was between the advocates of egoism and the advocates of altruism. Hobbes had maintained that self-preservation is the first law of nature, and that men are by nature selfish, since they but follow "that ancient law that they who have may hold." Cumberland, on the contrary, seeking to refute Hobbes, maintained that the nature of things, as continually governing by its First Cause, imprints on our mind some practical propositions concerning the study of promoting "the joint felicity of all rationals." This has been called the theological argument, whose weakness consists in trying to solve the problem by an appeal to religion as a last resort. This weakness Cumberland as much as admitted by switching to another line of argument, the laws of nature as such which reduced themselves to one universal law which may be expressed as follows: "The endeavour, to the utmost of our power, of promoting the common good of the whole system of rational agents conduces, as far as in us lies, to the good of every part, in which our own happiness, as that of a part, is contained."

This general formula had an intricate and interesting history. The notion of the common good, as based upon supposedly universal laws of nature, had existed as far back as the time of the Stoics and had been finally embodied in the Roman law. In turn, a more modern exponent of this notion, the Dutch jurist, Grotius, had sought to show that consideration for others was universal, since even animals manifest an altruistic instinct in caring for their young, while children show compassion at a very early age. But in adult man, that which in the lower stages of development had manifested itself as instinctive altruistic conduct becomes self-conscious and rational. Furthermore, this natural law has divine sanction, because it lies back of the divine nature itself. Thus the act was not just because God commanded it, but God commanded it because it was just. In other words, social justice lies "in the nature of things," for precisely as God cannot make twice two not to be four, he cannot make that which is intrinsically bad not to be bad. According to Grotius, then, the social and rational nature of man are one, for the primitive altruistic instinct is based on reason.

This plausible view, it is needless to say, hardly fitted in with the selfish theory of Hobbes. It smacked too much of mediæval logic, and to his jaundiced eye was too good to be true. Does man love society for its own sake? Hardly, he replies, for all society is either for gain or for glory; that is, not so much for love of our fellows, as for love of ourselves.

At this point Cumberland comes to the rescue of a maligned humanity, since to say, as does Hobbes, that men are "wolves, bears, and serpents" is a libel on human nature. If it were true, it were evidently impossible to reduce such beasts of prey, always thirsting after the blood of their fellows, into a civil state. Again, when Hobbes declares that man is unfit for society and so must be constrained because of his selfishness, Cumberland claims that he is fit, since sympathy is as much an attribute of nature as a desire for one's own happiness.

Of course on all these points there are valid differences of opinion, and as much might be said on one side as on the other. The contest threatens to be as long drawn out as a knightly tournament, except that at the last the champion of altruism finds one weak joint in the armour of the champion of egoism. Cumberland stands for universal benevolence as against universal selfishness, and the felicity of others against the exclusive happiness of the individual. Hobbes denies that there existed such universal benevolence, since man, being fundamentally a creature lacking right reason, must be governed by law as clearly promulgated by a competent authority. The first part of this proposition may be granted, says Cumberland, but the second does not follow. Even man in a nonrational state of nature had within him principles that were to develop into an inner law. Benevolent feeling first came to a human life as sexual love, while the parental instinct to protect the young gradually grew into an instinct for the preservation of society.

In one way Cumberland sounds old-fashioned—universal benevolence and the felicity of others were principles of an age of sentiment and not of science. But in another way, especially in his recourse to arguments from primitive society, he sounds highly modern. As Charles Darwin later expressed it: Man is a social animal, since the more enduring social instincts conquer other less persistent instincts. Indeed, as the author of the *Descent of Man* concluded, the social virtues are alone regarded by savages, while the self-regarding virtues are acquired at a later stage of development.

To return to the attack on Hobbes and his theory of the state of nature as one of original egoism and pure selfishness. The controversy begun by Cumberland was continued by Lord Shaftesbury, who contended that such a system was artificial and one-sided. Nothing, he argues, is so natural as that which conduces to preservation, whether the creature in question be animal or man. If eating and drinking be natural, herding is, too. If any appetite or sense be natural, the sense of fellowship is the same.

Writing at the beginning of the Eighteenth Century, Lord Shaftesbury represents the attitude of the age of reason. In these remarks, taken from his *Inquiry Concerning Virtue*, he exhibits that judicial frame of mind which, while attacking the absolutist Hobbes, would not go over entirely to the sentimentalist Cumberland. The latter, as befitted a bishop in the Church of England, had made use of theology to bolster up morality. Thus he utilized the so-called police argument which sought to drive men to seek the kingdom of heaven because of the fears of hell. As to this, coolly remarks the noble lord, there is no more of rectitude, piety, or sanctity in a creature thus reformed than there is meekness or gentleness in a tiger strongly chained, or innocence and sobriety in a monkey under the discipline of the whip.

In like manner Shaftesbury attacks the sentimental argument in regard to universal benevolence. Hobbes, as an egoist, may be one-sided, but so is his clerical opponent. What is needed, then, is to strike a balance between the two sets of impulses. "Self" affections are not only permissible, but necessary, while the "natural" affections, social and benevolent, may exist in excess and thus defeat themselves. Or, put in another way, the harmony of the whole consists in the excellence of the parts, since the good of all tends to become realized through the enlightened efforts of each to obtain his own true happiness.

In attempting to strike a balance between the natural and self affections Shaftesbury appears to have let the scales go up in favour of the latter. But this is not quite what he meant, for he had started with a proposition that, since man is originally a social being, he derives his greatest happiness from that which makes for the existence of society and the common weal. These two sets of statements are really not contradictory; they only appear so because they are dealing with different things, namely, ends and means. Here the good of all must be the end, but virtue is the means. If "the good man is his own best friend," he is also more than that—he is the very material out of which a successful society is constructed. In fine, the greater the happiness of the parts, the greater will be the happiness of the whole; consequently, virtue is identical with benevolence.

Shaftesbury's equation between virtue and benevolence is carried on in a curious way by his successor, Francis Hutcheson, who developed a kind of moral arithmetic in terms of the net benevolence of the agents; that is, the excess of benevolence over self-interest. This means that in equal degrees of happiness—expected to proceed from a proposed action—the virtue is in proportion to the number of persons to whom the happiness shall extend and, in equal numbers, the virtue is as the quantity of the happiness, or natural good; or that the virtue is in compound ratio of the quantity of good and the number of enjoyers.

This is moral arithmetic at its worst, and such dry calculations would have had little significance were it not that Hutcheson appended to them the fundamental formula of the entire utilitarian movement, namely, that that action is best which procures "the greatest happiness of the greatest number." Except for the final formula, all this, it is needless to say, has been criticized as too mercantile, and as a lowering of high ideals on the part of a nation of shopkeepers. To reduce benevolence to bookkeeping and the subtle motives of moral conduct to the black and white of debit and credit appeared monstrous to many. But there was a reason for this. England of the Eighteenth Century was undergoing a revolt against sentimentalism, and the satires of Jonathan Swift against current politics were matched by the sarcasms of Jeremy Bentham against current ethics. As the latter remarked, "The *summum bonum* —the sovereign good—what is it? It is this thing, and that thing, and the other thing—it is anything but pleasure—it is the Irishman's apple-pie made of nothing but quinces." What Bentham was attacking here was not morals as such but the "elbow-chair" moralist who talks glibly of the sense of duty and benevolence and so misses the real motives at work in the advancements of mankind. To Bentham it is an open question whether the unadorned desire to better one's condition is not on the whole a more effective tool of social reform than appeals to idealism and philanthropy, however noble.

The hard-headed Bentham, writing about the time of the American Revolution, presented with clearness the conflict between the two suggestive principles, that of enlightened self-interest and that of the greatest happiness of the greatest number. Nevertheless, he failed to work out their mutual connections. This task remained for the mid-Victorian John Stuart Mill, who followed his father James Mill in exploiting the possibilities of the "expediency" philosophy. Here the younger Mill was like the elder in taking as the exclusive test of right and wrong the tendency of action to produce pleasure and pain. In this he acknowledges that for several years he was under the influence of Bentham, who sought to prove that the immoral action is a miscalculation of self-interest, as if a crime were not a crime, but merely a mistake. But this selfish and calculating principle he considered too narrow; a wider outlook was needed and this was to be found in employing the word "utilitarian" as denoting an application to society as a whole. There thus arose in his mind the possibility of a science of human nature, based on the principle that human actions are conformable to law. As there is a theory of the tides, by which the attraction of the sun and moon can be predicted with fair accuracy for definite parts of the earth's surface, why should there not be a theory of morals, by which one may forecast with fair accuracy the results of human action? There is need, then, for a new science to be called "Ethology," or the science of the formation of character. This science, a kind of social statics, is further defined as that which corresponds to the art of education in the widest sense, including the formation of national or collective character, as well as that of individuals.

Mill's proposed new science was an ambitious scheme which he never carried out. It might apply in a general way, but not in a particular. It is true that that which is probable for individuals becomes almost certain for masses, but the reverse is not true. Statistics show, for example, that there are periodical crime waves and seeming epidemics of suicide, but plotting curves does not prevent crimes and suicides. Because of this Mill is forced back to the ancient principle that ethics is more an art than science, when he says that sympathy, though in a sense natural, requires a good deal of cultivation; that veracity, one of the highest virtues, is plainly artificial, for all savages are liars; and that the same might be proved of all the other virtues.

This earlier ambitious scheme of a science of conduct was thus modified by the latter reflection that, while nature may have its inflexible laws, human nature has not. It may be possible to predict the ebb and flow of the tide, but to speak of the rising and falling of periods of virtue and vice is to confuse prediction with retrospection. Again, Mill's scheme was modified by a touch of pessimism derived from his father, when he said of the latter, "He thought human life a poor thing at the best. . . . He would sometimes say that if life were made what it might be, by good government and good education, it would be worth having; but he never spoke with enthusiasm even of that possibility."

The younger man was, however, not such a cynic as the older. He grants that there may be an admissible moral theory of creation in which the principle of good does make man capable of carrying on the fight against the powers of evil with vigour and with progressively increasing success. And so, he continues, if it be said that there must be the germs of all these virtues in human nature, otherwise mankind would be incapable of acquiring them, I am ready, with a certain amount of explanation, to admit the fact. But the weeds that dispute the ground with these beneficent germs are themselves not germs but rankly luxuriant growths, and would, in all but some one case in a thousand, entirely stifle and destroy the former, were it not so strongly the interest of mankind to cherish the good germs in one another, in so far as their degree of intelligence allows.

"To cherish the good germs in one another"—this notable phrase may be taken as Mill's modest paraphrase of that creed which accepts as the foundation of morals utility, or the greatest happiness principle, and which holds that actions are right in proportion as they tend to promote happiness, and wrong as they tend to produce the reverse of happiness. Such is Mill's famous definition of "What Utilitarianism Is." Writing in 1861, four years before he was elected member of Parliament for Westminster, Mill proceeds to expound the meaning of utilitarianism and to show what it is not. The common herd, including the herd of writers, interpret the utilitarian principle of happiness as referring everything to pleasure in its grossest form. Like the ancient critics of Epicureanism, they claim that it is a doctrine worthy only of swine, forgetting that there is no known Epicurean theory of life, from Epicurus himself to Bentham, which does not assign to the pleasures of the intellect, of the feelings, of the imagination, and of the moral sentiments a much higher value as pleasures than it assigns to those of mere sensation. These critics also confuse quantity with quality; they ignore the fact that few human creatures would consent to be changed into any one of the lower animals for a promise of the fullest allowance of a beast's pleasures; or that any intelligent person would consent to be a fool because a fool is better satisfied with his lot. It may be indisputable that the being whose capacities of enjoyment are low has the greatest chance of having them satisfied, but it were better to be a human being dissatisfied than a pig satisfied; better to be Socrates dissatisfied than a fool satisfied.

In these trenchant remarks Mill shows that utilitarianism, as a doctrine of happiness, does not mean low pleasures, nor does it mean selfish pleasures, for its standard is not the agent's own greatest happiness, but the greatest amount of happiness altogether. When people who are tolerably fortunate do not find in life sufficient enjoyment to make it valuable to them, the cause generally is that they care for nobody but themselves. On the other hand, those who have cultivated a fellow-feeling with the collective interest of mankind maintain as lively an interest in life on the eve of death as in the vigour of youth and health. The main constituents of a satisfied life appear to be two: tranquillity and excitement. Tranquillity frees one from the excess of anxiety concerning the evils of life and enables one, like many a Stoic in the worst times of the Roman Empire, to cultivate the sources of satisfaction accessible to him; excitement, on the other hand, arises from the very contest against these evils. In a world in which there is so much to correct and improve all the grand sources of human suffering are, in a great degree, conquerable by human care and effort. Here education and opinion, which have so vast a power over human character, should be so used as to establish in the mind of every individual an indissoluble association between his own happiness and the good of the whole. Thus the greatest recorded victory which education ever achieved over a whole host of natural inclinations in a people was that of Sparta. Furthermore, that victory was reënforced by public opinion in its two aspects: its attractive power was the love of glory, praise, and admiration; its deterring power the fear of shame and ill repute.

## PERSONAL LIBERTY

When Mill speaks of the power of education to achieve victory over man's natural inclinations, and of that victory as being reënforced by public opinion, he marks the transition between the old and the new utilitarianism, and also raises anew the profound problem of the conflict between self and society. Thus Hobbes, in the Seventeenth Century, had stood for the selfish theory of the moral motive, and Hutcheson, in the Eighteenth, in fighting this theory, had hit on the famous formula of the greatest happiness of the greatest number. It remained for the Nineteenth Century to attempt a reconciliation of the two conflicting principles. Mill essays this task by showing how utilitarianism is connected with justice. Justice, he explains, in dealing with wrong doers is in large measure connected with the problem of punishment, while the desire to punish a person who has done harm to some individual is a spontaneous outgrowth from two sentiments—the impulse of self-defense and a feeling of sympathy. Here Hobbes was right when he spoke of the "natural" instinct of self-protection, for the sentiment of justice appears in its first step to be based on the animal desire to repel or retaliate a hurt or damage to oneself. But this instinct, sentiment, or desire is not moral. It only becomes so when it is widened to include all persons, by the human capacity of enlarged sympathy.

It is through this principle of sympathy, as the ultimate sanction of the principle of utility, that the objections of the anti-utilitarians may be met. First they say that the standard is too high; it is too much to expect that people shall always act from the inducement of promoting the general interest of society. Then they turn around and declare that utilitarianism is irreligious. But the truth of the matter is that in the Golden Rule of Jesus of Nazareth we read the complete spirit of the ethics of utility. To do as you would be done by, and to love your neighbour as yourself, constitute the ideal perfection of utilitarian morality. As the means of making the nearest approach to this ideal, utility would enjoin, first, that laws and social arrangements should place the happiness, or (as speaking practically it may be called) the interest, of every individual as nearly as possible in harmony with the interest of the whole; and secondly, that education and opinion, which have so vast a power over human character, should so use that power as to establish in the mind of every individual an indissoluble association between his own happiness and the good of the whole.

Of course, a man may say to himself: I feel that I am bound not to rob or murder, betray or deceive; but why am I bound to promote the general happiness? If my own happiness lies in something else, why may I not give that the preference? If the view adopted by the utilitarian philosophy of the nature of the moral sense be correct, this difficulty will always present itself, until the influences which form moral character have taken the same hold of the principle that they have taken of some of the consequences—until, by the improvement of education, the feeling of unity with our fellow creatures shall be (what it cannot be denied that Christ intended it to be) as deeply rooted in our character, and to our own consciousness as completely a part of our nature, as the horror of crime is in an ordinarily well-brought-up young person.

In this account it might seem that Mill has gone back to the religious sanctions of morality repudiated by Bentham. But a distinction has to be made. What he was really after was not the external sanctions but the internal; not the hope of favour, or the fear of displeasure of the Ruler of the Universe, but the feeling of unity with our fellow men. Like that high priest of the religion of humanity, Auguste Comte, Mill believes that it is possible to give to the service of humanity, even without the aid of belief in a Providence, both the psychological power and the social efficacy of a religion.

So much for the ultimate sanctions of utilitarianism; now for the means. If we propose, continues Mill, that this feeling of unity be taught as a religion, and the whole force of education, of institutions, and of opinion directed, as it once was in the case of religion, to make every person grow up from infancy surrounded on all sides both by the profession and the practice of it, I think that no one, who can realize this conception, will feel any misgiving about the sufficiency of the ultimate sanction for the happiness morality.

In this programme Mill has proved to his own satisfaction, first, that the expediency philosophy is not immoral, and second, that moral feelings are not innate. By the latter tenet he gets rid of the difficulty of those selfish exceptions among mankind who ask why they are obliged to promote general happiness. Yet such persons, he admits, whose minds are moral blanks, are comparatively few. This is because most persons could not bear to lay out their course of life on the plan of paying no regard to others, except so far as their own private interest compels. We may grant that the feeling of unity in most individuals is much inferior in strength to their selfish feelings, but to those who have it it possesses all the characters of a natural feeling.

This feeling of unity, this sentiment in favour of the greatest happiness of the greatest number, may be deemed a virtue, but a practical question remains: How can the will to be virtuous, where it does not exist in sufficient force, be implanted or awakened? The answer is only by making the person desire virtue, by making him think of it in a pleasurable light, or of its absence in a painful one. Further, the cultivation of this desire is a prerogative of man. Here human beings differ from other animals in two particulars: first, in being capable of sympathizing, not solely with their offspring, or, like some of the more noble animals, with some superior animal who is kind to them, but with all human, and even with all sentient, beings. Secondly, in having a more developed intelligence, which gives a wider range to the whole of their sentiments, whether self-regarding or sympathetic. . . . The same superiority of intelligence, joined to the power of sympathizing with human beings generally, enables him to attach himself to the collective idea of his tribe, his country, or mankind in such a manner that any act hurtful to them raises his instinct of sympathy, and urges him to resistance.

It is here that Mill places himself in the higher reaches of ethics, for this discussion shows how he had come under the influence of two of the greatest minds—that of Aristotle in his doctrine that man is the noblest of the animals, and that of Charles Darwin, who at this very time was pointing out that the origin of sociability lay far back in the records of natural history and that man as an animal was a social animal.

But this point is not pressed, possibly for the reason that universal social sympathy resembles too closely the earlier sentimental notion of disinterested benevolence toward all mankind. Mill as a practical reformer is less interested in sentiments than in rights. Here utility, or the greatest-happiness principle, follows Bentham's dictum, "everybody to count for one, nobody for more than one." This, then, is the highest abstract standard of social and distributive justice, that both the legislator and the moralist should acknowledge the equal claim of everybody to happiness. Unfortunately, this great maxim of justice has by no means been applied universally. Ideas of social expediency have interfered with its application. Yet in reviewing this very struggle between justice and expediency there is considerable hope for the progress of humanity. The entire history of social improvement has been a series of transitions, by which one custom or institution after another, from being a supposed primary necessity of social existence, has passed into the rank of a universally stigmatized injustice and tyranny. So it has been with the distinctions of slaves and freemen, nobles and serfs, patricians and plebeians; and so it will be, and in part already is, with the aristocracies of colour, race, and sex.

Such is the struggle between expediency, or the principle of the best for the time being, and utility, or the principle of the greatest happiness of the greatest number. But intimately connected with this is the struggle between authority and liberty. This is the same problem that troubled the soul of Nietzsche. But while the German cut the Gordian knot by putting master morality above slave morality, the Englishman was more patient and tried to disentangle the various strands. Thus he reasons that wherever there is an ascendant class a large portion of the morality of the country emanates from its class interests and its feelings of class superiority. The morality between Spartans and Helots, between planters and Negroes, between princes and subjects, between men and women, has been for the most part the creation of these class interests and feelings; and the sentiments thus generated react in turn upon the moral feelings of the members of the ascendant class, in their relations among themselves. Where, on the other hand, a class, formerly ascendant, has lost its ascendancy, or where its ascendancy is unpopular, the prevailing moral sentiments frequently bear the impress of an impatient dislike of superiority.

Here, then, arises the conflict between the feeling of class superiority and the popular dislike of superiority, or what, in a larger sense, may be called the struggle between authority and liberty. In old times this contest was between subjects, or some classes of subjects, and the government, and by liberty was meant protection against the tyranny of the political rulers. Here the aim of patriots was to set limits to "the king of the vultures, bent upon preying on the flock." In modern times the tyrant is public opinion, the tyranny of the majority that enslaves the soul itself. In the old days, again, patriots obtained certain immunities called political liberties or rights; in the new the struggle concerns the inner domain of conscience and man's liberty of conscience, liberty of thought, and absolute freedom of opinion on all subjects, practical or speculative, scientific, moral, or theological. But at this juncture public opinion comes in with its deterring power, and, as the public is made up of a few wise men and many fools, individual progress is slow.

The tyranny of the majority is real and it is dangerous. Society, explains Mill, can and does execute its own mandates: and if it issues wrong mandates instead of right, or any mandates at all in things with which it ought not to meddle, it practises a social tyranny more formidable than many kinds of political oppression, since, though not usually upheld by such extreme penalties, it leaves fewer means of escape, penetrating much more deeply into the details of life, and enslaving the soul itself. Protection, therefore, against the tyranny of the magistrate is not enough: there needs to be protection also against the tyranny of the prevailing opinion and feeling; against the tendency of society to impose, by other means than civil penalties, its own ideas and practices as rules of conduct on those who dissent from them; to fetter the development and, if possible, prevent the formation, of any individuality not in harmony with its ways, and compel all characters to fashion themselves upon the model of its own.

Here is a new and subtle danger. Democracy threatens to bring about a deadly uniformity in mankind, for nowadays the power of public opinion is fostered by the growth of the press and by the increasing influence of masses of voters upon legislation. The leaders in reform have been caught napping. They have occupied themselves rather in inquiring what things society ought to like or dislike than in questioning whether its likings or dislikings should be a law to individuals. Thus even liberty of conscience in religious matters has a disappointing history. Those who first broke the yoke of what is called the Universal Church were in general as little willing to permit differences of religious opinion as that church itself. In the minds of almost all religious persons, even in the most tolerant countries, the duty of toleration is admitted with tacit reserves. One person will bear with dissent in matters of church government, but not of dogma; another can tolerate everybody, short of a Papist or a Unitarian; another, everyone who believes in revealed religion; a few extend their charity a little further, but stop at the belief in a God and in a future state. Wherever the sentiment of the majority is still genuine and intense it is found to have abated little of its claim to be obeyed.

Such is the problem. Public opinion, which, with its positive power fostered the common defense against tyrants, now, with its negative power of disapprobation, threatens itself to become the tyrant. In the English-speaking countries not only is public opinion growing, but it is controlled by the spirit of Puritanism and by some of those modern reformers who, while placing themselves in strongest opposition to the religions of the past, have been no way behind either churches or sects in their assertion of the right of spiritual domination. There is an instance of this in the curious infirmity in English minds which makes them take a preposterous pleasure in the assertion of a bad principle; for example, in the assumption that the oath of a person who does not believe in a future state is worthless, a kind of intolerance which, though it kills no one, nevertheless induces men to disguise their opinions.

Among Americans a similar state of things obtains in legislation prohibiting the use of liquor, as if legal enactment made drinking a wrong in itself. This, declares Mill, writing when only one half the United States was under such restrictive legislation, is a monstrous principle since it violates the more fundamental principle that every man is free to do that which he wills, provided he does not infringe upon the equal freedom of any other man. It therefore behooves the lovers of liberty to examine the pass to which the tyranny of the majority has brought them. The United States of America, the most extensive of the democracies, may now perceive that such phrases as "self-government" and "the power of the people over themselves," do not express the true state of the case. The "people" who exercise the power are not always the same people with those over whom it is exercised; and the "self-government" spoken of is not the government of each by himself, but of each by all the rest. The "will of the people," moreover, practically means the will of the most numerous or the most active part of the people—the majority, or those who succeed in making themselves accepted as the majority; the people, consequently, may desire to oppress a part of their number; and precautions are as much needed against this as against any other abuse of power.

In guarding this abuse of power one precaution which should never be forgotten is liberty of discussion. If all mankind minus one were of one opinion, and only one person were of the contrary opinion, mankind would be no more justified in silencing that one person than he, if he had the power, would be justified in silencing mankind.

This may seem an extreme statement of the case of Athanasius against the world, but Mill has plenty of other cases where the suppression of individual opinion disproves the pleasant falsehood that truth always triumphs over persecution. History teems with instances of truth put down by persecution. If not suppressed forever it may be thrown back for centuries. To speak only of religious opinions: the Reformation broke out at least twenty times before Luther, and was put down. Arnold of Brescia was put down. Fra Dolcino was put down. Savonarola was put down. The Albigeois were put down. The Vaudois were put down. The Lollards were put down. The Hussites were put down. Even after the era of Luther, wherever persecution was persisted in, it was successful. In Spain, Italy, Flanders, the Austrian Empire, Protestantism was rooted out; and, most likely, would have been so in England, had Queen Mary lived, or Queen Elizabeth died. Persecution has always succeeded, save where the heretics were too strong a party to be effectually persecuted.

Mill grants that there have been, and may again be, great individual thinkers in a general atmosphere of mental slavery, but, on the other hand, he contends that there never has been, nor ever will be, in that atmosphere an intellectually active people. Still, when the dread of heterodoxy of speculation has been for a time suspended a generally high scale of mental activity has made certain periods of history remarkable. Of such we have examples in the times following immediately the Reformation, in the age of reason headed by Voltaire in France, and in the intellectual fermentation of Germany during the period of Goethe and Fichte. In fine, the lesson of history is this: Liberty fosters individuality and in turn individuality breaks the yoke of authority. There is need, then, for us to reassert our mental freedom, to fight against the encroachments of narrow public opinion, to be independent, to be strong. Strong impulses are but another name for energy. Energy may be turned to bad uses; but more good may always be made of an energetic nature than of an indolent and impassive one. Those who have most natural feeling are always those whose cultivated feelings may be made the strongest. The same strong susceptibilities which make the personal impulses vivid and powerful are also the source from whence are generated the most passionate love of virtue and the sternest self-control. It is through the cultivation of these that society both does its duty and protects its interests—not by rejecting the stuff of which heroes are made because it knows not how to make them. A person whose desires and impulses are his own—are the expression of his own nature, as it has been developed and modified by his own culture—is said to have a character. In conclusion, it is not by wearing down into uniformity all that is individual in themselves, but by cultivating it, and calling it forth, within the limits imposed by the rights and interests of others, that human beings become a noble and beautiful object of contemplation; and as the works partake the character of those who do them, by the same process human life also becomes rich, diversified, and animating, furnishing more abundant aliment to high thoughts and elevating feelings, and strengthening the tie which binds every individual to the race, by making the race infinitely more worth belonging to.

## II. EVOLUTIONARY ETHICS

"TURNING now to the social and moral faculties. In order that primeval men, or the apelike progenitors of man, should have become social, they must have acquired the same instinctive feelings which impel other animals to live in a body; and they no doubt exhibited the same general disposition. They would have felt uneasy when separated from their comrades, for whom they would have felt some degree of love; they would have warned each other of danger, and have given mutual aid in attack or defense. All this implies some degree of sympathy, fidelity, and courage. Such social qualities, the paramount importance of which to the lower animals is disputed by no one, were no doubt acquired by the progenitors of man in a similar manner, namely, through natural selection, aided by inherited habit. When two tribes of primeval man, living in the same country, came into competition, if the one tribe included (other circumstances being equal) a greater number of courageous, sympathetic, and faithful members, who were always ready to warn each other of danger, to aid and defend each other, this tribe would without doubt succeed best and conquer the other. Let it be borne in mind how all-important, in the never-ceasing wars of savages, fidelity and courage must be. The advantage which disciplined soldiers have over undisciplined hordes follows chiefly from the confidence which each man feels in his comrades. Obedience, as Mr. Bagehot has well shewn, is of the highest value, for any form of government is better than none. Selfish and contentious people will not cohere, and without coherence nothing can be effected. A tribe possessing the above qualities in a high degree would spread and be victorious over other tribes; but in the course of time it would, judging from all past history, be in its turn overcome by some other and still more highly endowed tribe. Thus the social and moral qualities would tend slowly to advance and be diffused throughout the world."—CHARLES DARWIN, *The Origin of Species*.

## THE ASCENT OF MAN

In the history of evolutionary ethics there is to be found a perfect case of the spirit of coöperation. Here three distinguished men had three separate tasks. To prove that man is a social and moral animal was the task of Charles Darwin in his *Descent of Man;* to determine man's place in nature as that of a fighter against the cosmic processes was the task of Thomas Huxley in his *Evolution and Ethics;* to gather together the evidences for the gradual evolution of morals and to show how slow was the emergence of the ethical sense was the task of Herbert Spencer in his *Data of Ethics*. Of course all these tasks had been essayed before, but it remained for the Nineteenth Century to attempt to bind under one conception the great masses of material offered by the old doctrines and the new sciences. Here Darwin stood first. In his epoch-making book, *The Origin of Species*, he ventured the prediction that by this work "light would be thrown on the origin of man and his history," but he confessed that he feared to pursue this subject lest it should only add to the prejudices against his views. In the meanwhile, the battle royal against his antagonists had been won and the principle of natural selection, through the struggle for existence and the survival of the fittest, had been accepted by the majority of scientists. Using this great principle of transformism, Darwin saw fit in 1863 to publish his evidence, collected during many years, on the descent of man from some lower form. This evidence is of three kinds: first, concerning the bodily structure; next, concerning the mental faculties; finally, as growing out of the latter, the evidence that man has affinities with his "poor relations," who have progressed in certain moral qualities, such as good temper, affection, and trustworthiness.

Darwin now proceeded to build his bridge of evidence in order to show that there is no impassable barrier between man and the lower animals. The general proposition is this: that however wide the gap between the lower and the higher, the difference is one of degree and not of kind, since countless intermediate links imply that exalted mental and even moral powers can be traced step by step back into the remote past. Man and his animal ancestors, though of course in very different degrees, have the same senses, intuitions, and sensations, similar passions, affections, and emotions, even the more complex ones; thus they feel wonder and curiosity;

finally, they possess the same faculties of imitation, attention, memory, imagination, and even reason.

In constructing this bridge of evidence, which would close the supposed gap between animal and man, Darwin had to lay certain foundations. These he found in the proofs of physical affinity, now familiar to all. These proofs were three: first, as to the bodily structure of man it is notorious than man is constructed on the same general type or model with other mammals; all the bones in his skeleton can be compared with corresponding bones in a monkey, bat, or seal. So is it with his muscles, nerves, blood vessels, and internal viscera. Next, as to embryology, the development of the embryo of man at a very early period can hardly be distinguished from that of other members of the vertebrate kingdom; thus the wings and feet of birds and the hands and feet of man arise from the same fundamental form. Lastly, as to rudiments, not one of the higher animals can be named which does not have some part in a rudimentary condition; such in man are the incisor teeth, the twitching muscles of the eyebrows, and the useless and troublesome vermiform appendix.

These physical affinities between man and beast are evident to the senses, but what of the mental and moral affinities? The naturalist had a harder task in dealing with these seemingly impalpable qualities. While man bears in his bodily structure and bodily development clear traces of his descent from some lower forms, yet it may be urged that, as he differs so greatly in his mental power from all other animals, there must be some error in this conclusion. No doubt the difference in this respect is enormous, even if we compare the mind of one of the lowest savages, who has no words to express any number higher than four and who uses no abstract terms for the commonest objects or affections, with that of the most highly organized ape. Nor is the difference slight in moral disposition between a barbarian, such as the man described by the old navigator Byron who dashed his child on the rocks for dropping a basket of sea urchins, and a Howard or Clarkson; and in intellect, between a savage who does not use any abstract terms, and a Newton or Shakespeare.

Here are two great difficulties which Darwin presents with his usual fairness and at the same time meets with his usual ingenuity. This is his way out of the dilemma. Just as the colours of the spectrum appear distinct when taken separately, but coalesce when taken together, so here. While the mental and moral differences between the highest men and the lowest savages are immense, they are nevertheless connected by the finest gradations, hence it is possible that they might pass and be developed into each other. Let us take these gradations in order, from the lower to the higher. Man has the same senses with the lower animal; he also has some instincts in common, as that of self-preservation, sexual love, and the love of the mother for her new-born offspring. These instincts in turn blend insensibly into the emotions, for here the lower animals manifestly feel pain and pleasure, misery and happiness, the latter, for example, being never better exhibited than by young animals, such as puppies, kittens, and lambs playing together like our own children. This fact, that the lower animals are excited by the same emotions, continued Darwin, is so well established that it will not be necessary to weary the reader by many details.

Here it may be said that Darwin was by years of training such a careful observer and at the same time such a lover of animals that his details will not weary the reader. As to the simpler emotions, little need be said, he proceeds. Terror, for instance, acts in the same manner on animals as on us, causing the muscles to tremble, the heart to palpitate, and the hair to stand on end. Still further, most of the complex emotions are common to the higher animals and ourselves. Everyone has seen how jealous a dog is of his master's affection if lavished on any other creature; and I have observed the same fact with monkeys. This shows that animals not only love, but have the desire to be loved. Animals manifestly feel emulation; they also love approbation or praise; and a dog carrying a basket for his master exhibits in a high degree self-complacency or pride. There can, I think, be no doubt that a dog feels shame, as distinct from fear, and something very like modesty when begging too often for food. A great dog scorns the snarling of a little dog, and this may be called magnanimity. But another step must be taken, another transition made. We may therefore turn to the more intellectual emotions and faculties, which are very important, as forming the basis for the development of the higher mental powers. Animals manifestly enjoy excitement and suffer from ennui, as may be seen with dogs and with monkeys. All animals feel wonder, and many exhibit curiosity. They sometimes suffer from this latter quality, as when the hunter plays antics and thus attracts them; I have witnessed this with deer, and it is the same with the wary chamois, and with some kinds of wild ducks.

And so the story goes in tracing the development of the higher mental powers and affinities between men and animals. It is almost superfluous to state that the latter possess attention, memory, and imagination, but when it comes to reason, which stands at the summit of all the faculties of the human mind, it is often difficult to distinguish between the power of reason and that of instinct. Animals may constantly be seen to pause, deliberate, and resolve. But when, for example, Arctic sledge dogs diverged and separated when they came to thin ice, so that their weight might be more evenly distributed, did these dogs act from the rational experience of each individual, or from the example of older and wiser dogs, or from an inherited habit, that is from an instinct? Questions of this kind are most difficult to answer, observes the naturalist, but here is the evidence for the affirmative. So many facts have been recorded in various works showing that animals possess some degree of reason that I will here give only two or three instances, authenticated by Rengger, and relating to American monkeys, which stand low in their order. He states that when he first gave eggs to his monkeys they smashed them and thus lost much of their contents; afterward they gently hit one end against some hard body, and picked off the bits of shell with their fingers. After cutting themselves only once with any sharp tool, they would not touch it again, or would handle it with the greatest care. Lumps of sugar were often given them wrapped up in paper; and Rengger sometimes put a live wasp in the paper, so that in hastily unfolding it they got stung; after this had once happened, they always first held the packet to their ears to detect any movement within. Anyone who is not convinced by such facts as these, and by what he may observe with his own dogs, that animals can reason, would not be convinced by anything that I could add.

Granted a modicum of reason in animals and Darwin is enabled to meet the great objection that man is separated in his mental faculties from all the lower animals by an impassable barrier. In similar fashion he meets the particular objections of Archbishop Sumner that man alone is capable of progressive improvement, and of the Duke of Argyll that no animal uses any tool, and of still other critics that animals have no sense of property, no dress, and no architecture. The latter objections can be answered by the specific instances of monkeys who hide their playthings in the straw; of orangs who cover themselves with leaves, and of the anthropomorphous apes who build themselves temporary platforms. In these latter habits we probably see the first steps toward some of the simpler arts as they arise among one of the early progenitors of man.

With numerous examples gathered by himself and a host of other accurate observers, Darwin builds the foundations of a system which binds together into one structure the human and the subhuman. Yet all this work is but preliminary to a far more difficult problem, namely, that of the moral sense. This great question has been discussed by many writers of consummate ability, he grants, and my sole excuse for touching on it is because, as far as I know, no one has approached it exclusively from the side of natural history.

Here the prime argument is that of sociability. It has been often assumed that animals were in the first place created or rendered social, and that they feel as a consequence uncomfortable when separated from each other and comfortable while together. But this argument of special creation puts the cart before the horse. It is a more probable view that these sensations were first developed in order that those animals which would profit by living in society would be induced to live together. With respect to the origin of these affections it is hopeless to speculate, but we may be sure that those individuals which took the greatest pleasure in society would best escape various dangers, while those that cared least for their comrades and lived solitary would perish in greater numbers. So this extension of the affections may be in chief part attributed to natural selection, but perhaps in part to mere habit.

Whatever the origin of sociability, it is evident that out of it grew sympathy, for it is certain that associated animals have a feeling of love for each other which is not felt by non-social animals. It is, of course, obvious that some animals and some men lack sympathy, because cattle will expel a wounded member from the herd, or gore or worry it to death, while certain North American Indians have been known to leave their feeble comrades to perish on the plains. Although sympathy may be often lacking it is of high importance to all those animals which aid and defend each other, and it will have been heightened through natural selection, since those communities which included the greatest number of the most sympathetic members would flourish best and rear the greatest number of offspring.

It may now be granted that animals are social because a sufficient reason has been found in the usefulness of sociability. Most people also admit that man is a social being; but is he a social animal? That is the main point which, if proved, bridges over the principal gap between man and animals. Although man, as he now exists, has few special instincts, having lost any which his early progenitors may have possessed, this is no reason why he should not have retained from an extremely remote period some degree of instinctive love and sympathy for his fellows. We are indeed all conscious that we do possess such sympathetic feelings; but our consciousness does not tell us whether they are instinctive, having originated long ago in the same manner as with the lower animals, or whether they have been acquired by each of us during our early years. The problem is perplexing. We may grant that most of our sympathetic feelings have been gained in our early years, but what about the early years of the race? If the social instincts were acquired by man in a very rude state, and if the same instincts were shown by his early apelike progenitors, there is then to be traced in dim outline an actual transition between man and animal. Just as the evidence of bodily structure and intellectual faculties pointed to a real connection between man and his humbler ancestors, so does the evidence of moral faculties. Of course, the actions of animals, though done for the good of others, are called instinctive and not moral; but why should animals be deprived of the benefit of the doubt which is granted to man? An action repeatedly performed by us will at last be done without deliberation or hesitation, and can then hardly be distinguished from an instinct; yet surely no one will pretend that an action thus done ceases to be moral. This being so, we can turn the tables and perceive that, as far as deliberation and the victory over opposing motives are concerned, animals may be seen hesitating between opposed instincts, as in rescuing their offspring or comrades from danger. This same condition of affairs is also to be seen in the early and undeveloped stages of mankind. Here the strictly social virtues alone were at first regarded; that is, the virtues which must be practised by rude men so that they may associate in a body, since no tribe could hold together, if murder, robbery, and treachery were common. This, reasons Darwin, is at the bottom of that former school of morals which assumed that the foundation of morality lay in a form of selfishness. But even in the case of the lower animals it would be absurd to speak of these instincts as having been developed from selfishness. The truth is they have rather been developed for the general good of the community.

At this point Darwin, the naturalist, makes some observations upon the more speculative writers on morals. Thus he disposes of the claims of the Hobbites by removing the reproach of laying the foundation of the most noble part of our nature in the base principle of selfishness. He also disagrees with the utilitarians, who assumed that the foundation of morality lies in the greatest-happiness principle. He grants that this may be a most important secondary guide and object, but contends that a more moderate and truer statement would be to say that when a man risked his life to save that of a fellow creature, he acted for the general good or welfare rather than for the general happiness of mankind.

Darwin does not press this point of difference with the later utilitarians. What he has done is to show that natural history supplies the missing links in the previous genealogy of morals. From Aristotle to John Stuart Mill numerous writers had assumed the social affinities between men and animals; it remained for the genuine evolutionist to show by countless examples that, in order that primeval men, or the apelike progenitors of men, should become social, they must have acquired the same instinctive feeling which impelled other animals to live in a body. In conclusion, this means that in studying the descent of man we are also studying the ascent of man, in other words, that "the great tree of life" indicates not only man's physical genealogy, but his moral genealogy.

## THE STRUGGLE OF SYSTEMS

In his *Descent of Man* Darwin showed, as no one else before him, how intimate was the connection between human nature and animal nature. The next task was to study the relation of human nature to nature as a whole. This task was undertaken by Thomas Huxley, who, as a devoted adherent of Darwin's, employed the latter's principles of natural selection, through the struggle for existence and the survival of the fittest, in an attempt to clarify the problem.

As to the moral meaning of nature, if any, and of man's place in nature, there was a veritable struggle of systems, and as an arbiter of this contest Huxley was peculiarly fitted to sit in the seat of judgment. He knew the philosophical systems both profound and popular, from that of Gautama Buddha to that of Alexander Pope in his "Essay on Man"; from the Oriental philosophy of despair to the Occidental statement that "whatever is, is right." Writing in his Romanes Lecture of 1893, Mill thinks that this modern speculative optimism is not so current as it was forty years before, nevertheless that there still exist the notions of the perfectability of the species, the reign of peace, and lion and lamb transformation scenes. Curiously enough, the early Victorian complacency was later reënforced by the doctrine of evolution as popularly understood, for the phrase the "survival of the fittest" was interpreted to mean the "survival of the best." This is, of course, erroneous; all that the fittest means is adaptation to the changing conditions of nature. Thus, if our hemisphere became hotter the pleasant valley of the Thames might be uninhabitable by any animated beings save those that flourish in a tropical jungle.

Properly interpreted, evolution does not mean that this is the best of all possible worlds; nor does it mean that it is the worst possible. If the optimism of Leibnitz is a foolish though pleasant dream, the pessimism of Schopenhauer is a nightmare, and more foolish because of its hideousness. Still even this extreme reaction can be explained. An age which sought sermons in stones and good in everything was not unnaturally succeeded by an age which looked on the dark side of life. Thus the old-fashioned arguments of the Bridgewater Treatises for the nervous system, as a wonderful contrivance for pleasure, might be turned about to prove an equally effective contrivance for pain, and if the pessimists had their say the preponderance of suffering in the world might appear to be overwhelming.

While both optimism and pessimism are to be rejected, a compromise may be made. This means that still another combination may be imagined. This was done by the ancient believers in a cosmic dualism, where there was a perpetual conflict between the powers of benevolence and the powers of malevolence, between Ormuzd and Ahriman, between deity and devil, or whatever names were given to the principles of good and evil. Curiously enough, this notion was revived by James Mill and even held in part by his son, despite the latter's acceptance of the greatest-happiness principle. But, as Huxley reasons, the conclusion of the whole matter seems to be that, if Ormuzd has not had his way in this world, neither has Ahriman. Pessimism is as little consonant with the facts of sentient existence as optimism. If we desire to represent the course of nature in terms of human thought, and assume that it was intended to be that which it is, we must say that its governing principle is intellectual and not moral; that it is a materialized logical process, accompanied by pleasures and pains, the incidence of which, in the majority of cases, has not the slightest reference to moral desert. Looked at from an impartial standpoint, the course of nature will appear to be neither moral nor immoral, but simply non-moral. So the old evidences of design, whether for good or evil, need no longer trouble us. Thus a deer may owe its ability to escape to its organization, but there is at least equal skill in the bodily mechanism of the wolf which enables him to track, and sooner or later to bring down, the deer. In short, deer and wolf are alike admirable, "viewed under the dry light of science."

In a way this reasoning seems too impartial, too cold-blooded. It resembles almost verbally the frigid formula of Spinoza when he attempted to look out upon the world "under the aspect of eternity." However, Huxley, in taking this neutral view of nature, is not aiming to be inhuman, but to work toward a solution of several difficulties. This he does by a distinction between cosmic nature and social nature. The vast and varied procession of events which we call nature, as he says, appears to us to have a governing principle which is intellectual and not moral, whereas those parts of nature in which man plays the part of immediate cause are more than intellectual. This means that human society differs from nature in having a definite moral problem. And a further distinction must be made. The course shaped by the ethical man—the member of society or citizens—necessarily runs counter to that which the non-ethical man—the primitive savage, or man as a mere member of the animal kingdom—tends to adopt. The latter fights out the struggle for existence to the bitter end, like any other animal; the former devotes his best energies to the object of setting limits to the struggle.

By this double distinction between cosmic nature and social nature, and between non-ethical man and ethical man, Huxley not only clears up several difficulties, but also harmonizes previous views. He agrees with Hobbes that among the very primitive men —first cousins to the "beasts"—life was a continuous free fight, since the war of each against all was the normal state of existence. He also agrees with Darwin that the first men who substituted the state of mutual peace for that of mutual war created society. Finally, he agrees with John Stuart Mill that, in gradually limiting the war of individual against individual, the ideal of the ethical man is to limit his freedom of action to a sphere in which he does not interfere with the freedom of others.

Such is the progress of man from sheer savagery to personal liberty, but in reaching toward the final stages of this progress the eternal conflict with nature as such is not eliminated. As Darwin had already pointed out, natural selection affects civilized nations as well as savage, and the more we try to eliminate the struggle for existence the more it returns to baffle us. With savages, says Darwin, the weak in body or mind are soon eliminated; and those that survive commonly exhibit a vigorous state of health. We civilized men, on the other hand, do our utmost to check the process of elimination; we build asylums for the imbecile, the maimed, and the sick; we institute poor-laws; and our medical men exert their utmost skill to save the life of everyone to the last moment. . . . Thus the weak members of civilized societies propagate their kind. No one who has attended to the breeding of domestic animals will doubt that this must be highly injurious to the race of man. But excepting in the case of man himself, hardly anyone is so ignorant as to allow his worst animals to breed.

The results of all this Huxley now proceeds to point out. In doing away with the old checks on population we but increase the population; we declare infanticide murder, and punish it as such; we decree, not quite so successfully, that no one shall die of hunger; we regard death from preventable causes of other kinds as a sort of constructive murder, and eliminate pestilence to the best of our ability; we declaim against the curse of war and the wickedness of the military spirit, and we are never weary of dilating on the blessedness of peace and the innocent beneficence of industry. Let us be under no illusions, then. So long as unlimited multiplication goes on no social organization which has ever been devised, or is likely to be devised, no fiddle-faddling with the distribution of wealth, will deliver society from the tendency to be destroyed by the reproduction within itself, in its intensest form, of that struggle for existence the limitation of which is the object of society. And however shocking to the moral sense this eternal competition of man against man and of nation against nation may be, however revolting may be the accumulation of misery at the negative pole of society in contrast with that of monstrous wealth at the positive pole, this state of things must abide, and grow continually worse, so long as Istar holds her way unchecked. It is the true riddle of the Sphinx; and every nation which does not solve it will sooner or later be devoured by the monster itself has generated.

These words may appear to be a surrender to pessimism, but such is not the way Huxley really looked at the problem. His was a combative character. As a defender of the doctrine of evolution he had been called "Darwin's bulldog," and now, although well-nigh beaten by the logical outcome of natural selection, he will not give up the contest. His motto is not flight from the world, but fight the cosmic processes. And so he concludes; while the theory of evolution encourages no millennial speculations, yet the cosmic nature which is born in us, and, to a large extent, is necessary to our maintenance, is the outcome of millions of years of severe training, and it would be folly to imagine that a few centuries will suffice to subdue its masterfulness to purely ethical ends.

Huxley's conclusions are largely borne out by Herbert Spencer, the third in the triumvirate of evolutionists, who shows how slow has been the emergence of the moral sense and also attempts to explain this retardation. The perplexed moralities of the past, he says, while severally justified as approximately the best under the circumstances, by no means belong to conduct that is fully evolved. The reason for this is that they all suffered from an incomplete idea of causation. All the schools, whether theological, political, intuitional, or utilitarian, display the effects which result from this lapse. The first school which though most ancient still has its representatives, recognizes no other rule of conduct than the alleged will of God. This point of view originated with the savage whose only restraint, beyond fear of his fellow men, was fear of an ancestral spirit. If in more modern form the divine will is the only standard of right and wrong, the assumption would be suicidal, for any act might be committed under this belief by one ignorant of such will.

The second school, the political, represented by Hobbes, holds that there can be neither justice nor injustice till a regularly constituted coercive power exist to issue and enforce command. In more modern times this would imply that moral obligation originates with acts of Parliament and can be changed this way or that by majorities. As for the intuitionalists, they affirm that we know some things to be right and others wrong by virtue of a supernaturally given conscience, which recognizes the right just as the bee recognizes honey. This is tacitly to deny any natural relations between acts and results, since there is not of necessity any causal connection between feeling and consequences. Finally, strange as it may appear, even the utilitarian school does not recognize natural causation as much as it might. Its followers think of final ends, it is true, but not of remote beginnings since they fail to deduce their principles from the very processes of life as carried on under established conditions of existence.

In criticizing the main systems of current morality Spencer implies that he has a better one, because he can push it back to the very nature of things. Ethics he considers to be the final fruit of the evolutionary process, the last part of the task to which all preceding parts were subsidiary. In a complete system of synthetic philosophy, then, we must trace the ascent of man as a moral being through the various steps in the ladder of the sciences. These steps furnish broadly four main views—the physical, the biological, the psychological, and the sociological.

Spencer's treatment of the first of these views is not important; it merely repeats the ancient analogies as to harmony and balance, as when it is declared, in more ponderous language, that complete life, in a complete society, is but another name for complete equilibrium between coördinated activities of each social unit and those of the aggregate of units. This is vague and inconclusive, but what is said next is better. From the biological point of view we see that the connections between pleasure and beneficial action and between pain and detrimental action, which arose when sentient existence began, have continued among animate creatures up to man. This is a general proposition, nevertheless it has particular applications. To ignore these phenomena of life at large leads men into grave errors as to those special phenomena of human life with which ethics deals. That pleasure increases vitality and pain decreases vitality is a truth much disregarded nowadays because of certain sentiments and ideas at variance with this truth. These adverse sentiments and ideas have several roots; there is first the theological root resulting from the primitive conception of deities who were propitiated by the imfliction of pains. There is another root in the primitive and still surviving militancy. Here, while social antagonisms continue to generate war, it is needful that physical suffering should be thought little of, and that among pleasures, recognized as most worthy, should be those that victory brings. Finally, partially developed industrialism furnishes a root. With social evolution, which implies transition from the life of wandering hunters to the life of settled peoples engaged in labour, there comes an underexercise of faculties for which the social state affords no scope. Hence, along with that growth of population which makes the struggle for existence intense, bearing of pains and sacrifice of pleasure are daily necessitated.

Spencer has often been criticized as making such vast generalizations as to put himself out of touch with reality, as if he dwelt high up in a speculative skyscraper, far above the life of the streets. The facts are quite the contrary. With all his aloofness, both social and speculative, he was at heart deeply sympathetic with the hardships of others, for he himself had suffered from undertaking too much. His vast *Synthetic Philosophy*, projected in 1850, was not finished until forty-six years later. In the meanwhile, in the midst of this gigantic undertaking which he himself had called "almost insane," he broke down from overwork. It was with this in mind that he could speak of people on all sides who yield examples of lives blasted by persisting in actions against which their sensations rebelled. Here are some specific cases: The careworn man of business too long at his office, the cadaverous barrister poring half the night over his briefs, the feeble factory hands and unhealthy seamstresses passing long hours in bad air, the anæmic, flat-chested schoolgirls, bending over many lessons and forbidden boisterous play, no less than Sheffield·grinders who die of suffocating dust, and peasants crippled with rheumatism due to exposure show us the widespread miseries caused by persevering in actions repugnant to the sensations and neglecting actions which the sensations prompt.

The synthetic philosophy as applied to moral problems is a philosophy of sympathy; it is also a philosophy of insight, for the author sees into the motives by which men justify to themselves the untoward conditions about them. Now always and everywhere, continues Spencer, there arises a theory conforming to men's practice. With the savage there originates the conception of a cruel deity enjoying the sufferings of the victims offered him; with submission to despotic government there grows up a theory of divine right to rule and the duty of absolute submission; with the industrial system, if the life is one that necessitates habitual denial of pleasures and bearing of pains, there emerges an answering ethical system under which the receipt of pleasures is tacitly disapproved and the bearing of pains avowedly approved.

With this broad theory of moral disapprobation, summed up in the paradoxical statement "pleasant but wrong," Spencer connects the current belief that the pleasures of the present must be sacrificed to the pleasures of the future. Thus the man of business hurrying over his breakfast that he may catch the train, snatching a sandwich in the middle of the day, and eating a late dinner when he is so worn out that he is incapacitated for evening recreation, pursues a life in which not only the satisfactions of bodily desires, but also those of higher tastes and feelings, are, as far as may be, disregarded, that distant ends may be achieved; and yet if you ask what are these distant ends you find that they are included under the conception of more comfortable living in time to come. So ingrained is this belief, that it is wrong to seek immediate enjoyments and right to seek remote ones only, that you may hear from a busy man, who has been on a pleasure excursion, a kind of apology for his conduct. He deprecates the unfavourable judgments of his friends by explaining that the state of his health had compelled him to take a holiday. Nevertheless, if you sound him with respect to his future, you find that his ambition is by and by to retire and devote himself wholly to the relaxations which he is now somewhat ashamed of taking.

In these acute observations as to the workings of the human mind Spencer has passed from the biological to the psychological point of view, for the science of right living has to take account of all consequences in so far as they affect happiness, personally or socially, directly or indirectly. But there remains the last, the sociological point of view, which is not reached until the various controls already spoken of have been moralized. The hard-working business man just mentioned was one whose actions were guided by a half-conscious fear of public opinion. But it is not until there arises a conscious relinquishment of immediate and special good, in order to gain distant and general good, that such self-restraint may be called moral. The same is true of the other restraints, not only fear of society at large, but fear of the visible ruler, and of the invisible ruler. Thus the truly moral deterrent from murder is not constituted by a representation of tortures in hell as a consequence, or by a representation of the horror and hatred excited in fellow men, but by a representation of the necessary natural results—the infliction of death agony on the victim, the destruction of all his possibilities of happiness, the entailed sufferings to his belongings.

In all this we are prepared to see that the restraints, properly distinguished as moral, are unlike the restraints out of which they evolve, and with which they are long confounded, in this respect— they refer not to the extrinsic effects of actions, but to their intrinsic effects. Thus, to take another instance, neither the thought of imprisonment, nor of divine anger, nor of social disgrace is that which constitutes the moral check on theft; but the thought of injury to the person robbed, joined with a vague consciousness of the general evils caused by disregard of proprietary rights.

It is here that the feelings called moral have their origin. The vague consciousness of general evils grows gradually clearer, until, in the realm of sociology, the true ethical motive is not determined by incidental consequences—such as legal penalty, or supernatural punishment, or social retribution—but by consequences which the various acts naturally produce. The sociological view, then, alone takes full account of natural causation and strives always to ascertain the necessary connections between cause and effect. And so, concludes Spencer, the sociological view is at the same time synthetic, in that it attempts to harmonize the struggle of systems. After observing how means and ends in conduct stand to one another, and how there emerge certain conclusions respecting their relative claims, we may see a way to reconcile sundry conflicting ethical theories. These severally embody portions of the truth; and simply require combining in proper order to embody the whole truth. The theological theory contains a part. If for the divine will, supposed to be supernaturally revealed, we substitute the naturally revealed end toward which the power manifested throughout evolution works; then, since evolution has been, and is still, working toward the highest life, it follows that conforming to those principles by which the highest life is achieved is furthering that end. The doctrine that perfection or excellence of nature should be the object of pursuit is in one sense true; for it tacitly recognizes that ideal form of being which the highest life implies, and to which evolution tends. There is a truth, also, in the doctrine that virtue must be the aim; for this is another form of the doctrine that the aim must be to fulfil the conditions to achievement of the highest life. That the intuitions of a moral faculty should guide our conduct is a proposition in which a truth is contained; for these intuitions are the slowly organized results of experiences received by the race while living in the presence of these conditions. And that happiness is the supreme end is beyond question true; for this is the concomitant of that highest life which every theory of moral guidance has distinctly or vaguely in view.

Hence, recognizing in due degrees all the various ethical theories, conduct in its highest form will take as guides innate perceptions of right duly enlightened and made precise by analytic intelligence, while conscious that these guides are proximately supreme solely because they lead to the ultimately supreme end, happiness special and general.

## III. WILLIAM JAMES (1842–1910): PRAGMATISM

"PERHAPS the chief reason for the popularity of James's philosophy is the sense of freedom it brings with it. It is the philosophy of open doors; the philosophy of a new world with a large frontier and, beyond, the enticing unexplored lands where one may still expect the unexpected; a philosophy of hope and promise, a philosophy that invites adventure, since it holds that the dice of experience are not loaded. The older monistic philosophies and religions present by contrast stuffy closed systems and an exhausted universe. They seem to pack the individual into a logical strait-jacket and to represent all history as simply the unfolding of a play that was written to its very last line from the dawn of creation. These old absolutisms go with the old order of things.

"James is an interpreter of the new order of democracy. The most important and interesting thing about a nation, or an historic epoch, as about an individual, was, he held, its 'ideals and over-beliefs.' And if he is our representative philosopher of democracy, it is not because of his individualism, his appreciation of the unique, the uncommunicable, his hospitality of mind, his respect for humanity in its every honest manifestation, his support of the doctrine of live and let live, his tolerance of all that was not itself intolerant; it is not because of his insistence that professions be measured by their 'cash value' in experience, and men by their ability to 'make good'; but it is, above all, because of his skill in interpreting those ideals and over-beliefs of his nation and epoch. For these are the things that save democracy from vulgarity and commercialism, that preserve the higher human qualities, and insure for the citizens of a free land the fruits of civilization—more air, more refinement, and a more liberal perspective."—CHARLES M. BAKEWELL, *Selected Papers on Philosophy, by William James.*

At a certain meeting of the American Philosophical Association William James was introduced as "one whom we all love and all delight to honour." These words were not excessive; James was loved because of his sympathy and honoured because of his liberality. As he wrote to a friend: "We have no revelation but through man. . . . So that it seems to me that a sympathy with men as such, and a desire to contribute to the weal of a species, which, whatever may be said of it, contains all that we acknowledge as good, may very well form an external interest sufficient to keep one's moral pot boiling in a very lively manner to a good old age."

James's sympathy, in the sense of insight into the workings of the minds of others, was evident in all his works, from his *Principles of Psychology,* through his *Varieties of Religious Experience,* to his final *Essays in Radical Empiricism.* This sympathy and its kindred liberality of spirit were in turn fostered by the settings and events of James's life. His father, Henry James, Sr., was a man of means who could afford to give his children the perfect education of the cosmopolite, the education of foreign travel and foreign languages. As William James's own son puts it: "There was profit for him also in the restlessness which governed his father's movements and which threw the boy into quickening collision with places, people, and ideas at a rate at which such contacts are not vouchsafed to many schoolboys. From so far back as his nineteenth year (there is no evidence to go by before that) William was blessed with an effortless and confirmed cosmopolitanism of consciousness; and he had attained to an acquaintance with English and French reviews, books, paintings, and public affairs which was remarkable not only for its happy ease, but, in one so young, for its wide range."

William James enjoyed what few young Americans of his day were afforded and that was the "grand tour" on the Continent. So from his various sojournings in France, Switzerland, and Italy he gained that insight into European character which later made him the first American philosopher who knew at first hand the Old World as well as the New. All this came out in his enthusiasms, as for Agassiz, the Swiss naturalist, for Wundt, the German psychologist, and for various representatives of the French school of thought from Renouvier to Bergson, and the English thinkers from John Stuart Mill as a libertarian to Ferdinand Schiller of Oxford as a humanist. These varied contacts were matched by an equally varied choice of careers which were offered him. Although several of these were rejected they left their traces. From his experience as an artist he gained that subtlety of style which strives to give an impression by constant, minute touches; from his companionship with Agassiz and his voyage with that naturalist to the Amazon he derived not only a taste for collecting, but a power of observation which stood him well in his later studies of human nature. Finally, from his medical studies at Harvard he came to emphasize the realistic and emotional side of life, which in turn made his outlook not one of cold reason, but one of warm vitality.

These three possible careers as artist, as naturalist, and as medical man were in turn each rejected, but what an unrivalled preparation they formed for his coming career as psychologist and philosopher! The gift of many tongues, plus the gift of much learning, explain the apt saying that while William James's brother Henry wrote novels like a psychologist, he himself wrote psychology like a novelist. Here one of his pupils has remarked that James was always asking: "How does the world feel to you? What emotional thrill do you get out of it?" The answer lay particularly in James's works like the *Will To Believe, and Other Essays in Popular Philosophy*, in his *Talks to Teachers on Psychology and to Students on Some of Life's Ideals*, and especially in his most widely read work entitled *Pragmatism*. Although this bore the subtitle of "A New Name for Some Old Ways of Thinking," it was a novelty in its original combination of factors. Just as William Penn founded in Pennsylvania a colony open to all creeds and classes and called it the "Great Experiment," so William James founded a philosophy which would reconcile the clash of opposing human temperaments, a philosophy which would find good things on both sides of the line of division; in short, a philosophy of insight and of sympathy.

## THE MORALS OF PRACTICALITY

As the morals of utility is typical of England of the Nineteenth Century, so the morals of practicality is typical of the America of the Twentieth. Westward the course of speculation has taken its way, and a system which combines the principle of the greatest happiness of the greatest number with the principle of individual efficiency appears the dominant system of the day. This system, generally known as pragmatism, may be summed up in two words— democracy and dynamism. As men have a share in the making of their policy so they have a share in the making of their morality, for in both there is shown the irresistible might of united personalities, in the one case as to how they should govern their public affairs, in the other as to how they should govern their private concerns.

The theory of democracy is one thing, its practice another; paper constitutions and book morals seldom work successfully, unless they have power behind them. Here the dynamic force is furnished by the principle of individualism in its best sense. As a doctrine of personalism, pragmatism is aggressive; it emphasizes self-sufficiency as against self-surrender. It differs from these older world philosophies whose adherents sought refuge in the bosom of the church or the bosom of the Absolute. In this sense it is highly self-reliant; it cares less for meditative saints and contemplative mystics than for practical inventors and pushing men of affairs. As regards tradition it is iconoclastic; if the old systems will not work it treats them like obsolete machinery and casts them on the scrap heap. To the European, who cherishes those treasures which are marked by the patina of the past, there is something repellent in this attitude. Pragmatism seems to him an unfinished philosophy of life, just as the American city is never completed but always being built. But while in tearing down sound buildings to make way for new he may see but restlessness and confusion, yet he cannot deny the feeling of vast vitality behind it all. In other words, to emphasize the destructive is to forget the constructive, for apparent iconoclasm may conceal powerful forces at work. Here the radical pragmatists have had the same attitude toward traditional system that the men of the Renaissance had toward colosseums and the palaces of the Cæsars, both asking why, if the old buildings have outgrown their original purposes, should they not be used for new structures?

However, in this very reconstruction something was preserved; that is, while the vast piles erected by former generations might be counted less valuable as antiquities than as quarries, yet from the antiquarians' point of view one can find fragments of older moralities in the present morality of pragmatism. Take these as typical examples among the leaders old and new. Aristotle considered man a

JEAN-JACQUES ROUSSEAU
"Our morals are corrupted in proportion as our arts and sciences progress"

political animal; so does John Dewey, provided the polity is democratic. Kant had his categorical imperative; so has William James in
the form of the "will to believe." Emerson said: Hitch your wagon
to a star; Charles Peirce as much as says: Hitch any star to your
wagon, since any theory that has practical consequences is good.

This process of reconstruction and modification goes still further.
In its broadest aspect pragmatism is the product of two modern
movements, utilitarianism and evolutionism. Because of its affilia-
tion with the former James dedicated his book to John Stuart Mill
as one whom his fancy liked to picture as "our leader were he alive
to-day." As for the doctrine of evolutionism, it furnished that very
"intellectual climate," as James would put it, in which we live and
move. But here the process of change, as in the weather itself, is
inevitable, and old Darwinism becomes the new Darwinism, where
less emphasis is placed on the influence of environment and more
on the plastic principle of modification. Thus the radical pragmatist
advises not so much an adaptation of oneself to the environment as
an adaptation of the environment to oneself. Obviously, this may be
carried too far. Relying on such instruments of science as could subdue a fever-ridden jungle and build a Panama Canal, some of the
American thinkers exhibit a spirit of daring and adventure which
verges on the presumptuous. James was modest in calling his pragmatism "a new name for some old ways of thinking," but the radical
pragmatist in his attitude toward high historic systems seems much
like the Yankee pioneer who would cut down fine old timber to grow
a patch of corn.

Here a contrast arises. The pragmatisms of Europe have had no
great success, largely because of the dead hand of the past. That of
Giovanni Papini in Italy was a flash in the pan, while that of F. C. S.
Schiller in England had the mischance of originating at Oxford—
Oxford "anchored in the stream" of time. In bearing the disarming
name of humanism, it was packed full of explosives, nevertheless it
failed to move that ancient hulk, the wooden system of English
Hegelianism. But in America pragmatism, when once started, was a
decided success. James was its sponsor and broke the bottle of his
effervescent wit at its launching. Riding now on the front of this
wave of scientific logic, Messrs. Schiller and Dewey, he says, appear
with their pragmatistic account of what truth everywhere signifies.
"Any idea upon which we can ride, so to speak, any idea that will
carry us prosperously from any one part of our experience to any
other part, linking things satisfactorily, working securely, simplify-
ing, saving labour, is true for just so much, true in so far forth, true

instrumentally. This is the instrumental view of truth taught so successfully at Chicago, the view that truth in our ideas means their power to 'work,' promulgated so brilliantly at Oxford."

This instrumental view, which insists that truths are truths only in so far as they are effective tools, James considered the mark of what was hailed as the Chicago school. In this, he adds, Dewey's favourite word is "situation," and the situation is one which is getting perpetually reconstructed. Just as the old Chicago was burned down and a new city built in its place, so must it be with various social and moral reforms. Take, for example, the problems of the "new education." It is useless, insists Dewey, to bemoan the departure of the good old days of children's modesty, reverence, and implicit obedience, if we expect merely by bemoaning and by exhortation to bring them back. It is radical conditions which have changed, and only an equally radical change in education suffices. The problem, therefore, is one of instrumental logic. The usual school has been so set apart, he explains, so isolated from the ordinary conditions and motives of life, that the place where children are sent for discipline is the one place in the world where it is most difficult to get such experience. Contrast with this the old days when the household was practically the centre in which were carried on all the typical forms of industrial occupation. The clothing worn was not only made in the house, but the members of the household were generally familiar with the shearing of the sheep, the carding and spinning of the wool, and the plying of the loom. In short, the entire industrial process stood revealed, from the production on the farm of the raw materials till the finished article was actually put into use. Not only this, but practically every member of the household had his own share in the work. The children, as they gained in strength and capacity, were gradually initiated into the mysteries of the several processes. It was a matter of immediate and personal concern even to the point of actual participation. Such was the old household system which furnished an intimate acquaintance with nature at first hand, with real things and materials, with the actual processes of their manipulation and the knowledge of their social necessities and uses.

In contrast with this, consider the school of the present day, which appeals for the most part simply to the intellectual aspect of our natures, our desire to learn, to accumulate information, and to get control of the symbols of learning; not to our impulses and tendencies to make, to do, to create, to produce, whether in the form of utility or of art. Against this conventional modern conception, which is merely a survival of a false mediævalism, the age revolts. One of the most striking tendencies at present is toward the introduction of so-called manual "training," shop work, and the household arts—sewing and cooking. This has not been done "on purpose," with a full consciousness that the school must now supply that factor of training formerly taken care of in the home, but rather by instinct, by experimenting and finding that such work takes a vital hold of pupils and gives them something which is not to be got in any other way.

All this is but an illustration of the pragmatic methods where experience is continually enlarging, situations always getting problematic, thus making old truths unsatisfactory and obliging new ones to be found. In short, pragmatism is a programme for more work, for, as Dewey points out, in the century of changes between the household and factory systems one can hardly believe there has been a revolution in all history so rapid, so extensive, so complete. Through it the face of the earth is made over, even as to its physical forms, political boundaries are wiped out and moved about, as if they were indeed only lines on a paper map; population is hurriedly gathered into cities from the ends of the earth; habits of living are altered with startling abruptness and thoroughness; the search for the truths of nature is infinitely stimulated and facilitated and their application to life made not only practicable but commercially necessary.

To meet these rapid changes and cope with these new necessities Dewey drew up a programme for the intellectual control of these needed adjustments on the practical side. These might be called the five points of progress common to all societies. The bearing of psychology upon educational procedure has already been treated. In addition there is the problem of the value of the research for social progress; the mutual relation of fine and industrial art; the question of the extent and nature of specialization in science in comparison with the claims of applied science; and finally the adjustment of religious aspirations to scientific statements.

When Dewey laid down this programme, just a quarter of a century ago, he became in large measure the prophet of many coming changes in American life. Here are some of the new instruments to meet new conditions: in social research child clinics, charity organizations, and personnel boards; in the relations of fine and industrial art the beautifying of banks and the erection of skyscrapers, those cathedrals of commerce; in the application of pure science to practical needs staffs of experts working on improvements in the airplane and the radio. These four points are obvious, but the last is not—the adjustment of religious aspirations to scientific statements is one which has scarcely been made in the Western world. In material achievements such as school equipment, business architecture, and technical laboratories, the country has more or less successfully met novel situations, but in spiritual achievements the same cannot be affirmed. The story of the Fundamentalist fight against the teaching of evolution is a case in point. Yet here, as Dewey says, Darwin, in laying hands upon the sacred ark of absolute permanency, upon notions of fixed and perfect types of creation, introduced a mode of thinking that in the end was bound to transform the logic of knowledge and hence the treatment of morals, politics, and religion. The influence of Darwinism has been to shift interest from an intelligence that shapes things once for all to the particular intelligences which things are even now shaping, from an ultimate goal of good to the direct increments of justice and happiness that intelligent administration of existent conditions may beget.

The final creed of the Chicago school thus resolves itself into the belief that the world is plastic, a world in the making, and that the law of social success is one which demands the choice of relations which work. The thinker, like the carpenter, is at once stimulated and checked in every stage of his procedure by the particular structure which confronts him; materials, price of labour, credit at the bank—all are varying factors demanding constant readjustment. Instrumental adaptability, then, is opposed to belief in perfect, absolute, complete, finished forms of thought because the facts of life are crude, raw, unorganized, brute. This being so, a certain spirit of adventure is demanded in the pragmatist. As the pioneer ran physical risks in the winning of the West, so the pragmatist must run the risk of criticism in leaving behind old forms of thought and in striking out into new fields. The pragmatist is not one who is satisfied with ancient institutions, with what James would call adherence to truths grown petrified by antiquity. The proof of this is that Dewey himself and his followers have variously protested against reactionary movements such as mediæval sumptuary legislation like that of Prohibition, obsolescent laws of literary censorship, fixed notions as to marriage being indissoluble, and more explicitly, American interference in Hayti and Nicaragua, the Scopes trial on the teaching of evolution, and the notorious Sacco-Vanzetti case of a judge judging his own judgments.

The Chicago school has been called radical pragmatism and such it was. It was never the school of contentment and acquiescence, but always the school of adventure and protest. The reason for this was

not an irritable discontent, or adherence to the pessimistic formula
that whatever is, is wrong, but rather to the spirit of those early
utilitarians who helped to bring about the Reform Bill, and to those
fighters among the followers of Darwin who saw that social progress
is a process of trial and error among struggling human beings.

## PERSISTENT PROBLEMS

Pragmatism as a philosophy of practicality has well merited the
name of humanism, but it demanded the genius of William James
to bring out its implications in regard to the last point in the
Chicago platform, namely, the adjustment of religous aspirations to
scientific statements. Dewey, indeed, had taken the first step here
in asserting that the modern age is marked by a refusal to be satisfied with the postponement of the exercise of reason to another and
supernatural sphere. This is a negative criticism; James makes one
more positive in declaring that the place of the divine in the world
must be more organic and intimate than in the older monarchical
theism which placed God apart from the world, like a king above
his people. As he further explains it, the vaster vistas which scientific
evolutionism has opened and the rising tide of social democracy run
counter to the mediæval notion that God is our magistrate, and
that mechanically to obey his commands, however strange they
may be, remains our only moral duty. The old theism makes us
outsiders and keeps us foreigners in relation to God; his action can
affect us, but he can never be affected by our reaction; our relation,
in short, is not a strictly social relation.

But the same defect which exists in the mediæval form of thought
is to be found in a more modern form, namely, scientific materialism.
Here materialism defines the world so as to leave man's soul upon it
as a sort of outside passenger or alien; it holds the foreign in things
to be more primary and lasting; it sends us to a lonely corner with
our intimacy. But from a pragmatic point of view the difference
between living against a background of foreignness and one of intimacy means the difference between a general habit of wariness and
one of trust. One might call it a social difference, for, after all, the
common *socius* of us all is the great universe whose children we are.
If materialistic, we must be suspicious of this *socius*, cautious, tense,
on guard. If spiritualistic, we may give way, embrace, and keep no
ultimate fear.

In attempting the pragmatic adjustment of religious aspirations
to scientific statements James appears to have gone over at once

to the anti-scientific side. But this is really not so. He is but pointing out the "present dilemma in philosophy," a dilemma which arises from the very constitution of human nature. To him people seem to be divided into two camps, two opposed types of mental make-up which may be called the tender-minded and the tough-minded. The marks of the former are rationalistic (going by "principles"), idealistic, optimistic, and religious; the marks of the latter empiricist (going by "facts"), materialistic, pessimistic, and irreligious. Now each of you, continues James, probably knows some well-marked example of each type, and you know what each example thinks of the example on the other side of the line. They have a low opinion of each other. Their antagonism, whenever as individuals their temperaments have been intense, has formed in all ages a part of the philosophic atmosphere of the time. It forms a part of the philosophic atmosphere to-day. The tough think of the tender as sentimentalists and soft-heads. The tender feel the tough to be unrefined, callous, or brutal. Their mutual reaction is very much like that that takes place when Bostonian tourists mingle with a population like that of Cripple Creek. Each type believes the other to be inferior to itself; but disdain in the one case is mingled with amusement, in the other it has a dash of fear.

This contrast can be carried too far. Few of us, as the lecturer points out, are tenderfoot Bostonians pure and simple, and few are typical Rocky Mountain toughs in philosophy. Most of us have a hankering for the good things on both sides of the line. Facts are good, of course—give us lots of facts. Principles are good—give us plenty of principles. The world is indubitably one, if you look at it in one way, but as indubitably is it many, if you look at it in another. It is both one and many—let us adopt a sort of pluralistic monism. Everything, of course, is necessarily determined, and yet of course our wills are free: a sort of free-will determinism is the true philosophy. The evil of the parts is undeniable, but the whole can't be evil: so practical pessimism may be combined with metaphysical optimism.

This is the compromise generally made by the philosophic layman; but we are amateur athletes in philosophy, insists James, and it therefore behooves us to tackle these problems more strenuously. Here the first point to be made is that there never were as many men of a decidedly empiricist proclivity in existence as there are at the present day. Our children, one may say, are almost born scientific. But our esteem for facts has not neutralized in us all religiousness. It is itself almost religious. Our scientific temper is devout. Now take a man of this type, and let him be also a philosophic amateur, unwilling to mix a hodge-podge system after the fashion of a common layman, and what does he find his situation to be? He wants facts; he wants science; but he also wants a religion. And being an amateur and not an independent originator in philosophy, he naturally looks for guidance to the experts and professionals whom he finds already in the field. A very large number of you here present, possibly a majority of you, are amateurs of just this sort.

Now what kinds of philosophy do you find actually offered to meet your need? You find an empirical philosophy that is not religious enough and a religious philosophy that is not empirical enough for your purpose. If you look to the quarter where facts are most considered you will find the whole tough-minded programme in operation, and the "conflict between science and religion" in full blast. Either it is that Rocky Mountain tough of a Haeckel with his materialistic monism, his ether-god and his jest at your God as a "gaseous vertebrate"; or it is Spencer treating the world's history as a redistribution of matter and motion solely, and bowing religion politely out at the front door.

If now, on the other hand, you turn to the religious quarter for consolation, and take counsel of the tender-minded philosophies, what do you find? The more absolutistic philosophers dwell on so high a level of abstraction that they never even try to come down. The absolute mind which they offer us, the mind that makes our universe by thinking it, might, for aught they show us to the contrary, have made any one of a million other universes just as well as this. You can deduce no single actual particular from the notion of it. It is compatible with any state of things whatever being true here below. And the theistic God is almost as sterile a principle. You have to go to the world which he has created to get any inkling of this actual character: he is the kind of god that has once for all made that kind of a world. The God of the theistic writers lives on as purely abstract heights as does the Absolute. Absolutism has a certain sweep and dash about it, while the usual theism is more insipid, but both are equally remote and vacuous. What you want is a philosophy that will not only exercise your powers of intellectual abstraction, but that will make some positive connection with this actual world of finite human lives. You want a system that will combine both things, the scientific loyalty to facts and willingness to take account of them, the spirit of adaptation and accommodation, in short, but also the old confidence in human values and the resultant spontaneity, whether of the religious or of the romantic type.

And this is then your dilemma: you find the two parts of your *quæs-itum* hopelessly separated. You find empiricism with inhumanism and irreligion; or else you find a rationalistic philosophy that indeed may call itself religious, but that keeps out of all definite touch with concrete facts and joys and sorrows. And this last, this absolutistic philosophy, is no explanation of our concrete universe; it is another thing altogether, a substitute for it, a remedy, a way of escape like a marble temple shining on a hill. But the universe itself is a colossal universe of concrete facts, of awful bewilderments of surprises and cruelties. This being so, the optimism of present-day rationalism sounds shallow to the fact-loving mind. The universe is a thing wide open, not a closed system of perfection internally complete as the absolutists say; for men in practical life perfection is far off and still in process of achievement. It is here that pragmatism comes in and seeks examples of revolt against the airy and shallow optimism of current religious philosophy. It may be that the belief in an Absolute Mind with whom "all is well" may yield religious comfort to a most respectable class of mind, but from the human point of view no one can pretend that it does not suffer from the faults of remoteness and abstractness.

When one picks up the daily paper, continues James, and reads of crimes of passion, and suicide from despair, to talk of such a world being "In Tune with the Infinite" is sheer absurdity. Absolutism is reared upon pure logic and spurns the dust; pragmatism says that in this real world of sweat and dirt when a view of things is "noble," it is noble in a bad sense, in the sense in which to be noble is to be inapt for humble service. The absolutist may say that his view is both true and good, but the pragmatist retorts that the test of the truth is that it must be good for something. In this world, just as certain foods are not only agreeable to our taste but good for our teeth, our stomach, and our tissues, so certain ideas are not only agreeable to think about, or agreeable as supporting other ideas that we are fond of, but they are also helpful in life's practical struggles.

Truth, then, being to the pragmatist a class name for all sorts of definite working values in experience, let us pass, says James, to some metaphysical problems pragmatically considered. There is first the dilemma between present-day materialism, which may better be called naturalism, and theism, or what in a wide sense may be termed spiritualism. This kind of materialism says that nature operates through blind laws of physics, whereas spiritualism says that mind not only witnesses and records things, but also runs and operates them; the world being thus guided not by its lower, but by its higher element. Treated as it often is, this question becomes little more than a conflict between æsthetic preferences. Matter is gross, coarse, crass, muddy; spirit is pure, elevated, noble; and since it is more consonant with the dignity of the universe to give the primacy in it to what appears superior, spirit must be affirmed as the ruling principle. To treat abstract principles as finalities, before which our intellects may come to rest in a state of admiring contemplation, is the great rationalist failing. Spiritualism, as often held, may be simply a state of admiration for one kind, and of dislike for another kind, of abstraction. I remember a worthy spiritualist professor who always referred to materialism as the "mud-philosophy," and deemed it thereby refuted. To such spiritualism as this there is an easy answer, and Mr. Spencer makes it effectively. In some well-written pages at the end of the first volume of his *Psychology* he shows us that a "matter" so infinitely subtle, and performing motions as inconceivably quick and fine as those which modern science postulates in her explanations, has no trace of grossness left. He shows that the conception of spirit, as we mortals hitherto have formed it, is itself too gross to cover the exquisite tenuity of nature's facts. Both terms, he says, are but symbols, pointing to that one unknowable reality in which their oppositions cease. To an abstract objection an abstract rejoinder suffices; and so far as one's opposition to materialism springs from one's disdain of matter as something "crass," Mr. Spencer cuts the ground from under one. Matter is indeed infinitely and incredibly refined. To anyone who has ever looked on the face of a dead child or parent the mere fact that matter could have taken for a time that precious form ought to make matter sacred ever after. It makes no difference what the principle of life may be, material or immaterial, matter at any rate coöperates, lends itself to all life's purposes. That beloved incarnation was among matter's possibilities.

This, according to James, is the intellectual answer to the conflict between materialism and spiritualism; it needs to be completed by the pragmatic method. What do we mean by matter? What practical difference can it make now that the world should be run by matter or spirit? Here our attention is called to a curious fact: it makes not a single jot of difference, so far as the past of the world goes, whether we deem it to have been the work of matter or whether we think a divine spirit was its author. Imagine, in fact, the entire contents of the world to be once for all irrevocably given. Imagine it to end this very moment, and to have no future; and then let a theist and a materialist apply their rival explanations to its history. The theist shows how a God made it; the materialist shows, and we will suppose with equal success, how it resulted from blind physical forces. Then let the pragmatist be asked to choose between their theories. How can he apply his test if a world is already completed? Concepts for him are things with which to come back into experience, things to make us look for differences. But by hypothesis there is to be no more experience, and no possible differences can now be looked for. Both theories have shown all their consequences and, by the hypothesis we are adopting, these are identical. The pragmatist must consequently say that the two theories, in spite of their different-sounding names, mean exactly the same thing, and that the dispute is purely verbal.

The problem is only half stated. We have been dealing merely with a past world, a supposedly completed world. Let us therefore place ourselves in the world we live in, in a world that has a future, that is yet uncompleted. In this unfinished world the alternative of materialism or theism becomes intensely practical. How, indeed, does the programme differ for us, according as we consider that the facts of experience up to date are purposeless configurations of blind atoms moving according to eternal laws, or that on the other hand they are due to the providence of God? As far as the past facts go, indeed, there is no difference. If philosophy were merely retro-prospective the matter would be settled with a stalemate, but philosophy is prospective also, and after finding what the world has been and done, and yielded, still asks the further question, What does the world promise?

Here the contest between materialism and spiritualism repeats itself, and materialism must be given the first innings. But what is the outcome here? According to the theory of mechanical evolution, the laws of redistribution of matter and motion, though they are certainly to thank for all the good hours which our organisms have ever yielded us and for all the ideals which our minds now frame, are yet fatally certain to undo their work again, and to redissolve everything that they have once evolved. In the words of Mr. Balfour, the energies of our system will decay, the glory of the sun will be dimmed, and the earth, tideless and inert, will no longer tolerate the race which has for a moment disturbed its solitude. Man will go down into the pit, and all his thoughts will perish.

According to James, it is this "utter final wreck and tragedy" which is the essence of scientific materialism as at present understood, and the true objection to it is not positive but negative. We make complaint of it, on the contrary, for what it is not—not a permanent warrant for our more ideal interests, not a fulfiller of our remotest hopes. The notion of God, on the other hand, however inferior it may be in clearness to those mathematical notions so current in mechanical philosophy, has at least this practical superiority over them, that it guarantees an ideal order that shall be permanently preserved. This need of an eternal moral order is one of the deepest needs of our breast. And those poets, like Dante and Wordsworth, who live on the conviction of such an order, owe to that fact the extraordinary tonic and consoling power of their verse.

James, it is evident, does not absolutely settle the problem of the conflicting claims of materialism and spiritualism. Considering these claims pragmatically means simply that they are matters of choice, the choice being determined by the consequences which would result from holding this or that form of belief. Choice in turn implies free will, and thus another burning problem arises. The free-willists and the determinists have been at one another's throats for ages and in James's opinion both have been arguing from a low moral standpoint, namely, that of accountability. If our acts were predetermined, if we merely transmitted the push of the whole past, the free-willists say, how could we be praised or blamed for anything? We should be "agents" only, not "principals," and where then would be our precious imputability and responsibility? On the other hand, if a "free" act be a sheer novelty, that comes not from me, the previous me, and simply tacks itself on to me, how can I, the previous I, be responsible? How can I have any permanent character that will stand still long enough for praise or blame to be awarded?

Both these arguments are futile, contends James, because the point of view is antiquated. To hear some persons one would suppose that all that ethics aims at is a code of merits and demerits. Thus does the old legal and theological leaven, the interest in crime and sin and punishment, abide with us. Who's to blame? whom can we punish? whom will God punish?—these preoccupations hang like a bad dream over man's religious history. To make our human ethics revolve about the question of "merit" is a piteous unreality— God alone can know our merits, if we have any. The real ground for supposing free will is indeed pragmatic, but it has nothing to do with this contemptible right to punish which has made such a noise in past discussions of the subject.

What is the real ground for supposing free will? At this point James employs a utilitarian doctrine, arguing that fatalism is not a formula that leads to the greatest happiness of the greatest number.

There are two kinds of fatalism, with neither of which he is in sympathy. There is crude naturalism, which reduces all action to physics, and there is transcendental absolutism, which makes history merely the unrolling of a cosmic film already developed in the divine mind. Now persons in whom knowledge of the world's past has bred pessimism, he argues, may naturally welcome free will as a melioristic doctrine. It holds up improvement as at least possible; whereas determinism assures us that our whole notion of possibility is born of human ignorance, and that necessity and impossibility between them rule the destinies of the world.

Free will is thus a general theory of promise, a doctrine of relief, and by attaching it to a theory of meliorism furnishes an antidote against not only the pessimism of the past, but the equally extreme optimism of the present. The Hindu and the Buddhist, explains James, are simply afraid, afraid of more experience, afraid of life, and Nirvana means safety from this everlasting round of adventures of which the world of sense consists. On the other hand, many of the modern idealisms try to make this world out as a "Lubberland of happiness." Here James might have pointed out that the idealistic New Thoughters were also prompted by a subconscious fear, a sense of inferiority, a desire to get away from the difficulties of this dark and wicked world. But he had already done so in his famous picture of Chautauqua, that "middle-class paradise without a sin, without a victim, without a blot, without a tear." Here, he continues, you have kindergartens and model secondary schools. You have general religious services and special clubhouses for the several sects. You have perpetually running soda-water fountains and daily popular lectures by distinguished men. You have the best of company, and yet no effort. . . . This order is too tame, this culture too second rate, this goodness too uninspiring. This human drama without a villain or a pang; this community so refined that ice-cream soda water is the utmost offering it can make to the brute animal in man; this city simmering in the tepid lakeside sun; this atrocious harmlessness of all things—I cannot abide with them. Let me take my chances again in the big outside worldly wilderness with all its sins and sufferings. There are the heights and depths, the precipices and the steep ideals, the gleams of the awful and the infinite; and there is more hope and help a thousand times than in this dead level and quintessence of every mediocrity.

It is evident that James reacted against all this as too good to be true, just as he did against the historic optimisms like that of Leibnitz with its best possible of all worlds. The world of Chautauqua,

like the world of Candide, is a fool's paradise, false to total reality
and ethically impossible. In a frivolous moment James compares
evil to "the bitters in the cosmic cocktail"; in a more serious
moment he asks this question: Will not everyone instantly declare a
world fitted only for fair-weather human beings susceptible of every
passive enjoyment, but without independence, courage, or fortitude, to be from a moral point of view incommensurably inferior to
a world framed to elicit from the man every form of triumphant endurance and conquering moral energy? Yes, is the answer, given by
the sentiment of rationality. As philosophers aiming at clearness and
consistency, and feeling the pragmatistic need of squaring truth
with truth, the question is forced upon us of frankly adopting either
the tender or the robustious type of thought. In particular this
query has always come home to me: May not the claims of tender-
mindedness go too far? May not the notion of a world already
saved *in toto* anyhow be too saccharine to stand? May not religious
optimism be too idyllic? Must all be saved? Is no price to be paid in
the work of salvation? Is the last word sweet? Is all "yes, yes" in the
universe? Doesn't the fact of "no" stand at the very core of life?
Doesn't the very "seriousness" that we attribute to life mean that
ineluctable "noes" and losses form a part of it, that there are genuine sacrifices somewhere and that something permanently drastic
and bitter always remains at the bottom of its cup?

In spite of what his critics call his surrender to the "genteel
tradition," to the trilogy of God, freedom, and immortality—as
respectively a seeing force that runs things, a principle of self-
determination, and a hope for a future life—James really belongs to
the tough-minded group. Here is his creed, the creed of the fighter
and at the same time, it may be, the creed of the good loser: I find
myself willing to take the universe to be really dangerous and adventurous, without therefore backing out and crying "no play."
I am willing to think that the prodigal-son attitude, open to us as it
is in many vicissitudes, is not the right and final attitude toward
the whole of life. I am willing that there should be real losses and real
losers, and not total preservation of all that is. I can believe in the
ideal as an ultimate, not as an origin, and as an extract, not the
whole. When the cup is poured off the dregs are left behind forever,
but the possibility of what is poured off is sweet enough to accept.
As a matter of fact, countless human imaginations live in this moral-
istic and epic kind of a universe, and find its disseminated and
strung-along successes sufficient for their rational needs. There is a
finely translated epigram in the Greek anthology which admirably

expresses this state of mind, this acceptance of loss as unatoned for, even though the lost element might be oneself:

> A shipwrecked sailor, buried on this coast,
> Bids you set sail.
> Full many a gallant bark, when we were lost,
> Weathered the gale.

The philosophy of James is that of the fighter. It is based on what he calls the element in reality which every strong man of common sense willingly feels, because it calls forth powers that he owns— "the rough, harsh sea-wave, north-wind element." It is because of this temperamental test that James declares that fatalism, whose solving word in all crises of behaviour is "all striving is vain," will never reign supreme, for the impulse to take life strivingly is indestructible in the race. Moral creeds which speak to that impulse will be widely successful in spite of inconsistency, vagueness, and shadowy determination of expectancy. Man needs a rule for his will, and will invent one if one be not given him. It is on the above grounds that one can estimate the respective success or failure of the historic systems. The Epicurean notion that "all is vanity" is the watchword of the moral skeptic brought to bay; the energy of the Stoic is that of the real moralist. The same thing holds true of the romantic movement. How did Kant and Fichte, Goethe and Schiller inspire their time with cheer except by saying, "Use all your powers; that is the only obedience the universe exacts."

James is to show later how far these energies, these powers of man, can be brought out in a practical way. Meanwhile, he takes up a more general problem and meets those critics who call him an irrationalist by arguing that the sentiment of rationality is not inconsistent with the sentiment of faith. Faith means belief in something concerning which doubt is still theoretically possible; and as the test of belief is willingness to act, one may say that faith is the readiness to act in a cause the prosperous issue of which is not certified to us in advance. It is, in fact, the same moral quality which we call courage in practical affairs; and there will be a very widespread tendency in men of vigorous nature to enjoy a certain amount of uncertainty in their philosophic creed, just as risk lends a zest to worldly activity. Now in such questions as God, immortality, absolute morality, and free will, one can always doubt his creed. But his intimate persuasion is that the odds in its favour are strong enough to warrant him in acting all along on the assumption of its truth. His corroboration or repudiation by the nature of things may be deferred until the Day of Judgment. The uttermost he now means is something like this: "I expect then to triumph with tenfold glory: but if it should turn out, as indeed it may, that I have spent my days in a fool's paradise, why, better have been the dupe of such a dreamland than the cunning reader of a world like that which then beyond all doubt unmasks itself to view. . . . Suppose, for example, that I am climbing in the Alps and have had the ill luck to work myself into a position from which the only escape is by a terrible leap. Being without similar experience, I have no evidence of my ability to perform it successfully; but hope and confidence in myself make me sure I shall not miss my aim, and nerve my feet to execute that which without those subjective emotions would perhaps have been impossible. But suppose that, on the contrary, the emotions of fear and mistrust preponderate: or suppose that, having just read the *Ethics of Belief*, I feel it would be sinful to act upon an assumption unverified by previous experience—why, then I shall hesitate so long that at last, exhausted and trembling, and launching myself in a moment of despair, I miss my foothold and roll into the abyss. In this case (and it is one of an immense class) the part of wisdom clearly is to believe what one desires: for the belief is one of the indispensable preliminary conditions of the realization of its object. There are then cases where faith creates its own verification.

Such is James's doctrine of the will to believe. His critics dubbed it the will to make-believe, and implied that under its sanctions all sorts of superstitious beliefs might be justified. But James retorted that the proper title of his doctrine should have been the right to believe, and that along with it should be put his view that life, being more or less an experiment, the faith experiments of the race should be put among scientific data. To indulge in private "overbeliefs" may be hazardous, but hazards are of the essence of manly virtue. Faith is a form of courage, and urging men to forego overbeliefs is like a general's informing his soldiers that it is better to keep out of battle forever than to risk a single wound. Of course there are countless examples of faith that have ended in failure, but there are also countless examples where it has resulted in success. The great evidence of this is the social organism. Whenever a desired result is achieved by the operation of many independent persons, its existence as a fact is a pure consequence of the precursive faith in one another of those immediately concerned. A government, an army, a commercial system, a ship, a college, an athletic team, all exist on this condition, without which not only is nothing achieved, but nothing is even attempted.

Exceptions might be taken to all these cases by saying that mere faith will not create a government unless there are funds, an army unless there is ammunition, a commercial system unless there is credit. But that is not precisely the conclusion that James draws. He does not say, as some of the romanticists said, that faith in a fact creates the fact, but that faith in a fact can help create the fact. And another modification should be noted. The facts in this case are not facts in the sense of being already in existence, but rather ideas of what it is hoped will come into existence. Now these ideas are realities, not in the sense that mere thoughts are things, but in the sense that certain tangible things cannot come into existence without certain ideas. Without enthusiasm, for instance, there could be neither governments nor armies, colleges nor athletic teams. The will to believe in the success of one's future undertakings, then, has a certain creative value. As James put it in his notable address, "The Energies of Men," certain sorts of ideas may be considered as dynamogenic agents, as stimuli for unlocking what would otherwise be unused reservoirs of individual power. Here the physiologists call a stimulus "dynamogenic" when it increases the muscular contractions of men to whom it is applied; but its appeals can be dynamogenic morally as well as muscularly. It is notorious that a single successful effort of moral volition, such as saying No to some habitual temptation or performing some courageous act, will launch a man on a higher level of energy for days and weeks, will give him a new range of power.

Of course, confesses James, ideals may fail to be efficacious, just as a wire at one time alive with electricity may, at another time, be dead. Here our insight into causes fails us, and we could only note results in general terms. But apart from such individually varying susceptibilities there are common lines along which men, simply as men, tend to be inflammable by ideas. As certain objects naturally awaken love, anger, or cupidity, so certain ideas naturally awaken the energies of loyalty, courage, endurance, or devotion. When these ideas are effective in an individual's life, their effect is often very great indeed. They may transfigure it, unlocking innumerable powers which, but for the idea, would never have come into play. Fatherland, the Flag, the Union, Holy Church, the Monroe Doctrine, Truth, Science, Liberty, Garibaldi's phrase: Rome or Death, are so many examples of energy-releasing ideas.

The greatest example of the energy-releasing capacity of ideas is war, and in wrestling with this problem, James gives a final example of the pragmatic method of seeking for a programme of behaviour for modifying the existent world. In his search for the "moral equivalent of war" James, as is his custom, first presents the difficulties of the question in order at the last to suggest the solution. The war against war, he admits, is going to be no holiday excursion or camping party. The military feelings are too deeply grounded to abdicate their place among our ideals until better substitutes are offered than the glory and shame that come to nations as well as to individuals from the ups and downs of politics and the vicissitudes of trade. There is something highly paradoxical in the modern man's relations to war. Ask all our millions, North and South, whether they would vote now (were such a thing possible) to have our war for the Union expunged from history, and the record of a peaceful transition to the present time substituted for that of its marches and battles, and probably hardly a handful of eccentrics would say Yes. Those ancestors, those efforts, those memories and legends, are the most ideal part of what we now own together, a sacred spiritual possession worth more than all the blood poured out. Yet ask those same people whether they would be willing in cold blood to start another civil war now to gain another similar possession, and not one man or woman would vote for the proposition. In modern eyes, precious though wars may be, they must not be waged solely for the sake of the ideal harvest. Only when forced upon one, only when an enemy's injustice leaves us no alternative, is a war now thought permissible. As things stand, I see how desperately hard it is to bring the peace party and the war party together, and I believe that the difficulty is due to certain deficiencies in the programme of pacificism which set the militarist imagination strongly, and to a certain extent justifiably, against it. In the whole discussion both sides are on imaginative and sentimental ground. It is but one utopia against another, and everything one says must be abstract and hypothetical. Subject to this criticism and caution, I will try to characterize in abstract strokes the opposite imaginative forces, and point out what to my own very fallible mind seems the best utopian hypothesis, the most promising line of conciliation.

Reflective apologists for war at the present day, explains James, all take it religiously. It is a sort of sacrament. Its profits are to the vanquished as well as to the victor; and quite apart from any question of profit, it is an absolute good, we are told, for it is human nature at its highest dynamic. Its "horrors" are a cheap price to pay for rescue from the only alternative supposed, of a world of clerks and teachers, of coeducation and zoöphily, of "consumers' leagues" and "associated charities," of industrialism unlimited and feminism unabashed. No scorn, no hardness, no valour any more. Fie upon such a cattle yard of a planet. . . . It is obvious that the United States of America as they exist to-day impress a mind like General Lee's as so much human blubber. Where is the sharpness and precipitousness, the contempt for life, whether one's own or another's? Where is the savage "yes" and "no," the unconditional duty? Where is the conscription? Where is the blood tax? Where is anything that one feels honoured by belonging to?

The war party, confesses James, is assuredly right in affirming and reaffirming that the material virtues, although originally gained by the race through war, are absolute and permanent human goods. Patriotic pride and ambition in their military form are, after all, only specifications of a more general competitive passion. They are its first form, but that is no reason for supposing them to be its last form. Men now are proud of belonging to a conquering nation, and without a murmur they lay down their persons and their wealth if by so doing they may fend off subjection. But who can be sure that other aspects of one's country may not, with time and education and suggestion enough, come to be regarded with similarly effective feelings of pride and shame? Why should men not some day feel that it is worth a blood tax to belong to a collectivity superior in any ideal respect? Why should they not blush with indignant shame if the community that owns them is vile in any way whatsoever? Individuals, daily more numerous, now feel this civic passion. It is only a question of blowing on the spark till the whole population gets incandescent, and on the ruins of the old morals of military honour a stable system of morals of civic honour builds itself up. What the whole community comes to believe in grasps the individual as in a vise. The war function has grasped us so far; but constructive interests may some day seem no less imperative, and impose on the individual a hardly lighter burden.

Let me illustrate my idea more concretely. There is nothing to make one indignant in the mere fact that life is hard, that men should toil and suffer pain. The planetary conditions once for all are such, and we can stand it. But that so many men, by mere accidents of birth and opportunity, should have a life of nothing else but toil and pain and hardness and inferiority imposed upon them, should have no vacation, while others natively no more deserving never get any taste of this campaigning life at all—this is capable of arousing indignation in reflective minds. It may end by its seeming shameful to all of us that some of us have nothing but campaigning, and others nothing but unmanly ease. If now—and this is my idea, concludes James—there were, instead of military conscription a conscription of the whole youthful population to form for a certain number of years a part of the army enlisted against nature, the injustice would tend to be evened out, and numerous other goods to the commonwealth would follow. The military ideals of hardihood and discipline would be wrought into the growing fibre of the people; no one would remain blind as the luxurious classes now are blind, to man's real relations to the globe he lives on, and to the permanently sure and hard foundations of his higher life. To coal and iron mines, to freight trains, to fishing fleets in December, to dish washing, clothes washing, and window washing, to road building and tunnel making, to foundries and stokeholes, and to the frames of skyscrapers would our gilded youths be drafted off, according to their choice, to get the childishness knocked out of them, and to come back into society with healthier sympathies and soberer ideas. They would have paid their blood tax, done their own part in the immemorial human warfare against nature, they would tread the earth more proudly, the women would value them more highly, they would be better fathers and teachers of the following generation.

THE END

# INDEX

# INDEX

Academy, Plato's, the influence of, 68; aim of, 130.

Academy of Dijon, 265.

Activity, Bruno's moral message, 212.

Adams, President John, definition of the deist's creed, 251.

*Addresses to the German People*, 310.

Adultery, Thomas Aquinas on, 186.

Æsculapius, 145, 146.

Æsop, 115.

Æsthetics, Schopenhauer's theories of, 328.

*Against the Gentiles*, Thomas Aquinas's, 180.

Agassiz, James's associations with, 381.

Agathocles, 202.

Agathon, 50.

Alaric the Goth, 5, 168.

Albertus the Great, Thomas Aquinas under, 179.

Albigensian Crusades, 191.

Albigeois, the, 363.

Alcibiades, 24; a disciple of Socrates's, 49, 58; his estimate of Socrates, 52; saved by Socrates, 57; 77, 339.

Aldington, Richard, his *Voltaire* quoted, 245-246.

Alembert, D', Rousseau's break with, 263.

Alexander the Great, 86; a pupil under Aristotle, 87; Diogenes's remark to, 131.

Alexander VI, Pope, 196.

Amyntas II, King, 87.

Ananias, 76.

Anaxagoras, his theory of life, 53.

Ancestor worship, defined, 118.

"Angelic Doctor," Thomas Aquinas the, 6, 180.

Animals, Darwin on instincts and emotions of, 367; the social affinities between men and, 369 ff.

Animism, its survival in Buddhism, 105.

Anne, Queen, 247.

Anselm, his definition of Deity, 222.

Antisthenes, founder of school of Cynicism, 132.

Antoninus, Marcus Aurelius, a representative Stoic, 132; writings of, 132-133; on death, 136-137; on the vicissitudes of fortune, 145-146; 170, 173.

Anytus, 63.

Apathy, the Stoics' armour of, 145 ff.

*Apology*, Socrates's Defense of Himself in the, 61 ff.

Aquinas, St. Thomas, successor to St. Augustine in the history of the church, 6; life, 6; method of reconciliation, 176; Scholastic philosopher, 179 ff.; his aim, 179; titles, 180; the *Summary of Theology*, 180, 181 ff.; his moral system, 180; foundations of the system, 181; conception of nature, 181; compared to St. Augustine, 182; on free will, 182, 188; doctrines of, 183; the "Ethics," 184 ff.; Hellenic influences, 189; influence of Aristotle, 189; sin and its punishment, 191-192; on natural law and the tranquil association of man, 241; his place in Kant's table of moralities, 305.

Aquino, Count, 6.

Argyll, Duke of, Darwin's reply to, 368.

Aristophanes, 50; satirizes Socrates, 52; quoted, 71.

Aristotle, 4; in Raphael's School of Athens, 23; his principle of the golden mean, 25, 92; Lyceum of, 67; influence of Plato's Academy on, 68; shares Plato's admiration for Greece, 77; his theory of over-population, 78; life and philosophy, 86 ff.; his association with Plato, 86; teacher of Alexander the Great, 87; founds Lyceum, 88; death, 88; keynote to his system of morality, 88; compared wtih Plato, 89; theory of moral education, 89; the *Nicomachean*

361; William James the interpreter of the new, 379; pragmatism the system of, 382.

*Democracy and Liberty*, quoted, 349–350.

Democritus, comments on the Skeptics, 52.

Demosthenes, 68.

Descartes, René, suppression of his works, 10; the "seat of the soul," 225; man a machine, 228; doctrine of innate ideas, 249; Hume influenced by the innate ideas of, 278.

*Descent of Man*, 352; Darwin's task in, 365; evidence presented in, 365 ff.

"Description of the Methods Adopted by the Duke Valentino when Murdering Vitellozzo Vitelli, Oliverotto da Fermo, the Signor Pagolo and the Duke Di Gravini Orsini," 196.

Desire, the stress of Buddhism on the absence of, 109; the Stoics on, 140.

Destiny, as a primitive force, 32; the problem complicated, 41 ff.; the Brahmanic conception of, 103; the Epicureans on, 159.

Devonshire, Earl of, 235.

Devotion, Stoic insistence upon, 131.

Dewey, John, 317; his protest against reactionary movements, 368; Dewey, the Chicago school, 384 ff.; his five points of progress, 385; on the influence of Darwin, 386.

De Witt, the brothers, 220.

"Dialogue, A," David Hume's summary of morality, 285.

*Dialogues on Natural Religion*, Hume's, 309.

Dickens, Charles, 321.

Diderot, Rousseau's break with, 263; his explanation of Rousseau, 275.

Diocletian, 173.

Diogenes, 4; in Raphael's School of Athens, 23; not a true Socratic, 56; incident of Alexander the Great, 131; personal habits, 132; his rejection of Greek civilization, 135; foundation of his conduct, 287.

Diogenes of Cappadocia, inscription by, 157, 161.

Dionysius I, 67; Plato's experiences under, 80.

Dionysodorus, 53.

"Discourse on Equality," Rousseau's, 265.

"Discourse on Inequality," 273.

*Discourse on Man*, 252.

"Discourses Concerning Unlimited Submission and Non-resistance to the Higher Powers—With Some Reflections on the Resistance Made to Charles I," 240.

*Discourses of Livy*, 197.

*Discourses, or Rousseau Judge of Jean-Jacques*, 263.

*Discussion on Estate Management*, quoted, 73.

*Divine Comedy*, 191.

"Doctor of the Church," Thomas Aquinas the, 180.

*Doctrine of Religion, footnote*, 315.

Dolcino, Fra, 363.

Dominicans, Thomas Aquinas a member of the, 179; 191, 206.

Domitian, Emperor, 160.

Dostoyevski, Feodor M., 4.

*Downfall of Western Civilization*, 112.

Drake, Sir Francis, 7, 213.

Dred Scott Decision, 98.

Drinking, John Stuart Mill on the principle of prohibition, 17; Socrates on, 50, 56; J. S. Mill on, 362.

Dualism, St. Augustines' doctrine of, 170, 178; of Zoroaster, 171; cosmic and moral, 211; revival of cosmic, 372.

"Dumb Ox," Thomas Aquinas the, 179.

Dürer, Albert, 322, 329.

Duty, Socrates on, 56; of men and women, advocated by Plato, 75; of children to their parents, defined by Confucius, 116; the five relations, 117; Stoicism's insistence upon, 131.

Dynamism, pragmatism the system of, 382.

Earnestness, Confucius on, 123.

Eckhart, Meister, 326–327.

Eclectics, their policy of expediency, 144; banished from Rome, 160.

Economy, David Hume's principle of, 277, 280.

Education, Protagoras on, 54; Plato's system of, described, 70 ff.; Aristotle's